The Obituary as
Collective Memory

Routledge Advances in Sociology

1. Virtual Globalization
Virtual Spaces / Tourist Spaces
Edited by David Holmes

2. The Criminal Spectre in Law,
Literature and Aesthetics
Peter Hutchings

3. Immigrants and National Identity
in Europe
Anna Triandafyllidou

4. Constructing Risk and Safety in
Technological Practice
Edited by Jane Summerton and Boel
Berner

5. Europeanisation, National
Identities and Migration
Changes in Boundary Constructions
Between Western and Eastern Europe
Willfried Spohn and Anna Triandafyllidou

6. Language, Identity and Conflict
A Comparative Study of Language in
Ethnic Conflict in Europe and Eurasia
Diarmait Mac Giolla Chríost

7. Immigrant Life in the U.S.
Multi-disciplinary Perspectives
Edited by Donna R. Gabaccia and Colin
Wayne Leach

8. Rave Culture and Religion
Edited by Graham St. John

9. Creation and Returns of
Social Capital
A New Research Program
Edited by Henk Flap and Beate Völker

10. Self-Care
Embodiment, Personal Autonomy and the
Shaping of Health Consciousness
Christopher Ziguras

11. Mechanisms of Cooperation
Werner Raub and Jeroen Weesie

12. After the Bell – Educational
Success, Public Policy and Family
Background
Edited by Dalton Conley and Karen
Albright

13. Youth Crime and Youth Culture
in the Inner City
Bill Sanders

14. Emotions and Social Movements
Edited by Helena Flam and Debra King

15. Globalization, Uncertainty and
Youth in Society
Edited by Hans-Peter Blossfeld, Erik
Klijzing, Melinda Mills and Karin Kurz

16. Love, Heterosexuality and Society
Paul Johnson

17. Agricultural Governance
Globalization and the New Politics of
Regulation
Edited by Vaughan Higgins and Geoffrey
Lawrence

18. Challenging Hegemonic
Masculinity
Richard Howson

19. Social Isolation in Modern Society
Roelof Hortulanus, Anja Machielse and
Ludwien Meeuwesen

**20. Weber and the Persistence of
Religion**
Social Theory, Capitalism and the Sublime
Joseph W. H. Lough

**21. Globalization, Uncertainty and Late
Careers in Society**
Edited by Hans-Peter Blossfeld, Sandra
Buchholz and Dirk Hofäcker

22. Bourdieu's Politics
Problems and Possibilities
Jeremy F. Lane

**23. Media Bias in Reporting Social
Research?**
The Case of Reviewing Ethnic Inequalities in
Education
Martyn Hammersley

**24. A General Theory of Emotions and
Social Life**
Warren D. TenHouten

25. Sociology, Religion and Grace
Arpad Szakolczai

26. Youth Cultures
Scenes, Subcultures and Tribes
Edited by Paul Hodkinson and Wolfgang
Deicke

27. The Obituary as Collective Memory
Bridget Fowler

The Obituary as Collective Memory

Bridget Fowler

Routledge
Taylor & Francis Group
New York   London

Routledge
Taylor & Francis Group
270 Madison Avenue
New York, NY 10016

Routledge
Taylor & Francis Group
2 Park Square
Milton Park, Abingdon
Oxon OX14 4RN

© 2007 by Taylor & Francis Group, LLC
Routledge is an imprint of Taylor & Francis Group, an Informa business

Transferred to Digital Printing 2009

International Standard Book Number-10: 0-415-36493-0 (Hardcover)
International Standard Book Number-13: 978-0-415-36493-5 (Hardcover)

Library of Congress Cataloging-in-Publication Data

Fowler, Bridget, 1943-
    The obituary as collective memory / Bridget Fowler.
       p. cm. -- (Routledge advances in sociology ; 27)
    Includes bibliographical references and index.

    ISBN10: 0-415-36493-0 (hbk)
    ISBN10: 0-415-87130-1 (pbk)

    ISBN13: 978-0-415-36493-5 (hbk)
    ISBN13: 978-0-415-87130-3 (pbk)

    1. Collective memory. 2. Obituaries. 3. Obituaries--United States. 4. Collective memory--United States. 5. Celebrities--Obituaries. 6. Death--Social aspects. I. Title.

HM1025.F69 2007
920.001--dc22   2006038300

Visit the Taylor & Francis Web site at
http://www.taylorandfrancis.com

and the Routledge Web site at
http://www.routledge-ny.com

IN MEMORY OF

PIERRE BOURDIEU

rdieu est mort

Matthews: the Peter Pan of sport in 1939

ophe est décédé mercredi. Mondialement reconn in engagement aux côtés des mouvements socia

ash dispute, nering per-e manager over into ransfer re-gned at the of the city's an extent claimed the oduction. A ed by 3,000 ore waving all, under-lebrity and ded by such amicable

thèmes aussi divers que la l'art, la littérature, la politi médias, la haute fonction que, la misère sociale, la tion masculine, etc. Di d'études à l'Ecole des haut des en sciences sociales (E élu au Collège de France en réunit autour de lui une sociologique dont la revue *la recherche en sciences s* fondée en 1975, sera la vitri

Pour ses disciples, sa thé monde social constitue une *lution symbolique* », sembl celles qu'ont pu connaître d disciplines. Pour ses détra l'originalité de la sociologie

World War, AF as a fit-nk with the nd Tommy cy England he most ex-s of his ca-, wartime ere against ere never atthews re-

he let it be known he really would move this time, but only to Blackpool where he owned a hotel, the Seasiders were happy to snap him up for a mere £11,500. It proved to be one of the biggest transfer bargains of all time.

Matthews relished the North-West, where he maintained a rigor-

deniably the leading light as pool reached three FA Cup fin six seasons.

The first, against Matt Bu Manchester United in 1948 billed as the 33-year-old's last istic opportunity of pocketin winner's medal he craved, bi Seasiders lost a breathtaking

Bernie Grant

ltered through had been select-Tottenham, the ur Party gulped. to do whatsoever was black. That that he was cur-No 1. The council ed the Metropol-adwater Farm –

so many diverse cultures, a cham-pion not only of those who were black but brown, yellow, white and all colours of the proverbial rainbow.

He was an MP for the underdog. I never ceased to be amazed at the amount of casework from all over the country that he managed to con-duct with the hugely efficient support of his partner and second wife.

alent-spotter

would have become what they became even if he had never come to Queen's. It would, of course, be absurd to suggest that such as Heaney, Longley and Muldoon would have remained mute, inglorious Miltons but for Philip's poetical midwifery. But it would also be absurd to minimise the impor-tance of the Belfast group in bringing about change. What seems indisputable is that Philip was an important influ-ence upon the development of these writers (see, for example, how Heaney's *Death of a Naturalist* (1966) manoeuvres between particular techniques of Larkin and Hughes), that they became different poets because of him, that if he did

trade secretary, he would incorrigibly illiberal, refu landing rights to Freddie Laker's Skytrain and beli duly overruled by the hig court. Weirdly for a one-t unilateralist, he argued f purchase of Chevaline w heads to update Polaris.

In 1976, he became envi ment secretary. The usefu things he believed in – lit protection of inner city ar from degeneration – he p claimed, but did little abo The recurring adjective us about him as a minister w "indecisive". Politically, he keeping the company of th left, with a furious campa against a "Yes" vote in the Europe referendum and h support for Michael Foot the 1976 leadership electi

new labour la in the change when moder ism" in policy with a Conse gaining grou provincial n legal action a cal Associatio ing at his W TUC was di agreed to sup law, but its E tee voted to strike that th Murray recal had that supp ally repudiati lawful activit

In retrospe mark of his a the Prime M and the news and lampoor in the eulogi

maximum envious focus, mimum disposable power. act, he was so little reg-that, within 18 months, son was giving serious ughts to dropping him ogether, settling in 1969 esolving the department shifting him to minister hout portfolio and deputy ler of the house. But re's failing was political, ministerial. characteristically, he had

to Richard Crossman was the more deadly for lacking anger: "I over-promoted him. He's no good."

Drab attachment to the wrong idea would be a con-stant feature of Shore's political life. But it would also, periodically, give his ca-reer an uncalculated boost. In 1970, he launched himself as an inveterate anti-European, making thundering speeches and getting thunderous ap-

But like another uncert but more comfortable poli cian, John Silkin, with wh he was associated at this t Shore did not belong with new rabidry which would soon suffuse the rank and A phrase of George Orwe

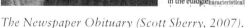

The Newspaper Obituary (Scott Sherry, 2007).

Contents

Acknowledgements   xi

PART I
Theoretical, historical and quantitative studies of the obituary   **1**

Introduction   3

1 Collective memory   25

2 The historical sociology of death   41

3 Bourdieu's social theory and the obituary   59

4 *The Times'* obituaries in 1900 and 1948   81

5 The social value of death: The microworld of the editors   105

6 The lives we choose to remember: A quantitative analysis   129
   WITH ESPERANZA BIELSA

PART II
**Memories burnished at the shock of death: Discourse analysis
of newspaper obituaries**   **157**

7 The politicians' obituaries (1999–2006)   159

8 The writers' obituaries (1999–2006)   181

9 The artists' obituaries (1999–2006)   197

10   The sports obituaries (1999–2006)   217

11   The trade unionists' obituaries (1999–2006)   233

Conclusion   243

Notes   251
Bibliography   273
Index   285

Acknowledgements

An advance might be made in the sociology of knowledge by analysing acknowledgements pages. These, like obituaries pages, if gleaned studiously and addressed imaginatively, provide an untapped source of sociological information. Gathered together systematically, these often off-guard accounts of debts incurred in the process of undertaking research would provide fascinating and important field-studies of underlying patterns of influence and interaction. They would reveal, in particular, how peripheral or metropolitan, national or cross-national are interchanges of ideas and might in this way provide a valuable corrective to mechanistic approaches via citations indexes.

In my own case, whilst I am solely responsible for what appears in these pages, I would like to thank many people who have helped me to chart what is still academically virgin territory. I am grateful to the obituary writers and editors for communicating, via interviews, their unparalleled experience about the production of these symbolic goods. Others have been generous with their time, especially in offering criticisms of the manuscript based on their specialist knowledge of different fields. I thank yet others for their very practical help, not least via the invaluable obituaries cuttings they sent to me regularly over the years of this research.

My chief debt is to Esperanza Bielsa, my research fellow on the project, who never failed to be both resourceful and supportive, and with whom I enjoyed collaborating on the quantitative study. I also feel grateful to Robert Gibb, Andy Smith, Harvie Ferguson, Susan Tennery, Ann and Philip Nicolson, Rob and Kirstie Maslen, Mike Gonzalez, Mary-Ellen Browne, Scott and Kirsten Meikle, Ruth and Chris Madigan, Gill Scott, Mary Dottridge, Emmanuelle Guibé, Stephen White, Hélène Lipstadt, Georgia Giannakopoulou, David Frisby, Alasdair Clark, James Fergusson, Jim McCue, Colin McDiarmid, Andrew McKie, Phil Osborne, Chuck Strum, Nadine Avelange, Adam Bernstein, Alastair Stephen, Mo McQuillan, Herminio Martins, Hillel and Lindy Ticktin, Terry Lovell, Miklos Hadas, Bert Moorhouse, Anna McLaughlin, Sarah Lowndes and Tam Dalyell. Meg Fowler provided literary guidance, Daniel Fowler help with the computer,

Luke Fowler suggestions for the artists' obituaries and frontispiece and Ben Fowler advice on sports obituaries: all of them sustained me in too many ways to mention.

Earlier versions of some chapters of this book have appeared in a different form in *Theory, Culture and Society* (chapter 1 (*Collective Memory and Forgetting*, Vol. 22, No. 6, December 2005) and chapter 3 (*Autonomy, Reciprocity and Science in the Thought of Pierre Bourdieu*, Vol. 23, No. 6, November 2006), in *Sociological Review* (May 2007) chapter 6 *The Lives We Choose to Remember*, with Esperanza Bielsa) and also in Lisa Adkins and Beverley Skeggs' edited *Feminism after Bourdieu* (Blackwell, 2004). I thank their publishers for permission to use them. Finally, I could not have seen this project through without the grant to aid the research from the Leverhulme Trust, for which I am also very grateful.

PART I

Theoretical, historical and quantitative studies of the obituary

Introduction

> Lives are supported and maintained differently [....] Certain lives will be highly protected [....] Other lives [...] will not even qualify as "grievable".

> A hierarchy of grief could no doubt be enumerated. We have seen it already in the genre of the obituary, where lives are quickly tidied up, and summarised, humanised, usually married or on the way to be, heterosexual, happy, monogamous. [...].
>   [...] we have to ask, again and again, how the obituary functions as the instrument by which grievability is publicly distributed. It is the means by which a life becomes, or fails to become a publicly-grievable life, an icon for national self-recognition, the means by which a life becomes noteworthy. As a result we have to consider the obituary as an act of nation-building. (Butler 2003: 32; 34)

This book concerns the selection and depiction of the lives chosen for enduring memory. Butler, despite the power of her writing, is somewhat dated in her view of contemporary obituaries: not all of them have subjects who are heterosexual and 'married or on the way to be'. Although the focus of the obituary is on the public sphere, the distinguished are often now acknowledged to be in private, somewhat transgressive figures. Even those who have committed suicide are no longer excluded automatically as they once were.[1] Further, it has to be conceded that certain figures appear now who would never have been given obituaries one hundred years ago, such as the Nigerian-born hot-water fitter and anti-colonial activist Michael Akintaro (*The Guardian*, 7 October 2000), Irene Thomas, the daughter of a meter-reader, who won Brain of Britain (4 July 2001) and the working-class Cumbrian climber, Alice Cross, whose partner made her boots (*The Times*, 13 March 2004). Even leaders of Hamas have had favourable obituaries, such as Abdel Aziz Rantisi (*The Independent*, 19 April 2004).

Due to these changes, obituary editors often discuss 'the revolution in the obituaries' since the 1970s. According to them, *anyone memorable* can now be given an obituary. Indeed, the figure of Akintaro seems to bear this out. This small African arrived in London as an immigrant seafarer-turned-caretaker, in the 1930s, and started a club where black GIs could dance with white women, leafletted for George Padmore (the champion of colonial freedom), and, later, acted as the repository of migrant collective memory in Camden. Paradoxically, he ended his anti-colonial career with an Imperial Services Medal for his duties as a hot-water fitter in Whitehall and even Buckingham Palace.

Yet, despite such vivid evidence of occasional democratisation, there *is* an underlying validity in Butler's view that some lives are more to be mourned than others. In this book I shall seek to explore the principles and taken-for-granted practices through which Western obituaries continue to be oriented particularly to the dominant discourses — and thus to elites, a Eurocentric location and to masculine achievement. This will be undertaken by obituary studies adopting both quantitative and qualitative analyses, alongside interviews with the obituary editors. Further, I will explore the wider theoretical significance of the obituary not just in relation to issues of national memory, but also for the light it continues to shed on the social relations of class, gender and ethnicity.

THE SOCIOGENESIS OF THE OBITUARY

The first *modern* obituaries in newspapers or periodicals or death announcements accompanied by brief biographies, appeared in 1731,[2] in the London-based *The Gentleman's Magazine*. Under the editorship of John Nichols in 1778, this magazine: 'established a standard of necrology for modern times' (Fergusson 1999: 149). Interestingly, the eighteenth century net of 'eminent persons' was cast unusually widely, including in one issue — as Fergusson shows — an astronomer, a well-known widow, a man with thousands of descendents, a 'wild man' who lived by poaching and John Wesley (an obituary of eight pages) (1999: 149–50).

The precursors for these magazine obits were earlier books of short biographies. Particularly influential were John Aubrey's *Brief Lives*, written from 1669–96 (Clark, 1898). In uncanny resemblance to today's obituaries, Aubrey focuses especially on philosophy, the arts, the sciences and the political field — mainly delineating men, but with a minority of scholarly woman.[3] However, Aubrey's seventeenth century actors existed within a wider cosmos that is radically different from our post-Enlightenment universe. It is not just that he views his subjects' lives as profoundly affected by the astrological conjuncture at the precise minute of their birth, and by their predominant humour (phlegm, choler, melancholia, sanguinity) (1898: 48). A more profound contrast is that most of his subjects pursued their work in highly unstable political structures, in which they were imminently in danger of being exposed and forced into ideological conformity or exile. In the Civil War, especially, these actors experienced a 'world turned upside down', a social reality more changeable than was the Second World War for today's obituary subjects. The 2000–2001 subjects had fewer temptations to be 'turncoats and opportunists'.[4]

There is also a striking historical difference in the portrayal of the arts. From the 1850s' emergence of modernism, these have been constructed as a refuge or 'pure world', based on the practice of art for its own sake. Aubrey, in sharp contrast writes vividly of contemporary artists' *interests* — their need for money and their deep fear of material insecurity — adopting a practical tone quite remote from the later ethos of idealised cultural production. Moreover, Aubrey's subjects inhabit a noticeably less specialised world, where thinkers can be at once mathematicians and philosophers (Descartes), or Lord Chancellors and epistemologists (Bacon). In our sample, Iannis Xenakis, both an experimental composer and architect, was alone in having two concurrent specialisations.

Aubrey's biographies were sparked off through his personal acquaintances, centring especially on Oxford and Cambridge. The eighteenth century journal, such as *The Gentleman's Magazine*, provided a broader framework for its obits. It is no coincidence that the secular obituary, this 'first stab at biography' (Fergusson 1999: 150), emerged at the same time as the coffee-houses and the new reading public within Habermas's democratic eighteenth century public sphere (Habermas 1989; Houlbrooke 1998: 329–30[5]; Sennett 1984; Lara 1998):

> However much the [...] salons and coffee-houses may have differed in the size and composition of their publics [...] they all organised discussion among private people that tended to be ongoing [...] First, they preserved a kind of social intercourse that [...] disregarded status altogether...Laws of the market were suspended as were laws of the state [...] Secondly, discussion within such a public presupposed the problematisation of areas that until then had not been questioned [...] Thirdly, the same process that converted culture into a commodity [...] established the public as in principle inclusive. (Habermas 1989: 36–37)

Here the male members (p. 33) of the bourgeoisie and artisans jostled next to the aristocracy, whilst new forms of evaluation, notably literary criticism, emerged out of the expanded cultural maelstrom (Eagleton 1984: 12–13). As Habermas points out, this was a public space in which the press was freely available, cheap and radically anti-hierarchical.[6]

The Gentleman's Magazine was to pass the obit baton in1785 to *The Daily Universal Register* — better-known later as *The Times* — which was another staple of the coffee-houses. This paper was to revolutionise production by its early use of the steam press and by a network of foreign correspondents. It early acquired a reputation for impartial, independent journalism[7] (Anon.1935, 18).

When *The Daily Universal Register* first appeared in 1785, it carried only death notices. By 1835, retitled, it had begun to feature obituaries: unpaid commemorations which focussed on the individual significance of its subjects' public lives (see the obituary for the Headmaster of Harrow, 7 November 1835). But for a considerable period *The Times* obituaries took a highly conventional and formulaic form. 'The Obituary' listed deaths in order of precedence, as part of an *annual* record of 'Death's Doings'. Thus the list for 1869 started with the names of those in the House of Lords, followed with those of baronets, then those in the worlds of art, literature and science, the legal world, the professional army and the House of Commons and ended with the medical world, with a coda containing 'foreign royalty and dignitaries'. Concurrently, detailed obituaries of an individual, modern type appeared as *occasional* separate entries (see Prof. Jukes, 3 August 1869). Their appearance did not become a regular feature until 1879, when 515 individual deaths were noted in this form throughout the year, sometimes taking the shape of a specialised obit column. Today's obituary was in fact inaugurated under the editorship of Delane (1841–1877) who expanded the form, making obituaries 'the first drafts of history' that they are now (Brunskill 2005: xiii).

The obituary thus became linked to class. Indeed, as Fergusson nicely comments: 'for many years [*The Times*] was the only place to be seen dead in' (1999: 152). Aristocrats would make sure their servants informed *The Times* of their impending demise. Despite its middle-class founder, who had made his money as a coal merchant (Anon., 1935: xii–6), *The Times*, by the twentieth century, had become staffed by the haute bourgeoisie or minor aristocracy. Possessing, themselves, an 'effortless authority' (Fergusson, 1999: 152), this assurance became transferred to the impersonal judgements and dignity of its post-mortem judgements. In fact, as will be shown in chapter 4, this Establishment character had produced in its entries for the year 1900 an apparent return to the traditional order. For obituaries appearing in *The Times*, the dissenting and pacifist tradition of the progressive bourgeoisie were entirely absent from the agenda of power.[8] What was at stake instead, then, was not just the invention of the nation, but of new 'feudal' traditions, of which the obituary, ordered by hierarchical precedence and genealogical pedigree, was one.[9] Its tacit rules of operation now turned on these regular circuits of elite information and canons of eligibility,[10] far from the expansive curiosity of *The Gentleman's Magazine*. In the late nineteenth century and through much of the twentieth, no paper seriously competed with it: 'the paper's obituaries were matchless' (Fergusson 1999: 153).

It has become conventional to see the command *The Times* had over obituaries as shattered by two changes. Firstly, the birth of *The Independent* in 1985 went hand-in-hand with author-attributed contrbutions, as opposed to the anonymous form that had prevailed in *The Times*. Secondly, at *The Daily Telegraph*, Hugh Montgomery-Massingberd took office as obituaries' editor, inaugurating a new informality and directness of style, even a 'sepulchral hilarity' (Fergusson 1999: 155). In brief, by the 1980s, the form is claimed by contemporary newspaper editors to have entered a 'brave new world'. In this symbolic revolution, the obituary had made the transition from the closed universe of *The Times* Establishment to the open cosmos ushered in by *The Independent* and Massingberd. A new set of evaluative criteria and a plurality of voices had replaced the old, 'subverting the traditional obit from within'. The Massingberd revolution engineered a reactive shift even in *The Times*. If Rupert Hart-Davis had complained (in 1956) of the space for the 'Sewage Disposal Officer for Uppingham' — read, the routinised appearance of The Establishment — by the 1990s the Sewage Officer had been whisked away (Brunskill 2005: xii–xiii). Similarly *The Guardian* Obituaries editor, when interviewed, refers to the stringent reappraisal of who should get such a notice. Challenges began to appear to the traditional procedures, such as the rule that every diplomat who had completed two tours was entitled, after death, to such dignified inclusion in the obituary columns (on obituaries editors, see ch. 5).[11]

In America, other innovations appeared — Alden Whitman (the *New York Times*) interviewed subjects for their entry before they died, thus giving an entirely new meaning to the obituary writer as 'the recording angel'. This gave an extra gravitas to an interview with an actress or artist, as Bette Davis was quick to appreciate (BBC, Radio 4, 3 February 2006).[12] In France, *Le Monde* broke new ground by extending highly critical obituaries even to former Prime Ministers — such as Chaban-Delmas — whilst at the same time, their language changed, even sometimes permitting those disruptions of grammatical rules that are typical of avant-garde styles.

The consensus on the part of the obituary writers is that 'a great flowering at the end of the twentieth century' has occurred (Fergusson 1999: 151). The transformations of the genre, since Aubrey's *Brief Lives*, have been sustained. The leitmotif of all this is that the 'general reader' has now been assumed to consume the columns of the obit where before he/she was missing. In other words, the obituary has opened up, just as Liz Stanley has detailed the expansion of auto/biography more broadly to ordinary working-class lives, to women, and even to those whose lives are characterised by disorder, waywardness or fragmented experience (Stanley 1992: 12–13).

Yet the auto/biography as such is under the expressive control of its author and is thus as profound (or simplistic) as he or she is. In contrast, one characteristic of the *obituary* is that these lives are *selected* as particularly memorable, distinguished or newsworthy. For figures in the arts in particular, the obituary features as a crucial benchmark of later consecration or canonisation. Hence, the tension at its heart, so that the obit, despite its democratic ambitions, could still be described recently by a sociologist as limited to 'the upper classes, the famous and the socially mobile' (Walter 1994: 183).

It will be argued in the following chapters that this 'great flowering', associated with the increased democratisation of the obituary under the editors of the 1980s, is merely a further stage of the inclusiveness which started with the *Gentleman's Magazine* and saw the blooming of working-class autobiography in the nineteenth century. Yet this is still a localised and restricted flowering, since the obituary is deprived of a fully universalistic character by the persistence of social inequalities in new forms (see ch. 6). Indeed, it is argued here that the democratisation of the national newspapers is in this respect less extensive than is commonly believed, being principally limited to certain narrow fields, such as jazz and the blues, or football and boxing.

Given, the epoch-making claims for the current period by both Johnson (2006) and the obituary editors,[13] the greater scepticism about the obituaries amongst academic writers, such as Butler (2003), Walter (1994), Bytheway and Johnson (1996) and Hume (2000: 147), needs to be explained. Moreover, such conflicting claims are arguably part of a wider dialectic of life and death, at stake within other fields. Without neglecting the disparities, for example, the same *rhetoric of equality* is noted in a different context, the treatment of patients by medical practitioners in an Accident and Emergency ward. Sudnow's unusual ethnomethodological study of one such hospital, based on covert participation in the 1960s, laid bare a reality subtly divergent from the rhetoric within the emergency ward. Certain categories of incoming patients — all provisionally 'dead on arrival' — were in fact shown to be more equal than others in staff resuscitation efforts (1967: 100–105). Young people, for example, were privileged over the middle-aged or elderly (especially older women), whilst those defined as reputable were privileged over those with spoilt moral careers: alcoholics, drug-users or prostitutes. For the elderly or 'disreputable', resuscitation attempts were less urgent, less fervent and less prolonged.[14]

In the rather different case that is in question here, that of the 'obituary chances' of the dead, the main dynamic is neither the moral career nor, of course, age. Rather it is talent, and behind that, ongoing class or elite reproduction. The obituary has a two-fold significance. In the first case, such a notice is itself one of the stakes of class reproduction in that it is one of a series of material and symbolic rewards for lives considered well lived. The obituary offers the rare accolade of public recognition, the first step towards posthumous memory. Yet it is not just a *store of value*, it is also a *measure* of value: the obituary as a biographical form illuminates the social reality of dominance and distinction, whilst only rarely shedding light on the world of subordination. It thus complements what is known about class and its contingent hierarchies, being linked to the subjects' advantageous spatial positioning (especially large houses), precocious achievements, and use of the standard linguistic form from infancy. In fact, everything suggests that the obituaries still continue to feature those privileged by high class origins, as we shall show in chapter 6 when discussing the proportions of contemporary British subjects who have been to public school.

There is another, gendered, dynamic, based earlier on the systematic exclusion of women from the public sphere, which Walby has labelled 'private patriarchy' (1990: 177). In the 1900 newspapers, this was sufficient to screen out women as such — bar the most ground-breaking pioneer — from the usual tests of distinction for potential obituaries, (ch. 4). In contemporary Western societies, when girls are doing better at school than boys and sex discrimination legislation is in place, it might be presumed that such gendered exclusion has been relegated to the past. Indeed, the more broad-brushed view — for example, of Greer — that women are *systematically* hidden from view within this public space is no longer true. The papers, as Jacqueline Rose argues, had not lacked obituaries of her sister, the philosopher, Gillian Rose:

> Charting the invisibility of women was historically crucial, but I don't think that it is the only thing that feminism should be doing, and it certainly shouldn't be doing it if it means passing over the vibrant, brilliant presence of a woman philosopher. (Jacqueline Rose 2003: 23)

Yet — as I shall show — there are still only a very small proportion of obituaries awarded to women. Why might this be?

Despite the shift to a 'public patriarchy' from a 'private patriarchy', women's position has been and continues to be rendered more precarious by their greater caring responsibilities (Jamieson 1998). It is not simply that women's labour is rewarded differentially — with Scandinavian gender divisions noticeably less significant than other countries (Bradley 1989:18). Women's — or carers — domestic roles continue to affect them detrimentally, especially in an economy founded on labour flexibility (Beck and Beck-Gernsheim 1995: 22–24, Bradley 1996: 94–95). Gershuny, for example, has revealed the damaged promotion hopes and reduced material life-chances of women who have taken lengthy work-breaks, as against those who do not (2000: 61). It has also been argued that women tend to cluster in particular areas where they can be more autonomous in determining their hours: in general practice rather than brain-surgery; in pharmacy rather than banking (Crompton 2000). Yet even in such autonomous professional jobs, women have notably fewer children than their male co-workers; further, the more engaged they are within the long hours' culture (as in banking), the fewer children they have (Crompton 2000: 171).

Those who have made deductions about an imminent end to patriarchalism — surely relevant to women's minority appearance in obituaries — have cited trends based on women's declining number of children, their later age of marriage and the 'gender-blind' nature of capitalism and bureaucracy (Castells 1997; MacInnes 1998). Yet these trends were linked, more importantly, to a series of interlocking social forces between the mid-1960s and 1990s. These produced conciliatory managements rather than the aggressive style of the ultra-competitive workplace in the 2000s. Thus, underlying all of these factors for parental carers, is the issue of *time sovereignty* and the degree of overall control such carers possess in their combining of employment and children (Crompton 2000: 175). In turn, these questions are fundamentally linked to women gaining another type of autonomy (more or less cherished): the autonomy that allows them to afford to invest in similarly serious 'stakes in the game' to those of men (see Bourdieu 2001b). It is this notable independence that Gillian Rose's position-takings presupposed, as was recognised in her obituaries.

Of course, where women *have* experienced more gender equality in the recent past, it is partly because in some professional and bureaucratic sectors they have been able to substitute their domestic labour for that of less educated working-class women, not least by resurrecting a servant class. But even in these sectors, those in employment are challenged in general by the neo-liberal imperative of short-run returns on capital (Dixon 1998; Ingham 2000: 68–73). In this environment, men can be expected to do better than women carers, such that 'men will continue to dominate the higher levels of the occupational structure' (Crompton 2000: 168).

With the exception of *Le Monde*, all the obits editors interviewed were male. They emphasise their own impartiality vis à vis gender and anticipate a much greater inclusion of women in future obituaries. Yet they may perhaps be unaware of the long history of underestimating the importance, learning and skill of work associated with women (Bradley, 1989). They neglect the all-too-fragile nature of the conditions fostering their recent improvement (Crompton 2000; Brenner 2000; Walby 1997).

THE OBITUARY AS COLLECTIVE MEMORY

The obituary might also be said to occupy a site within Nora's 'realms of memory': archives, museums and libraries (see Nora 1996). Such realms plunge us into the *querelles de mémoire* — raging in France in particular — on collective memory and history and especially focussed on the work of Halbwachs.[15]

It has recently been claimed that collective memory is merely a fashionable alternative to concepts of social myth and that there are ultimately only individual memories, myths and history (Gedi and Elam 1996). It is argued here, on the contrary, that the importance of cultural products such as historical films and novels — or obituaries — is precisely that they mould collective memory. Gedi and Elam are wrong to see Halbwachs' collective memory as going one step beyond Durkheim and ending up with a metaphysical group mind. Halbwachs never denied that individuals alone are the repositories of memories. Indeed, because he did not think of collective memory as located in a collectivity sui generis, it is unnecessary to rephrase his concept as 'social memory', so as to sound more inoffensive (Fentress and Wickham 1992: ix). What is essential is that, for Halbwachs, any image of the past of purely individual origin would be no more memorable than a dream. For him, it is only in coming together to repeat and reaffirm the past that a group survives, most strikingly in the absence of written history (Coser 1992: 43).

Now the contemporary obituary similarly recapitulates the past, not just by delving into the bare bones of *Who's Who* but — increasingly — via memories of the subject's unique experience, gathered from those in his or her group networks. It simultaneously reflects on an individual's concrete, indeed unpredictable life, while also revalorising a certain view of the past. Adopting this view of the obituary as collective memory does not dispute the parallel need for *history*, with its own collective tradition of theories together with its rigorous individual analyses of archival sources. But it does suggest that Gedi and Elam are mistaken that there are only either *individual* vivid memories or history. Rather there is a great tension between collective memory, vested in individuals, and history/ies.

Perhaps the most important and brilliant plea for the concept of collective memory is Osiel's *Mass Atrocity, Collective Memory and the Law* (1997), which argues that in liberal show trials there is certainly room for narrative indeterminacy (conflicting stories) *but this does not amount to legal indeterminacy* (unresolved courtroom conflicts over judicial truth). Different narratives can be accepted, as can differences in the interpretation of certain events or in the frameworks that have produced such narratives. But Osiel argues persuasively, against extreme relativists, that the existence of corroborated testimonies is crucial in the struggle towards the truth and, moreover, that this is fundamental for structuring collective memory.[16]

I am proposing that the obituaries — coming as they do as an overall verdict on a life — have provoked their own increasing demand for similarly authoritative accounts. Paradoxically, the more the obit has become stripped of its euphemistic codes, the higher are readers' expectations for its judicious assessments.

Osiel writes about the need for the rediscovery of a usable past with voices other than those of the dominants alone, relating his demand especially to the newly-opened Eastern European societies. Collective memory has indeed been *spectacularly distorted* in certain places. A totalitarian or larger power 'uses the method of organised forgetting', notably in Czechoslovakia, in 1618, 1948 (and again, in 1968), sacking historians and silencing writers (Connerton 1989:15). But Eastern Europe has had no monopoly on distortion; with good reason Simon, one of the main protagonists, remarks in the Ireland of *Ulysses* 'History...is a nightmare from which I am trying to awake' (Joyce, 1968:40). Some obituaries, such as those of Reagan in Britain, arguably also represented an occasion for forgetting within collective remembering, forgetting, not by deliberate falsification, but rather by silences and by adopting narrow interpretations of crucial facts (*The Guardian* 7 June 2004, *The Independent* 7 June 2004).[17]

It *is* possible, even in this newspaper form, to write of 'abusive memory' and 'manipulated memory'. In other words, certain obituaries are based on more authentic testimonials and witnesses than others and a future study, based on a wider study of the evidence, would hope to demonstrate this. Here, we will merely show that in the obituaries addressed in these samples, the obituarists occasionally side authoritatively with a dissident 'voice', *even against State power.* An example is the obituary for the eminent lawyer, William Wade, who championed Clive Ponting (a civil servant who leaked certain secret documents on the grounds of public interest) at his trial.[18]

Furthermore, although obituaries are often written by journalists or professional obituary writers, it is possible to make an initial, elementary differentiation between them. The obituaries can usefully be distinguished in terms of their different origins, between dominants' memory, popular memory, counter-memory and occupational memories (compare Fentress and Wickham 1992: 92–127). Thus, whilst the obituaries, like other ceremonies of death, serve to bind people together (Simmel), they also hint at concealed social divisions and schisms (Ben-Amos 2000: 29; Simmel 1964: 17–20). This classification by social origin is further developed in chapter 2, and in the qualitative studies of Part II.

THE OBITUARY AND DEATH

For some, the award of an obit is part of the ritual of death. It is paradoxical that although the conception and nature of death plays a significant part of classical social theory, this has largely been neglected in contemporary theorists' expositions. Despite the work of Elias (1985) and Bauman (1992), sociology has been virtually blind to the sphere of death in contemporary society. This is certainly a striking omission in comparison with both anthropology from Hertz (1960) onwards, and social history, stimulated by Ariès (1984, 1991) and Vovelle (1983), which has produced a rich analysis of the underlying mentalités of death. In order to understand the role of the obituary, we need to turn particularly to the latter.

Throughout the history of death, the commemoration of the holy and the dominants has always been a constant, in death rites and monuments aiming to prolong or even eternalise the memory of certain socially-valued lives (Hertz 1960). The obituary, in its newspaper form, is in this respect merely one of a series of human devices which honour the memory of noble individuals, to the extent even of sacralising them. What we shall show, however, is the initiation of *new secular rituals*, from the French Revolution on. In France, the emergence of memorialising through the grand state funeral and the committal of revered bodies to the Panthéon is particularly significant because it parallels the simultaneous appearance of lengthy and elaborate obituaries. Moreover, from French nineteenth-century history onwards similar divisions appear between those on the Right versus those on the Centre/Left over the type of hero to be honoured as are now found in the choices of obit subjects by different newspapers. Characteristic social schisms then came to light: military heroes and aristocrats were honoured in conservative monarchies and the Second Empire, whilst scientists, philosophers, artists and politicians were pantheonised in the Enlightenment and progressive Republican periods (Ben-Amos 2000: 61, 83). These earlier eighteenth and nineteenth century controversies about pantheonisation tellingly prefigure the twentieth century changes within the obituary (2000: 273).

BOURDIEU'S THEORY OF PRACTICE AND THE OBITUARY

It is Bourdieu, in particular, who has most purchase for the study of the obituary, not least because his entire theory of practice addresses questions of social reproduction, domination, endurance and time. The concept of collective memory never figures here explicitly. Yet the habitus for Bourdieu is shaped, amongst other social relations, by family and class, thus possessing strong affinities with Halbwachs' theories.

Bourdieu's detractors argue that his is a 'socio-ideology', merely concerned with domination. If this were true, his work would be intrinsically alien to building the sociology of admiration or distinction that an analysis of the obituary requires. Yet fundamental to Bourdieu is the necessity for both an 'objectivist' situating of actors in terms of their interests and a *phenomenological* understanding of the *meanings* that are actually significant for them. Amongst the latter are beliefs about distinction. Moreover, contrary to some claims, it is not the case that Bourdieu can only explore reproduction. He has always addressed a margin of liberty where transformative agency can have its place.

In this context, his understanding of cultural iconoclasm is telling. He argues, paradoxically, that those with the greatest knowledge of the history of a given cultural field — hence its collective character — have been those most disposed to artistic or literary originality. It is they who transform the field. Further, against reading his work as relativist, Bourdieu's sociological study of the diversity of tastes does not entail the necessary abandonment of any theory of Enlightenment universalism. What he dismissed was ' a hypocritical universalism',[19] that is, an imaginary universalism, a product of sectional interests, and one that can only be replaced by ensuring general access to the means of understanding the legitimate works. More specifically, in relation to production, Bourdieu has always argued for a universalistic approach to cultural value that is also based on a historical theory of the socio-genesis of works (1993a: 263–64, 1996a, 1998a; see also Bennett 2005, 150–51).[20]

Bourdieu was both the writer and the reader of obituaries. His own use of these in the academic field serves to bring out certain fundamental theoretical concepts — such as the *cognitive machine* of education and its misrecognition (1996b: 32). This cognitive machine should not be understood literally as mechanistic, because it takes place via the spontaneous working of the habitus (1990a: 55–56). It does mean, however, that the position of the dominant class and gender tends to be inherited from one generation to the next (2001b).

This theory of reproduction or domination will be addressed throughout this book, both in the qualitative approach to the obituaries, grouped under different fields, and in the quantitative analysis of the obits samples. It will be claimed that Bourdieu's model of capacities, assets and resources is crucial for producing a contemporary theory of class. This would be in the spirit of Marx, yet without relying on a base-superstructure theory (Savage, Warde and Devine 2005: 41, 43, see also Savage 2000, x, ch. 5). Bourdieu's innovative analysis in this respect has always been critical of Althusserian theory for its elimination of agency and reduction of actors to passive bearers of structures (1990a: 41), but it has also been distanced from certain over-voluntaristic aspects of phenomenology (1990a: 21). It emphasises both actors' possession of economic or cultural capital as well as the principles of symbolic vision and division (class, religious or nationalist) with which they structure their mental world.

Fundamental to this book is Bourdieu's criticism of 'the biographical illusion' — the individualist assumption within the orthodox biography of a unified self and a steady mountain climb to the ascent (see also Stanley, 1992: 6–10). But, Bourdieu rejects also the simple antithesis of this view — an extreme assumption of fundamental contingency and the unpredictable fragmentation of the self ('"In each one of us" [he quotes from Durkheim] "is contained the person we were yesterday"' (1990a: 56)).

To summarize, the main theories and concepts for the analysis of the obituaries are drawn from Bourdieu's logic of practice, the structured mentalités of death and the notion of collective memory (see chs. 1–3). However in order to understand the contemporary, 2000–2001, obituaries, the sociogenesis, or history of the obituary must be sketched further. Chapter 4 thus shows that the 1900 *Times* revealed the hegemony of the upper-class military leader and the subordinate status of the industrial bourgeoisie: at this point, women are almost entirely contained within the constrained space of the private sphere.[21] By 1948, however, *The Times'* obituaries span a group of new heroes — notably the American banker, as in the case of Pierpoint Morgan, but also national figures who stand for Keynesian popular welfare — most prominently, an innovative judge, a plant scientist, an expert on potato yields and a regional planning officer.

The interviews with the obituary writers and editors (ch. 5) are intended to illuminate the microworld of obituary production. This focuses on their taken-for-granted assumptions as well as their dilemmas. In chapter 6, this is followed with quantitative research into the 2000–2001 obits, written with Esperanza Bielsa, which addresses systematically *whose* 'lives we choose to remember' and what attributes they have. These findings are drawn from a sample of a minimum of one hundred obituaries from different newspapers, chiefly from Britain, but also, for cross-national comparison, from the United States and France. Amongst the more unexpected discoveries are not just that a high proportion of the British subjects of obituaries continue to have been to public school[22] but also that — in the British newspapers — a large number of obits subjects have been to Oxford or Cambridge universities. Indeed, in recent years the obituary subjects have possessed a disproportionately high level of academic cultural capital, a level that was unnecessary for distinction in a previous epoch.

Along with the privileged education, we see reflected back in the obituary mirrors of mortality societies with a high degree of class immobility. It is evident that almost all of these subjects of the quantitative samples can be classified as members of the dominant class (using Bourdieu's broad definition). Moreover, it will be shown that a much higher number than expected also had *social origins* in the dominant class. Conversely, only a small proportion of the sample had been upwardly-mobile. However, the obituary subjects do show consistent variations in relation to newspapers, since each newspaper has an implicit 'contract' between their readers and the editorial staff (Bourdieu and Passeron 1990: 25).

Another unexpected discovery is the prevalence of *migration* across national boundaries on the part of the obits subjects or their parents. This unusually high number includes, of course, those who were forced into exile by Nazism, Stalinism or Francoism, such as the Spanish poet, Jose Valente, (*The Times*, 27 July 2000). But it also includes those migrants whose social origins were in postcolonial societies and whose 'double vision' or cognitive breadth has stimulated both acute responses to modernity and new cultural production, such as the writer, Ola Rotimi, *The Guardian*, 17 October 2000) (Ahmad 1992, Bhabha 1994, Casanova 2004, Smith 2004). Indeed — against the expectation of Judith Butler, quoted above — there now appear occasional British obituaries for Palestinian refugees, such as the striking memorial for the Palestinian poet, Fadwa Tuqan (*The Times* 3 January 2004).

Yet despite the post-colonial migrants, the obits still include extremely few subjects from the global South. These figures only represent a significant transition at all if seen against their total invisibility in 1900. Moreover, today's memorialised citizens, at least as consecrated by the obituary, have not become noticeably 'blackened' or ethnically diverse, even in recent years. At 4 per cent black overall (mainly popular musicians and sports figures) and only 4 per cent explicitly Jewish, this is a conspicuously homogenous elite.[23]

In brief, there is a noticeable discrepancy between the views of the obituary editors that these columns have been opened out to anyone who had had a memorable life and the social reality that has been uncovered here. Despite certain elements of undoubted democratisation of the obituary since 1900, our assessment suggests that the group with 'grievable lives' still remains socially very limited.

The remaining chapters seek to illuminate this discrepancy further. The interviews with the obituary editors and writers are remarkably clear that there is a politics of recognition at play here. The obituary for them is clearly a distinction, yet they are united in their avowals of universalistic openness. Given this, they may be surprised by the findings of this research. The disparity of the results from the editors' stated aims can be explained partly in terms of their own widely-held ideology of natural talent, a mystifying understanding that neglects the (highly unequal) access to investments in time and money to nurture or even produce talent. But the discrepancy also derives from the editors' daily procedures for choosing subjects, with their regular resort to the most prestigious universities, the higher ranks of the Church of England and the top Army circles. They systematically underestimate the degree to which such daily procedures narrow down all possible 'distinguished lives' to those of the dominant social group.

Part II consists of qualitative studies of the obituaries. These are based not just on the systematically sampled obituaries, but also on further obituaries collected in the period 1999–2006, which allow a better coverage of subjects from different social fields. Although only part of the critical investigations into specific newspaper traditions, like *Le Monde* and the *New York Times*, and into specific fields, these studies have had to be restricted, for reasons of space, to politicians and trade unionists (chs. 7 and 11), writers, artists and sportspeople (chs. 8–10). However, these fields are sufficiently broad to reveal any developments towards the democratisation of the obituary. Thus in these chapters we elaborate further the divisions that we have already introduced between dominants', popular and counter-memory.

Brockmeier has rightly claimed that '[t]here is no in principle separation between intentional and unintentional, official and vernacular, dominant and subversive memory' (2002: 10). Indeed, on the phenomenological level of experience, this is true. It is reinforced by the fact that obituaries are frequently written by journalists, who sieve memories from very divergent sources through a single mesh. Thus in the case of 'popular memory', it cannot be argued that there is an *unmediated link* between the subordinate classes and the publication of the obituary. Even if an obituary relies for its content on popular memory, it is likely to be elaborated, softened and sweetened by passing through the hands of middle-class, educated journalists. These professionals sometimes have to censor themselves internally, the worst of all censorships. For all this, it is important analytically to distinguish these various sources of memory, just as Halbwachs himself did when he noted the very different memory of the Paris Commune possessed by servants as against the bourgeois élite (Namer 1987: 26). Mechanisms such as incorporation and nation-building often result in *all* groups coming to acknowledge the significance of the dead individual by the time he dies. This is true especially of a radical hero, who may be in the initial processes of being recuperated as 'national heritage', his thought sanitised in the process. Nevertheless, it makes sense to ask who were the bearers of the person in their formative years, whose needs did he or she express (Ben-Amos 2000)? Thus in writing about obituaries, we should distinguish between *different perspectives on greatness*. We include, therefore, trade unionists such as Jack Dash, or sporting figures such as the athlete Emil Zatopek (or the Belgian cyclist, Alberic Schotte) who are venerated within folk or popular memory. In some cases, these made a transition in their heyday to 'national memory' (see, for example, George Best, *The Times*, 26 November 2005).

The abundant obituaries of those who came from the dominant elite will be illustrated in many fields. But we also include a group of rare obituaries that are nourished by a counter-memory, deliberately offered against the alternative 'indignity [that] of speaking for others' (Foucault). These are founded on a counter-discourse, of a kind that circulates amongst outsiders. Writing of a group that lacks all official representational powers for example, Foucault delineates 'a discourse against power, the counter-discourse of prisoners: those we call delinquents' (Foucault, 1977: 210). We shall designate, for example, one such outsider, and his obituary as "counter-memory", the sculptor from waste materials, Howard Finster, in ch. 9).

THE GENRES OF THE OBITUARY

The obituary and its positive form

However, a further classification of these obits now appears essential. Despite the fact that the obituary is perceived as a mark of esteem, the individual portrayal ensures that they are by no means always an accolade. Against a naively positivist content analysis of narratives, in which, amongst other things, a lengthy obituary is invariably 'better' than a short one, it is crucial to understand their meaning more profoundly in relation *to the genre* used. Obituaries, on occasion, possess understated or secret subtexts which at the least add ambivalence and may introduce a clash between right and right, thus subtly transforming a celebratory recollection into an indictment.[24] Of course, what might be called the 'default' model is the traditionally *positive* or neutral form, close to the eulogy. This signifies the first and most usual mode of commemoration.[25] But, there is a second mode that is fundamental to the understanding of certain obituaries.

The negative obituary

This includes a form of critical discourse. By revealing the subject's subversion of legal or ethical rules, the writer effectively undercuts the obit's
ostensible objective: to praise. Take the typical case: that of the Fiat heir,
Giovanni Agnelli. Here the reader's positive stance towards the dead industrialist is gradually undermined, initially by doubts about his misogyny,
provoked by the obituary's narrative about his youthful philandering. These
are further reinforced by accounts of his company's backstage control of
the agenda for political power. Doubts finally crystallise into critique with
the accounts of Agnelli's complicity in his own managing director's bribing
of magistrates.[26]

Another instance is the obituary for the Harrow/ex-Irish Guards' stock-
broker, Sir Maurice Richardson, whose Establishment origins might have
been expected to offer a guarantee of appreciation. Yet — at least in *The
Guardian* (20 May 2003) — this again is a critical assessment fuelled by
Richardson's fraudulent practices and his association with discredited financiers and inside traders, amongst them, Robert Maxwell and Asil Nadir.
It delineates him as

> The most consummate city fixer of the 1980s and 90s [. . .] Richardson
> had a suave ruthlessness and used his regular table at the Savoy to spin
> his web.[27]

Today's obituaries offer no theodicies (justifications of God) but they do
supply 'sociodicies' (justifications of *society*) (Bourdieu and Passeron, 1979:
206–28).[28] The obits that obey the usual conventions are tiny, exemplary
tales of our times. These narratives are expected to reveal the heroic individuals of our society, even if accomplished observers of human societies
take their distance from them and recognize the many possible hermeneutic
layers beneath the surface. Yet each positive obit simultaneously implies
the potential for critical biographies of the fallen or 'the other' — those
of dictators, the venal, demagogues. Of course, the specific genres of the
obituary that are discussed here — negative, ironic etc — are not pregiven
as an inherent part of the form. Rather, they are meaningfully interpreted
by their readers, with all the differences in readers' standpoints that this
implies. Nevertheless these variations are crucially important.

The late Minister of Defence in South Africa, Modise, can serve as
another powerful, yet typical, negative obituary. Unsurprisingly, in 2000–
2001, while post-colonial writers have been celebrated, post-colonial politicians have often been castigated. Joe Modise can stand for many (*The
Guardian*, 29 November 2001). His obituary charts his rise from street-
fighter to chief of the armed wing of the ANC, noting forbodingly that in
this capacity he had the Communist, Chris Hani, killed in the brutal Quat-

tro camp. Becoming Defence Minister, he came to amass £5.6 million in shares. He died, nevertheless, decorated by Mbeki with the South African Grand Cross.

The obituarist progressively sows seeds of doubt about Modise: references to his 'staggering brutality, extraordinary abuse of power' are followed by subsequent evidence of corruption. He ends, using Shakespearean innuendo to reinforce Modise's critics: 'So his friends say, for all his sins, Joe Modise served the new South Africa well'. By this mustering of the evidence, the reader realises that the verdict should not rest with his friends.

A parallel narrative of accumulating misuse of power is deployed in the case of Jack Dash, the dockers' leader, in *The Daily Telegraph* (ch. 11). Dash is presented as seductive and charming, but an ultimately irresponsible trade-unionist. He is said to have priced his own London members out of the market.[29] In this case, in *The Telegraph,* the individual critical obituary has to be linked to a series of others for militant trade unionists, all derogatory. These men offer the reverse image, as it were, of this newspaper's glorious soldiers.

That the obituary is more geared to celebration than defamation can be seen clearest when its 'rules' are flouted. This is the case with the prominent obituary of Lord Shore (Edward Pearce, *The Guardian*, 26 September 2001), so harsh that it provoked readers' protests. Pearce's obit used the impersonal gravitas granted to each individual obituarist for an unusually destructive judgement of his subject's entire personal and political reputation. The obituary breaks radically with the usual authorial goodwill. Thus, writing off its subject for 'dullmindedness', it reassesses Shore's entire political odyssey as unsuccessful, offering a series of barbed attacks on his radicalism, consistency and intellectual credibility:

> But Shore's political career involved a long dwindling without there ever having been quite a solid achievement to dwindle from. [...] He might even have had a reputation for magnificent independence like Tam Dalyell, but the melancholy truth was that undoubted courage, furious contradictions, and some force as a speaker were never enough to make Shore interesting ....

The obituary includes phrases all the more savage for having the authority of a direct quotation: 'Wilson's comment to Richard Crossman was the more deadly for lacking anger: "I over-promoted him. He's no good" '.

And much more. This is the point-zero of the critical genre.

In other words, there are certain obituaries that the subject's family might have preferred had not been published at all, the converse of the appreciative mode. In the succeeding chapters a beginning is made in tracing out the parameters of these, as well as the occupational fields where such critical obituaries are most likely to be found. As might be expected, these have certain common elements — involvement in corruption, past support for Nazism and, especially in the context of Eastern Europe in the 1980s, a refusal to adapt to market economies.

The tragic obituary

Certain portrayals reveal contradictions or social clashes which possess tragic dimensions. Such tragedy revolves around a man or woman who has had some success in their projects, but who is brought down by a fall (see Frye 1957). It is his/her decisive act in breaking rules or even, simply, in assuming leadership that 'has thrown a switch in a larger machine than his own life, or even his own society', sometimes — but not necessarily — for moral omissions (Frye 1957: 211). The tragic element — as opposed to purely negative — lies in the recognition of the structural forces stacked up against him or her. Such heroes' deaths sometimes usher in further descent into mutilation and torture —worlds of shock and terror (Frye: 219–22).

Applied to the obits, there is the ancient tragedy of the barren wife, rejected in favour of a fertile successor, as in the case of the exiled and melancholy Iranian Princess of the ruling Bakhtiari tribe, Soraya (*The Independent*, 1 November 2001). There are also obituary figures of distinctly modern tragedy: women, for example, whose pure commitment to social justice led them into Soviet espionage and thus to be caught between two sets of ethical rules. Typically presented as deeply flawed, these are mistaken rather than monstrous or pathological types, as in the case of Ruth Werner, the accomplice of the physicist spy, Klaus Fuchs. Thus *The Times'* obituarist writes of Werner, whose mother was Jewish and whose birthplace was Berlin, that 'her love affair with the Soviet system had been born of a painful consciousness of the gulf between rich and poor, bred in the economic conditions of Weimar Germany'. This was only heightened by her observation of dead and live babies abandoned in the gutters of Shanghai after World War I (10 July 2000). In other words, her betrayal was mitigated by the extreme situation.

Note lastly that there are within this type, obituaries of subjects whose projects of power and social mobility turned from triumph to resentment. Who, for example, would have expected that Sir Larry Lamb, editor of *the Sun*, would receive a notice with tragic undertones? Yet this is the case, his obituary revolving round his resentment that he was never permitted by Murdoch to be editor of *The Times (The Guardian*, 20 May 2000*)*.

The ironic obituary

Fourthly, obituaries may be ironic, thus subtly subverting common obituary conventions by inviting a contrasting and distanced reading of the subject's actions. In the mode of classical irony, as Moi points out, the writer possesses a privileged angle of vision and his subject appears as naïve. Such was the case with the 'spiteful obituaries' for Simone de Beauvoir, which denigrated her as merely an aesthetic shopgirl (*midinette*): a 'false intellectual' (Moi 1994: 90–92). Paradoxically, despite their very different subject, Barbara Cartland's obituaries, too, were ironic in this way, as will be shown in chapter 8. So also — more gently — was that for the author of *Jennifer's Diary* in *The Tatler*, Betty Kenward (*The Independent*, 27 January 2001). Kenward had developed an idiosyncratic set of grammatical rules which permitted the immediate linguistic registration of a person's importance in the social hierarchy — a prince uniquely receiving double inverted commas, and so on down the ladder.

In the ironic genre the obituary subject is subtly objectified: she or he can be safely mocked for elitism, but not excluded as a monstrous other. This satirical form is found in all newspapers occasionally and is often used with great wit to point to personal — or social — foibles (see Fergusson on Waugh, ch. 8). A more profound satirical form develops into 'sour irony', in which the obituary writer attacks the rules and conventions themselves and points out that they benefit the institutions or actors who run them (see Frye, 226–27). While this is very rare, it becomes a prominent feature of the negative obituary of Primo Nebiolo (ch. 10), whose presidential control over the International Amateur Athletic Federation is summed up by his obituarist as *inimical to a just social order* in athletics (*The Guardian*, 8 November 1999).

Satirical obits also cover a subgenre which is at present unique to the *Telegraph*, where it is interspersed with their more heroic obituaries, often of Second World War servicemen. This is an irreverent, comic mode in which the lesser deviancy of eccentricities is humoured but pretensions curbed (Frye 1957: 164–70). It offers a series of obituaries which are comparable to the French nineteenth century *Physiologies of Parisian life*. One such is for the anarchist aristocrat (Lord Russell) who used to appear in the House of Lords dressed in trousers he knitted himself. Others include the Dickensian student landlady, Sadie Barnett, the deerstalker, Patricia Strutt, whose toughness was legendary, the specialist in criminal escape, Alfred Hinds, who delighted in long legal disputes with judges, and Christopher Lubbock, a barrister and cricketer, who drove so slowly that he would be overtaken by combine harvesters (22 June 2000). In the distinctive *Telegraph* form, relish for the unique individuality of their subjects combines with a parody of their frailties. Thus, running through these obits is a broad vein of subjects selected as 'characters', judged to be beloved or dangerous according to the degree of subversive threat they represent.

THE UNTRADITIONAL POSITIVE OBITUARIES

The fifth and final category breaks the mould of the Establishment masculine trajectory pinpointed by Bourdieu and offers a positive portrayal, yet one stripped of the usual obituary conventions. Increasingly numerous, these miniature biographies abandon the assumption of a steady ascent upwards, as in the classical career. Instead, their subjects have been thrown by a roller-coaster of experience, sometimes fêted, at other times marginalised.

One such obituary is the imposingly celebratory essay for Joan Littlewood. Her life had been an unlikely one. Coming from an East End, working-class Catholic family, she was what would Bourdieu would call a 'miraculous survivor'. In the course of launching her own Brechtian theatre group touring factories in the North East, living in poverty, she married Ewen MacColl and, when she became pregnant, decided not to have the baby. Although she won great esteem for her *Oh What A Lovely War*, Littlewood never thought that subsequently that she was given sufficient support, especially the official subsidies due to her. Nevertheless, she remarked with some pride at the end of her life, looking back at the numerous touring groups that she had inspired: "I have many children — all over the world" (*Guardian* 23 November 2002). Littlewood is presented as having a new kind of vision and tenacity.

****

Each paper frames its obits to harmonize with its own readers' 'horizon of relevance' whilst often being influenced by other newspapers that a given actor is worth, or is not worth, a news obituary. However, in the case of great political or national obituaries, as we have seen in the case of Reagan, obituary editors and writers were surprisingly muted in their criticism, even in the radical newspapers (see for example, *The Guardian*, 7 June 2004).[30] We shall argue that on these ceremonial occasions where raisons d'Etat operate with maximum visibility, the obituaries still remain important as part of the diffuse techniques by which governmentality is ensured. Although being creditable testaments, based on objective documentation of front-stage events, they also become instruments of 'gentle' or symbolic violence' by diverting the attention from back-stage scenarios. Orwell, it will be remembered in chapter 2, describes similar news euphemisms as relying on omissions and, on occasion, outright lies.

This study aims to demonstrate that contemporary obituaries have changed noticeably from the narrow seam mined by *The Times* in 1900. The genres of the obituary have become more diverse; the ethos developed for each newspaper's obits is in some crucial ways distinctive. Currently, obituaries embrace women in their own right, politicians and writers from the Third World or South and figures from popular culture and sport, virtually all of whom were excluded earlier. Nevertheless, despite the obits editors' claims that everyone who has lived a 'memorable' life may be included, the evidence produced here suggests that the orbit of the memorable and the routines for discovering them are still very narrow. In this sense, we agree with Butler, quoted at the outset. Categorising the social and educational backgrounds, ethnicity and gender of these subjects reveals the small span from which these subjects continue to come.[31] Indeed, this research shows that those absent from these pages at present are not only the working-class but also the lower professions of the middle class en bloc. Clearly, nobody expects obituaries to provide quotas reflecting proportionately the different social groups, as in some inappropriate new model of Equal Opportunities law. Yet some of the fresh air of the 'history from below', that challenged academic history at an earlier point, is still overdue in the sphere of the media.

1 Collective memory

[T]he struggle of man against power is the struggle of memory against forgetting. (Kundera 1982: 3)

Memory is life. It is always carried by groups of living people, and therefore it is in permanent evolution. It is subject to the dialectics of remembering and forgetting, unaware of its successive deformations, open to all kinds of use and manipulation. Sometimes it remains latent for long periods then suddenly revives. History is the always incomplete and problematic reconstruction of what is no longer there. Memory always belongs to our time and forms a living bond with the eternal present... (Nora 1984: xix)

Far from being a series of random recollections of individuals, obituaries represent the activities of social or collective memory. However, the concept of collective memory has acquired a certain contemporary seductiveness. I shall pose a sceptical question about whether this is an intellectual tool which is really good to think with, or whether it is merely an empty, but fashionable, phrase (see Gedi and Elam 1996:30–31; 47). Rejecting the latter argument, I shall explain why by first introducing the *fin de siècle* concept of memory, with Bergson, in 1896. I shall then explore the role of 'collective memory' in the theory of two canonical interwar and wartime writers: Halbwachs, on the social frameworks underpinning memory and Benjamin on the decline of traditional memory. Their work frames the contemporary 'quarrels over memory', which will be assessed by drawing on the thought of Nora, Ricoeur and Osiel.[1] Clarification completed, I shall return to the problem of the obituaries as collective memory and offer a theory of their social determinants, meaning and types.

It is impossible to analyze social memory without alluding — however briefly — to the philosopher and psychologist, Henri Bergson. His *Matter and Memory* introduced a genuinely new way of thinking at a period when the sciences of memory were being founded in late nineteenth century Paris. Bergson is important for challenging the early medieval notion of memory as a storehouse or a great central depository of ideas and impressions. Instead, he advanced a model more adequate to modernity: the mind is like a telephone exchange into which nerve-cells in the entire body play a key role (1991:30). Memory, for Bergson, derives from the necessary interaction of mind and matter (1991:13). Perception is itself inseparable from memory-images, although it is our practical action that crucially conditions what we perceive rather than the requirements of contemplation (1991: 73–74). The entire processing of perceptions depends on a complex selection, in which nerve-cell information from the outside world is sieved or filtered through memory-images of the past, within the visual centres of memory in the brain: '[I]n all psychical states', Bergson argued, '[...] memory plays the chief part' (1991: 43).

However, and here I agree with Lawlor, Bergson should not be understood as a subjectivist (2003: 29). He also thought that such perceptions — filtered through memory- images — must fit the test of externality: that is, they must be adequate to the object that is perceived. Memory then, was neither a container nor a camera (1991: 38–39), but made up a circuit, rather like an electrical charge, between mind and matter.

Bergson also made a key distinction between two kinds of memory, voluntary or motor-memories (as when we learn our multiplication tables by heart) and memory-images in the form of crystallised, sensual impressions (1991: 80–81, 88). These second, involuntary images emerge uninvited, as in dreams, but enrich each everyday act of perception. Indeed, perception is 'like an immense keyboard on which an external object executes at once its memory of a thousand notes' (1991:128).

Although Bergson was one of those thinkers whom Durkheim regarded as making a great leap forward in psychological terms, he had discussed only individual representations or memories. What, then, are *collective representations*? In Durkheim's view this term was used to denote those categories and systems of classification which are fixed and carefully delimited due to the long and steady influence of the collectivity (Stedman Jones 2001: 70). Only in individual representations are signs and symbols purely elective or chosen (1965: 25). Of course, collective representations can exist only through the medium of individual interaction, but they are socially situated and are thus 'social facts'. In the case of fields such as religion or metaphysical beliefs, they are conditioned by other representations as part of a wider grammar of ideas and are thus to a certain degree independent of socio- economic structures (1965: 31). How do we recognise collective representations apart from this quality of obligation? First, simply by their proliferation: we have *more images* of the great, those at the centre of sacred cults the powerful. Second, collective representations are often learnt by heart, as in the catechism or the Ten Commandments.[2] In short, for Durkheim, memory-images, like other forms of collective representations, only have resonance and authority because they are attached to social and group realities. Such patterns of collective consciousness might be attenuated in modernity but they are never entirely forgotten.

TWO PIONEERS OF COLLECTIVE MEMORY: HALBWACHS AND BENJAMIN

Halbwachs' 'path breaking' (Coser 1992: 21) concept of collective memory is profoundly influenced by these Durkheimian arguments and by the notion of collective *mentalités* or structures of feeling, developed particularly by the Annales historians, Marc Bloch and Lucien Febvre. Halbwachs takes issue with Bergson's individualistic conception of memory, however dynamic and interactive the latter's model of the mind. Yet Halbwachs also goes beyond Durkheim's notion of periodic 'collective effervescence': the intensified force of sentiments and creativity which emerges from great conferences, demonstrations and gatherings (Durkheim 1984: 99). As in the Marxist concept of collective revolutionary action and its re-enactment in popular festivals of liberty, such collective effervescence serves to revitalize the social in the minds of individuals (Marx 1995 (1852), Bloch 1986 II: 908–09). However, in between these periods, Halbwachs suggests, collective memory acts to recreate events, for example, imaginatively re-embodying the past within a whole topography of sanctified places. Indeed, it is collective memory itself which enhances the depth and clarity of individual memories:

> One cannot in fact think about the events of one's past without discoursing upon them. But to discourse upon something means to connect within a single system of ideas our opinions as well as those of our circle [...] the framework of collective memory confines and binds our most intimate remembrances to each other. (Halbwachs in Coser 1992: 53)

Halbwachs' most sensational proof of the power of the social is that we only exceptionally remember our dreams, since the dream has too much purely individual content:

> No memory is possible outside frameworks used by people living in society to determine and retrieve their recollections. This is the certain conclusion shown by the study of dreams.... (Halbwachs in Coser 1992: 43)

For Halbwachs, collective memory is actively sustained through place memory, especially through the social construction and reconstruction of sacred group landmarks (Halbwachs in Coser 1992:193–235). For example, Halbwachs discusses 'walking a city' such as London, accompanied on different occasions by an architect, surveyor and painter. These representative figures allow him to enter temporarily into their social circles, so as to grasp their different ways of seeing London's history (1980: 22–24). Thus there are different collective memories, which may mutually illuminate a scene, crisscrossing it from their different perspectives.

Collective memory also has a certain distance from public memory or history. Deploying Halbwachs' own imagery, it can be said that while history fixes dates and places precisely on the river-banks, collective memory offers a social current within which we 'bathe midstream'. In the same vein, collective memory often possesses a certain fuzziness, as in the child's evolving views of the father. Only in the days after the father's death is a clearer focus gained, argues Halbwachs (1980: 72). I would argue, similarly, in relation to the obituary, that the death of those we know crystallizes the individual memory-images of their presence, structured by a group framework. Such memories, often poignant, may be recalled within these columns by friends, colleagues or even journalists. Yet in this obituary context, the theorised rupture between public history and collective memory is too total. We might accept the Halbwachs point that the former has more rigorous procedures. Nevertheless, collective memory imperceptibly influences the problematic of all historians to some degree, while it has its most notable effect on the 'new' historians of mentalities (see also Hutton 1993: 77). Doesn't the collective memory encompassed within these miniature biographies — the obituaries — both feed back and shape public historical assessments?

Halbwachs extended his concept of collective memory from the familiar family memories and the culture of religious groups, such as Jews, to the new phenomena of bourgeois society, identifying certain dispositions and cultural inheritances with specific social classes. Thus he writes persuasively of the transformation of the aristocracy from the 'nobility of the sword' to a nobility of public service, and of bourgeois lawyers' adaptations to the once-aristocratic inns of court. Or again, he focuses on the co-operative project, which, through the medium of shops, building societies and temperance hotels, had become part of everyday life for millions of British working-class people (Halbwachs 1958: 88) Here, collective memory incorporated the rational foundations of group experience into new traditions (Coser: 183–84).

However, Halbwachs' outstanding strengths in the study of *groups'* collective memories do not transfer easily to the concept of collective memory in *nations*: nor are all his views persuasive (Namer 1987). Schwartz notes acerbically, yet convincingly, that Halbwachs, and especially his followers, adopts an overblown historical perspectivism at this level, in which the needs of the *present* entirely colour the collective memory of the past (1982: 375, 1990: 104). Schwartz's own studies, which address issues such as the choices of American leaders for statues in the Capitol and the changing image of Abraham Lincoln, provide impressive evidence for some historical continuity rather than constantly renewed choices, according to the latest fashion. Schwartz plausibly argues that, despite a perennial, present-oriented, revaluation of values, the past always imposes a set of determining limits (1982: 395–96). In the case of Lincoln, for example, the earliest collective memory partly survived, although a subsequent, Progressive-era memory of his epic nobility was fused with it:

> From the initial conceptions of Lincoln as a man of the people we know that later generations subtracted little; they only superimposed new traits [...] The new Lincoln's dignity and remoteness thus subserve rather than undermine the old Lincoln's simpleness and intimacy. Correspondingly, the collective memory comes into view as both a cumulative and an episodic construction of the past. (Schwartz 1990:104)

Further, the Halbwachian antithesis between collective memory and history has rightly been criticised for presupposing a positivist conception of history as absolute and unchanging truth (Hutton 1993: xxv, 77; 97). More tendentiously, Halbwachs has been depicted in some quarters as a Burkean conservative, whose conception of the collective memory bears a resemblance to the organic notion of collective traditions branching out from the tree of order (Osiel 1997: 213–14; cf Ricoeur 2000: 146–51). Halbwachs' theoretical ordering of the memories of different groups is argued to be too closely-integrated with the memory of the powerful (Misztal 2003: 55). He has been held to have been over-influenced by Durkheim's notion of 'mechanical solidarity' and by the importance of a solidarity based on emotional and moral consensus rather than reasoned argument (Osiel: 213–14). Finally, despite his fruitful notion of the dependence on the social in memory, he has been criticised for an 'over-reliance on the collective nature of social consciousness' [rendering the individual an] 'automaton, passively obeying the interiorised collective will' (Fentress and Wickham 1992: ix)

However, these contentious interpretations are coloured too exclusively by the guiding concept of the social framework of memory, ignoring Halbwachs' further qualification that 'everyone does not draw on the same part of this common instrument' (1980: 48). Thus Stendhal, he says, has a distinctive rendering of *details* of the French Revolution, although his main recollections converge with the general pattern (1980: 60) Moreover, critiques of Halbwachs as a regressive Romantic forget his inconvenient recognition that some groups, such as newly-formed families, use collective memory to buttress an *innovative* turn towards the future (Halbwachs, quoted Namer 1987: 87). They neglect, too, the stress in his thought on the rational principles underlying group ideas (see Halbwachs 1958, also Coser, 81–83; 44–45, Namer 1987: 41).

This being said, the greater complexity of memory at the level of a whole society rather than in terms of Halbwachs' families, churches and occupational groups has engendered important new concepts in the writings of a later generation. Halbwachs himself started this by emphasising that the memory of the subordinate classes is fragile. Where there is a conflict with the dominant memory, the dominateds' recollections are vulnerable to being reduced to: 'a memory outside memory' (quoted Namer 1987: 73). Subsequently, in Foucault's thought, 'counter-memories' or oppositional memory, play a distinctive role, as we have seen. Counter-memories are also analogous in some respects to Bourdieu's group cultural inversions or 'worlds in reverse', such as that of 1850s' bohemians (Foucault 1977: 160–61, 206–11; Bourdieu, 1993a: 39).

The second great interpreter of collective memory is Walter Benjamin. His most accessible and compelling account of such memory, for him 'arti-sanal' in character, is perhaps in *The Storyteller*. There he links the flour-ishing of the story-telling tradition to two conditions, both disappearing in contemporary societies (Eiland and Jennings 2002: 143–66).[3] The first is the link between the story and lived experience, which always has its roots in the past. For this reason, soldiers returning from the First World War could not tell stories to communicate the qualities of the war, so unimagi-nable was the nature of the social reality that greeted them. Virtually all were condemned to silence (as noted also in Ferguson 2004).

The second condition for storytelling is epic wisdom, which, once again, is based on tacitly-accepted moral assumptions. Yet, in societies dominated by Taylorist production and the allure of fashion, these moral assumptions are shared by progressively fewer people. Thus the storytellers, with their funds of wisdom, hang on only in less developed areas. Here they derive their acceptance either from being long-settled inhabitants, with years of unten-ded observation, or from the more variegated experience of the seaman or traveller. In both cases, the stories told are fed by collective memory.

In contrast, the main cultural source of the modern, deskilled city-dweller is the newspaper. Now in Benjamin's view — with which I shall disagree — the newspaper can never be the vehicle for collective memory. Rather, newspapers merely process information, governed by 'evident ver-ifiability': 'Every morning brings us news from across the globe yet we are poor in noteworthy stories' he remarked (Eiland and Jennings 2002: 147). The only exceptions are the Soviet newspapers of the 1920s where an attempt was being made, via readers' letters, to make a collective product by collating the old form of the story with the medium for the new literacy (Benjamin 1973: 90).

Benjamin's unfinished masterpiece is his extraordinary sociological analysis of the modern city in *The Arcades Project* (1999). This focuses on the city of Paris to reveal the vicissitudes of collective memory. Benjamin's method lies in a demystification of the new 'religions' that emerge in the capitalist city, most notably the religion of consumption ('commodity fetish-ism'). It also lies in the exploration of the accompanying utopia, advocating the dramatic transformation of existing social relations, which go hand in hand with these new religions: the technological utopia of Fourier and the progressive bourgeoisie, ironically treated in Offenbach's operetta (eg, *La Vie Parisienne*; *Orphée aux Enfers*) 1999: 4–5; 8) or the revolutionary uto-pia, of Blanqui, which ended abruptly with the Commune (1999: 26)

Writing in 1936, amidst the shabby decay and destruction of the *quartiers* of the modernist city, Benjamin's archaeological exploration is intended to reveal the contrasting newness — in the mid-nineteenth century — of the material and symbolic culture of the city, particularly the architecture that shaped its iron and glass arcaded shops and its great straight boulevards (see Frisby, 1985: 240–41). For Benjamin such physical forms went hand-in hand with the unprecedented social relations of the modern metropolis. No longer shaped by feudal hierarchies but by invisible differences, these social relations were founded increasingly on both social levelling and the new divisions of the money economy, as well as in the stratification created by fashion. These created the irresistible allure around material (and intel-lectual) consumption: 'The phantasmagoria of capitalist culture attains its most radiant unfolding in the cycle of fashion....', he argues (Eiland and Jennings 2002: 37).

Benjamin proceeds to link these new sources of collective elation to the collective imagination of past utopia (2002: 33–34). His words still have the power to startle, when he writes of: '[the religious] intoxication of the great cities: the department stores are temples consecrated to this new intoxication' (1999: 61) — as though the commodity were the hash avail-able in Indian temples for spiritual exaltation. Indeed, he displays from angle after angle the impact of the commodity on collective memory, not least the new colonial goods, displayed especially in the World Fairs, and the factory-made cups-and-saucers to commemorate events, collected by ordinary citizens (1999: 7, 206).

Perhaps, however, Benjamin is most prescient in formulating his distinc-tive notion of the 'cultural inheritance', which implicitly acquires its salience as a form of collective memory. Now, on the surface, the standard process of consecration or canonisation of a body of national works seems innocu-ous enough. Yet Benjamin thought to the contrary, not least because his immediate problematic was more harsh than ours. This was due to the mid-1930s appropriation of all cultural goods for surveillance by the German State, a process in which any 'unselected' intellectual property was exposed to destruction. Benjamin's response to all such canonisation was incisive: thinkers should distance themselves from such decontextualised celebration and 'the idea of a stock of cultural goods inventoried and available once and for all. Above all, they should strive to form a critical concept that will coun-ter the "affirmative concept of culture"' (Eiland and Jennings 2002: 312).

This 'affirmative concept' was the stance that divorced culture from any practical significance. It thus segregated it, in particular, from popular collective memory, which, as Halbwachs recognised, has always had its forms of remembering focused on solving dilemmas of action. Indeed, for Benjamin, a 'genuine tradition' would perform this function better, since it would be organised to focus on the use of defamiliarising techniques in cultural production and would be more alive to cultural reception (1973: 98–101, 2002: 312).

Despite its seeming resonance in terms of social memory, Benjamin sees the implementation of cultural policies around the concept of 'cultural inheritance' as fraught with difficulties. For a start, he emphasises the danger that only those works narrowly defined as 'art' (consecrated or fine art) will become part of such an inheritance. Thus against the bureaucratic procedures of rationalised museums, he places the insightful expansiveness of collectors who pursued a personal vision, such as Eduard Fuchs. Fuchs had gathered together objects such as *unsigned* pots, despite narrow contemporary concerns revolving mainly around individual authenticity in artists' work (Eiland and Jennings 2002: 283). Moreover, at odds with the then current contemplative awe towards art works supposedly embodying the great tradition or national inheritance, Benjamin follows Fuchs in emphasising a wider body of work. Famously, he was one of the first to draw attention to those films and plays which were intended to galvanise the minds of those watching, even if in a distracted mode: Chaplin's cinema, for example (Eiland and Jennings 2002:141). Indeed, Benjamin's sociological gaze taught him that the transient tastes of museum-directors, pursuing 'showpieces', or the consumption patterns of a polite élite might all too easily become *substituted* for the collective inheritance (2002: 282, 284).

For Benjamin, then, the collective memory of the rural and artisan community had become transformed with the new technologies of the city, so that collective dreaming and a mythic nature had replaced the simpler older forms (Buck-Morss 1991: 23–24). Disabused of the bourgeois notion of continuous progress, Benjamin nevertheless also sees the cultural superstructure with eyes unblinkered by the constraints of traditional materialist aesthetics. On the one hand, he develops Proust's notion of involuntary memory, applying it more widely to the popular experience of everyday life, where it might be triggered off by material objects, such as the arcades themselves or the bizarre chignons and crinolines from a past fashion (Buck-Morss 1991: 462, n.125). On the other hand, reflection makes it possible, in his view, to retrieve memories and by interweaving them into new dialectical constellations, to dissipate the myths of a post-Enlightenment modernity. Both the shocks of popular actors like Charlie Chaplin and the politicising of aesthetics, in the hands of photomontage artists like John Heartfield might contribute to this. Thus unlike the Surrealists — with whom he shared the notion of collective dreaming — Benjamin accepted the potential for *collective awakening*: 'dialectical images' could stimulate a different and enlarged socio-historical framework for memory. These images and the wider dialectical constellations which they made up, could thus provide the fuse to "blast out the continuum of historical succession" (1999: 475, Buck-Morss 123–24, Frisby 1985: 237).

To sum up, Benjamin associated the switch away from storytelling, and towards those impersonal, urban forms of narrative offered in European newspapers, with a *decline* of collective memory and epic wisdom. I have disputed certain aspects of this transformation. Indeed, everything that

Benjamin himself wrote about the city in modernity suggests that disparate elements of collective memory still persisted within the new context, admittedly often only in estranged or utopian forms. Further, Benjamin's distinctive critique of the affirmative concept of culture rests on the unspoken premise that literature (or cultural production in general) *does* contribute to a wider, non-parochial tradition of collective memory. In fact he himself had edited and published in a newspaper, the *Frankfurter Zeitung* in 1931–32, a series of letters that commemorated notable German men and women — philosophers, writers, surgeons, chemists; this series suggests that he might well have envisaged certain developments of the obituary form as a renewal of collective memory (Eiland and Jennings 2002: 167–220), see especially 220, Benjamin 1973: 86).[4] Finally, against the insistence on old academic models of realism, Benjamin usefully expands a theory of cultural production in which development in the artistic 'forcefield' occurs through developing new techniques of production — such as Brecht's epic theatre — not just through distinctiveness of ideas (1973: 87). In brief, as with his critique of the canonisation apparatus of bourgeois aesthetics, we see how cultural production might be moved beyond the restricted channels of a formalist aesthetic, redeeming it as a vehicle for a wider collective memory and thus as a break with mythic dreaming.

* * * * * *

We have so far introduced a notion of collective memory distinct from (official) history and from newspaper information. Since the interwar writing of Halbwachs and Benjamin, further intellectual developments have been made, some wrapping the topic in chic cultural pieties, others advancing into important new terrain. New dangers have been cited: '[w]e have forgotten our own forgetting' remarks Casey (1987: 2; see also Ferguson, 2004: 26–27). More specifically, memory has fragmented even further, alongside the fragmentations inherent in metropolitan modernity itself (Frisby 1985; Matsuda 1996; Nora 1992, 1996). In the context of these multiple realities, the conception of 'counter-memory' has been introduced and has become vital within the field.

MEMORY CRISIS AND FISSION: POPULAR MEMORY AND COUNTER-MEMORY

The social frameworks for memory in capitalism become fractured by rival constructions of the past (Popular Memory Group 1982: 211; Fentress and Wickham 1992: x). Now in the present book, the enduring significance of popular and dominants' memory is registered with much greater frequency than counter-memory. We shall classify as 'popular' any memory which emerges from the settled subordinate classes, whether peasant or working-class in origin. While certain popular memories are purely kin-based and local, the popular memories that are linked to representative figures featured in the obituaries are those that are long-established and linked to collective recreations, carnival festivities and to popular movements for autonomy or opposition.[5] Popular memory has, of course been linked with workers' support for strikes or occupations, and to movements extending to a classical working-class consciousness, but it may also be rooted more straightforwardly in factory-based work-memories, or memories of urban poverty framed through interpretations of personal failure or fate. In periods where open opinion has been dangerous, popular memories may revolve round factory work, but are also censured via silences and gaps, whilst being interspersed with memories of deeply concealed acts of defiance (Passerini 1987). Moreover, collective popular memory is often rooted in forms of community expression linked to leisure, not least games and athletics. In the succeeding chapters, the obituaries incorporating such forms of memory are predominantly those for footballers, cyclists and Hollywood and television celebrities — only rarely does the popular memory of trade unionism or of movements such as anti-imperialism surface within these newspapers.

Nevertheless, public memory has sometimes been subject to a politics of spectacular fission, as in the case of the destruction, in 1871, of the Vendôme Column, the official commemoration of Napoleon I. The Parisian workers and artists' Commune, which came together after the Prussian defeat of France, was built on a powerful counter-memory of the first Empire, a memory that fuelled their anger against the second Emperor, Louis-Napoleon III (Matsuda 1996: ch. 1). Here remembrance led not to enduring memorials, but — by means of organised and grave symbolic action — to the toppling of monuments, a graphic enactment of the limits to usurped power.

Such 'counter-memory' evokes dramatic symbolic struggles over the meaning of events in which the leadership of the subordinated people actively contests the dominants' coding of historical acts. But memory, as has been pointed out dramatically by Foucault, is also a control over those whose practices and knowledge do not fit taken-for-granted historical assumptions:

> Memory is ... a very important factor in struggle ... If one controls people's memory, one controls their dynamism... It's vital to have possession of this memory, to control it, to administer it, tell it what it must contain. (quoted Osiel, 1997: 210)

Despite Foucault's later 'discursive inflationism',[6] his enduring early importance is in having reinstated various forgotten others — homosexuals, the mad, prisoners, inhabitants of work-houses — whose voices had been systematically silenced, misheard or neglected (1977: 160–61; 206–11). Yet when such marginalised others confront their atomised condition, it is often only with an impoverished memory of different earlier voices.

Certainly, they possess a counter-memory, but it is guided only by the imperfect resources of the 'reverse discourse', in other words, based on a wholesale inversion of State or dominant discourses, whilst also structured around a demand for recognition. Yet such reverse discourses can still serve as a powerful social technology for repudiating official control.

Paul Connerton has usefully linked various forms of memory with economic and political power, including entire genres such as odes, or monuments such as war memorials. His research valuably links memory to forms incorporated into the body itself via physical rhythms and into the mind via ritualised phrases, as in liturgy (1989: 85). Such celebratory forms, I would add, also characterised the traditional, highly coded form of the obituary, now dying out. Connerton further argues that when a dominant group wants to remove another from power, it does so by refusing that group access to social memory (1989: 1). Here we have the 'structural amnesia' which Misztal has so illuminatingly researched (2003: 30).[7]

Yet perhaps the most compelling arguments against collective forgetting have been made by Orwell. It is paradoxical that in a period when collective memory has acquired a new interest, Orwell is himself strangely forgotten. He addressed systematized oblivion in his fictional *1984*. But his essays of the period were already pioneering in revealing the distortion of an active forgetting as an instrument of Soviet power, with — for example — the Stalinist erasure of the ignominious Soviet-German pact of 1939 from subsequent 'public memory'. Less comfortably for some British readers, he recounts exactly the same processes at work in the West:

> Material facts are suppressed, dates altered, quotations removed from their context and doctored so as to change their meaning. Events, which, it is felt, ought not to have happened are left unmentioned and ultimately denied. In 1927 Chiang Kai-Chek boiled hundreds of Communists alive, yet within ten years he had become one of the heroes of the Left when he joined the Anti-Fascist camp, so that his acts 'didn't count.' (Orwell 1965:166–67)[8]

In these ways organised forgetting creates an indifference to reality, or an ease in negotiating inconvenient facts.

THE 'QUERELLE DE MÉMOIRE' (MEMORY STRUGGLE) IN FRANCE AND ELSEWHERE

Nora et al's collaborative publication, entitled *Realms of Memory*, plumbs a series of historical transformations, from the innocent continuities of *collective memory* to the ruptures characterising the *era of history*, and finally, to an *era of commemoration*. This last era is characterised by a proliferation of voices deserving an audience, along with an inversion of the order of importance between public and private. Moreover, for Nora, even the *Realms of Memory* project had become sucked into the vortex of the commemorative frenzy, instead of acting as its critique. The passage from social memory to history is depicted with great pathos:

> If we still dwelled among our memories, there would be no need to con-secrate sites embodying them. [...] [E]very one of our acts, down to the most quotidian, would be experienced, in an intimate identification of act and meaning, as a religious repetition of sempiternal practice' (Vol I: 1996: 2).

Nora is here defining once again the disenchantment of the world with the entry into modernity, just as Marx and Weber had so notably done beforehand.

For Nora, the last expression of collective memory is linked to that of the French nation itself, a nation that was defined chiefly through its extraordinary breaks and transformations. Instead of the long-standing obligation to identify with the collective history of the nation or at least its Republican tradition, memory has at present become endlessly differentiated, or, in his terms, 'alienated' and 'atomised'. Gut attachments to the earlier 'conscience collective' still exist but they are in full decline, overridden by the more vigorous tradition of critique and masked by the study of memory itself.

This decline of a national collective memory is charted by Nora in a rich and suggestive manner, which can be used by sociologists whatever their response to Nora's specific ethical/political perspective. He is undoubtedly correct that there has been a profound move to *democratize* the archive, so that hitherto unheard subjects can now be heard, amongst them the voices of women, the working-class, and (in France) Corsicans. Marx once described the founding logic of market society as 'Accumulate! Accumulate! This is Moses and all the prophets!' (*Capital*, Vol. 1), but for Nora there is now a supplement '[Archive!] Archive! There is always something left out.'(1996, Vol I: 9). Against Nora, I would see democratisation and national collective memory as not necessarily mutually exclusive but as rather played out in a complex dynamic, one with the other.

For Nora, there has been an 'alienation' of collective memory, which results from the loss of a clear sense of the past, coupled with a parallel loss of any sense of a future towards which humanity or the nation might be progressing. It is this, he argues, which leads to the undiscriminating character of the archivising drive. Thus whereas in the past the memories of the dominants alone were preserved (as in Sacré Coeur, a church built as a thanksgiving for the ending of the Commune), now we preserve those of the dominateds' as well (as in the diaries of housemaids, like Hannah Cullwick). Memory now may be communal in its expression — like Armistice Day — yet also 'totally individualistic' (as in prostitutes' memoirs). Memory in once-flourishing groups, like the peasantry, may be in decline, yet in other areas, memory has new inducements (museums of photography). Nevertheless, despite this proliferation, a recurrent social concern is still the desire to remember itself: '[to] resurrect old memories and generate new ones...this is what makes them [collective memory] exciting' (1996, I: 15).

There are telling insights derived from this framework, and important studies contained in some individual essays.[9] Nevertheless, there are certain difficulties with the project, which emerge most clearly with the third volume, where the new 'era of commemoration' is debated. In Nora's view, the commemorative epoch — luxuriating in classifications, typologies and hierarchy — is intended to compensate for the fragmentation of experience in modernity (cf Matsuda 1996: 7). Yet Nora delineates also its simultaneous loss of monumental scale, most visible in the disappearance of an earlier epoch's proud 'statumania'. Accompanying this is the proliferation of little narratives, and a shift from the reaffirming of historically-significant events to the cult of the old as such (Nora III: 997, 1003).For this reason, Nora ends with a striking critique of 'the era of commemoration' as a new *tyranny of memory*: 'The tyranny of memory will only have lasted for a while but it is our time' (Nora III: 1012).

For all its sharp observation, there is a lack of analytical power in Nora's model. His sociological history hovers uneasily between a lament for a lost history of spontaneous revolutionary fervour, with its still-living heroes, and regret about the varied politicisations of memory, including migrants' memories, which are virtually absent. This ambivalence is notable in his barbed comments about the commemoration of 'memory from below' (Nora III: 986). Moreover, although he rightly acknowledges a contemporary silence concerning any *rational anticipation of the future*, he fails to explain adequately why a feverish drive for commemoration and heritage should be linked with such a reluctance to debate alternative social visions (Nora III: 1009). Nora's own reluctance to explore more profoundly how these two senses of time, past and future, are yoked together may itself represent a form of mystification. If so, his is a nostalgic Republican mystification, dependent on a particular interpretation of the Enlightenment and unprepared to acknowledge its sectionalist use of universalism (Spivak 1999, Bourdieu 2000: 122–27).

As has been seen, for Halbwachs, memory operates imperceptibly and can never be totally expropriated. Yet for him, too, collective memory — the historical glue of each group — is gradually declining. For Benjamin, in contrast, an 'archaeological' project can discover hidden caches of older forms to inform memory. In particular, traces of the earlier city of modernity remain, partly in old architecture, as Victor Hugo suggested, partly also in literature and art. From these we can gain unexpected insights, even 'epiphanies'. Cultural documents may be passed into the repositories of tradition, but they often register also forms of oppositional consciousness (or counter-memory), which might otherwise be expunged.

If the *fragmentation* and *attenuation* of collective memory that has occurred constitutes — for some — a crisis of social meaning, for others these constitute a struggle of a radically different order. For many late-Foucauldian texts, only a multiplicity of memories is apparent, promoting a retrospective of radically-incompatible pasts. Yet certain more recent enquiries have concluded that, for the most important issues, such analytical fragmentation is deeply problematic (Ricoeur 2000: 26, Osiel 1997). Indeed, Osiel contends that vis-à-vis the wars and mass atrocities which make up the grand narratives of history, we cannot simply let a 'hundred interpretative flowers bloom' (1997: 265; Winter 1995: 5). Instead, going beyond fragmentation, major trials seek to base both legal processes and subsequent collective memory on the careful search for witnesses and reliable testimony.

Osiel argues that the postmodernist case has merit when it draws attention to 'narrative indeterminacy': the existence of many different stories about the same events. However, he argues that certain, crucial stories receive an authoritative endorsement by means of demanding standards of witnessing and judges' summings-up. As opposed to peasant memory, which is self-identical 'from time immemorial', modern memory *is* conflictual and social agents expect *some* disparity of accounts (Osiel 1997: 214). The authoritative legal judgement about a mass atrocity defined above need not be totally compatible with all the other stories told in and outside the court, but these latter stories are necessarily constrained by the master-narrative sanctioned in the courtroom[10]: It is *still* the case that '[L]arge-scale administrative massacre is not the kind of event about which we feel comfortable about letting a hundred interpretative flowers bloom' (Osiel 1997: 265).

In brief, this author writes with powerful invective against the view that all we have are little 'islands of indeterminacy' in a sea devoid of metanarratives. '[I]n the face of this century's abundant horrors, people are not incredulous towards all metanarratives', he remarks 'only toward illiberal ones' (Osiel, 275). People need to 'ventilate' their 'disagreements' and this requires the role of reason in constructing social solidarity: a 'discursive solidarity' (Osiel, 283). It implies a terrain, the law- court, where agents are constrained to operate according to a 'constitutional patriotism' (Habermas, cited Osiel 1997: 208).

Of course, such rules are themselves constantly endangered by factors such as the divergent symbolic capital of different linguistic codes. Following Bourdieu (1991), Osiel accepts that linguistic representations are indeed a key, and often clashing factor in the defining of reality. Nevertheless his argument is persuasive that, after all, the court can be seen as the equivalent of a Brechtian theatre of ideas, where, in the dramatic collision of interpretations the public becomes capable of accepting a concluding resolution at a higher level of rationality (Osiel 290–91). Developing from this, my argument is that the obituary form itself offers a new ingredient for national collective memory, which can also foster this higher level of rationality.

It is in this context that Paul Ricoeur has tellingly expanded the Freudian notion of memory-distortion at the individual level, to the concept of memory-clarification and distortion at the social level (2000). Ricoeur is illuminating about collective memory: he says that we remember most clearly those individuals who are defined as great when they are seen against their background of social time.[11] The memorial service and the funeral are for him part of collective memory, standing midway between private and social memories (2000: 53n). However, in Orwellian terms, he also accepts that the dominants — and especially tyrants — taint collective remembering with narratives of their own glory; such abuses he calls 'manipulated memory' (2000: 83, 103). Yet ultimately, Ricoeur strongly endorses Osiel's conclusion that what distinguishes history and grounded legal judgement from mere collective memory is the presence of a witness: 'the witness constitutes the fundamental structure of translation between memory [...] and history [which can have trust placed in it]' (2000: 26). This means that we should speak not just of the abuses of history but of history's use also in shaping collective memory in its turn (2000 381–82; 450).

In this way, the active shaping of collective memory becomes a stake in a wider enquiry into ideological mystification or Orwellian history-control. Following Ricoeur, it is necessary to delineate 'blocked memory' or 'manipulated memory' on a practical plane and 'memory abusively commanded' on the ethico-political plane (2000:83–111). Such wounded memory is a fundamental component of ideology.

The need to evaluate a record accurately is an element that characterises not just trials but the obituaries (Bytheway and Johnson 1996). As has been seen, *The Times* editor has recently called obituaries 'the first drafts of history' (Brunskill 2005: xiii) Of course, there are practical limits to the obituary as a form of witnessing, in part because of constraints on criticism due to respect for the dead, in part due to the conflicting perspectives of different newspapers. However, not unlike Osiel's great trials, obituaries supply evidence and furnish procedures for a higher, Brechtian resolution of clashing viewpoints (1997: 290–91). This is particularly apparent where various 'voices' conflict within the same obituary and have to be reconciled, where newspapers have two obituaries by two different authors or, finally, where a variety of authors write in different papers, some offering forms of resistance to the dominant representations of an individual. In thus supplying factual materials — which can be interpreted through a wider socio-historical perspective — these exemplary instances, offered in the format of the obituaries, contribute a vital resource for actively shaping and demystifying collective memory (see Ricoeur 2000: 381–82, 450).

CONCLUSION: THE OBITUARY AS A REPOSITORY FOR COLLECTIVE MEMORY

Let me return to the significance of the obituary and pull these threads together. What do the authors introduced contribute to an understanding of the components of the obituary? Halbwachs is helpful for the selective group filters that are used when some operate as the representatives of the collectivity in deciding whose memory should be preserved. The obituary editors can be seen as crucial gatekeepers in this respect. Benjamin's notion of collective memory is useful for several reasons — the atrophying of customary wisdom within modernity, coupled with the decipherable presence of collective memory in various monuments and buildings, and finally, the survival of certain authors via a decontextualising consecration or museumisation process. The rapidly-increasing trend to feature cultural producers in the obituaries is a testimony to this second aspect of collective memory.

Nora describes the drive to gather archives, so as to offset the accelerating transformations of modernity. This allows a framework to address the contemporary obituaries as such an archive, illuminating their dual nature as both samples of cultures from the fragmented occupational fields and portraits conferring 'eternal life' on an elite. Further, Orwell and Osiel are crucial in providing resources for vigilance about repressed memory. These collective memories of marginalised or publicly-denied experiences are of the type which surface in the demonstrations of the mothers of the disappeared, and which in the end create the raw materials for the obituarists of authoritarian power.[12] The defendants in Osiel's liberal show trials cannot sustain their narratives against the voices of their victims.[13] As we have seen, it is chiefly these men and women who receive negative, or critical obituaries after death, when the balance-sheet of justice and truth is found to be weighed against them.

Ricoeur is telling, in similar terms, for the importance he attributes to witnesses, testimonies and procedures for testing which narratives will hold. The obituarist has a lower profile but an analogous responsibility. Since the obituary is the first station to canonisation or more permanent memorialisation, he or she needs to balance telling the truth against those more sycophantic discourses that flatter the family, the elite or — even more uncomfortably — the fond images of newspaper publics.

2   The historical sociology of death

The historical and sociological study of death is of relatively recent origin (Gittings 1984: 4). But despite that, it is pivotal, and cannot be reduced to a mechanistic epiphenomenon of the relevant material base. For key symbolic processes occur at the point of death which serve to legitimate the great and thus to justify the social order. Such symbolic processes of death also encapsulate human struggles against the fear of ghosts, hell, and the putrescent power of nature. Indeed, at root, social confrontations in relation to death are battles over insignificance or meaninglessness. Paradoxically, the greater our scientific-technological victory over death, the weaker we are in attributing meaning to death, as indeed, to life (Bloch 1986: 1172–176). It is within this nexus of the symbolic significance of death that the homage of the obituary plays its part.

The obituary is part of the social apparatus for the selective 'justification' of certain individuals at death. It has its earliest roots in the religious framework in which people might assess the saved ('saint', or a member of 'the elect'), or the perpetrator of 'venial sins' as opposed to mortal, irredeemable sins. The obituary makes an identical case for the merits of an individual, but now within a purely secular space. In this sense, the obituary has made the same cultural transition from spiritual to secular as the auto/biography (Vincent 1981; Smith and Watson 1998).

The origins of the obituary can be traced via a series of religious and secular cultural histories, which come together at a secular crossroads. First and most simply, it belongs to a wider group of monuments or memorial objects, part of a social technology for remembering individuals. Its older precursors include the statues of the dead on tombs. The early medieval statues represented the dead as recumbent and highly conventionalised figures but, by the thirteenth to fourteenth century, these had become more realist, portraying the commemorated individual standing or kneeling. Indeed, by the seventeenth century, they had become naturalistic personal images, often within the context of a family group (Ariès 1994: 46–48). This loss of impersonal status characteristics and the growth of more individuated qualities parallels the later development of the written obituary.

Secondly, narrative forms that originated in Christianity's handling of death have had a powerful ancestral role in contributing to the shaping of the obituary. The spiritual biography is crucial here — at first surfacing as oral tales and then as written hagiographies of the saints. These appear with particular importance at the point of death: engravings show the dying remembering the deficiencies of their past like film flashbacks to earlier episodes of one's life. Later, as in Bunyan's *Pilgrim's Progress*, such biographies take the form of a spiritual trajectory — a dramatized story of a life, with a powerful climax and the invariable achievement of a peace with God after earlier struggles. The early obituary has a similar standard form: if it often lacks the transgressiveness of the early 'life of sin', it typically conveys the underlying sense of a meaningful journey through society. What is at stake in this biographical form is not the discovery of grace in the face of recollected mistakes but rather the demonstration of a magnificent political career or national military glory.

Thirdly, certain aspects of the obituary appeared initially in forms such as the will (or testament). This mechanism for allocating inherited property and gifts went through the same evolution as the biography or the obituary: thus its early religious provision for gifts to the Church and donations to charity became progressively overshadowed by the prosaic order of material gifts of goods to individuals, family and others.

Now all these earlier forms and conventions — the growth of naturalistic tomb sculpture, engravings of a life, and testaments — might suggest that when the obituary emerged in the eighteenth-century public sphere, it would be as part and parcel of a mobile, individualistic and bourgeois society, revealing the same formal realism and the same luxuriating growth of middle class authors and readers as were apparent in the rise of the novel or the autobiography. To a degree this is true, but things are more complex than that: for, as we shall show, *The Times* obituary column, even in 1900, is still a living, hierarchical product of a small elite, underpinned by the status and family ties of an ancien regime. In this respect, the obituary was clearly the descendent also of a quite different medieval document, the *heraldic certificate*,[1] a notice at death issued by the State heralds' office to guarantee the title and pedigree of the deceased individual. Heraldic notifications were still current in the early modern period, for example, in sixteenth- and seventeenth-century England (Gittings 1984: 168). Such genealogies hung on into modernity, being subtly adapted to recognise the ennobling of the industrial bourgeoisie. Surprisingly, even the 1900s' newspaper obituary, with its curiously aristocratic focus on pedigree, retains the traces of this thoroughly feudal role (see chapter 4). In the case of the nobility, it can be accepted, with Connerton, that 'the blood relation is crucial in the mechanisms and celebrations of power' (Connerton 1989: 86 cf Foucault 1978): unexpectedly, the genealogy composes part of the 'urhistory' of the contemporary art of the obituary.

Thus the obituary appears as a form with certain internal tensions, derived from its synthesis of spiritual biography, epitaph, testament and heraldic certificate. These tensions explain its curious variety and its potential for transformation. On the one hand, in keeping with the heraldic status-certificate, the themes and language of the obituary have been highly coded through most of its history, thus protecting the private identity of an aristocrat from appearing in the public gaze. On the other hand, recent developments, as in the case of the spiritual biography, reveal a trend towards ever-greater realism, not least, the inclusion of more transgressive actions (racism, extramarital affairs, alcoholism).

To understand these forms further, a certain dichotomy between different ideological visions of death needs to be introduced. In the first, there is the traditional display of a distinguished dominant class. Its existence is established *in perpetuity* as though it never dies. The family and the institution survive despite the contingent death of this individual. This was what was at stake with the well-known idea of the King's two bodies: *this* King's physical flesh might succumb to death but in the wider sense the king, representing kingship, was still very much alive (The King is dead! Long live the King!) (Kantorowicz 1957: 383–451, especially 412; Gittings 1984: ch. 8) Indeed it was not merely the King who had two bodies — so did bishops, popes and even great nobles (Vovelle 1983: 151–52). Certain symbols at death acted as emblems or silent parables to underlie these truths.

One such was the effigy, a model of the dead King or noble, typically displayed publicly as still alive and 'eating' a meal at the funeral, showing its continued presence despite physical death (Vovelle 1983: 153; Gittings 1984). Here the individual features of the person pale into insignificance and only their noble or kingly role appear in public.[2] Perhaps the obituary reveals the later cultural inheritance of this feudal public-private split? For its initial, highly conventional, form is peculiarly suited to celebrating public activities and splitting off the private, more 'accidental' life.[3] Moreover, just as the nobility were obligatorily compelled to perform certain charitable acts, so the obituary writer offers the nobility an obligatory language of praise. In this sense the obituary serves — like the King's two bodies — to make the social existence of the dominants seem natural and essential, a second skin as it were.

Secondly, however, there exists as well a secular culture of the distinguished. In this, as we shall see, meaning is ostensibly divorced from the struggle for the soul, or the physical defeat at death. Finitude has become severed from the great theodicies or religious debates over the point of death and is associated instead with a secular, this-worldly cult of greatness. If the effigy is the ideology-soaked symbol of *kingly* power, the new symbolic structures associated with *secular republican* culture are the various national Panthéons — which received the bodies of the distinguished — the neo-Egyptian memorial obelisk, and the American Hall of Fame. These monuments prefigure the language of originality and sacrifice celebrated in the contemporary obituaries.

The obituary is thus a commemorative form which possesses its precursors and parallels in other cultural emblems, especially religious forms. Nevertheless, it only appears alongside modernity and it signals a death which is itself conceived vastly differently in modernity. Drawing on Ariès (1981; 1994), I shall briefly survey four key historical moments shaping the experience and cultures of death, of which the secular obituary is one late facet. I shall lean on complementary research, notably by Le Goff (1984), Vovelle (1983), Gittings (1984), Dollimore (1998) and Ben-Amos (2000). Unfortunately, I am limited by the Western ethnocentrism of these sociological histories. They cover only Anglo-Saxon and European histories: in other words, neither those of the Middle/Far East and Judaism, nor the Islamic world as it influenced the West.

PRE-CHRISTIAN AND EARLY CHRISTIANITY: THE TWELFTH CENTURY 'TAME DEATH'

Ariès famously distinguishes between the tame death (*mort apprivoisé*) of pagan or early Christian communities and the subsequent cultures of death through Western history. He isolates four succeeding phases which will appear in this chapter in the form of jump-cuts — death feared as *loss of the self* (*le moi*), death as loss of the other (*le toi*), the beautiful death and the shameful or invisible death of our own period. These categories should not obscure a certain uneven development in the understanding — or doxa — of death and especially the long persistence of the tame death in some areas. This latter attitude, which underpins the writing of Homer, and also Tolstoy's peasant valet in *The Death of Ivan Illich*, has now disappeared. Ariès comments — and we are reminded of Hertz (1960):

> It has by now been so obliterated from our culture that it is hard for us to imagine or understand it. The ancient attitude in which death is close and familiar yet diminished and desensitised is too different from our own view, in which it is so terrifying *that we no longer dare say its name*.
>
> Thus when we call this familiar death the tame death we do not mean that it was once wild and that it has become domesticated. On the contrary we mean that it has become wild today when it used to be tame. The tame death is the oldest death there is. (Ariès, 1981: 28, my emphasis)

The apex of the tame death was the warrior's death.[4] Mortality here was experienced as a relatively non-individualised event to which its survivors were resigned. Nor was it illogical to hold that the bereaved simultaneously rebelled against an individual death — say, of a four-year-old child — but also *submitted to death as a fate*. Such submission has to be grasped within the limits set by the old demographic regime, dominated by an average expectancy of life as low as thirty-two years, in which a high birth rate and high death rate went hand in hand. The death of children, and especially new born babies — was particularly common: indeed, infants were typically not even registered in parish burials. Yet certain categories of death were more significant than others: the death of the adolescent was particularly hard to bear.

Associated with this culture, was a wide-ranging social technology that paradoxically at once created and softened death's impact. This centred on a powerful set of collective ritual actions. The world in such folk communities was, in Weber's words, a 'magical garden' (Weber 1964: 200) and until the twelfth century, only partially Christianised. It was also the sphere of custom: custom that served not to eradicate fears of death, but to make such fears surmountable. Thus a whole set of beliefs and practices relating to these magical ideas existed: that the soul after death might wander and needed to be watched, that demons might steal the body, that the night before the funeral the whole community must pay its respects. This was accompanied by drinking — sometimes erupting in fighting — around the body and giving presents to the dead to help it on its way[5] (Ragon 1983). In the period after the physical death, there was a constant intermingling of the living and the dead, not least in the churchyard burial place. Thus the living went about their business as a community in the cemetery surrounded by the atrium, the cloisters for the ossuary (deposit for bones), or charnel house. It is a strange irony that the word *atrium* today signals the one place where the community now meets — the shopping arcade. The original atrium, within the church precinct, was the centre for the living as well as the dead.

A deeper cosmological framework underpinned the chain of being which was implicit in this tame death. The soul of the recently deceased person might temporarily wander, but it ultimately slept. Bar the very wicked, all such sleepers would collectively awaken at the last judgement (Ariès 1994: 28). This was also a world of little written commemoration, except on tombstones, and even these were often absent in the cemetery. As early as in the twelfth century, there was *some* differentiation — the saints, clerics and great nobles were buried in the cemetery or in the church itself — the rest were outside (Vovelle 1983: 44–45). Yet except for a brief death notice in abbey books or short commemorative plaques, this was a world without any equivalent to the modern honouring of the distinguished dead, as in the obituary form.

DEATH FEARED AS LOSS OF THE SELF (ARIÈS)

The invention of hell dates from the twelfth century. Or rather, then hell — once insignificant —became the subject of theological and geographical debate. Its rise was accompanied by the decline of the earlier world as a 'magical garden' and with this, the increasing fear of death. High feudalism ushered in for many — even rich peasants — a new sense of attachment to possessions. Hence death was now the imminent tragic loss of family, house, vineyards and orchards — the increased sense of worldly pleasures made it harder to bear (Aries, 1981).

The key feature now is the pervasive Christianisation of death, with the shift of control over its treatment from the community itself to the supreme monopoly of the Church, a body of religious professionals. Earlier, hell and paradise had been seen as this-worldly enclosures, much like a battleground or the plenitude of a beautiful garden. Now there was a division of the after-life into hell and heaven. The collective imagination flourished with terrifying doctrinal images of death — demons, burning oil, an eternity of suffering.

Alongside this was a crucial eschatological shift from a collective Last Judgement to an individual Last Judgement: each judgement now based on evidence rather than a single ordeal. Linked to the greater individualisation of late feudalism, this was a fundamental change. Where once everyone was thought to wake at the final trumpet and join in the bosom of Jesus at the Apocalypse, now there was an emphasis on the separation of the ways.

A key precursor of the literary obituary form later was the appearance, from the twelfth century, of the individual spiritual record as opposed to the earlier entry of sins in a large collective book (Vovelle 1983: 62; Ariès 1981). Already narrated for saints in the form of popular hagiographies, this spiritual record acted, as it were, as the instant video replay of the life of each individual at the point of their physical death. By the thirteenth century there had emerged a new emphasis on evidence, with God, the Devil and intercessionary angels consulting a large book at the bedhead. The Devil read out each dying person's sins — from the fifteenth century depicted as condensed into a one-page *biography* (Ariès 1981: 105). It was this evidence that then allowed the Angel Michael to ordain whether the dying went to heaven or hell. Indeed, at the end of the medieval period, few were believed to be saved. If, by the twelfth century:

> the individual biography no longer appears as part of a long uniform development but as compressed into that moment [of death], when it is recapitulated and personalised (Ariès 1981: 106)

by the eighteenth century such individualisation had progressed further:

> the big collective book of the main entrance of [the cathedral of] Conques has become an individual booklet, a kind of passport or police record that must be presented at the gates of eternity. (Ariès 1981: 106)

Interestingly, alongside this, went the first appearance of the weighing of individual souls in a balance, not unlike the weighing of goods for exchange or the assaying of metals for their purity.[6] Such precise weighing is also linked to judicial weighing, and especially to the late medieval emergence of legal courts or assize circuits, with crucial roles for judges and juries. Both Ariès and Le Goff emphasise that this battle over the soul on the death-bed is underpinned by the growth of the new organisation of monarchical sovereignty — kingly justice: the Divine Court of justice is imagined in its form (Aries 1981: 103, Le Goff 1984:211, cf also Vovelle 1983: 144). The spiritual world now possessed its own analogy to the socio-legal process that was so vital as the 'political accumulator' of the lords' feudal power, namely, the new royal courts[7] (Brenner, in Aston and Philpin 1987: 241, 249), Corrigan and Sayer 1985: 32–35)

From the second half of the twelfth century, another new element appeared in the medieval eschatology: the 'invention of Purgatory' (Le Goff 1984; Vovelle 1983).This 'intellectual revolution' (Le Goff 1984: 2) was a move from a logic of two places — heaven and hell — to a logic of three. For all — except the exemplary saints who go straight to heaven, or the irredeemably evil, who go straight to hell — the sacred journey is now perceived as a journey to Purgatory, a purificatory place before angels take the purged soul to heaven.

With Purgatory, came the greater ritualisation of the moment of death, including the making of mandatory testaments or wills — later the memorial service or the obituary. Along with the emergence of indulgences, the testaments became vital vehicles for transmitting the gifts which would lessen the individual's time in Purgatory. From the twelfth century — spreading widely in the fifteenth century — paying for masses after one's death became a vital extension to the concept of indulgence (Le Goff 1984; Vovelle 1983: 150.) At once a spiritual and a material technology for mastering the new terroristic discourses of hell and purgatory, indulgences ensured for certain privileged strata *conspicuous consumption of reduced purgatorial time*. Is this to be linked to the (thirteenth century) growth of an urban merchant class and their increased circulation of commodities? Probably: Le Goff identifies the binary thinking of hell-heaven or lords-peasants as displaced by the 'three places', which, in turn, could be conceived more easily alongside the growth of the bourgeois in towns. For the bourgeois, in particular, the tendency to the elaborate quantification of Purgatorial accountancy made sense in a world ordered increasingly, from the thirteenth century, by urban life and, within it, by commercial and fiscal book-keeping (Le Goff 1984: 226, 229).

Indeed one historian has gone so far as to argue that the entire seigneurial crisis at the end of the medieval period needs to be linked to the cult of purgatory, with its monetary means for handling it (Vovelle 1983: 173)[8]. Less disputable is the emergence of 'galloping inflation in the economy of purgatory', from the fourteenth to sixteenth century. Thus paradoxically, inflation first began as a phenomenon *not of a capitalist economy* but of the cost of reduced Purgatorial time (Vovelle 1983:174)! This underlines the place of the Catholic Church as one of the world's first bureaucracies (Weber 1978: 1172–173). For like all bureaucracies — including that created by the contemporary British universities' Research Assessment Exercise — the Catholic Church needed precise *quantification* of the remitted Purgatorial years created, in this case by the saying of certain prayers:

> Domine Jesu Christe [. . .] only valued at 14,000 years of remission of pain for St. Gregory, is reevaluated by Sixtus IV at 46,012 years and 40 days. From the moment when one introduced human time into the tariff assessment of the pains of purgatory, it was inevitable that a precise amount of money would be invented to bring it to an end. (Vovelle 1983: 174, my translation)

Death feared as remote and yet imminent

Gradual individualisation of the meaning and rituals around death developed, associated with the interests of priests and other religious professionals. Increasingly, the collective consciousness of the village community was replaced by a sense of the soul as 'the advance-guard of the self'[9] (Aries 1981: 286). In Ariès's words, the 'spontaneous solidarity of the living and the dead has been replaced by a solicitude on behalf of souls in danger' (Ariès 1981: 155).

Nowhere was this more evident than in Europe as a whole at the time of the Black Death in the second half of the fourteenth century, until the sixteenth century. Now preparation for death began to *penetrate the whole of life*. At the same time, the living and the dead were torn apart by the frequency of death, reducing the life expectancy in most European societies yet further, from thirty-two to as low as twenty-seven years in England (Vovelle 1983: 89). This created a growing horror of physical death, expressed in the arts of the macabre. Not the least of these were depictions of the dance of young, pregnant women coupled with their hideous inverse images: living skeletons with bellies like the young girls, but split and full of worms. This cataclysmic explosion of deaths created a whole outbreak of *idées noires* which was immediately evident in the multiplying of flagellants' sects and attacks on Jews, thought to have been responsible for the Plague (Vovelle 1983: 101).

Certain historians associate this 'wild death' with the growth of melancholy. Yet it would be wrong to assume that this melancholy had its origins in the greater presence of death alone. As Brenner and others argue, these Malthusian interpretations ignore the deeper roots of social conflict (1987). Such convulsive episodes need to be understood also in the intensifying surplus-extraction of goods, labour and money from the peasantry, as well as early movements for enclosure of the common land (Brenner 1987: 284

–95). Nor was this conflict restricted only to the country. It is evident in the growing separation of the rich guilds from the poor ones, in the Italian cities like Florence and Siena, and the emergence there of a precocious, and ultimately doomed, development of bourgeois guild masters. These were the patrons and peer group of artists like Giotto, who, in tune with the contemporary pope's denial of Christ's poverty, increasingly adopted neo-Platonist pagan ideas, in which death was devalued, secular values celebrated and a more modern and realist style of painting developed (Antal 1947: 159 –79). In the artists of the poor guilds, however, who were forced into an early proletarianisation and revolt, anguish took the form of more traditional, stereotyped representations of the Day of the Last Judgement at Death, with figures massed together at the apocalyptic time. These Last Judgements, especially the frescoes by Nardo di Cione (1320–365), were spiritual expressions of the anger and ressentiment of the little men: they showed the great cardinals of the Church, the nobles and the richer masters all doomed to hell while the poor were saved (Antal 189–91, 199).

The anguish of 'your death' but also the 'beautiful death' (the late eighteenth and nineteenth centuries)

'Until the idea of scientific progress', argued Ariès, 'humans accepted the idea of a continued existence after death' (1981: 96.) After this, aided by the transformation of the demographic regime, the old ideas of death and hell as necessary torments of the passage from life began to recede. Indeed, death itself was no longer constructed as a judgement on one's life. The traditional classification of this-worldly and other-worldly values began to be rethought. The Enlightenment produced a new culture of death, a new 'great game', in which the older, terroristic discourse had no place.

Eighteenth-century philosophes and nineteenth-century rationalists: progressive bourgeois thought and new institutions of death

Especially with the developments of the eighteenth-century materialist philosophers, La Mettrie and d'Holbach, it became possible for the first time to think of human beings *whose lives ended with their death*. Simultaneously, immortality was interrogated in Enlightenment terms. A new culture of death emerged with a mixture of non-supernatural sacred and secular elements. The main form this took — important later for the obituary — was a heightened awareness of collective memory, conceptualised in terms of national greatness. As in Renaissance Italy earlier, national memory was to become extended to other forms of greatness than simply political or military leadership — to philosophical originality, artistic importance and subsequently, scientific innovation. It is hardly surprising, then, that the French Revolution was the first to institute an entirely secular building, the Panthéon, to memorialise the nation's heroes. It was to create the focus of the first Western debate over what *new forms of distinction* might be honoured in a radically modern society, a debate that still haunts theorists of secular canonisation and the obituary today. Along with the Great Men and Women of the French Republic came the birth of a new civic order, made concrete in the Panthéon, objectified in monumental statues and in memorial books.

Death now heralded a battle over collective memory: the struggles over individuals' images of their society's past. The ceremonies linked to death — the new State Funeral or the immediate appearance of a lengthy obituary — are also ceremonies identified with social solidarity or integration. Yet such deaths also exposed fierce antagonisms which undermined further the 'conscience collective' (Ben-Amos 2000). Although dominant groups sought to organise such official interpretations and ceremonies and to draw benefit for themselves from the outburst of national unity, rival interpretations could never be entirely repressed (Ben-Amos 2000: 10). It is precisely this clash of memory and counter-memory, within the immense wave of national mourning, that is present today in the form of either positive or negative, critical, obituaries. And it is this that makes Ben-Amos's analysis so particularly fertile for discussions of modern collective memory.

The anguish of 'your death'

Marx writes that the bourgeois order has always been subjected to a Romantic critique that will accompany it as its 'legitimate antithesis right up to its blessed end' (1973:162). We might also note within Romanticism the recurrent alternation of positive, inventive structures of feeling in relation to death, as against the periodic reappearance of despair, or sorrowful death. If Enlightenment thinking in the eighteenth century and the mid-nineteenth century represented one such positive period, when the terroristic ideology of death and the anthropomorphism of the symbolic world were subdued, in contrast, the end of the eighteenth century, and the beginning and ending of the nineteenth century were periods orchestrated around the omnipresence of death. The threat of death and the ravages of social order, preoccupied Europe from the Gothic novel to Goya's black murals, depicting the mad and the sleep of reason. There was an implicit call for the traditional order of things here, or, alternatively, for a new, ethical order strengthened against the excessive unfolding of technology and the feared transgression of all precautionary principles (Martins 1993, Lovell 1987: 65–68).[10]

Death played a counterpoint to bourgeois rationality. On the one hand, the early nineteenth-century Romantic celebration of love through suicide pacts refused as illusory the conventions of the bourgeois life-trajectory. Flouting the religious terrors of hell, it willingly accepts the sweetness of death (Douglas 1967; Vovelle 1983: 516). On the other hand, the 'Belle Epoque' — despite an unprecedented decline of mortality and of improved working-class prosperity — was to witness, in the rise of Symbolism and the Decadents, a fascinated return to death. This preoccupation with mortality was at stake once again in Expressionism, whose artists and writers responded with portrayals of mutilated or murdered figures to the mass deaths in the First World War trenches and to the sharp polarisation of life in the great metropolises (Frisby 2001: ch. 6).

But first, we refer to a new cult, not only what Aries calls 'the anxiety about your death' — 'le mort de toi'' — but also anxiety about life. Against the crises of traditional religion, which provoked both the rupture of Enlightenment hopes as well as subsequent despair, there also emerged in the nineteenth century a conservative revival of religion. With it went a new fear of death. Such fears were intensified by the fragmenting of wider public and social relations and the enhanced focus on the private sphere of the family alone. At its heart was the desolating loss of loved ones: its only mitigation, the belief in their rediscovery 'on the other side'.

The 'beautiful' death

An idealised portrayal of such loss was expressed in what Ariès calls the 'beautiful death', in which servants and family gather round the bedside of the dying person. The dying man or woman reconciles themselves to those from whom they are estranged and offers them a blessing. The antithesis of the beautiful death was the one that lacked the bedroom ceremonial, the funeral coach, procession, orderly burial and the soul left undisturbed in the family plot (Ben-Amos 2000).

Yet another social reality gave this proper death its peculiar allure. This was the practice of grave-robbery and the selling of bodies for dissection in the new anatomy schools. Such a trade was particularly disturbing for literal believers, since folk Christianity viewed the bodily integrity of the person after death as a prerequisite for the subsequent salvation of their soul and resurrection (Richardson 1989). The heightened risks for the poor with respect to grave-robbery, as against the aristocracy and the bourgeoisie, were the consequence of their inability to pay for the three-layered, lead-lined coffins and for the watchmen to guard their graves.

The immediate source of this conflict, the long-lasting problem of procuring bodies for science, was resolved by the passing of the Second Anatomy Act in 1832 (Richardson 1989, Strange 2005: 7–8, 131–33, 266). Yet this law only served to strengthen the penalisation of poverty produced by incarcerating the 'undeserving poor' in workhouses. The Anatomy Act produced new terrors by allowing any unclaimed pauper's body to be used for post-mortem dissection in the interests of medical research.[11] Not only, now, was unemployment likely to produce eviction and forced labour in the workhouse, it tapped deeply into working-class fears that they would not be able to protect even the dead bodies of their pauper kin from stigma and desecration (Strange 2005: 144–149,154–159).

Death, in the nineteenth century, was thus structured by multiple social inequalities. The conspicuous consumption surrounding the funeral ceremonies, such as undertakers' coaches and the lavish food at wakes, now extended to the bourgeoisie and even — arguably — to the labour aristocracy (Strange 2005: 2 –12; 154 –55). It was coupled by elaborate rites of mourning in the dominant classes, one form of that conspicuous waste, to which Veblen refers when discussing the unproductive inactivity of strong, and vigorous male domestic servants as footmen or valets.[12]

Nineteenth-century bourgeois death was increasingly tied to the commercialisation of activities once done in the home. We could see the birth of undertakers and funeral parlours, jet necklaces and black paisley-bordered shawls as simply the extension of the vast network of consumption symbolised by the rise of the department store, with its money-mediated culture of hidden levelling. But the phenomenon of death cannot be reduced solely to the widening sphere of such material goods. For new layers of inequalities in status had emerged, illustrated in symbolic goods such as the obituary, the epitaph and, for professional families (such as Sir Leslie Stephens'), the Mausoleum Books (Strange 2005: 213). In France, also, by the end of the nineteenth century, a significant change had occurred and the obituaries relaying a death to the wider social network, had already spread from the monarchy and aristocracy to ordinary middle class people and rural notables (Vovelle 1983: 629).

Yet however outdated by 1875 the earlier binary division between the paupers and the prosperous in death,[13] such a divide is still correct in one respect. The fear of dying in the workhouse served to create a structuring of working-class experience in which the newer apparatus of civic commemoration, as in the Panthéon, the Mausoleum Books or — from the late nineteenth century — the obituaries, *was passed over as only for the elite*. These features never became an element of the mental maps of the poor for themselves. No obituaries appeared of working-class men and women. Nor later, did obituaries feature in the Harmsworth/Rothermere newspapers that they read. It is to this newer apparatus of civic commemoration that we now turn.

Civil memory

If Diderot, in the eighteenth century, originated the conception of the secular survival of the great in memory, the inauguration of a national house of memory like the Panthéon, in the midst of the French Revolution, served to embody Diderot's rationalist ideas in a new form. These ideas were elaborated further in the mid-nineteenth century by Comte, perhaps the first to argue that the cult of ancestors found in so many simple societies should not be rejected as simply a tradition of the uneducated. Rather he argued for the existence of 'subjective immortality': a 'Great Being' in which everyone had a part — the dead, the living and their descendents to come.

Of course, on the national level, the 'Great Being' did not mean that everyone was remembered, but that *significant individuals* were selected for memory. Ben-Amos's recent analysis of the underlying implications of this is particularly illuminating. The Paris Commune specified all the chosen by engraving on their coffin plaques 'the just man never dies'. But, before and after the Commune, Comte's 'subjective immortality' in practice preserved an elite at the cost of the others. Indeed in this sense modernity offered a break with a universalistic conception of salvation, open to every believer. If Heaven had appeared in the medieval artistic imagination as a ranked and ordered microcosm of the feudal order, at least in principle everyone was entitled to salvation. The same can be said of seventeenth-century Britain, even if the universalistic funeral rites were accompanied, for the great alone, by a new, modern phenomenon — the printing and sale of their funeral eulogies (Gittings 1984: 138).[14] In contrast, as the Republican order advanced, it served particularly to shape a *selective elite* of heroes. And it is this that we shall also see in the secular obituaries too.

From 1789 on, all French regimes gave homage to the great with a State funeral, often linked to a day of national mourning. However, this ceremonial of death at State expense provoked several issues, at stake also in other forms of collective memory. Which categories of individuals were to be given State funerals? In the "rosy blush" of the Italian Renaissance, the former feudal privileges of Kings, such as epitaphs and eulogies, first spread to the rich and worldly elite: to merchant-princes and humanist creators. Now they combined for the first time *living well* and *dying well* (Vovelle 1983). With the 1789 French Revolution and Napoleonic Directorate, new conceptions of charismatic heroes arose to repossess old ceremonials, even, for example, poor poets. Understandably, national memory tended to substitute in each case the abstract qualities required in a great Republican for those of a particular individual (Ben-Amos 2000: 285). Yet, despite this, the individuals who received a State funeral or Panthéonisation only belonged to certain social categories.

First — until Marie Curie, in the twentieth century — none of these are *women* (Ben-Amos 2000).[15] As is well-known, the gendered private sphere, which spread from the bourgeoisie into every class in France in the nineteenth century, was incompatible with the recognition of women as possessors of marks of political heroism, artistic or literary distinction (Landes 1988). Second — and this is particularly telling for the study of obituaries — the great man, especially in the Third Republic, was one whose personal achievement was through *hard and long labour in the service of humanity*:

> the great man did not inherit his title, nor was it given to him by God; he owed it to his merit and his talents. A philosophe and a legislator, an artist, an orator – these figures were fit the role of the great man, but not the military hero, who gained his fame in an instant and

had something of the supernatural about him. Nor was the great man a unique and solitary creator, towering above other human beings. He belonged to the company of his peers [...] and together they constituted a sort of assembly to which anyone could aspire [...] and they all worked for the same ideal of man's progress...His universalism easily crossed geographical boundaries and historical epochs. (Ben-Amos 2000: 22)

Here is a familiar dichotomy that becomes clearer when the Restoration and anti-Commune 'Moral Order' State funerals are contrasted with the Republican funerals. The dead stood in the funerals of Right and Left for contrasting values. On the one hand, we have monarchs, aristocrats and military heroes — including those who won their honours by a single act of courage on the battlefield. On the other, we have meritocratic public figures: politicians, writers and men of letters, and scientists. In an uncanny way, the State Funerals awarded to the Republican figures — such as Victor Hugo — look forward to the figures that are most numerous now in the obituaries of *The Independent*, *The Guardian* and *Le Monde*. The former category, in which birth and military valour predominate, still makes up the bulk of *The Daily Telegraph*, and to a lesser extent, *The Times'* obituaries.

Ben-Amos (following Simmel on secrecy) argues that 'In general, a death is propitious for the effacement of conflicts, since a community gathers all its forces to overcome the blow inflicted upon its forces' (2000: 29). Nevertheless, a distinction can be made between those occasions where a death produces triumphant rituals of national inclusiveness as against those occasions where it produces a more complex movement, not just a moment of integration but also a closing of ranks against enemies, internal or external. Calling the first *integrative* and the second *exclusive* funerals, Ben-Amos notes the appearance of the latter in the French Revolutionary Terror, and later, also, in the days of the Commune (2000: 29 –30).

In the French Third Republic, the funerals became fundamental moments of the invention of *new traditions of Republican modernity*. Central to this of course was the invention of the nation — Renan had stressed: 'the life of man is short but the memory of man is eternal — it is in this memory that one really lives' (quoted Ben-Amos 2000:159). Within the 'sacred time' (Leach) of the period of death, heightened emotions may have extraordinary results. Such profound social ruptures and antagonisms emerged most dramatically in the ceremonies in which popular leaders could be mourned, on occasion provoking the government into State funerals. Funerals are always dangerously volatile occasions, in which events could be orchestrated in ways that favour both those possessing State power and those hostile to it. Thus in *subversive funerals* the subordinate classes sought to impose *their* priorities on a State event. Benjamin Constant's funeral (12 December 1830), for example, was the scene for a dramatic confiscatory intervention within an existing ceremony, as students and workers tried to reopen the

Panthéon and to deposit the body of Constant, their great man, within it. But the State funeral also on occasion played a key role in *redirecting* the anger expressed by the popular masses, especially through the funeral oration, which might be listened to in respectful silence by half a million mourners. And here again there is an analogy with the obituary. These frequently — but not always — recuperate individuals, portraying them in a light that fits the interests of the elite in an imaginary community.[16]

It will be argued here that the obituary form, similarly, has this potential for both integration *and* exclusion, in other words, for the reassessment at the time of death, of profound social rifts. In the obituary, this usually takes the form of a 'balanced' appraisal of the dead individual: different perspectives are offered in the same obit. On occasion it may also produce, as already indicated in the introduction, a disturbingly critical or negative obituary. In these cases — as in Ben-Amos's exclusive funerals — death is shaped by political circumstances. Here we are going further than just arguing, as Foucault does, that death can be linked to forms of symbolic violence in which legitimation occurs, at some remove from the State (1977). State funerals, it is clear, have had in France a vital role in the haemorrhaging of a Government's power. Our argument is that despite their frequent euphemisms, obituaries play a similar role: as weather vanes of popular antagonisms, they serve to crystallize memory-images for collective remembering — and forgetting — sometimes fiercely antagonistic to the government.

The obituaries of the late twentieth century also allow unknown readers to empathise with a great man, and now, also, woman, to some degree. Fleetingly, readers acquire a 'fictive kinship' in their existence and loss. However, in sharp contrast to the wider social inclusiveness of nineteenth-century mass nationalism, in late modernity, the obituaries are read by educated publics only. Further, in contrast to the nineteenth century, this form of celebration is typically more individuated, only rarely linking the great scientist, writer or musician with any specific concerns for social justice or social goals. The obituary is a device, like the great funeral speeches, for elucidating the inheritance left behind to the nation. The obituaries of the late twentieth and twenty-first centuries have also revealed as in the case of the State Funerals, underlying social gulfs, not least those little-noted divisions such as those which follow from clashing definitions of the public sphere.

THE 'INVISIBLE DEATH' OF LATE MODERNITY (ARIÈS)

Death in late modernity is typically medicalised and thus removed from the home, secularised and thus removed from the doctrine of the churches, commercialised and thus removed from the personal body-care of women or servants. The double meaning of individualisation is at its most apparent here. Death in modernity is freed from obligatory customs, yet the dying are also free from — or abandoned by — their family and friends (Sudnow 1967; Baudrillard 1993; Elias 1985: 86–91). Delivered to homes and hospitals, the terminally ill typically experience solitary deaths:

> The crisis of death is probably the most severe of all problems resulting from an individualistic philosophy. (Gittings 1984: 10)

One consequence of the critique of religion is that death has been stripped of its supernatural meanings. The rationalist critique has not been matched, however, by any equally powerful subjective understanding of death. The reflections of Enlightenment philosophers, such as Diderot, Comte, and the utopian socialists, had produced powerful frameworks for *rethinking* the intertwined lives of successive generations. These have since waned. Ariès puts the issue in sharp relief:

> Death, so omnipresent in the past that it would become familiar, would be effaced, would disappear. It would become shameful and forbidden. (1984: 85)

Death has always provoked problems of sociodicy — or crises in explaining the supernatural or the social order — but such meaninglessness is especially heightened in a society constructed around anticipations of desire and consumerism. In this context, death is experienced without the old priest-induced terrors,[17] but often also without fulfilment and hence any consolation for survivors.[18] Indeed, for some social theorists, such as Walter Benjamin, the new modes of consumption in modernity betray a deep affinity for this meaningless death. *Fashion* and *death*, for Benjamin are analogous, both inexorably mechanisms of change (1999: 62, 79). Death now has become increasingly stripped of its ethical theatre to be reduced mechanistically to its biological degree zero:

> Dying was once a public process in the life of the individual and a most exemplary one: think of medieval pictures in which the deathbed has turned into a throne towards which people press… Today people live in rooms that have never been touched by death, dry dwellers of eternity. (*Illuminations*, 93–4, cited in Dollimore 1998: 119)

One further reason — ignored by Ariès — for the wild death of our time lies with an often forgotten feature of modernity: war. I refer specifically to the mass deaths of the First and Second World Wars, which are best treated as a single event, linked together by a period of peace. Hundreds of millions of avoidable deaths resulted, in Ferguson's words, from an unprecedented reign of terror launched by governments on their peoples (Ferguson 2004; Winter 1995; Mosse 1990). So corrosive were these wars of Enlightenment ideas of reason, cosmopolitanism and universal peace that they provoked, for those in combat, a powerful sense of the deformation of the familiar and a supreme ordering by the forces of fortune, or luck, of the parameters of the known world (Ferguson 2004: 27–33). Experiences of death and near-death were understood overwhelmingly in terms of chance.[19] This widespread experience of mass warfare itself has until now been given extraordinarily little attention by sociological theorists, yet it has contributed ineradicably to the critique of eighteenth-century Reason.

In 2006, a generation after Aries first wrote, it has become something of an orthodoxy to write of death in modernity as a shameful taboo or a source of silence. However the terms of the so-called 'rediscovery' also need to be challenged.

Death in the twenty-first century is certainly still a subject of medicalisation, sequestration and secularisation, as from the late 1960s. If there has indeed been a *rediscovery of death* and a slight diminution of the taboo around it, this has taken incompatible forms. First, there has occurred a heightened set of demands for this-worldly autonomy in the last stage of life — not least via organisations such as Dignitas and Exit, which facilitate the suicide, at their own hand, of the terminally ill. Second, a different ethos of death has emerged, a return to the macabre, just as Goya's disturbing monsters, emerging from the sleep of reason, appeared *after* the eighteenth-century Enlightenment (Williams 1976).

No doubt the global epidemic from AIDS has fuelled this linkage of death to the irrational and the arbitrary. Yet there has been an unprecedented explosion of contradictory beliefs, in which the Enlightenment project of prioritising the living over the dead and rethinking doxic immortality has encountered a surprising irrationalism. While New Age religiosity flourishes in the West, the occult is reborn in societies of corruption and dictatorial interventions, as in the case of Nigeria. Such fears of ghosts and vampires are sustained by a deeper social 'mal de vivre' (Smith 2003; Vovelle 1983: 761).

The pessimism of the nineteenth century fin de siècle had its origins in the growth of an imperialistic bourgeoisie allied to the partial rehabilitation of the feudal *ancien regime*, coupled with the determinist analyses of blockages to reason (Mayer 1981). In parallel, renewed fears of death in the late twentieth and twenty-first centuries have occurred. It is no accident that this is a period of revived international inequality and of anomie in the Durkheimian sense — unregulated insecurity (Bourdieu 1998d: 24–28).[20] Moreover, despite the existence of occasional exemplary hostels for the terminally ill, the segregation of the dying in nursing homes or hospitals has failed so far to satisfy their psychological and social needs (Elias 1985; Walter 1994).

The taboo about death is sometimes now said to be merely a journalists' cliché, more observed in its defiance than compliance (Walter 1994). It is undeniably true that there is a growing discussion and differentiation of death and burial practices, including those addressing the non-religious, or concerned with ecological imperatives (Davies 2004: 81 –82). But the debate raised so poignantly by Ariès is hardly limited to the mode of dying and of funerals, or even the distribution of obituaries: it is more about a series of interlocking cultural and social aspects of modernity that, together, create the crisis over modern death. Certainly, there are signs of a revival of a new philosophical anthropology of death, developing from writers who have offered secular reinterpretations of immortality, including that of collective memory. But is abandoning Ariès's wild death in modernity possible? If he and other historians are right, steel-hard communal supports were what once tamed death and such supports cannot be combined with an ultra-individualist social order.

More fundamentally, we would suggest, only greater social justice for the living can ultimately generate a new form of 'tame death'. For taming *secular* death requires a solution to the arbitrary fortunes, alienation and hence meaninglessness of modernity (Ollman 1976; Elias 1985).To reappropriate Max Weber, a new pattern of dying would be one sated with the completeness of modern life.[21]

3 Bourdieu's social theory and the obituary

> All the manifestations of social recognition which make up symbolic capital, all the forms of perceived being which make up a social being that is 'known', 'visible' , famous, admired, invited, loved, etc. are so many manifestations of the grace (charisma) which saves those it touches from the distress of an existence without justification... (2000a: 241)

Bourdieu's 'logic of practice', perhaps the most powerful synthesis of contemporary social theory, focuses especially on strategies of distinction within late capitalism. It is a particularly useful instrument for illuminating the character of obituaries, since these are concerned centrally with individuals who have 'made their mark'. For Bourdieu, the study of obituaries would not have signalled an over-narrow angle of vision on modern societies. Not only did his sociology often take the apparently peripheral, such as photography, and reveal its centrality, but he himself wrote obituaries for those whom he admired, amongst them homage to Foucault (2002b: 178–81), Canguilhem (1998b) and Goffman (1983). Further, Bourdieu turned obituaries to surprising new uses, by analysing them as empirical case studies for his own theories (1988a: 210–25; 1996b: 5–53.). Indeed, the whole of Bourdieu's thought could be seen as a meditation on time, endurance and social domination, the wider issues at stake in interpreting the obituaries. In this chapter we shall consider the Bourdieusian theory of the obituary as a microcosm of specific regions of social space, exonerate him from the common critiques of his work, and show how his theories of the obituaries, death and canonisation require both an unflinching socioanalysis of the social world and a recognition of the power of the canonising collectivity in motivating agents to extraordinary asceticism. Without accepting the view that his sociology is merely a 'sociology of domination', his fruitful initial theory can be further strengthened by supplementing his concepts of 'symbolic capital' with Ricoeur's phenomenological approach to the imagination and the future.

Bourdieu, at his most sardonic, regards some individuals as able to elude death itself:

> Death, from the point of view of groups, is only an accident, and per-
> sonified collectives organise themselves in such a way that the demise
> of the mortal bodies which once embodied the group — representa-
> tives, delegates, agents, spokesmen — does not affect the existence of
> the group [...]
>
> If this is accepted [...] then capital makes it possible to appropriate
> the collectively-produced and accumulated means of really overcoming
> anthropological limits. The means of escaping from generic alienations
> include representation [and] the portrait or statue which immortalises
> the person [....] Thus it can be seen that eternal life is one of the most
> sought- after social privileges. (Bourdieu 1984: 72)

The obituary, I argue, is another such representation — like the 'portrait
or statue' mentioned above — which offers an escape from some of the
'generic alienations' imposed by death.

A central reason for being drawn to this approach is that in a period
sometimes labelled the 'auto/biographical society', Bourdieu offers a critique of underlying 'biographical illusions' (1986a, 1994: 81–89). In a
sense his whole theory of practice offers an approach to this, especially its
tight-rope passage between Sartrian voluntarism and mechanistic materialism. An article in *Actes de la Recherche en Sciences Sociales* allows us to
pinpoint more exactly his precise critique of commonsense life-histories,
which is especially productive for those studying popular biographies or
the newspaper obituary.

This *Actes* essay offers us a vantage point from which to criticise the
atomised, pre-Freudian, unified self of liberal humanism, without abandoning altogether the notion of an authentic (Kantian) 'me'.[1] In applying
this to the obituary, I accept Bourdieu's view that we must avoid the seductive common-sense inherent in the unitary view of the subject. Clarifying
what he calls the 'biographical illusion', Bourdieu elucidates this by label-
ling as 'contraband' or smuggled ideological goods, the view depicting life's
route as like a mountain path. Such a 'rhetorical illusion' assumes that
life makes up a homogeneous whole, a coherent, directed ensemble, which
can be understood as the arena of a single subjective — or even 'objective'— intention. Signalled by terms like 'already', or 'from a very young
age' this implies an

> original project in the Sartrean sense...This life organised like a history
> unrolls according to a chronological order which is also a logical order,
> from a beginning, which is [...] a first cause, but also a raison d'être, to its
> final point, which is also its goal. (Bourdieu 1986a: 70, my translation)

Against this, Bourdieu argues, in an act of 'rhetorical revolution', that
the biography might be better seen as Macbeth's "tale, told by an idiot,

a tale full of sound and fury, but signifying nothing"(Bourdieu 1986a: 69–70).Yet he retreats from such nihilism. Thus his own, distinctive, critique of the biographical illusion does not imply that agents are merely clusters of fleeting refugee fragments, caught up in an endless, mobile flux. The concept of the habitus saves us from total contingency. This concept, which stresses the specific mode of perceiving, dividing and evaluating the world is understood as a group's experience of successfully adapting to its objective material and social necessities. Although never an eternal destiny, the notion of habitus identifies durable dispositions which inform agents' 'feel for the game' (Bourdieu and Wacquant 1992, Bourdieu 2002a). These durable dispositions are partly composed of collective memory — the collective memory of family, classes and ethnic groups — and in this lies Bourdieu's debt to Halbwachs.

Bourdieu's general critique of the biographical illusion serves to remind us that the 'life history approach' has been shaped overwhelmingly by a certain habitus, that possessing the structuring mechanism of youthful anticipation and educational investment, followed by steady progression within a career. But such an upward ascent is more typical of an aristocratic or bourgeois elite than of lower social classes, whose less controlled existence forcibly attunes their members to more cyclical or disrupted rhythms (see also Connerton 1989: 19; Maynes 1989: 105; Stanley 1992: 11–14, 214–15; Plummer 2001: 17–46).[2]

It follows, as Bourdieu has taught us, that when we confront the study of obituaries, we must be wary of those constructions that identify success too much with an individual's self-avowed objectives and 'natural gifts'. Instead, we shall focus on *empowerment* as a result of birth into an elite and induction into the esprit de corps within great public schools, Oxford or Cambridge. In France, the key mechanisms are the *grandes écoles*; in America, the Ivy League universities (Bourdieu 1996b). In assessing this empowerment, Bourdieu's distinction between various forms of capital is helpful, economic and cultural capital, of course, but also social capital, that capital based on networks and bonds — which bring credit and creditability, another form of material and immaterial profit. It should however be recalled here that family bonds and local networks do not count as capital for Bourdieu, excluding small-scale societies where there are few inequalities. Thus he stresses that such immaterial profits are based on *rarity*: 'the practices and assets thus salvaged from the 'icy waters of egotistical calculation' (and from science) are the virtual monopoly of the dominant class' (1986b: 242). Or again 'social capital [is] made up of social obligations ('connections') which is convertible under certain conditions into economic capital and may be instituted in the form of titles of nobility' (1986b: 243). The working class community, however stable, regulated and even able to offer job-connections, cannot institutionalize such titles of nobility.

The last reason for turning to Bourdieu to understand obituaries is that the contemporary form — European, American and British — are dominated by those with careers in the arts and media (55 per cent of all current obits). Bourdieu's sociological account of the artistic field offers a promising beginning here. In particular, his approach to the 'world in reverse' of the bohemian avant-garde and the range of position-taking available to them opens a new path for the qualitative study of the artistic biography and obituary.

BOURDIEU'S STUDY OF OBITUARIES

Bourdieu uses obituaries as valuable keys to academic or professorial understanding. In his studies of Grandes Ecoles students he uses two empirical content analyses, coupled with detailed quantitative analysis. The first is a content analysis of the philosophy essays of Ecole Normale Supérieure students' (ENS) and the comments on these by a philosophy teacher in the *khagne* (preparatory) classes. The second is an analysis of the obituaries that appeared in the ENS magazine.[3] Bourdieu suggests that each document is founded on a set of ordered classifications of intellectual judgements, like Durkheim's primitive classifications. The obituaries in the *Annuaires* represent, he comments, 'the final test' of one's life (Bourdieu, 1996b: 45). From these thirty-four male former-pupils, whose obits appeared from 1962–65, a hidden academic classification can be reconstructed, directing the connotations of these euphemistic recollections.

For example, in such obituaries, a term like 'aristocratic' — used of a philosopher — does not mean 'unacceptably privileged': rather it means 'distinguished', that is, the opposite of a 'vulgar' or popular understanding. In this way, academic linguistic codes have become shaken free of their original social context and have gained a specialized university or disciplinary meaning.[4] Nevertheless, the workings of the habitus do ensure that there remains a remarkable statistical correlation between a students' performance, their family cultural capital and hence their social origins. This was clearly revealed when Bourdieu matched the students' essays with their fathers' occupations. Without any intended elitism on the part of the professors, both the students' initial academic classification and their later academic destinies — recounted in the obituaries — match their family's position hierarchically (1996b: 34, 43). Higher education teachers thus misrecognise their own use of university codes of assessment. Given that such codes are cleansed of the *obvious* terms indicating hierarchical position — slavish, plebeian, kingly, etc. — they therefore assume them to be socially neutral. Nevertheless, academic descriptions retain the wider connotations linked to classes — especially those flourishing in the nineteenth century — yet neutralize them. So a student who produces essays said to be mediocre, earnest and conscientious turns out to come from the petty-bourgeoisie; a student judged brilliant, scintillating, original, turns out to possess the self-confidence and other dispositions that are the mark of the assured haute bourgeoisie. And so on.[5]

Bourdieu makes another — equally Durkheimian — argument that has not been picked up in other discussions of these obituaries (Reed-Danahay 2005; of Durkheim 1984, 1992). The obituaries, he suggests, reveal with great clarity the *occupational ethics* of the academic and teaching profession. Because these short essays were written by fellow-students or professors, the whole ethos or raison d'être of the group emerges in this set of judgements as an idealized form or ethics. The obituaries — like eulogies — suspend divisive conflicts: the death of an individual makes him/her harmless. This penetrating comment on the obituaries' recasting of a professional *ethos* into an *ethic* needs to be remembered. It is a telling source of that 're-enchantment' of the world to which the obituary also contributes.[6] Yet unlike Bourdieu's Ecole Normale Supérieure obituaries, the newspaper obits sometimes allude to bitter conflicts, both internal and external to the academic world. In certain rare circumstances, then, the taboo on speaking ill of the dead has been challenged.[7]

Sadly, Bourdieu is right that most 'choices' still emerge as a love of one's perceived 'fate' (*amor fati*) — 'that funereal virtue celebrated in obituaries' — which always makes something positive out of necessity (1996b: 45). Yet, contrary to Bourdieu's sample, obituary writers do not simply record the verdict of the institution on the individual. They may also leave traces within this portrayal of earlier hopes that were later dashed. A Nobel Prize may have been unjustly withheld; a celebrated university made life so hard that another post was taken up (see for example, Fred Hoyle, *The Guardian*, 30 August 2001). Obituaries may even stoke the flames of criticism of structures viewed as over-bureaucratic or even corrupt (see Margaret Simey's obituary on the Liverpool police or the reorganization of the Labour Party, *The Independent*, 29 July 2004). As has been seen, a similar phenomenon has been shown by Ben-Amos in his study of French State funerals, where funeral speeches and obits on occasion turned, on occasion, into passionate anti-government outbursts or even the erection of barricades (see the funeral of Victor Noir, 12 January 1870; Ben-Amos 2000: 97–9). Resentment still leaves its after-image in the muted indictments of the obituary.

Given the whole array of ENS obits, each tiny biographical mosaic offers a dual set of perceptions and evaluations — they reveal what these men (sic) were but also what they might have been. Thus Bourdieu is illuminating on the ranking of academic virtues, where he distinguishes between *lesser virtues* and *higher virtues*, quoting from three named obits to display how these operate in typical cases. These illustrate, first, those who possess the so-called lesser virtues — being a good father, being committed to their students and gaining respect for their good lectures. Or there are those, secondly, with lesser academic virtues: accomplished translators or writers of textbooks, who do not aspire to independence or originality. Third and finally, there are those whose lives express the greater intellectual virtues: members of the 'noble race of philosophers', possessing, in the words of one ENS obit, an 'aristocratic' distance from the commonplace. To describe such a man, as in the case of Merleau-Ponty, the professor of philosophy at the Collège de France, a distinctive academic content is decanted into the bottles of the older feudal language that described exemplary figures. It is Bourdieu's claim that this code of courage, dignity and distance is linked with much greater probability to those with distinguished origins: thus it is no surprise that Merleau-Ponty himself was the son of a high-ranking artillery officer (1996b: 47).

However compelling this argument, it *is* specific to men. Such a compensatory language of 'lesser family values', applied to the good male *lycée* teacher is in fact not available for women. For them, the private sphere represents a fraught arena contesting with the public world — to *fail* at being a good housewife/mother is a devastating verdict, yet to be *exemplary* in the performance of these rule-governed activities is to risk not being taken seriously as a public figure. Hence, women are in a 'double bind'. They *turn inside out* the categories of these obituaries.

By introducing distinctively Bourdieusian concepts like habitus and classification, we now need to approach more centrally his own logic of practice. Indeed, Bourdieu's self-baptised 'trinity formula' (capital + field + habitus) invite us to concentrate on these three concepts, and they can be found often enough as catechisms in the proliferating introductory books on Bourdieu. But there is a danger in this literature of serious reification or of vulgarization. Rather, Bourdieu's conceptual tools should be understood as linked to Bachelard's philosophy of science, and distilled into a distinctive and unified theory by means of the classical sociological theorists, as well as the subsequent work of Panofsky, Mauss, Merleau-Ponty and Elias. Ultimately Bourdieu's theory of practice or 'constructivism structuralism' (1990b: 25) rests on an entire architecture of theories and method from which particular elements cannot be torn away without endangering the other structural elements. For equally as central as habitus, field and capital are his notions of symbolic power, misrecognition,[8] a gift economy, illusio, interests within disinterestedness, doxic or taken-for-granted understandings of the world, orthodoxy, heterodoxy, strategy, rites of institution and so on. To give one instance: rites of institution by which a person is inducted via certain words and ritual actions into membership of an organization are crucial 'acts of consecration' (1991: ch. 4). Not only do they *make* certain artists Academicians and certain couples married, but they create all the difference between an act of State mass murder and legitimate conflict, as when the House of Commons or the UN passes (or does not pass) a war motion. Obituaries offer a parallel 'act of consecration'.

MISAPPROPRIATIONS OF BOURDIEU

As already suggested, from *Outline of a Theory of Practice* (1977) to *Science of Science and Reflexivity* (2004), Bourdieu walked along a precipitous path, with the abyss of mechanistic or fatalistic materialism on one side and that of voluntaristic individualism on the other. Other, easier, routes opened up instead: Levi-Straussian structuralism, Sartrian existentialism, rational action theory. For Bourdieu, these were inviting but ultimately arid alternatives, which would not deflect him from his chosen path, later amended as a 'realist constructivism' (1999: 618).

In his poignant settling of accounts with social theory, *Pascalian Meditations*, Bourdieu criticises the fatalistic determinism or objectivism which his accusers level at him (2000a: 234–36).[9] At first glance, it could be argued that he had created his own hostages to fortune here, for his works invoke, more than once, the Nietzschean motif of *amor fati* (fated love). This offers a graphic understanding of the tendency within the subordinate habitus to be complicit with its own mystification and to accommodate to domination (1984, 2000a). Despite this, he insists that while habitus should always be seen as durable, it is not a destiny (Bourdieu and Wacquant 1992: 133). If the unconscious is in part the forgetting of history, reflexivity or self-monitoring offers us the possibility of recovering this buried knowledge. With it, we control at least our second, if not our first, moves. It is within this context that Bourdieu founds his sociological refusal to accept conservative forms of elitism. It is this potential for reflexivity that fires also his political commitment to 'rational utopianism', adding that such utopianism must be in accordance with the 'objective possibilities' of the epoch[10] (1998a:127–8).

In general, the mistake of his critics have been to interpret what Bourdieu called the 'internalisation' of external necessity in a simplistic and mechanical manner. Bourdieu always insists that this takes place over several generations, not just in the course of the parent-child socialisation. What he is defining as habitus are not specific, rule governed actions, but a *generative* matrix, based on classifications homologous with the relations of power. Thus it cannot be right to claim, as Margolis does, that practical action in Bourdieu is 'triggered *by a finished and familiar script*' (whereas in reality the ordinary human agent 'creates a fresh script nearly always and continually') (Margolis 1999: 69). Bourdieu's 'scripts' are, as he patiently explained, sometimes based on written scripts (as in a musical score) sometimes based on improvisation, as in a jazz-player's solo, a performance which itself presupposes a rich understanding of the history of jazz. This is understood very well by Bouveresse who notes that Bourdieu's model of action involves more creativity than do intellectualist models of rule-governed action (Bouveresse 1999: 56–57; 62). Bourdieu allows intelligent *rule-breaking* by ordinary individuals (see, in this vein, his unjustly neglected discussion of his model of practice deployed in relation to how bureaucratic apparatuses work (2000b: 162–63,165)).

This is also what is at stake in Bourdieu's rejection of the objectivist/ subjectivist division. Fundamental to the habitus is a distinctive experience of time. For some, benefiting from generations of material mastery, the habitus engenders the 'protension' (anticipation) of a rationally-achievable future; for others — from families of impoverished peasants or casual labourers — the habitus conceptualizes the future only fatalistically, in terms of a deep-rooted affinity with what has already passed. This is not merely a reworking of Weber's notion of rational socialism (1962). It is also a creative social incorporation of the delicate logical categories of perceived time addressed by Husserl which, as the latter reminded us, always felt like nature.

The habitus with its pre-reflexive, bodily *accommodation* to the social order is succeeded in certain circumstances by a habitus of *malaise*: a sense of the painful contradictions of racial slurs, an awareness of rational alternatives and a perception of injustice (see particularly *The Weight of the World* (1999) for this emphasis on a sense of oppression).[11] The main arenas for this malaise are first, the clash of doxa — or taken-for-granted assumptions — with new heterodoxies; second, the emergence of specialised fields. It is not the case that, having rejected charismatic leader-precipitated transformations, Bourdieu resisted *all models of change*. Further, despite his general discussion of the remarkable complicity with which the oppressed and impoverished reproduce the social order which profoundly marginalises them, he also emphasized at many points that inequalities of capitals (economic, symbolic and cultural) are also the breeding ground for crises. The Dreyfus Affair was one such well-known crisis, as were the later struggles for anti-colonial emancipation, or crises that deployed the language of class with programmes for radical structural transformation. What outcomes took place depended, on the one hand, on the type of *heterodox leader*, especially defrocked priests (the *bas clergé*) or those proletarianised writers and philosophers who belonged to the corporation of the universal and demanded its logic (1990b: 45–46). On the other hand, these spokespersons depended themselves on *the interests of the masses*, who supported their ethics of resistance. For these reasons, Bourdieu's theoretical renewal, far from being conservative, is more adequately described in Pinto's words, as a 'Copernican revolution' in social thought (Pinto 1999: 106).

In his clearest break with the model of pitiless reproduction, *Pascalian Meditations*, Bourdieu elaborated on the 'margin of liberty' that exists (2000a: 234–36, 2002a). There are two sources of such liberty and transformation, he argues: the first is where there is an unstable *discrepancy* between the structured structure of the habitus and the experience of objective structures.[12] This is capable of producing some significant changes. Nevertheless, within a merely temporarily radicalised habitus, the weight of the reified world is still felt, slowly restructuring the agent to orthodoxy, via a lengthy call to order. Such a short-run, dislocating conversion from conservatism emerged in the students of bourgeois origins in May 1968, only to be followed later by a reconversion to conformity (1988a: ch. 5).

The second is where the dispositions in the habitus are out of sync with the positions available in a given field, especially a field of cultural production. Here, the dissident is able to play in a sustained manner on the resulting tensions and conflicts he or she experiences, so as to bring about world-historical changes. In 'the most extraordinary intellectual and artistic revolutions', he states, agents operate on 'a subversive habitus', connected with 'dynamic friction' to the field, so as to remake structures (2002a: 31–32).

From *The Rules of Art* on, Bourdieu was to be engaged in an unstated war with other philosophers, often over their common Bachelardian and Canguilhemian legacy of realist rationalism (Bachelard 1986: 8–10; McAllester Jones chs. 1–3). Bourdieu was to dissociate his theory from other analyses of discourses, such as those of Foucault, which, in starkly asserting a struggle between different 'knowledges' in relation to power, abandons any ordering of cognitive validity[13]. He aimed also to disentangle his theory of scientific and artistic autonomy from that strand of the philosophy of science which proposed that 'anything goes' (see, eg, Feyerabend 1993: 23; Bourdieu 2004: 69). It is the trajectory of this analysis of cultural production that should be reassessed with its endpoint in the short, but masterly, book, *Science of Science and Reflexivity* (2004). Here we move analytically from the questions above concerning the relative autonomy of the individual to the nature of the whole field of cultural production, and its potential to foster independence in relation to State and economic power.

THE CRITIQUE OF AN 'ABSOLUTIST' UNIVERSALISM (BOURDIEU AND HAACKE 1995: 62)

Bourdieu's studies of reception were initiated by a concern for cultural demystification. He disputed the notion that there was, in modernity, a single 'cultural inheritance', which was equally available to all. Taking as his examples the Kantian judgement of beauty, which should be valid for everyone, or the Kantian abhorrence of the facile and charming, Bourdieu argued that such aesthetic categories were neither equally distributed nor, indeed, equally available as elementary forms of the artistic life. For this reason, Kant's aesthetic criteria could better be understood as the specific social expression of an ascetic, professional bourgeoisie. This new, cultivated class fraction icily cuts itself off from the people on one hand and from the mundane tastes of the temporally-powerful courtly aristocracy on the other (1984: 491–94).

Thus, just as Spivak showed that Kant's politics of cosmopolitan pacifism had certain underlying limits, set by his incapacity to admit into 'the cosmopolitan' category any voice coming from the subaltern Third World, so Bourdieu argued that there were certain underlying limits to universalism, to which Kant was blinded by the doxa of the eighteenth century professorial middle class and his conception of a unified self (Spivak 1999). Such limits were at stake in the opposition underlying Kant's *Critique* between French worldly civilisation and German scholarly 'culture'.[14] It is crucial to note here that Bourdieu deliberately entitles his approach a 'vulgar critique' of Kant (1984: 485).

This sophisticated historical examination of Kant's philosophical anthropology is inspired by a classic sociology of knowledge or materialist analysis in terms of elective affinities. Bourdieu extends this into a *relational* analysis. This will address the socio-genesis of the aesthetic within a capitalist society (1993c: 264), showing how this produces a dichotomized relationship to culture. On the one hand, the aesthetic attitude simultaneously affirms but reifies 'culture', which is no longer interpreted as a close response to practical experience, but as a series of frozen, radically decontextualised art-works. The alternative — the naive gaze — is unconcerned with this play of form, but reduces works of art to their immediate ideological or moral meanings, in a utilitarian fashion.

Bourdieu labels his own critique of Kant 'vulgar' because by directly linking cultural expression to class experience and class interests, it still operates within a 'short circuit'.[15] Such a cultural model ignores the artistic rupture of the mid-nineteenth century modernists – in poetry, the novel and painting — and their foundation of a newly autonomous 'field of cultural production'. This is an economy of artistic practices based on symbolic revolutions. Within this symbolic economy, such 'heroic modernism' represents an undying refusal of the commercial and moralistic priorities of the urban bourgeoisie. But it also represents a 'terrorism of taste', especially a refusal of the working-class, whose inadequate literacy denied their entry to the artistic experiments of the bohemian world, a 'world reversed'. It should be clarified that Bourdieu's critique of Kantian universalism is *not* founded on a Zhdanov or Stalinist pseudo-aesthetic, in which a certain social/political vision is prized, irrespective of how it is expressed (1984: 566; Bourdieu and Haacke 1995: 73). Rather his criticism arises from the fact that in modernity there is no longer any *universalistic distribution of the conditions of access to the aesthetic sphere* (Bourdieu and Wacquant 1992: 88). The most important source of distorted communication, for Bourdieu, is the deep-rooted absence of an effective educational tradition for everyone. Moreover, a non-hypocritical universalism would have to acknowledge that even 'transcendental' artworks have their specific historical conditions of existence: '[i]t is in discovering its historicity that reason gives itself the means of escaping from history' (1990b: 25).

Bourdieu's later historical sociology concerns the nature of these cultural fields. Various forms of 'artistic salvation' are at play within such enclosed, generationally-distinctive 'worlds apart'. Hence the sociologist needs to understand *position takings* within the field of art or literature itself. 'Position taking' refers back to the Weberian opposition between sects and churches in relation to salvation doctrines: in art it refers to the Academy on one hand and the established avant-gardes, as well as the conflicts in the wider world of classes. In the new context, 'position taking' also led away from the passive ideological functionalism of Althusserian theory and theorised a more active concept of artistic production (Bourdieu and Wacquant: 102, 109; Bourdieu, 2002b: 113).

Bourdieu's claimed break with Western Marxism and the earlier sociology of literature and art should not be exaggerated, for all his dramatic critique of Lukács's, Antal's or Goldmann's short circuits. Bourdieu is certainly right about the importance of the artistic field or 'art-world' itself (see Dickie 1974: ch. 1, especially 33–34). In his telling example, the 'genealogical insult' that artists use, referring to a fellow-artist as the 'son of a bourgeois', is often a veil. Behind it, artists are condemned whose real crime is disloyalty to the manifesto of their artistic group, not their social origins (1996a: 83). It is also true that there is no exact 'reflection' between the state of social forces and works of art since artistic currents (in the form of museum curators, critics and reviewers) act as intermediaries, shaping the work (1996a: 204; Bennett 2005: 149). Yet his method still insists on a profound understanding of artists' agency in the light of their families' social trajectories in the field of power (1996a: 111). This is not to say, as Bourdieu's critics of *Distinction* did, that artists from higher social backgrounds are *consciously* and individualistically aiming to win distinction, as though art was merely another means of doing business or seeking status. Rather the reverse: Bourdieu emphasises that distinction often sits on actors as though it were natural to them, part and parcel of the pursuit of their principles. Insofar as there is a prompting from the habitus to make art-works differently, bringing, in turn, certain 'profits of distinction', the latter is unconscious.

Thus the social location of artists, often privileged, tends to produce an aristocratic style, plus a rebellious 'impatience with limits' (the constraints of bourgeois philistinism, oppressive tyrannies). Such a social rebellion is never entirely negated but is rather *refracted* via their access to specific techniques of art. Through such techniques — innovative poetic metre, imagery etc. — they incorporate mental structures into artistic forms. Further, it is their distance from material necessity — typically built up over several generations, which creates the precondition for the emergence of producers who possess an artistic habitus of great complexity. For them, the artistic tradition has become second nature, along with all its nooks and crannies. Those with the greatest volume and best-structured cultural capital are likely to find themselves within the most cutting-edge groups, such as Manet (1988b, 1996a) or the later 1860s' Impressionists. Bourdieu has here bound up together an 'institutional' theory of the importance of the conventions and history of autonomous fields with a Marxist theory of art, Dickie with Antal, so to speak.

******

Bourdieu always knew the dangers of his 'objectification', especially of the game of art (1984: 12; 2004: 69).[16] He had reason to be anxious, since his socioanalysis has been widely 'refused' as over-determinist (see, for example, Lamont 1992, Alexander 1995, Butler 1997, Bohman 1999, and Zangwill 2002). The most well-known critics, such as Judith Butler, have underplayed the complexity of habitus and strategy and claimed that Bourdieu's theory of practice has its unacknowledged origin is the base-superstructure model (1997:157). Against these, John Guillory has perhaps offered the most historically-rich and perceptive comments on Bourdieu's cultural theory (1993 and 1997).[17]

Guillory has distinguished in the work of Bourdieu three uses of the term market: the economic market, where the economic principle of profit maximization operates for its own sake; the mimetic market where certain goals stand analogously for material profits, such as accumulating solo exhibitions, and, thirdly, anti-mimetic markets (for example, the modern French literary field). Yet even Guillory is misleading about the role of what he calls 'anti-mimetic markets', those social structures or fields in which symbolic honour rather than economic accumulation is paramount (1997: 388–9). For Guillory fails to see that Bourdieu's key move is to eliminate altogether the misleading and stark opposition between altruism and ego-ism which lies behind such classifications. Instead, he aims to substitute a different dichotomy, between those types of society, which are founded on 'games' of honour — including knowledge — as the basis of their interests in distinction, and those on bourgeois criteria, production for production's sake. Typically, in the former, economic exchange is organised around reci-procity, while symbolic honour serves chiefly as the realm of competition.

Guillory succeeds emphatically in illuminating those sources of *inde-terminacy* — *hence agency* — which are present in Bourdieu's model of literary modernism (Bourdieu 1996a). As he says, it is at the heart of the anti-economic economy founded through modernism that the sociologist finds both determinism and pathos (see especially 1996a: ch. 3). But curi-ously, this same anti-economic bohemia confers also a type of freedom, which Bourdieu captures in the image of the author flying above all social circles. This is a reflexive indeterminacy, which a figure such as Flaubert acquires insofar as he is an artist, that is to say, also a sociologist. The novelist (Flaubert) thus possesses a 'geometrical angle on all perspectives'. By using such a margin of liberty through feats of 'social flying', the heroic modernist acquires — *not genius* — but singularity. Guillory is surely right that in the homage that he paid to Flaubert, Baudelaire and Manet,

Bourdieu indicated at the end of the day, how profoundly he was 'on the side of the artists' (1997:398).

The theoretical significance of a writer such as Zola also needs clarifying. Bourdieu's conception of Zola's 'invention of the intellectual' is of a figure who, in the politics of the Dreyfus Affair, refuses what the church, state and military demand. Unlike Sartre's 'intellectuel engagé', however, Bourdieu's socioanalysis of Zola is less idealised: Bourdieu emphasises realistically that Zola could not have made his historical political defence of the Jewish officer, Dreyfus, without having already won a popular, yet aesthetically 'compromising' success with his novels (1996a: 116). In other words, Zola's position in the literary field was within the expanded, commercial field, where monetary profits are typically high in the short run, but literary profits are minimal. His high-profile advocacy of Dreyfus via his compelling article, 'J'accuse!', might also be interpreted as a gamble on his own behalf: that it might make rather than break his *literary* reputation. Such a sociological objectivation rejects a cult of saintliness by recognising such wider interests, but it does not obscure the element of genuine disinterestedness in his action.

THE SOCIOLOGY OF SCIENCE: AUTONOMY REVISITED

From the early nineties, Bourdieu had become increasingly remote from one trajectory of post-structuralist theory, 'postmodernism', and contributed an alternative trajectory of great sociological power. As opposed to the important tradition of anthropological relativism (Boas and others), he critiques a *chic relativism* or 'nihilistic pseudo-subversion'. He protects his earlier criticisms of universalistic orthodoxies from attack, while openly repudiating a relativist stance in the philosophy of science (Bourdieu and Wacquant 1992: 153–5; Bourdieu 2000a: 71).

In the scientific field, Bourdieu seeks to oppose both the great divide between an idealised model of a communal unity and the Hobbesian model of a struggle of all against all.[18] Instead, Bourdieu proposes a realist rationalism, emphasising the common membership that scientists enact in their 'corporation' (2004: 50). These stem from lengthy, specialised apprenticeships and from peer review, which meant, historically, that 'gentlemen of honour' vouched for experiments as witnesses. Given the continued role for disinterestedness — as well as interest — and the centrality of specific, scientific symbolic capital such as (in the natural sciences, mathematicization (2004: 48), this field can be portrayed as a genuine gift economy[19]:

> The fact that producers tend to have as their clients only their most rigorous and vigorous competitors, the most competent and the most critical [colleagues], those therefore most inclined and most able to give all their critique full force, is for me the Archimedean point on which

one can stand to give a scientific account of scientific reason, to rescue scientific reason from relativistic reduction and explain how science can constantly progress towards more rationality, without having to appeal to some kind of founding miracle [God]. (2004: 54)

AUTONOMY AND DETERMINISM IN LITERATURE AND ART

A parallel argument is deployed by Bourdieu for the fragile autonomy of that other gift economy, the arts (1996a: 148; 2000a: 193). As we have seen, these gift economies depart from the 'economic economy' by being organised around production for the artists' professional honour, not for the sake of as high a price on the market as possible. These are universes which are founded on reciprocity, but where immediate cash returns or too sordid a pricing of presents is sanctioned (Bourdieu 1998a: 92–112). Now, the fact that artists also possess some *interests* in their disinterestedness should neither be surprising, given what we know of how traditional societies' reciprocal exchange works, nor should this be misunderstood as merely the cynical maximising of advantage. Artists give generously — but they also expect the return of favours in some indeterminate way, the nature of such exchanges being collectively mystified or misrecognised (1998a: 95).

For Bourdieu, the truly distinctive social invention of the post-1900s' art field is the emerging set of conditions for producing reasonable acts of disinterestedness. From now on, 'artistic follies' can be offered, such as Duchamp's 'readymades' (1998a: 112) or Haacke's artworks, critical of the art institution, such as *Framing and being Framed* (Haacke 1975, Bourdieu and Haacke 1995). For example, Haacke's conceptual assemblage consists in revealing to the exhibition public the secret history of many critical or disenchanted modern artworks: not least the paradox that these have moved, by subtle transitions of ownership, into the possession of those with great economic power.

Bourdieu stresses that the key demarcation of the *restricted field* from the *expanded field* lay in knowledge of these specific codes, as well as the artists' peer review mechanism, which was similar to that of the scientific field ('freedom under constraints': 1996a: 235, 339–40; Casanova 2004). Since the seventeenth century, the arts have been more of 'a world in reverse' than has science, that is, they have been organized around the restricted field. The epoch-making conquest of autonomy in the arts from 1850 on was constituted by a radical rejection of both commercial production and popular esteem, a dynamic that was much less marked in science. This division is crucial for analyzing the nature of the artistic obituaries.

In fact, there is a parallel between the world of science and the field of artistic production. In science, as we have seen, developments in the field are first structured by the autonomous scientific tradition of hard-won freedoms (peer review, experimentation, anonymity). They are also shaped by the scientist's position in the field, that is to say his standing in the departmental and university hierarchy.

Analogously, in art worlds, each poem's or painting's position-taking is a dynamic and reflexive element leading to newness entering into the world. It is because of such *indeterminacy* that symbolic revolutions can emerge, as in the invention of 'pure' painting or the sacrilegious interventions of surrealism (Bourdieu 1996a). Such action happens partly because of conflicts within the field itself. Artists' 'social flying' beyond their own socially-structured space is also a key aspect of such independence from temporal power. But, as Becker also suggested, art is still limited by the social traditions inscribed in certain kinds of language and hence 'the laws of images' (Becker 1982: 77–81). More crucially, it is shaped by the writer's very choice of form or genre.

Thus Bourdieu's argument stresses two main points. First, vis à vis time: while total originality is impossible, innovation can nevertheless occur, due to artistic autonomy and the transgression of tacit conventions. Second, artistic positions are linked indelibly, via their habitus, with material necessities. Those in the commercial genres — Bourdieu's 'industrial novels' — such as popular romance — are permitted less autonomy and are therefore less critical of power. Marx earlier had addressed the problem of consumption for modern art: the fact that the artist needs to create a taste and an audience for his work, not just the work itself (1973: 92–3). To this issue Bourdieu constantly returns, remarking, for example, on the material freedom for independent writing, which university employment gives. Yet he notes also its associated 'blind spot': academics possess a perspective from which they often fail to objectify their own cultural world.[20]

CRITICS OF BOURDIEU'S THEORY OF ART

The arch critics of Bourdieu in Paris are all ex-Bourdieusians. For the theory of cultural production, it is Heinich who is at the moment the most courted voice. Strengthening her own theory with that of Luc Boltanski and his colleagues, she has made a formidable attack from the position of a schismatic devotee on her former research director. You could call this symbolic parricide.

Her argument is that Bourdieu's logic of practice is merely a 'sociology of domination'. In particular she notes that this is a 'critical sociology' which has as its targets the 'illusions of the creator' — naturalisation of taste as an innate possession and the extreme individualisation of the notion of genius. However, while she views sociology as having importantly shown certain collective social actions at the heart of so-called independent art, she also sees sociology such as Bourdieu's, as now resting primarily on a 'socio-ideology' (Heinich 1998a: 9).

Implicit in this move, Heinich claims, is a 'generalised reduction', which shows the artist is nothing other than 'the product of an economic context, social class, habitus'. She argues that we need to know more about the subjectivity of the artist. In particular, we need to distinguish between a 'regime of singularity' (which relates to notion of inner gift, artistic vocation, sacrifice, disinterestedness) and the regime of community — often emphasised by artists in their rejection of the cult of individual genius — in which the artisanal character of creativity is introduced, ie, the team elements of artistic works (1998a: 14) The sociology of art has classically described the latter. Quite so, but one wonders what has become here of Bourdieu's very similar conception of the field?

What Heinich aims to forge is new 'pluralistic' turn, a 'descriptive', 'acritical' sociology' (1998a: 16–17). Breaking with Bourdieu's display of illusions (Heinich 1998a: 80), her sociology will offer an anthropology of admiration. Her main example is '*The Glory of Van Gogh*' (1996). Here, she addresses the founding moment of a new paradigm of the 'accursed artist' who is redeemed after his death by community devotion. In this new paradigm, art is seen as a gift or debt which has entailed the sacrifice of material and sexual interests — even sanity — and which needs to be repaid by a community. Thus, in the social construction of admiration, with its recognition of singularity after death, the crucial move is to stress the *spiritualisation* of the artist by later generations, as in the pilgrimages to Van Gogh's studio. Such an anthropology would make much of the different positions of the professional critics and the cultivated on the one hand as against the popular razzamatazz of the commercialised tours on the other.

Yet such a conflict between the scholarly, detached gaze and the naïve gaze surely owes much to Bourdieu. What is more, Bourdieu himself theorised, as early as 1975, the Romantics' invention of the artist as a Christ-like figure. Heinich is undoubtedly insightful in understanding that the social meaning of the new sociology of art must lie in grasping how religious consecration has been displaced onto the artist as a charismatic figure. Yet it was indisputably Bourdieu who first pointed out that Weber's studies of the field of religion should now be applied to art. Moreover, at the heart of Bourdieu's sociology there has always been a profound concern with time. Wasn't it he who developed a whole phenomenology of duration by applying Husserl's studies of the experience of the present and the future to certain key social relations? Those social relations in which individuals — such as Manet — strove to *make their mark in posterity* were his prime example.

The point should not be to deny at all the worth of the Heinichian analysis. Rather it should be to point to its origins in Bourdieu's own project, not least in his *The Rules of Art*, unreferenced by Heinich, which asserts the singularity of Manet, Flaubert and Baudelaire as heroic modernists. But a last, important point is necessary here — and it needs to be addressed to Heinich and others. Why did Bourdieu place at the centre of his sociology a critical stance, an ethic of suspicion? It was not, I have argued, that he utterly rejected the Kantian aspiration towards universalistic aesthetic judgements but precisely that he thought that with inequalities in educational access, some were always precluded from joining in this public sphere on the same level. Kant was thus guilty of an absolutist or false universalism. More tellingly than this, Bourdieu was suspicious of an 'affirmative attitude' to culture, as Marcuse once called it (1972: 122–131). As I have suggested, Walter Benjamin was also wary of this when he wrote of the 'cultural inheritance', for he feared that it would ossify into a canon the selective taste merely of *some* — the Germans, Aryans, the appointed mandarins of culture (1979: 356, 2002 267–8). In other words, what is at stake is precisely collective memory and who is — as Bourdieu put it — to 'create the creators' ('God is dead', he famously argued 'but the uncreated creator has taken his place' (1996a: 185)).

Bourdieu has other, less rebellious heirs, Sapiro and Casanova especially. Casanova is particularly useful for the study of the writers' biographies (see below, ch. 8). She has followed Bourdieu (1984, 1993a, 1996a) (and Braudel) in providing a historical analysis of the features of the literary world or 'international republic of letters', which has its own distinctive forms of domination — not reducible to economic or political domination (2004). Moreover, this world has own literary time (Greenwich literary mean time) according to which writings are judged as new or outdated, located in the great centres of 'universal' symbolic capital, initially Paris (seventeenth century), then joined by (eighteenth/nineteenth century) London and later by New York (twentieth century).

Casanova's research shows how the laws

> that govern this strange and immense republic — a world of rivalry, struggle and inequality — help illuminate in often radically new ways even the most widely-discussed works. (2004: 4).

Drawing on an extraordinarily wide range of writers — not just Joyce, Beckett, Kafka, Faulkner and the greatest literary revolutionaries of the twentieth century, but also Henri Michaux (Belgium), Emil Cioran (Rumania), Danilo Kis (Yugoslavia) and Arno Schmidt (German) — she reveals especially the struggle of writers from 'small literatures' (such as Belgian), or 'literarily-impoverished regions' such as pre-1960s' Latin America to gain a reputation or 'spiritual capital'. It is the 'miraculous survivors', writers from the least well-endowed literary spaces who are the most improbable.

Casanova distinguishes three major stages in the genesis of world literary space: the mid-eventeenth century's vernacular thrust of capitalism; the nineteenth century's philological-lexicographic revolution, with its the invention of self-consciously national languages and the emergence of the Romantic movement to isolate a popular consciousness of 'soul' and of myths; and lastly post- World War II, decolonisation, the entry into cultural space of new writers, previously debarred. She explores further the generational ruptures within these ex-colonial spaces, such as the movement of different generations of Irish writers from being focused on London (Wilde), to a Paris- or Triest-based Europeanising move, like Joyce or Beckett. Post-colonial literary positions however have all offered divergent opportunities — either *assimilationist* (like Naipaul's) or else radically *differentiating* the writer vis à vis the colonial metropolis, as in Ngugi's or Mahloud's choices. In general, she focuses on the greater inequalities facing writers in the most dominated spaces (Kenya, Algeria), which are usually ignored by focusing on the metropolitan Paris- or London-based writers. Yet even unendowed literary spaces may in certain cases be turned in the writer's favour by acts of 'symbolic alchemy': the slum tenements of Brooklyn, for example turned into 'literary gold' after the immigrant, Henry Roth, had educated himself.

Casanova's approach insists on turning away from the spotlight on the singular individual, and in bringing back into view all the collective traditions which shaped a writer.[21] In this respect — as well as in the struggles over literary space introduced above — she shows that the approach developed by Bourdieu and Becker continues to bear fruit. It is this tradition that will be pursued for the qualitative study of the obituaries.

BOURDIEU, PHENOMENOLOGY AND FEMINISM

Questions about time and the anticipation of the future are crucial to Bourdieu, as I have argued elsewhere (Fowler 1997). The profound obstacles in adopting a rational, future-oriented model of time on the part of the subordinate classes is a matter of frequent insistence in the early and in the very late work of Bourdieu (from *Travail et Travailleurs en Algérie*, 1964 to *Pascalian Meditations,* 2000a: 206–45). Indeed, in the picture of the unemployed given in *Pascalian Meditations*, with its recognition of a Kafka-like fragility in the possession of a justified social existence, we have Bourdieu's most compelling and convincing writing.

Many writers now want to adopt Bourdieu's phenomenological approach, which has more intellectual prestige than his work of objectivation. He himself grasped this, with a series of ironic comments in *Pascalian Meditations* (2000a:128). Many had been reluctant to objectify their own culture or academia; now a much wider recoil was at stake.

The study of obituaries requires both a 'moment of objectivation' and an understanding of agents' subjective worlds (see Bourdieu, 1999: 610–15).[22] And here I think that we need, as McNay has suggested, to elaborate on Bourdieu's models of time and experience, so as to describe the movement of women into the public sphere and the market (McNay 2000). Women have historically had fewer stakes than men within the 'illusio' of the public sphere. Women's time has been different.

One way to clarify further Bourdieu's notion of the vocational habitus is to take up, as McNay has done, Ricoeur's ideas about the phenomenology of time (Ricoeur 1984). This theorises further the transformative aspects of agency which may be aided in the obituary.[23]

The key determinant of whether or not women receive obituaries is not just the question of how active they have been in the artistic or political field. Nor is it just a consequence of the filters used in interpreting their action: those interpretative practices of women obituarists or feminist men that enhance their historical visibility. My view is rather that the fundamental issue for women concerns their own perception of time and their involvement in a specific game. This is another way of approaching the thorny problem of canonisation, or, in Terry Lovell's concept, the notion of 'literary survival value' (Lovell 1987). It is also another way of returning to the fact that over one-third of the women subjects at present do not have children (see below, ch. 6).

Bourdieu prompts us to ask: 'What stakes have women acquired in a game? To what degree has your fundamental sense of yourself and what you live for become tied up in that field?' Here he has some important points about the pre-reflexive 'protension' or imagining of the future, in which the future unfolds as part of the logic of the habitus, as in the case of the male State Nobility and their great world-making activities. In fact, as Bourdieu insists, it is only at a certain level of *distance from necessity* that *alternative projects for the future* can be anticipated: the future loses its doxic, taken-for-granted character and becomes a changed place, either as collectively achieved in the classic trade-union imaginary or through individual practice (2000a: 216–17). Such active projects for the future — along with obligations to others — serve to distinguish those individuals with a 'justified' 'social existence' from those without. The power of 'symbolic baubles' (entry to *Who's Who*, honours, etc) is to act *as a support for the social game*. That is, they act as buttresses for the decision to cope with one's own finitude or mortality, not by fleeing the world, but by seeking social esteem. This is the fundamental source of investment in a specific field:

> With investment in the game and the recognition that can come from cooperative competition with others, the social world offers humans that which they most totally lack, a justification for existing. (Bourdieu 2000a, 239)

The possibility of a celebratory obituary could clearly count as one of the long string of 'symbolic baubles'.

Earlier, Bourdieu had written about the harsher face of competitive struggles, for example, when the surrealist, André Breton broke Pierre de Massot's arm in an argument about the future of art (1996a: 383). Now when we raise questions about women and time, it is to these kinds of phenomenological questions about the future that we should be turning. The issue raised by Breton and de Massot's anger is this: when does your artistic or craft effort seem so important that you will dedicate your whole life to it? Such an engagement is in part a question of not being caught up in other, rival experiences of time, in revolutionaries' commitments, for example. In terms of those not so directly caught up — amongst them, many scientists, artists or philosophers — the passion with which you throw yourself into these disinterested fields or vocations is a key determinant of achievement. The performance of the work-in-hand becomes infused with an extraordinary importance. Undergoing *this* routine activity everyday, seeking, say, to understand cancer cells, may be your way of changing the world...

Bourdieu writes of the doxa which preserves noble tasks for men (2001b). But women — or caregivers of either gender — of very young children, cannot be involved in the same sense with the illusio of their work as a life and death struggle. Instead they are constrained to participate in other more pressing life and death struggles, such as their children's vulnerability to illness or to ontological insecurity. One might write without any essentialist presuppositions, of their deficit of professional engagement, for they show, reluctantly, a *suspension* of effort.

What I have called here the necessary suspension of professional effort is neither lifelong nor found in all professional working women. Sarah Checkland, for example, writes vividly of Barbara Hepworth being accepted for a Venice Biennale, and of her husband Ben Nicolson — who had *not* been picked — enviously smashing her sculpted maquette. Hepworth's young triplets did not impede her artistic 'worldmaking'activities, nor, indeed, her participation in the international constructivist group, The Circle, which enfolded both husband and wife (Bowness 1985; Checkland 2000).

Bourdieu took from Husserl and Heidegger certain approaches to time which he went on to fuse with a more relationist historical sociology. Ricoeur has developed further one aspect of this German phenomenology which may help theorise agency, as McNay also emphasises (McNay 2000: 85–96).

Ricoeur distinguished between the contrasting experiences of 'linear, calendar time' and 'eternal time' (Ricoeur 1984, vol. 1: 25). Now we might call such 'eternal time', following Bourdieu, the time of posterity, the future in which the scientist or artist might make his or her mark. More interestingly, for feminism, Ricoeur has also stressed the effects of the imagination and utopia in freeing agency (1991: 319–324). He has addressed Proust's *A la Recherche de Temps Perdu*, as a story about the author's oscillation between a vivid, sensual understanding of the lost childhood time and the adult sense of disillusionment and knowledge of power, via his narrator, Marcel. The novel culminates in a commitment to vocational time as Marcel learns to unify these different worlds in order to become a writer (1985: 144–45). Perhaps we can salvage something further about dedication and anticipated completion from this novel? This will reveal a general operation of the habitus in certain highly autonomous fields, which can be extended more broadly than the privileged milieu of aristocrats, bourgeoisie and modernist cultural producers of Proust's novel (see Dubois 1997, Casanova 2004). The role of this kind of narrative might reveal — particularly for women — the nature and dynamics of an engagement or illusio within modern fields of the public sphere.

Of course, the subjects of obituaries have often been — and still frequently are — authority figures, figures of state or nobility. As such, they are linked more closely to Ricoeur's 'monumental' and 'official time' than to 'eternal time' (Bourdieu's time of posterity) (Ricoeur 1985: 106, 112). The obituary genre as a whole is much broader than the depiction of original or distinctive achievements as in the meritocratic/French Republican model, caught up as it still is with the symbolic rewards for higher administration and other forms of elite 'public service'. But it also reinforces, as we shall see, the consecration of innovative cultural producers.

Now, with the narrowing of the gender difference in terms of a full engagement with the illusio of the field, the disparity between the numbers of obituaries for men and women will undoubtedly become less marked. Ricoeur's approaches to what he calls 'temporal refiguring', the enhancing of imaginative possibilities through the narratives in modernist novels (or film), clarifies those often transformative forms of agency on which the modern obituary draws (1988: 274). We are arguing then, that there is a benign circle — narratives of dynamic lives shaped by accomplishments, individual or collective, can encourage the imagination of others, and these in turn become the resources of further autobiographies, socioanalyses and obituaries :

> Unlike the abstract identity of the Same, this narrative identity, constitutive of self-constancy can include change, mutability within the cohesion of one life-time. The subject then appears as both the reader and the writer of its own life, as Proust would have it. (Ricoeur 1988: 246, see also Stanley 1992: ch. 6)

This is perhaps particularly crucial for women, as we know from Felski on the role of literature — confessional novels particularly — in this extension of imaginative possibilities (1989, Lara 1998). Post-colonial literature has had the same significance amongst African readerships for both men and women. A break with the resigned habitus of the subordinate classes has often occurred via such images of political radicalism, in a dedication to the collectively transfigured future.

But we would also have to remember that it is not simply the raising of *consciousness* about the range of possible futures that is at stake. It is rather, as Bourdieu has pointed out on numerous occasions, a hard and unrelenting *craft activity*, as remorseless as those 'involving repeated exercises [which alone] can, like an athlete's training, durably transform habitus' (Bourdieu 2000a: 172).

CONCLUSION: THE MEANING OF CANONISATION

We have argued that Bourdieu's theory of practice is a particularly fruitful resource for the study of the obituary, firstly, because of his own study of obituaries and biographical trajectories, secondly, because of his rich analysis of social reproduction and its misrecognition, and thirdly, because of his unsurpassed theory of cultural fields which ties together an interactionist analysis of the art institution with a historical understanding of the genesis of the modernist field.

It is noticeable that towards the end of his life, Bourdieu turned his reflexive understanding on his past, revealing in a socio-biography what had shaped his own experience as the grandson of peasants who became a 'miraculous survivor' (2004: 94–114; see Reed-Danahay 2005) . His last years also produced reflections about death and survival in the future, on what he had earlier entitled 'eternal life' and labelled the prerogative of the dominants. With his own death in sight, he reassessed the phenomenon in which a few live on, meditating on his own induction into Athens University with his honorary D.Litt. He, a 'singular' being, is transmuted into the collective being of the University. This process has an 'extraordinary effect' (2003b: 58): it seizes a person from a purely individual existence to be made into a consecrated figure. A 'discourse' (body of work) which was singular — perhaps even on occasion bizarre, mad — becomes something of the 'communal and divine'. In doing so, its producer loses his/her insignificance. In the ceremony of induction, he is assimilated into a dignity which does not die:

> The word institution has a double sense: it is simultaneously a collective, such as the University or the Universitas, which exists objectively and it is also an act which this collective accomplishes in instituting a person in a dignity. A dignity of which the canonists, the lawyers of the Middle Ages, said that it never died — dignitas non moritur. Put differently, it is a question, bizarrely it seems to me, of life and death, of the life and death of individuals, of the life and death of institutions. (2003b: 57)

I argue, in a Bourdieusian manner, that the obituaries are important because they seize a person from singularity and canonize or consecrate them. In this ultimate mode of showing respect, their name and their cause go on living after them.

4   *The Times'* obituaries in 1900 and 1948

The Times in 1900, more than any other paper, could be seen as the dominants' memory. The newspaper obituaries of the 2000s make some gestures towards encompassing a popular memory; they even acknowledge the most prominent of critical voices as a counter-memory. In 1900, by contrast, *The Times'* orbit is extraordinarily narrow. It is largely restricted to the aristocracy. Within that class, it features particularly the Army and the Navy and to a lesser extent, the second and third sons, who traditionally enter the clergy. Curiously, in a newspaper festooned in factory advertisements for an industrialist public, the bourgeoisie hardly feature at all.[1] When they do, they appear at best as having been functional for the economy, at worst as the objects of class condescension. The great are not yet found amongst their ranks.

Even more strikingly, the obituary in *The Times* of 1900 is a vital mechanism in keeping fresh the kinship memories of the élite. Of course, in this respect, the obits are programmed to recall the significant public acts of men. Women largely appear only as agents of family reproduction, or Lévi-Strauss's 'objects of exchange': indeed, in the 146 obituaries printed in 1900, there are only two precursors of today's more emancipated women.

This is a world, also, in which Catholics and Jews, Methodists or other Protestant sects, are notably absent, except occasionally as celebrated foreigners. Religion has so to speak, been nationalized to fit the interests of the dominants. Paradoxically, alongside this, *The Times* obits express an openness towards the activities of European and American elites — including the German nobility — indicative of the first period of globalization — which was to end with the intense inter-imperialist rivalries of 1914. Thus, although the 1900 *Times* obituaries, saturated by imperialist orthodoxy, screen out the entire population of the Third World, they are otherwise surprisingly cosmopolitan. An earlier intermarrying European elite is displayed, on which the vying nationalisms of the prelude to the First World War were later to be superimposed.

Into this world the death of John Ruskin produces resounding echoes. Ruskin, 'the Prophet of Brantwood', was the only figure in this collection of 1900 obituaries who created a rigorous and systematic form of critical thought and action. By his death he had already been incorporated into the dominants. Yet in 1900 he, more than anyone else in these columns, broke the mould of the comfortable 'union of blood and gold' that was repre- sented in the aristocratic- bourgeois compromise (Thompson 1968, 902). He did so by extending his critique of contemporary art and architecture into a fundamental attack on the division of labour. Ruskin was also cru- cially important in the *invention of art criticism* and heralded the new role that art was to take in the twentieth century, displacing to a large extent the traditional churches. He was, however, a backward-looking figure, who tried to resurrect feudalism and the role of the crafts within it. In this respect, however mythical and idealized the old order that Ruskin appealed to, his death only enhances the aura of a premodern society.

THE ARISTOCRACY

In the obits of the 1900 *Times*, the positioning of individuals within the obituary column is still in terms of an estate-ordered society. Literally, in terms of Bourdieu's categories, your position *in social space* dictates your rank order in the obit lists of precedence and — to a lesser degree — the number of inches awarded. The higher species — the dukes and barons — have priority over the mere gentry, as well as over the plebeian strata. Yet this is also an obituary column which registers the growth (since the late sixteenth century) of an individualist and increasingly capitalist, middle class society. Hence, the appearance of the new — the 'electrician' (Pro- fessor of Electrical Engineering, D.S. Hughes) or the liberal professionals — the surgeons, doctors and newspaper editors. It is this *fusion of new and old* — and the rival principles of the vision and division of the social order linked to it — that makes the obituaries of the turn of the twentieth century worth studying.

The 1900 obituaries delineate the current membership of the aristocratic great 'chain of being' much as the pedigrees of animals might be traced today. Thus the obituary for Sir Kenneth Mackenzie states that he was the thirteenth feudal baron of Gairloch, descended from the barons of Kintail (12 February 1900). There then follows a brief account of his diplomatic service and his service as Lord Lieutenant and Chairman of his County Council. Finally, there is a reference to his son succeeding him in the title. Or take Lord Lyveden: he 'was the son of the first baron, who was the son of Mr Robert Percy Smith by the daughter of Richard Vernon and who acquired a royal license to assume the name of Vernon on being raised to the peerage.' Lyveden abandoned a diplomatic career in order to act as First Secretary to a Duke. He then served his father, the first baron, when he was Secretary of State for War and subsequently, at the Board of Control (for India). The obituary describes his first marriage to another aristocrat, his second, to the daughter of a commoner and confirms which son was to become his heir (28 February 1900). Thus the obituary largely recapitulates the form of the heraldic funeral, the aristocratic celebration of the late feudal death (Gittings 1984). Yet not everything in the obituary is quite in keeping with this earlier order. Although other aristocrats with 1900 obituaries had still entered the arena of direct political power *uncontested* (see Lord Manvers, 17 January 1900), Lyveden unsuccessfully contested a seat.

Along with 'public service', the aristocracy of the 1900 *Times* spend their lives in the Army or Navy, much as feudal lordship was once premised on the aristocracy's monopolization of the martial arts. The obituaries' sons of county families are no longer described as vassals to barons. Yet they become members of the forces surprisingly early — at 10 or 12 years of age — and their careers acquire the pattern of ritualised ascent that Bourdieu describes as the 'biographical illusion' (1986). Entering the Army or Navy, they proceeded remorselessly up the ladder of seniority. In one case, promotion is described from Rear-Admiral via Vice-Admiral, to Admiral, and as in comic opera, it occurred seven years *after* retirement (Admiral Henry Blomfield, 6 June 1900).

In the mid-nineteenth century, to which these obits look back, this was overwhelmingly an imperial service: the litany of the services' obits includes a ritualized series of colonial theatres of war. The deceased is remembered for having been mentioned in dispatches after the Burma Campaign, or having distinguished himself in the Campaigns against the Kaffirs or Zulus. Such an officer is judged solely in terms of his war service and typically no other distinction is mentioned. He achieved the medal with three or four clasps or the Medjidieh Medal with service in India, Afghanistan, the Crimea and Africa (see inter alia, Vice-Admiral Richard Duckworth-King (8 January 1900), Major Alexander Cockburn (5 February 1900), Lieutenant-Colonel Sir Frederick Hervey-Bathurst, 21 May 1900). Although the defeat of the British in Afghanistan goes unrecorded in the obits, the bravery of the deceased, decorated with C.B. or medals, does require some narrative reference to *resistance to the British overseas*. Hence the obits chart the eternal return of shadowy 'rebels', whose motives are never considered and who are always vanquished by the valorous dead soldier (see, for example, Major-General George Hutchinson, Major-General Edward Saunders, Captain James Menteith Middlemist and Captain William Ernest Goff).

It is possible to see these aristocratic and gentry figures as playing out within the overseas imperial service the idea of the crusade. Everything suggests that these obits serve to further legitimate the ethos of the upper/upper-middle class, picturing them in a feudal landscape whose figures

> underwent a process of social differentiation through which specific social orders were symbolized. The aristocratic military elite not only looked distinctive because of their weaponry, armour and horses: they were essentially different, endowed with the natural valor and love of justice which they spread to the wilderness of non-Christian lands...

> The knight was tall, well-formed and clear-eyed, untouched by disease,
> strong, skillful and eternally youthful [....] The common people were
> rough, ill-formed, lumpy, fitted for work. (Ferguson 2000: 31)

Even before the Enlightenment Orientalism which justified the 'civilizing
mission' of social imperialism, there was a stock of feudal chivalric identities on which the aristocracy continued to draw. Traces of these are also
preserved in the lesser gentry, those figures who man the regional regiments
without ever going to war (see, for example, Mr.Robert Chaffey-Chaffey,
one time Captain of the Somerset Militia, whose wife was the daughter of a
Reverend Cobden Cobden, 18 June 1900). The paradox is that these ascetic
and well-formed knights of the obituaries now also inhabit the social relations of modern, industrial societies, based on commodity exchange. Thus
alongside the soldiers, and partially subsumed under their warrior ethos,
appear those elite figures with all the other functions of imperial rule —
civil servants in the Indian Board of Trade, judges, tax officials and district
commissioners (see Dr. Robert Collum, 15 January 1900, Sir Gregor Paul,
3 January 1900, Mr. Frederick Weaver, 17 May 1900). These are unim-
peachably virtuous and self-denying servants of the Crown.

The second or third sons of the aristocracy in this century frequently
entered the clergy or teaching. Some became well-placed (such as the Mod-
erator of the Presbyterian Church, 8 January 1900). But many, we are told,
died as scholarly and obscure vicars or underpaid schoolmasters, having
dedicated all their energies to being virtuosos of the work ethic and missionaries to the poor. In a sense we could see their obituary portrayals as
also leaning on medieval models of monks, who served to compensate for
the necessarily sinful lives of the feudal warrior (see eg, Southern 1970: 225;
Le Goff 1984). Thus there is the Reverend George Pownall, whose father
was a judge and who was a product of Rugby under Thomas Arnold. After
a period preaching in Australia and thirty-three years' work in 'one of the
poorest parishes of North London', he died, greatly esteemed by his parish-
ioners. Yet even more gloriously, 'he' (sic) brought up a family of ten — his
wife does not merit a reference — of whom six daughters were destined to
be missionaries (14 February 1900). Or there is the Reverend Hales, with
a Cambridge Classics degree and a period as secretary to Lord Verulam,
who became a Yorkshire preparatory school headteacher. Again, the stress
is on his piety and ascetic style of life: 'To his school he may be said to
have sacrificed his life …he hardly knew what rest meant' (14 February
1900). His unrelenting demands on himself are thus celebrated, alongside
his 'singularly stimulating' influence on the boys. In contrast to the intel-
lectualism of the urban bourgeoisie, the Reverend Hales was always concerned with the 'ordinary boy', not just those with the rare achievements
of gaining scholarships to Eton. Another typically sacrificial figure, Canon
Arthur Anstey, unwavering in his service within an impoverished district

of Bristol, died young of a heart attack. His parish alone had a population of 12,000 (15 January 1900).

The most clearly hagiographic amongst these obituaries describes the life of Father Dorgère of Paris, a Mother Theresa-like figure. He had acted as a valuable mediator in French imperial struggles, negotiating the capitulation of the King of Dahomey. He contracted a terminal and 'virulent smallpox', from burying a vagrant in Paris, his piety epitomized in his manner of death (28 February 1900). Given this general marginalization or exclusion of Catholics from the British national columns, it is all the more remarkable that the saintly life of Father Dorgère is included: perhaps it is his imperial political role that was decisive.

THE BOURGEOISIE: INDUSTRIAL CAPITAL
AND LIBERAL PROFESSIONALS

Following Weber, the work ethic and asceticism have typically been seen as both legitimating the bourgeoisie and facilitating the transition to a very new kind of rational order of capitalism and modern bureaucracy (1962, see Bauman, 1998). It comes as something of a surprise, then, to discover that the bourgeoisie is treated in a perfunctory and even denigratory manner in these 1900s obituaries. Such patronising portrayals serve to reinforce the interpretation of these obituaries as the dominants' memory.

Excluding the agrarian bourgeois (landowners running their farms as commercial undertakings) and bankers, who are by this time also public-school educated and gentry or aristocratic figures, there are only a very small number of bourgeois figures. The 146 in our sample for 1900 included very brief entries for a Reading alderman, head of a brewing company; a shipping owner, operating from Harwich; another operator of a ferry line; a publisher (Calman Levy, Paris); two bank chairmen and that is all.

The exception is the longer column for Joseph Cowan whose obit veers from irony to reluctant respect (19 February 1900). The tone distances him as a member of a class viewed as essentially alien to that of the implied reader. Cowan displays the 'peculiarities' of the Northern bourgeoisie. Yet, as will be argued, the qualities his obituarist defines as 'peculiarities' are to a large extent the consequence of *The Times* Southern gentry bias.[2] His obit starts by defining him as well-established in his city, Newcastle. His father, an engineer, had been knighted for deepening the Tyne for ocean-going ships and subsequently became a Liberal M P. His son, Joseph, a coal-owner, also became for many years a Liberal M P and is viewed against the backdrop of Newcastle as a 'radical city'. Eventually local political manoeuvres saw him ousted from Parliament, to the benefit of the Tories. He retrieved his civic position by becoming the proprietor of a newspaper, local brickworks and other concerns. The obituary focuses especially on

Cowan's stature as a 'Radical Liberal' MP, ambivalently remarking on his identity with working men:

> Though not a miner, but an owner of several mines, Mr. Cowan was not essentially different, either externally or intellectually, from some of the rough, keen colliers of Northumberland today [who possess] a mental activity and a grasp which are rarely to be found in working people in other parts...

The obituary goes on to denigrate him for this, pointing out how he used to wear a Northumberland miners' cloth cap. It then proceeds to a description of his bodily hexis and his gestures, including his accent. The tone is unexpectedly disparaging, a product of the physical anthropology and racist phrenology of the nineteenth century (Miles 1982: 10–15):

> Short in stature, uncouth in dress and figure and speaking a tongue the peculiarities of which are admired only to the manner born, he commanded in his early appearances in Parliament anything but respect.

There is an extraordinary openness in the obituarist's espousal of the 'magic' of dominants' bodily dispositions (hexis) here. Lest it appear entirely a feature of the past, it should be recalled that this is a magic which Bourdieu still partially credits for the power of today's French state nobility, reinforced by their educational qualifications (1996b: 117–18).

Although devoid of this social 'magic', Cowan did possess an outsider's capacity to make difficult choices: he had quickly championed Irish Home Rule, Mazzini's Italian nationalism and Kossuth's Polish nationalism. Moreover, he was ultimately someone who could be respected *for his social imperialism*. Hence the final assessment rises from the ironic to the positive:

> Though neither his appearance nor his disposition gave him any of those advantages which can help men forward in public life, he contrived during the dozen years which he represented Newcastle, to impress his individuality in a remarkable manner, not only on his constituents but also on the country at large.

Not a single working-class individual makes an appearance on the stage of the 1900 obits. This no doubt reflected the status of industrial labour as mere 'hands': indeed hands reduced in this period to an 'animated individual punctuation mark, as the living [...] accessory' to the machine (Marx, 1974: 470). The only exception is a groundsman at Lords Cricket Ground, who appears in the role of deserving and faithful servant (14 May 1900). He — and a man remembered as a 'brilliant cricketer' (8 January 1900) — appear denuded of title, not even the simple title of 'Mr.'.

On the other hand, there are various figures from the liberal profession-als. These are worth discussing briefly because they are the precursors of the many distinguished academics, surgeons and barristers of the contem-porary obituary. Some act as bridges between the patrician warriors and the more Enlightenment values of secular intellectuals.

Lieutenant-General Augustus Henry Lane-Fox-Pitt-Rivers is a descen-dent of an earl, conspicuously invested with the Name of the Father. He is praised for a dual career, both as a practical man who could inspire confi-dence as a great commander, and as a scholar. Awakened to other cultures while he was engaged in British Army campaigns (7 May 1900), his obit points out that as a soldier at Sevastapol and the battle of Alma he had been impeccable, having been mentioned in dispatches and granted two medals. His subsequent posts were as lieutenant general and then general. His mili-tary career crowned with laurels, he was to go on to acquire equal distinc-tion as a collector. His interest was in clothes, weapons and ornaments, or — as the obituary put it — of 'savage life and embryo civilisation'. These passions urged him into anthropological research, the obituary omitting that these became the seeds of the Pitt-Rivers Museum (founded 1886). His scholarly imagination was further broadened by studies of his own locality. These in turn came about by a distinctively aristocratic serendipity — archaeological research on his own estates.[3]

The 1900 columns also celebrate the lives of several doctors and sur-geons, specialists in physical pathologies. Unlike the other Oxbridge-educated obit subjects, these were trained at Edinburgh, Trinity College, Dublin and University College, London.[4] There are, it is argued, three main reasons why such a rupture appears in these obits. First, Oxford's medical training was predominantly restricted to studying classical and Renaissance texts in Latin, at a time when empirical research was advanc-ing rapidly. Secondly, small, university-dominated towns, such as Oxford and Cambridge, did not offer a sufficiently large range of clinical cases for training. Thirdly, the demand for Church of England conformity at Oxbridge impeded the advance of more radical Protestants, yet it was from these groups that many middle-class doctors, as well as industrialists, drew their roots[5] (Crowther and Dupree 1996).

The doctors in these obituaries, British and foreign, typically ended their lives with a practice in or near Harley Street, London. Further, they often traveled in a continental circuit, decorated with honours from European universities. In this respect, these professionals show the early signs of international consecration through prizes and honorary degrees, a pattern which would become the mark, in the 2000s obits, of other professions like architecture (Biau 2000).

A rather different profile emerges for the engineers, in Britain more than elsewhere, a career open to talent. Even when the individuals are upper-middle class in origin, their obituaries refer to the belated British acknowledgement of their innovations. Thus Professor Hughes, Chevalier de la Légion d'Honneur — labeled in his obituary simply as the 'electrician' — undertook pioneering work on the telephone. This eventually resulted in a Royal Society Gold Medal, but he had long been honoured in Europe before gaining British recognition (24 January 1900).

It is amongst the engineers that the rare upwardly mobile individual of 1900 emerges, standing out amongst the 92 per cent of the obituary subjects from the dominant class like members of an exotic species. Take, for example, Mr. William Lewis, who came from Merthyr Tydfil, 'a typical member of the industrial community of South Wales' (14 February 1900). Educated at Taliessin (Elementary) School, alongside other pupils who went on to be similarly illustrious, he is remembered for the invention of many 'useful appliances', including mechanical engineering on Welsh 'ocean' mines. Lewis is 'noted for the control he exerted without friction and over bodies of working men. He died in harness after a working life of 70 years, during which he never spared himself'. Yet although 'universally respected', and possessing control 'over bodies', Lewis notably 'took no part in public life'. In an aristocratically-oriented context like the obituary, this is registered as an omission. To today's reader, the obits for these members outside the traditional dominant class appear exercises in strategic condescension (cf Bourdieu 1991: 68–69).

WOMEN IN THE 1900 OBITUARIES

It has been noted that the lines of ascent and descent are studiously reproduced in the 1900 obit. In the case of men, genealogy leads into their careers. In the case of women, things are different. Here is Viscountess Newry:

> Viscountess Newry died on Saturday at her residence, 98, Eaton Place [London, it goes without saying], aged 80 years. Anne Amelia, Lady Newry was the daughter of General the Honorable Sir Charles Colville, and was married in 1839 to Francis, Viscount Newry and Morne, the eldest son of the second Earl of Kilmorey. She is the mother of the third Earl and was left a widow in 1851. (6 January 1900)

This is the whole obituary. She is significant — in other words — merely for her father and her husband and her son! The entries for women habitually and decorously present them as objects of marital exchange. Another will confirm the point, again the whole obit:

> A Reuter telegram from Bermuda states that Mrs Barker, the wife of Lieutenant-Gen George Digby Barker, C.B., Governor and Commander in Chief of Bermuda, died on Monday evening. She was Miss Francis (sic) Isabella Murray of Ross-shire and she was married to Gen. Barker in 1862. (13 May 1900)

This is by far the most common mode of entry for women (see Lady Lee, Lady Montague Pollock, Dowager Lady Beach, Isabella, widow of Sir Charles E. Lewin and the Dowager Princess of Hohernzollen). Occasionally they are included for their father's achievements, as in the case of Eleanor, daughter of William Cobbett, author of *The Political Register* (15 January 1900). They appear devoid of individual achievements (see Maybury 1995–96).

Only three women in the entire sample depart from this format. One is a good hostess and rider who made a mark amongst the expatriates in India. The other two are more lengthy accounts and are precursors of later obits of independent women. The first of these is more typical of an active upper-class woman within a patriarchal society, the second has escaped that set of constraints, only to die very young.

The Hon Mrs. James Stuart Wortley (7 February 1900) was legally a 'femme couverte' — entirely absorbed into her husband's status. Yet the obit makes it clear that she had, in fact, an independence and organizational skills far beyond the existence of 'decorative birds in their gilded cages', Wollstonecraft's image of aristocratic women. Indeed while Jane Wortley dedicated herself to facilitating her husband's career and shows the strategic role of her social capital in the process, everything suggests that she did so with remarkable flair. As her husband was moving up the judicial ladder, from Advocate-General, to Recorder, she was giving informal parties, indeed becoming, in the obituary's words: 'one of the most interesting women of the epoch'. In other words, to some extent Jane Wortley's house became part of the public sphere whilst appearing to be entirely confined within the bourgeois private sphere. Landes describes in the case of France, a clear Post-revolutionary rupture with the salon sociability of the eighteenth-century aristocratic woman (Landes 1988). This obituary suggests that in Britain the noble salon continued, in another guise, although no doubt, lacking the earlier sexual freedom of aristocratic hostesses. John Scott has noted, following Leonora Davidoff, the shift from the public sphere of coffee-houses and pubs in the eighteenth century to the private in the nineteenth century, allowing a greater social selection and exclusiveness to operate behind the walls of the family house (1991:99). This was a change which women especially superintended, as hostesses: a figure like Jane Wortley is typical of the trend.

Even more significantly, according to her obit, Mrs. Wortley participated outside the domestic confines within public associations, establishing the training of nurses for the poor in East London and arranging the emigration to Australia of women 'with good character'. In brief, if women were seen as restricted to the private sphere this is partly by the definitional fiat incorporated into the Census itself — *everything* done by women was private. As Gordon and Nair argue, despite the prevailing discourse, Victorian bourgeois women actively 'mediated and modified 'the rules'' by undertaking activities beyond the family sphere (2003: 233). This was because their practices could be legitimated by other ideologies and practical actions, such as running religious and imperialist organizations. Some of these today are unambiguously labelled 'work' but in nineteenth-century Britain they were the actively-constructed worlds of women. Such women have to be understood as possessing an angle of vision on suffering, which was derived from their own *subordination* (Lovell 1987) but also as blinkered by their own material and imperial privileges (Gikandi 1996: 119–156).

Mary Kingsley — a 'traveller, voluntary nurse and writer' received a long notice, especially for a woman (12 inches), delineating her as unusually independent (6 June 1900). She possessed a radical habitus marked by critical and anti-bourgeois thought, which the obit links to her uncle, the Christian Socialist novelist of the 1840s and 50s, Charles Kingsley. Although early death cheated Mary Kingsley of the influence that a figure like Pitt-Rivers was to acquire, her 'ethnographic' approach — based on verstehen and a rigorous empirical method — anticipated later breakthroughs in method (Gikandi 1996: 150).

She is announced as the author of *Travels in West Africa* (1897), notable especially for its studies of fetishism, and *West African Studies*, a memoir of her father and of other works on West Africa. The article starts off conventionally enough situating her as under the aegis of her father, Dr. Kingsley, who 'shared with his better-known brothers the literary facility that won them distinction'. By implication, Mary Kingsley merely inherited a family gene. However, this lively obituary has an account of Mary Kingsley's life as an independent and indeed highly critical woman who could 'project herself into the mind [singular] of the negro races' and who became one of the earliest critics in the continuing controversy over imperialism[6]:

> In West African Studies, Miss Kingsley set forth, with much array of facts and arguments, a strong indictment of the system of government by Crown colonies in West Africa.

Her sociological, political and scientific interests were strengthened by a strong work ethic and by her courage — 'pluck'. Her investigations — labeled here 'ethnography' required autonomous fieldwork, which she undertook, accompanied by native 'attendants' ('key informants?'). On this she founded her methodology, which — however empiricist — was based on personal experience and careful observation. Mary Kingsley refused to accept any report of a custom unless it had been authenticated by more than one person[7]. A good platform speaker, her writings were said to have literally shaped opinion:

> [she has] done more than any man or woman in recent times to foster a popular interest in West Africa.
>
> She died, as she had lived, struck down by the fever she had caught as a nurse, in the [Boer] War that had been launched by her ideological antagonists.

THE FIELD OF CULTURAL PRODUCTION IN 1900

The obituaries from the area of cultural production and the professions are a tiny proportion (30%) compared with current obituaries, in which newspapers such as *The Independent* and *Le Monde* publish over 70 per cent from these groups. The 'love of art' as the proof of the obituary subjects' spiritual soul has not yet appeared. Further, the arts represented in the 1900 obituaries are seen with an Academic eye: their columns are entirely unaffected by the transgressive rise of the avant-gardes.

They already exist in a state of tension with popular culture. The arts represented are chiefly elite genres, possessing elite publics; in this sense they are 'high culture' rather than low. Yet there is a subterranean conflict between the more advanced tastes of the critics and that of the wider, more middlebrow public. We would thus largely qualify the artists in the 1900 obituaries as representing in the broadest sense 'bourgeois' taste (always understanding that these sometimes also criticize the bourgeoisie (Bourdieu 1993a: 51, 102). In American terms, they can be linked to the movement studied by Levine in which drama like Shakespeare's or entire genres like opera or oratorio became adopted and colonized by cultivated elites such as the Boston Brahmans (Levine 1989). Imposed with an obligatory awe and silence, these performances were stripped of their popular side acts (jugglers, acrobats etc.) and the undemanding audience engagement which they had once possessed. Distanced from the common taste to which they had once been organically linked, these arts became both part of a legitimating style of life and the subject of cultural missions to the working-class.

There are no long and detailed obituaries in the 1900 field of music. Perhaps the most international of the arts, music, accounts for only 3 per cent of the obituaries, all classical. Amongst them we note a Viennese composer and the Director of Wagner at Bayreuth.

Of the performing arts, drama is represented solely by an actress from the Comédie Française, one of a long family line of actors. She brings to these columns the first breath of bohemianism: a divorced woman with children, she had still worked. Her obit describes her as famous for certain 'coquette' roles, while it simultaneously stereotypes and distances bohemianism as a French phenomenon.

A similar stress on sensuality and the decorative — reinforcing stock national stereotypes — is given for another French painter, Eugène Lambert (17 May 1900). He is the 'Watteau of chats', a famous watercolourist. Lambert's Academic skills are tailored almost to a single subject, (though a selling one) and he is universally recognized as having great powers of observation, even by 'the great public' (ie, the masses). The relationship between the art and a public possessing social capital is here transparently evident, in contrast with a century later, where it is disavowed (Bourdieu 1993a: 78–79). The observation that 'all the elite of Paris was at his funeral' carries the connotation that the elite public was a more desirable one.

Another painter, the Hungarian, M. de Munkácsy, is a more absorbing case since his obit has an ironic tone, acknowledging his capacity to get through to a wide public but simultaneously suggesting that his art is too facile (2 May 1900). It is worth noting in this connection that Munkácsy, apprenticed to a house painter at the age of ten, is one of the very few upwardly socially mobile within this whole sample (his father was a 'humble employee' of the Hungarian Government). He had to live off art, hence he could not afford to dispense with as many conventions as his obit writer would have liked. In this respect, he recalls the position of Renoir within the Impressionists' circle, the only member who was lower class and who was also more inclined towards an idealizing rather than a critical gaze (Bourdieu 1993a: 47).

Adopting a Kantian cultivated stance, the obituary writer's assessment of Munkácsy firmly distances art from any common-place pleasures. While on the one hand saluting the appeal of the religious subjects of the paintings, the obituarist subtly derides their banal and heavy-handed technical qualities ('bituminous tones' etc.):

> It is hardly necessary to say anything about the character of Munkácsy's art which has always had more success with the public than with [...] the artists or the critical few, for its virtue are those which appeal to the many and its faults are easily seen by the trained eye. He was the greatest of those who, in our time, have seen and expressed the dramatic effectiveness of the Gospel story [...] and by his scenic sense, his power of expressing contrasting types and his command of rich bituminous tones, he produced pictures which appealed to thousand of admirers as a revelation.

It therefore comes as no surprise to be told that on the one hand this Salon painter only produced a tiny number 'in modern genres', while, on the other hand, he sold well — one painting going for as high as £20,000 to a dry-goods retailer. This obituary bears all the marks of Bourdieu's 'aesthetic disposition' within the restricted cultural field — yet at this point, still within an Academic ambit (1984: 28–30).

The longest obituary columns are for the extraordinary figure of John Ruskin. His obituary writer chooses the language of prophecy — 'the prophet of Brantwood' to describe his life (22 January 1900). He clearly counts as a prophet in Bourdieu's terms, too, as the founder of a heterodoxy. Ruskin was a key figure, we are informed, in widening the scope of the artistic field. More than this, he was one of the outstanding critics of British society and especially of British industrial capitalism. He was also an architectural critic, a lecturer (so powerful that his lectures had to be given twice), and a founder of Ruskin College, a college for workers in Oxford. His obituaries say nothing about his private life.[8] His distinctive education was, however, linked to his childhood as the son of a strict Calvinist mother and a father whose work — as a London wine merchant — permitted his wife and son to travel throughout Europe with him, visiting art galleries and churches. This discordant combination of fundamentalist Protestant Ethic with Kant's aesthetic judgement — the sensuous, disinterested love of art as play — was to produce an explosive force and volume of writing. His public was similarly assembled beyond the restricted world of the intellectuals: he could move from lectures to Oxford professors to 'letters' to workers.[9]

From Ruskin came the importance of producing a theoretical base for landscape painting, one of the key genres of modernity which had not been theorised properly in Academic terms. The obituary calls it analyzing the nature of the 'sublime and the beautiful'. For Ruskin this was not a fully secularized idea. The *ethical* work of the artist in interpreting every tiny structured leaf or shell in nature is stressed. Elaborating on *The Times*, it could be added that this Ruskinian argument about the sublime in painting is analogous to the Newtonian and Protestant conception that revealing the scientific laws of God's universe operates to enhance the glory of God. In both cases there is a coming together of an intellectual and an ethical/religious project. This profoundly differentiates the artistic project of Ruskin from the aesthetic project of the Impressionists in France, who lacked this set of traditional religious meanings.

On the other hand, both the Impressionists and the pre-Raphaelites, (whose spokesperson Ruskin became) wished to see '*without Academic spectacles*'. In the case of Ruskin this meant abandoning the principles of vision and division to which the Academic rules were linked- from the hierarchy of the value of different types of painting — to the Academy as a source for commissions.

The obituary for Ruskin stresses not just his rupture with the classical conventions of art. It also stresses his genius:

> John RUSKIN (sic) [...] was what genius and fortune made him and the world is infinitely the richer for the product. (22 January 1900)

In this respect his obit belongs itself to that charismatic ideology of artists, now so familiar. But Ruskin's ubiquitously invoked genius is explicitly linked with the practice of an earlier 'genius', that of St Francis, not least in giving away his money.

Most important — and this is also at the heart of the obit by the Chief Rabbi (22 January 1900) — was Ruskin's brilliance in founding a new approach, social economy. Opposed to political economy with its free-trade liberal market doxa, Ruskinian social economy started off from the paradox of Great Britain's increasing inequalities — despite its great trading wealth — and its multiplying forms of alienated work — despite the earlier skill of its craftsmen. In brief, for Ruskin, the mission of art can only be furthered via a wider social transformation.

The obit conscientiously notes this 'social subversion' on a par with the attacks of Cobbett, his 'monstrous thinking to those who take self-interest as the mainspring of human action', which alludes to his earlier clash with the Manchester economic liberals. It does not, however, reveal the consequences of this dissent in which Ruskin was to be smeared as 'socialistic' and the influential Cornhill Magazine refused to publish his writing any further (Cook, II 1911: 8). In this respect, the obituary retrospectively *dilutes social conflict even as it remembers it*. However, it does claim — with some truth — that Ruskin would be remembered more for his 'social economy' and less for his ethical theories of art.

If Ruskin's general political economy is accepted in both obituaries, this still has to be understood as a certain type of social criticism. Ruskin's principle of vision and division is attached not to a further, socialist, transformation but to a conservative critique of industrial capitalism (Williams 1961, 151–53.). Neither Ruskin nor his obit writers make any systematic connection between the adoption in Victorian Britain of the laws of capital accumulation and the detail division of labour. Rather they look back to a lost paradise of craft autonomy, aiming to resurrect a dying feudalism into 'an orderly system of interdependence sustained by authority and obedience' (Ruskin's *Modern Painters*, quoted Williams 1961: 146).

1900: CONCLUSION

The 1900 obituaries still evoke a world where destinies are fixed by birth and people move within their prescribed orbits like planets. Exceptions are noted, most conspicuously Ruskin, Mary Kingsley and the Radical MP, Joseph Cowan. But in general the pattern is typical of the aristocracy, whose pedigrees are traced like horses. Even the death of the individual aristocrat pales into significance in the obit because the heir, the new holder of the title, has already taken their place. The obituary of 1900 then gives us in an archetypal manner the pattern which Bourdieu has described as 'the inheritance inheriting the inheritor' (1999: 522; 2002c: 24–25). This phrase, taken from Marx, captures the distorting effect of class relations. It is present in various portrayals of country baronets, who retire from their executive positions in banks or politics as soon as they inherit their title (cf Bourdieu 1993a: 150–1). Such descriptions are, as we have seen, particularly in evidence in the portraits of women. Within the obituary genre in this period, the women (except for Kingsley and Wortley) lack the noble victories of the warrior ethos; they lack also that characteristic of bourgeois modernity — autonomy — the revolt against tradition and the past (Ferguson 2000).

THE 1948 OBITUARIES OF *THE TIMES*

In 1948 many aristocratic figures appear, as in 1900. The stock portrait is still that of an aristocrat who fought nobly in various wars and served worthily in public office (see, for example, Brigadier-General Lambarde, 23 February 1948). Women no longer appear as significant purely for their kinship, yet may still be recalled only for the fame of the men to whom they were related. If others in 1948 are remembered in their own right, it is as largely as hostesses, responsible for a cultivated and refined style of life (Bourdieu 1984: 55).

Yet even *The Times* obituaries now register the unprecedented ethos of social reform and reconstruction of the post-First World War period, in the light of the Russian Revolution, the turn of both intellectuals and trade unionists to Marxism and the 1929–30s Great Depression. There are virtually no working-class obituaries — the sole exception is a much-revered telephonist at *The Times*. Nevertheless, a fresh choice of individual subject emerges as the herald of a new, utilitarian but socially-conscious world, the planner. Indeed, there is a general expansion of the liberal professionals; the *scientist* as genius begins to have an important place. For the first time also there appears a socialist politician (the leader of the Social Democratic Party and Deputy Premier, in pre-war Czechoslovakia (Rudolf Bechyne, 5 January 1948) and a radical judge, who — in the vision of the obit — arbitrates disputes with informed independence (Viscount Sankey, 9 February 1948).[10] Finally, other, differentiated fields of cultural production have been deepened. A writer from slave origins who would never have been legitimated in 1900, can now, after the eruption of the Harlem Renaissance, be championed in an obituary. Previously unthinkable — even a *critical* obituary for an aristocrat appears.

Thus while there is still a dominants' memory with a much more established financial bourgeoisie, there begin also to be the more diverse and even fragmented pattern of collective memory that is to be explored at length for the 2000s. Lines of social conflict begin to penetrate even the honorific form of the obituary, challenging definitions of ethical action at the heart of the most consecrated administrative elite (see Sankey, below).

THE ARISTOCRACY

The army officer and admiral still has his place even if the officer corps has shrunk from 34 per cent to 16 per cent. Indeed their actual names may denote past imperial exploits such as Sir Arthur Havelock Doyle (23 February 1948), whose second Christian name, Havelock, recalls — unmentioned here — the commander who ruthlessly put down the Indian Mutiny. In his portrayal, the continuity with the past is emphasized — the son has the same trajectory as the father, the identical Sandhurst training and identical action in colonial theatres of war. Just as the father wrote military poetry about his regiment's exploits, so the son in retirement writes on warfare and celebrates the long line of generals in his family.

In some cases, soldiers represent a new type, those who have served with distinction in the First World War. Nor is it essential that these individuals should even have had distinguished military careers. In a world in which social capital and cultural capital is difficult to distinguish, a positive obit may contain nothing about their actual military performance but praise their personal qualities — their 'good and original thoughts', or the gap provoked by their death for their Brooke's club friends. A new type of legitimation begins to creep in — their ratings' devotion to them, and a similar democratic concern surfaces with the frequent references to the various charities to which they dedicate their time, after the Second World War. Here is a revival of the gift economy of charity in which the obits hold up the upper class as disinterested. A more disenchanted sociological approach might enquire whether such conspicuous philanthropy did not serve certain interests in decorously veiling the capital accumulation or privileges of the elite.

Finally a new *structure of feeling* about war itself has emerged, even in these obits. Within the 1900 obituaries for officers, the medieval warrior ethos survived. But following the two World Wars, with their modern mass warfare, this ethos was challenged, as noted by Winter (1995). Ferguson points out that the literature of the First World War reveals certain elements of the experience of modern combat which can now be seen as a fundamental transformation. Whereas combat was once viewed in classical bourgeois modernity 'as the highest form of expressive will; an out pouring, growth and uprising of a meaningful commitment to an ultimate cause', by the First World War 'combat is seen in terms of the immediacy of an overwhelming experience: as terror and sublime' (2004: 4, 5). In terror, 'fear crushes the body rather than liberates the soul' (2004: 10), while survival is now interpreted as springing from 'chance' — from 'rationalized forms and experiential chaos' (2004: 17–18)

Certain elements of this interpretation might be questioned, not least the notion that the War was 'contingent' as opposed to a highly-determined consequence of the market's over-production and consequent nationalist antagonisms. Ferguson, however, is concerned exclusively with establishing the *phenomenology* of modern warfare (2004: 10)[11]: hence what he exposes is *the experience* of a life jettisoned to a degree hitherto unprecedented into arbitrary fortune.

The 1948 obituaries do not share the terror and forced wager over existence that emerges in the collective memory of the First World War. The shared experience which plunged most surviving soldiers into silence, has as its testimony only the Expressionist or Vorticist paintings, the novels or poetry of the war (Winter 1995; Frisby 2001, ch. 6). In the 1948 obituaries of war, a few tiny fragments recapitulate these cultural memories. Col. Thruston's obit reveals that his only son's death in combat had blighted his life (28 January 1948). The aristocratic Lord Dunalley's habit of seeing war as an enjoyable type of sport is a mode of thought from which his obituarist distances himself (5 May 1948). Yet these feeble traces mark a new era and a new ethos.[12] They herald the later break with the military aristocracy in *The Guardian* and *The Independent* of the 2000s.

CLERGY AND SCHOOLTEACHERS

Even within the aristocracy, certain lives cannot be reconfigured in terms of the 'biographical illusion's' mountain ascent (Bourdieu 1986; 1994: 81–89). Despite the recurrent trends towards creating hierarchies in non-hierarchical occupations, the 1948 obituaries show that a strand of the aristocracy turns away from such 'worldly success': it rather adopts a life of innerworldly asceticism, quite different from the asceticism of the warrior ethic.

Some, perhaps, retreated from demands for which they were not suited and in Bourdieu's terms, made a virtue out of a necessity. One such might have been the brilliant Oxford Classics scholar who gave up school-teaching, to become a vicar in Argentina. Many are figures with a virtuoso work ethic, often influenced in the 1948 obits by the High Church Oxford Tractarian movement and geographically situated in the church settlements in the East Ends of cities[13] (see for example, James Moir, 23 February 1948) In this respect, 1948 brings nothing fresh. However, a distinctive element in this period is the fusion amongst the clergy of *religious activism* and *political radicalism*. An ideal-typical figure here is the Keble-educated, Bishop of Stepney, Bishop Mosley, whose analysis of the structural sources of poverty led him to adopt 'Poplarism'. This was the London (East End) based movement for municipal socialism, pioneered in Poplar by the working-class local politician, George Lansbury. Supported by the retiring bishop, who declared that Mosley was needed to 'Poplarise Hackney', the Bishop had engineered this movement as a Poor Law Guardian. Mosley, then, was a 'wise and just administrator, with a firm hand [....] natural [sic] dignity [and] stern self-discipline. [...] he was greatly trusted and greatly loved for he was so entirely in the service of other men.' In Hackney, according to Lansbury 'he stood head and shoulders above us all' (26 January 1948).

The judiciary appears in these obituaries as touched by a similar will to transformation. Not every case: a long obit for a judge may earn praise for his 'clear as crystal' delivery, independence (even nonconformity — cf his 'skil[l] with the knitting needles'), but also a coded censure for his imputed authoritarianism, summoned up by his 'talkativeness', 'aggressiveness and heat'. (Lord Thankerton, whose career ended, exactly as did his father's, as Lord of Appeal, (14 June 1948)).[14]

The longest obituary in 1948, also for a judge, reveals a quite different set of dispositions. Lord Sankey is another ascetic figure, but in this case championed an iconoclastic autonomy which helped established a quite different set of social structures (9 February 1948). Nothing in his origins — home in Moreton Court, Gloucester, school at Lancing, law at Oxford — suggested that he would be a radical judge. Yet he used the notion of judicial balance to put forward several important developments, not least his handling of a commission in 1919, which — agreeing with miners' representatives — proposed the nationalization and state management of the mines. More than this, it was Sankey's interwar negotiations with Indians which paved the way for independence, whilst he also oversaw the disestablishment of the Church of Wales. The obituary places explanatory weight on his experience in hearings of the Workmen's Compensation Act: 'The Workmen's Compensation Act was the making of him'. It also stresses the social conflicts around his decisions, despite his grave bodily demeanour in his bewigged obituary photograph. His unworldliness is the leitmotif of the whole obit: he had, we read, 'real piety'.

THE BOURGEOISIE, INCLUDING LIBERAL PROFESSIONALS

It would be wrong to give too monolithic a portrayal of the 1948 obits as testaments solely of a certain aristocratic asceticism. Unlike the 1900s, there are celebrated figures of the grande bourgeoisie here — a banker from J.P. Morgan's bank, Lord Hambro of Hambro's bank, a regulator of the Stock Exchange. Yet the obituaries are underpinned by the 1945 election promise of social renewal. This emerges especially in the prominence given to scientists, planners and to academics in new disciplines. Here, for example, are aircraft designers (including Sir Orville Wright of the Wright brothers), a professor who edited *The Journal of Pomology* (a branch of plant pathology dealing with the vital potato), a civil servant who encapsulates the spirit of post-war planning (Sir Gwilym Gibbon), an architect and town planner (Housing Commissioner for the Ministry of Health), a Chairman of the Metropolitan Water Board, and a Chairman of the Food Council and President of the Public Health Congress (Sir Allan Powell). Many of these are the educated sons of the unsung bourgeoisie of the 1900s. Implicitly, these obituaries negotiate critiques of the public sector's specific interests, routinisation and lack of democratic feedback. We are told, for example, in Gwilym Gibbons' obituary that the problem for planners as he defined it was that of 'sustaining unity of control without the loss of local knowledge and the diminution of local spirit and activity'. Still, officials cease to be grey and faceless figures and have become 'heroes of bureaucracy'. They are even attributed with innate 'gifts'!

Equally, whereas the scientist of the 1900s obits was a lesser human whose lack of elite background obscured his significance, by 1948 the scientist has acquired a reputation similar to that of a Romantic poet. Professor Baly is an ideal-typical scientist, whose otherworldliness and scientific work ethic is signaled in the obituary by his moments of illumination: points at which his 'noble head and glittering hawk-like gaze' embody entirely his galvanized resolution and lonely intellectual discipline. The obituary image of this scientist offers a Friedrich-like portrayal of a solitary figure surmounting a mountainous crag:

> To many who were unable to appreciate his gifts as a scientist, Professor Baly, with his noble head and glittering hawk-like gaze, will nonetheless remain the epitome of genius. His appeal to generations of students was magnetic and under a person at first impact formidable, lay a warm heart [...]. His feelings for his beloved mountains was almost mystic. His favourite story was of a solitary traverse of the Loire Lagan [Skye] peaks. [...] [A]s he approached each summit, the mist lifted from it and he found himself in sunshine. He was for ever afterwards convinced that he had been vouchsafed a vision.' (7 January 1948). (See also Dr. V. Cornish, 3 May 1948)

WOMEN

In 1948 there are a few more women than there were in 1900 (from 11% to 17%). Yet some who do appear steal into these columns solely because of their relation to more notable others — what is distinctive, then, about Anne de Gaulle, is solely her father, General de Gaulle (9 February 1948), and the same goes for Lady Ada Frederick (26 January 1948), Lady Boothby (12 May 1948) and Lady Hayter (7 June 1948), whose husbands are once more commemorated, as still happens today. And yet there has been a slight shifting of the techtonic plates of the obituary writing. Just as there are now scientists of genius, so a woman musician can be credited with the accolade of genius (the musician, Mrs. Gordon Woodhouse, 19 January 1948). There is some recognition of women who are carving out an independent stance, as in the case of Phylippa Fawcett (6 June 1948), who administered outreach education in South Africa or Mrs. G Atherton, whose 'feminist' novels critique patriarchal families.

Yet, paradoxically, in this period of post-World War II restructuring, women, whose lives had been so turned upside down by the war, were being encouraged to reacquaint themselves with 'eternal femininity' (Muel-Dreyfus 2001). Women chiefly appear in these columns in their traditional family roles: their individual distinction is acquired within home and the wider gift economy of aristocratic women.

A more poignant portrait is of a Miss Edith Olivier, a woman of great potential and cultural capital, who did not live up to her early ambitions (12 May 1948). Rather than see this obituary as part of a masculine detraction of her pretensions, it is more illuminating to see her as a woman who fails to fulfil herself for the sake of the duty to her family, as in Radcliffe Hall's *The Unlit Lamp*. Thus the obit recalls her student promise at Oxford and her ambitions to be an actress, which her imperious father, the canon of Salisbury, called 'grotesque' and killed in the bud. After he died, she 'suddenly' wrote three novels, then becoming once again deflected onto a more traditional way of life for an upper-middle class family. Rooted in her family's great house, she became a local mayor when she might have written sufficient works to acquire 'literary survival value' (Lovell 1987). Olivier is perhaps a George Eliot manqué: the obituary is in many respects a tragic one.

1948: THE FIELD OF CULTURAL PRODUCTION

There is one remarkable portrayal which also measures the clear distance with the 1900s obits. This is the obit for Claude McKay, a Jamaican, who emigrated to the States at the age of twenty-two, and was educated at the Tuskegee Normal Institute and Kansas State School (9 June 1948). After visiting the newly-socialist USSR (where he met Lenin and Trotsky) he settled in the North, working on the Pennsylvania Railway and financing his writing through Catholic Youth Organisation work. Settling in Harlem, New York, where he had an early *succès d'estime*, he wrote three novels — *Home to Harlem*, *Banjo* and *Banana Bottom*, the last a study of the 'intense yearning for English culture' in Jamaica ('not his most popular book'). The obit defines his more *subtle* work as *less popular*, thus locating the obituarist within the routinised high-low division of the restricted literary field: 'broader experience ripened his innate power, with the result that *Home to Harlem*, published in 1927 made him famous not only as the interpreter of the Negro mind but as a fine exponent of the craft of novelist'.

This is a medium-length obit, highly unusual in relation to other obituaries of writers in both 1900 and 1948, all of whom have very different social origins. It still uses the charismatic ideology — but in an unexpected way — as in the reference to his 'innate power' above. What the obituary fails to do, however, is to see his novels as only possible within certain new social institutions; McKay's attendance at the (Booker Washington) Tuskegee Normal School, established for Afro-Americans in the interwar years (Brinkley, 2000) and the brief flame of the interwar 'Harlem Renaissance', which circulated the work of Afro-American cultural producers, extending both novel and painting to include the new voices in their Northern urban districts. The Harlem Renaissance, and especially McKay's publication in the distinctive pro-trade union magazine *Messenger*, is omitted altogether, which turns the obit away from the cooperative field of cultural production and reverts instead to a formulaic Romantic discourse for its subject.

CONCLUSION

Obituaries are often said to identify figures on a national or international stage whose achievements have been significant. Yet they also inform the *collective memory* of particular groups and indirectly contribute to their doxic character. What do they therefore tell us about the capacity of different, antagonistic, classes to idealise their action?

The importance of the aristocracy in 1900 and its resilience even in 1948 can most easily be explained in terms of Arno Mayer's *The Persistence of the Ancien Regime*. This accounts for the 'Thirty Years War' of the First and Second World Wars as due to the hold on power by an authoritarian, anti-democratic, 'feudalistic' class whose trade was war and the collapse, after 1870, of the bourgeois challenge. Mayer accepts Schumpeter's argument that the

> human materials of feudal society continued to "fill the offices of state, officer the army and devise policies". Although capitalist processes, both national and international, generated ever larger shares of government revenue [...] the feudal element remained a classe dirigeante that behaved according to "precapitalist" patterns. (1981: 11)

Mayer himself goes farther and argues that from 1870–1914, the 'feudalistic element' fought off the bourgeoisie, so that, with the exception of Britain, the numbers in agriculture throughout Europe remained large, the progression to modern corporate capitalism was weak, merchant and artisanal capitalism was more powerful than capital goods or consumer commodity production and the power of 'high culture' lingered on. Even in Britain, the numbers in the industrial labour-force stayed relatively low, compared with the newly-unified Germany; throughout Europe, the aristocratic 'call to order' was supreme. The nobility represented itself through Academic art and were ostentatious consumers of classical ballet, opera and theatre. Hence the fierceness of the challenge from the artistic modernist movements, and the hostility or dismissiveness with which they and their supporters were treated — Tschudi, of the Berlin National Gallery, lost his job for buying Impressionists; modernism was so shunned by Academic curators that Monet, Degas and Rodin had to start a subscription to have Manet's *Olympia* bought by the Louvre; not a single Cezanne was bought by the Under-Secretary of State for the French Arts; in Vienna, Egon Schiele went to prison for his nude drawings (Mayer 1981: 227–35).

Mayer's book ends powerfully with the consequences of this feudal persistence[15]:

> The upper classes of Britain were prepared to take their peoples into a catastrophe from which they hoped against hope to draw benefits for themselves...To be sure there might be millions of victims, massive devastation...The politicians and generals were accomplices....What tied them together apart from shared social and political attitudes was a common commitment to struggle against political democracy, social levelling, industrial development and cultural modernism.' (1981: 321)

Eric Hobsbaum has a divergent view, however, and the significance of the aristocracy within the obituaries needs also to be assessed in the light of this. For Hobsbaum argues, in contrast, that the nineteenth century can only be seen as the triumph of capitalism and that the social imperialism it brought in its train was vital for gaining access to raw materials and to wider markets for exports. Indeed, for Hobsbaum the aristocracy itself was increasingly economically tied in to the destinies of capitalism. Princes and dukes exploited the coal-mines on their estates, invested in property and possessed shares in major companies, steel and otherwise. Equally, the bourgeoisie was no longer the puritan, frugal class it had once been, nor one linked by small networks of co-religionists. Vastly expanded, it had become increasingly permeated with a cult of money and luxury consumption. Moreover, it had sent its sons to the schools of the aristocracy — the public schools — which expanded from the nine ancient establishments to 'between 64 and 160 more or less expensive schools in the early 1900s' (1987: 178). There, as in the lycée and the gymnasium, they received a high culture based on Latin and Greek — in France and Germany, the classics together with a wider humanist culture.

The capitalist economy now organized production on an everyday basis for greater and greater numbers. Against Mayer, Hobsbaum argues that the public schools 'assimilated aristocratic values to a moral system designed for a bourgeois society and its public service' (1987:176). Indeed, the ennoblement of grocers and other commoners in both Britain and Germany — like Lord Lipton and Lord Leverhulme — could be seen as the powerful consecration of the bourgeois masters, rather than a sign of the 'supine' nature of the bourgeoisie. If the bourgeoisie increasingly withdrew into private life, leaving political leadership to others, its material position, perspective and vision was unassailable. Extending from a small plutocracy to an upper-middle class including liberal professionals, it had cohesion well beyond the seven hundred families of the peerage alone: the ancien regime had been decisively swept away.

Yet Hobsbaum is at one with Mayer that the older bourgeoisie's 'Enlightenment values', no longer survived. After democratization especially, 'progress, reform and liberalism were all in crisis' (1987: 188) — even more strongly — 'The fashion in the years before 1914, for rejecting an ideal of peace, reason and progress for an ideal of violence, instinct and explosion has often been observed' (1987: 190).

If Mayer's argument about the persistence of the ancient regime is accepted, it certainly explains the uncontentious fact of the pre-eminence of the aristocracy within the *politically dominant* fraction throughout the nineteenth century (see Hobsbaum 1987, Guttsman 1963, Corrigan and Sayer, 1985: 152–54). However, his argument eclipses from view the nineteenth-century changes in forms of government and economic life which from now on prioritised profitable property. It is a 'moral' and 'cultural revolution', developed through the British State itself, which created this outstanding rupture with earlier centuries. For as Corrigan and Sayer persuasively point out, there was a need to create new means by which 'Society' — now expanded to include the middle class — might moralise, discipline and channel the activities of the (wider) 'society'. They suggest that this was done particularly through the emergence of two new 'ideas', both apparently neutral — the resonance of *education* as a tool for moulding masses and the *statistical idea*, which measured 'civilized change' (in factory production, and the rates of births, marriages and deaths) (Corrigan and Sayer 1985: 125–136). The rise of independent middle class people to gather statistics and to pursue moral as well as material Improvement, has to be set against the simple unending regime of the aristocracy. This civic religion, it is argued, has been underestimated by Mayer.

The 1948 obituaries encapsulate a much greater fusion of the new with the old. If we regard Keynesianism as saving capitalism from itself then the nature and ethos of the 1948 obits have a strong Keynesian strand. The spread and the tone of these obituary profiles take all the ingredients of Keynesianism — large corporations, finance capitalism (those bankers from J.P. Morgan and Hambros), new science, new planning and new nationalization. It is going too far to see the 1948 obituaries as belatedly returning to the Enlightenment ideals of the middle classes — 'progress, reform and liberalism' (Hobsbaum, 1987: 188) Yet alongside the persistence of the old power bloc, more liberal and democratic voices were appearing, unthinkable earlier, like the African American writer, Claude McKay. If this interpretation is taken, it is not surprising that the *only* critical or negative obituary in this 1948 sample is for a young woman. She was Unity Mitford, who had added her aristocratic voice on Nazi platforms to that of Hitler and Goebbels (31 May 1948).[16]

5 The social value of death
The microworld of the editors

Obituary editors are confronted daily with the need to make delicate hermeneutic interpretations of the social meaning of individuals' deaths and to express these powerfully to their readership. This chapter seeks to throw some light on the world the editors inhabit and how, confronted with the multiplicity of deaths, they classify them, attributing to some an importance that others lack. It is essential not to be lured by the idea of 'obituaries for the great and the good' into positivist fantasies that there is an objective basis for such decisions. Daily, minor decisions have to be made by editors in the heat of rapidly- moving events, just as doctors have to decide when a 'possible death' should become 'pronounced [as] death' by ceasing resuscitation attempts (Sudnow 1967: 100–105). In order to undercut endless discussion, certain rules of thumb are adopted by obituary editors which guide them through this quagmire. It is these rules that we now aim to elucidate. Such practical rules or strategies are framed by the editors' wider reflections on the enhanced importance of the obituary in modernity as a countervailing force, which can in a small way offset the fragmented specialisation of the modern division of labour.

The editorial reflections on their procedures and experiences will be considered in relation to a sociological analysis — or 'objectivation' — of the obituaries in Chapter 6 (Bourdieu 1996b). Here I briefly anticipate the argument by drawing attention to a discrepancy that appears to exist between, on the one hand, the editors' subjective avowals about the openness of the obituary columns and, on the other hand, the objectively highly restricted origins and trajectories of the obituary subjects. This contrast occurs particularly sharply in relation to the privileged educational trajectories of contemporary British obituary subjects, of whom — as will be discussed — 77 per cent went to public school and 35 per cent went to Oxbridge. This study also raises questions about the higher visibility of 'whiteness', European and American citizens, and indeed, men.

This discrepancy derives from the complex and ambiguous nature of the editorial criteria for obituary inclusion, criteria which journalists are in practice forced to use to simplify the otherwise bewildering array of choices. As we shall show, despite the many confusing directions implicit in the rhetoric of openness, a set of doxic social classifications — about the best universities, the highest church positions etc. — impinges strongly on the editors. In other words, by means of a subtle symbolic violence, certain types of knowledge and power acquire an enhanced legitimacy and it is these attributes that define the people chosen to feature. Consequently, the net of subjects for the obituaries is in reality spread much less widely than the journalists might imagine in their more expansive rhetoric.

THE OBITUARY EDITORS ('THE EDITORS')

This account of the manufacture of news obituaries is based on interviews that the editors generously gave me. The reflections offered in the interviews have been supplemented with three essays, all of which address contemporary obituaries from the perspective of the newspaper journalist (Fergusson 1999; Massingberd 2001; Osborne 2003) The editors, for the most part, are employed by the broadsheet (or ex-broadsheet) British newspapers, based in London.[1] Two are working in the Edinburgh offices of *The Scotsman* and Glasgow offices of *The Herald*, respectively, whilst the obituaries editors or writers, in Washington, New York and Paris are for the most highly-reputable of their countries' papers. They are:

Obituaries Editor, *The Daily Telegraph*
Obituaries Editor, *The Guardian*
Obituaries Editor, *The Herald*
Obituaries Editor, *The Independent.*
Obituaries Writer, *Le Monde.*
Obituaries Editor, *The New York Times*
Former Obituaries Editor, *The Scotsman*
Former Deputy Obituaries Editor, *The Times*
Assistant Obituaries Editor, *The Washington Post*

With the exception of the *New York Times* and *Le Monde* interviews, which were by telephone and e-mail, the interviews took place in or near the editors' offices which are situated on extensive, busy, open-plan floors. Working in spatially-segregated departments, the editors, their deputies and assistant journalists are surrounded by their colleagues in other departments, like small obituary islands within the wider newspaper sea. The former editor of *The Scotsman*, who had had over twenty years' experience, pointed to this specialised emergence of the obits' department as a development within his own working life. When he had first become obituaries editor, writing obits had been alternated with a variety of other activities, notably court and social announcements.

METAMORPHOSIS OF THE OBITUARY

The editor of *The Independent* holds the view that 'There has been a revolution in newspaper obits.' Clarifying this, he argued in an earlier essay, that *The Independent* obituary columns are now open to any one who has made their mark in the world in a significant, striking or surprising way:

> I think [...] of the multitude who might never have had obituaries written about them if the *Independent* [...] had not come along. Of all the photographers, monks, bookplate designers, chairmakers, suffragettes, graffiti artists, jazz saxonophonists, lexicographers, cartoonists, pulp publishers, puppeteers, mimes, weavers, ferrymen, schoolteachers and master plasterers; of Tom Forster, Britain's oldest working ploughman; Roly Wason, 91, Professor of Archaeology turned Hartlepool bus conductor [...], Mr. Sebastian', 63, body piercer and tattooist [...]; Winifred ('Winnie the Hat') Wilson,88, fearless sometime picture dealer to Walter Sickert; ... Donald MacLean, 66, for twenty-five years director of the Crieff Highland gathering and 'the greatest of all private collectors of the potato'.' (Fergusson 1999: 159–60)

This transformation in today's obits is attributed often to Hugh Massingberd, *The Daily Telegraph* obits editor (1986–94). Certainly it is by the *Independent*'s editor, who honoured Massingberd for having made the really significant rupture with the old way of writing obituaries.

Massingberd's contribution, as he himself explained in one of his edited selections, was to heighten curiosity by 'colourful' hooks. This would draw readers into the obit and also 'celebrate' the lives of his subjects with an educated eye and a fresh honesty (Massingberd 2001). Judging from these selections, under his editorship obituaries ranged widely, revelling in cultivated allusions: an Old Etonian Belvoir Hunt Master, for example, is described as a Corinthian,[2] or the Bhagwan Rajneesh's followers are labelled as 'sannyasin' (Massingberd 2001: Lord Daresbury, 91, Rajneesh, 87). Moreover, Massingberd paid scant respect to bourgeois respectability or puritanism: the *Telegraph* obituaries are never reticent about the political or sexual peculiarities of their subjects.[3] In fact, it is clear from Massingberd's approach that the whole conception of his obituary column was to free it from that seriousness or earnestness alien to a comic world-vision. It is therefore essential in understanding this editor that he asked aspiring obituarists at recruitment interviews whether they were 'familiar with the Master' (ie, P.G. Wodehouse). Indeed, he was gratified by a reader who interpreted his new *Daily Telegraph* gallery of 'eccentric peers and dotty dowagers' as proof that 'the Master' had been dealing 'in realism rather than fantasy' all along (2001: ix).

The Massingberd 'revolution' in obituaries needs to be understood in terms of its historical anchorage in a specific social perspective. At this point we shall merely note a certain individualistic structure of feeling which encourages licensed idiosyncracies, framed within a wider 'organic' order. Coupled with this are certain honorific relics of a 'predatory' rather than a 'pecuniary' leisure culture — *The Telegraph*'s law-revering readers are regaled with exploits of huntsmen, marksmen and 'sporting' criminals. These are the marks of a distinctively aristocratic style of life, emulated more broadly by gentrified heirs whose money originated in industrial capital (Wiener 1985; Hobsbaum 1999).

The present obits editor of the *Daily Telegraph*, accepted Fergusson's view of a transformed, post-Massingberd obituary universe. Using a similar language of a break with tradition, he emphasised that the current changes embrace transformations of both form and content: 'The primary revolution in obits is stylistic, although it is content as well' (editor, *The Telegraph*). Moreover, following on rapidly from Massingberd's era of innovation in the 1980s, the birth of the *Independent* newspaper in 1986 reinforced this rupture with the past. The present *Independent* editor encapsulated the new era as 'breaking the mould', interpreting this particularly as a movement to expand the scope of obits:

> Obituaries aren't all the same. They have a duty to represent the person accurately and perhaps sympathetically. But there are a million ways of doing it. *The Independent* broke this mould: you could do it in a number of different ways, a partial interview, a dialogue and so on. There is no single genre of 'the obituary'. It should be an argument: it should be a question of why this person *deserves* to be remembered.

A similar emphasis on what he called the new 'warts and all honesty' in today's obits was detected by the editor of the *The Herald*. In this connection, we might even want to talk about a *modern movement* in the obituary world, which thus breaks decisively with the highly-conventional cultural obituary most characteristic of earlier periods and embraces popular worlds once spurned — such as cinema and jazz. *Le Monde* develops this further into literary modernism, abandoning grammatical rules in artistic obits, as well as adopting a less routinised manner of delineating the lives of obit subjects. An unprecedented informality and rupture with codes is undoubtedly spreading, illuminatingly interpreted by the American obituary writers as particularly characteristic of British obituaries. Readers' intensifying interest in this form is reflected in the enlarged space and length for obits.

In brief, the 'revolution' in obits is now said to be spreading to all the non-tabloid newspapers. *The Scotsman*'s editor speaks of an unmatched era of 'openness' and of the gradual inclusion of a new breed of celebrities, especially in football, cricket and modelling, mostly known to the public through television. *The Times*'s editor spoke of the new obit era as one which might now include the brick-worker who first suggested putting three holes in bricks before they were baked. In general, editors of both Right and Left-leaning papers saw the obits as utterly transformed, as though 'a new world was born'. The obits now are ruled only, they claimed, by the imperatives of portraying influential, interesting and distinctive individuals as their subjects, with an emphasis on their being 'interesting'.

Yet there are also divergent readings of such a 'revolution'. In its heartland, The *Telegraph*, the new obits could be seen as more like a rebirth of late Wordsworthian Romanticism , in which the poet stretched out, beyond the patrician world, to acknowledge the dignity of traditional rural figures. The familiar agrarian idyll of authenticity is *reenacted* in the *Telegraph* in gentrified accents (see Guillory 1993: 125–131). This newspaper's obits are magnetically drawn to independent small farmers in decline and also to those with 'old money' who could afford to indulge in political and aesthetic outrageousness, from sexual promiscuity to crocheting their own cotton trousers (see Lord Daresbury and Earl Russell, respectively, Massingberd 2001: 28–31, 91). In other words, on a more sceptical reading, the *Telegraph* 'revolution' has fallen far short of any more profound movement to represent wider circles, which might have moved decisively beyond the Establishment and its rural Arcadian preoccupations.

What does the 'revolution' mean to those who produce the obituaries? On this point, *The Herald* obits editor sketched out his paper's policy clearly and trenchantly. First, he filters out for obituary commemoration those whose 'status' is secure amidst a certain *constituency of his readers*, using obits written in-house or by specialist subject journalists. Secondly, he selects obits from those he is offered. These are often absorbing and memorable accounts of the lives of people of whom he had once been oblivious. He sums up: 'To merit an obituary one ought to have made a difference. Perhaps not a huge difference and maybe not to many people, but a difference all the same.' It is necessary, then, to show how such an idea might function in practice, for him and others.

ACTS OF EXCLUSION

The lived reality of the obit journalists' microworld can be illuminated with the help of their own accounts and views. What are the difficulties they are confronted with each day in terms of choices of subject? By and large they have to make these choices with well-tried rules of thumb for making sense of an otherwise infinite morass of possibilities. Practical rules, recipe knowledge, this they have; but also a rival awareness exists that ultimately 'there are no *real* rules of thumb' (*The Guardian*'s editor)

Nevertheless, all the interviewed editors argue, as has been seen, that they want obituaries to be about 'interesting' and 'important' individuals. Certain individuals are the product of a consensus: they are taken-for-granted choices —'doxic' in Bourdieu's terms — which a newspaper is obliged to make. Some of these men and women may have shaped directly the social order in which we now live. To use Lukács' term, they are 'world-historical individuals'; their power has made them so influential that they have had to be included, 'beyond good and evil', whatever their acts. Yet others have been important culturally — in working with Fermat's Last Theorem or pioneering analysis of DNA. Others, much less obligatory, are symbolic of a valued way of life that is passing, and which needs to be commemorated. Collective memory is here served by the dead representing a past that is being sidelined or destroyed. Lastly, regardless of the subjects' merits, the editors only include well-written obituaries, preferably those that contain an element of the 'unexpected'.

British obits may come from any quarter, from their own journalists, from regular writers on a subject, or from members of the public. American and French *news* obituaries are written solely by their own obituary writers or by other specialised correspondents. In all these cases there is a positive injunction — choose as subjects the distinguished, brilliant and respected individuals! There are also negative injunctions in interpreting 'respect' — avoid the worthy, 'boring' and the merely private virtues! In this connection, the editors see themselves as having to negotiate a new passage between tradition and modernity or, to use their language, between 'some you *have to have*' — a high-ranking diplomat, minor Royalty or 'the wife or mother of someone very well-known' — and those that they *really* favour.

On the one hand, all editors, without exception, possess a mission to open up the obit column beyond ascribed status, and in that sense they are contributors to democratisation. Yet, on the other hand, they are also guardians of the cultural canon. They are thus conscious that the truly significant individuals, whom posterity will remember, may be recognised at death by a minority of their peers only. For this reason they typically oppose any imposed levelling, interpreted as moves to equal representation of ethnic groups or genders irrespective of quality. There is, of course, a tension between these two concerns.

THE CASH NEXUS: THE MATERIAL BASE FOR THE OBIT

The uniformity of the British obits pages conceals variations in the economic relations behind their production. Moreover, the greater availability of the newspaper obituary for a general public in the States hides a quite different cash nexus from that prevalent in Britain. Balzac said 'Tell me what you earn and I will tell you what you think'; similarly, the economics of obits may alter who is represented and *how we will think of them*. Cross-cultural studies are important here, since they show a wide range of practice. These vary from Nigeria, where the obits are financed privately, costing sometimes a whole month's salary, to the professional journalists' publication of obituaries in Britain which costs the family nothing.[4]

In other words, the obituaries represent intersecting worlds, a commercial economy based on money and a 'gift economy' based on respect and honour. As *The Herald* editor pointed out, in American newspapers, the obituaries are frequently part of the advertising division, not the editorial division. Indeed, in the case of certain American papers, there is a 'grey area' where a given obit may be located in the territory of the editorial or of the advertising departments. In contrast, in *The Herald*, about 80 per cent of obituaries are produced in-house — 40 per cent by specialists, 40 per cent by the obituaries' department — whilst 20 per cent are provided as gifts, contributed by the friends and colleagues of the deceased. Contributors to *The Herald* often expect the editor to require payment and are surprised when the obituary is free. Conversely, as *The Independent* and *The Scotsman* editors remarked, many lay contributors think that they are undertaking a 'labour of love'. Not expecting any payment, they may even return their cheques. In fact, the payment for contributors is not negligible. A small obit ranges from £60 to £120 in all the newspapers, while *The Times'* editor cites the cost of a full page obit as between £800 and £1000[5].

Writers who specialise in a specific area, like Hollywood film, find editors frequently turning to them. They can more adequately provide an account of the significance of the dead person than their own journalists, who are necessarily confined to using the standard sources. This is particularly true where the writer might have met or worked with the deceased. Here we can differentiate between various types of writer to whom the journalists turn. First, one editor (*The Guardian*) spoke of his contacts with certain university academics, such as Jane O'Grady (a professor of philosophy at London University) who offered obituaries of philosophers whose circles she moved in, whilst a Scottish editor referred to Tam Dalyell's regular political obituaries for *The Independent*. Dalyell's subjects were MPs whom he had known in Parliament or Scottish footballers, preferably people for whom he had some affection.[6] Secondly, however, there was another category. *The Guardian* editor referred to the retired military man who made steady part-time earnings from the supply of military obituaries, most of them figures *unknown* to him personally. A writer based in London, Alasdair Stephen, was regularly asked by *The Scotsman* to write obituaries in a variety of fields.[7] Are we witnessing here the growth of a semi-professionalised specialist on the form who lives off the obituary? This is felt by the editors to be a possible — but not a very likely — outcome, partly because of the resilience of the specialist writing more broadly in any field. *The Herald* editor summed up for the others:

> There are people to whom I'll go to commission an obituary of X. Brian Pendreigh does quite a lot of film obits. He earns his living as

a film writer or critic, but he'll do obits for us and *The Times*. But I would hesitate to call him semi-professional. He has a knowledge of the film world — a good person to approach to estimate the *significance* of the contribution.

[...] I don't see any reason why it should become more professionalised in the future. In the cases where people write about their professional colleagues, they are only going to write one or two obits in their lives.

This is not an area that obits editors lose any sleep over — it is *routinised*. And yet there is a realisation that it is tied up in an intimate way with the power and artistic qualities of the obit. An author who has already done an important full-length biography of a given person may serve in turn as a good obituarist, whilst certain free-lance or specialist correspondents can be relied upon to write accurately and readably about a variety of people. However, in Britain, it is often felt that the best writers for this occasion are those who knew the individual on a personal basis. As *The Herald*'s editor put it, they should fall 'within certain parameters — neither as enemy nor as widow'.

NEWSPAPERS' POLITICAL IDENTITIES — CURRENT DOXA

The *Le Monde* editor separated her paper's obituaries sharply from the British ones, in terms of their own greater space constraints. She stressed her concern for 'objectivity', over and above the journalists' individual styles. Her approach was echoed by many of the others: 'it is a question above all of retracing a life, a career, a passage in the most objectively possible manner without being either hagiographic or negative.'

However, the world of the obituary editors is furnished by certain internalised classifications of their national newspapers and their own hierarchical position ('people would unquestionably prefer to be seen dead in the *New York Times*' (*Washington Post* editor)). After the obituaries that every editor 'must' run — Ronald Reagan, say, or (in Britain) a Cabinet minister such as Mo Mowlem — it is the newspapers' self-images that inform assumptions about the subjects for obits whom they will choose.

The Independent's editor distinguished its subjects from those of other newspapers:

The Times is still an Establishment paper, the *Telegraph* still has leanings towards those who ran the war, towards those from the Shires and those who are active in shooting and fishing. *The Independent* was a tabula rasa: we made it up as we went along. It is very strong on showbiz, the arts, foreign obits, science (we give an obit to every

FRS) academia. *The Guardian* [...] has similar interests, although it will have more Lefties, more school teachers.

In his (separate) interview, the Deputy Editor of *The Times* in effect contested this:

> I think that *we* are the most wide-ranging. There is a kind of *Daily Telegraph* eccentric Englishman, too many aristocrats and not enough foreigners, a bit upmarket, county good chaps. They turn their noses up at things which make good stories, such as the man who invented e-mail.

This reveals *The Times'* concern for 'inventive entrepreneurialism'; it may also illuminate why they include more entrepreneurs and financiers than any other newspaper.

The obituary writers' choices are inseparable from their readers' composition. Thus the editor of *The Guardian*, saw his own paper as at root 'more realistic'. It values arts obits over military ones, featuring the popular arts as well as high culture. Alternatively, *The Independent* obituaries editor was withering about the Scottish newspapers' openness to any obituary subjects whom their readers championed, defending the more discriminating practices of his own newspaper. '[T]he Scottish papers' he commented acerbically, 'receive pieces and gratefully print them all'.

The Scotsman's former obits editor was in this respect closer to *The Guardian* pole, although taking for granted the need also to feature 'top Scots'. Thus he identified a 'problem' with World War Two officers who had served in the war, retired to live in Perth and had done nothing since. Implicitly setting himself against earlier obit traditions, he expressed his willingness to include leading trade unionists and discussed his earlier writing of jazz musicians' obits with particular enjoyment.

Further, the editors incisively *differentiated* their approach to any given obit subject by pricking the balloon of the Left — or, conversely the Right — with which their antagonists' papers were identified. Here, for example, is *The Telegraph* editor on Eric Hobsbawm, whom he expects to get a very approbatory obit in *The Guardian* or *The Independent*: '[He is] a tremendously significant historian but *I* will say that he was foul in his acceptance of Stalinism at a time when other people were rejecting it.'

Distinguishing himself again from the despised 'orthodox radical consensus' of the latter newspapers, this editor goes onto tackle the shibboleth of Edward Said:

> I was quite critical of Said, especially for making things up [unspecified] about his childhood. He also wrote in a bizarre way about *Mansfield Park*: plantations in the West Indies and so on. But I would not have disputed that he was very important for post-colonial studies.

Many *Telegraph* obituaries thus subtly destroy the aura of prophetic figures of the Left, and vice versa. Here we can see the telling nuances that separate political positions, alongside more general agreement about the lines of culturally significant work.

Finally, a further obvious principle of division between the newspapers, following the 'golden age of journalistic anonymity', was over the matter of *authorship* (Fergusson 1999: 153). *The Times* and *Daily Telegraph* — true to their own traditions — continue to favour anonymity, but now in contrast with the other newspapers. This had become an issue for dispute ever since Andreas Whittam Smith had first broken the rules by naming the obituary column's authors. Tellingly, each side preferred its own paper's practices on this matter, justifying their own practices as a guarantee of greater freedom.[8]

EVERYDAY OBITUARY PRODUCTION: SOCIAL MECHANISMS FOR INCLUSION

As *The Times* editor pointed out, many more obituaries are written than are printed. Of about a thousand used by *The Times* each year, ten times as many are 'looked at' and four times as many are printed preliminarily. All of this occurs at speed, so that in high- profile cases an obit appears a day after the death. There are certain obit editors' routines that generate daily the resources for the next crop of obits.

Firstly, the editors and journalists survey obits and death notices in their own and other newspapers and second, read the death notices via overseas and London news agencies, such as Reuters.[9] Of these, one editor considered that: 'AP [Associated Press] is the best of them' (*The Herald*), perhaps referring to the global extensiveness of this news agency, the heir to the former Empire-based and American agencies which served London from the nineteenth century (Bielsa 2005).

Following the death notice, the obits department acts. Some obits will be taken from stock as 'advances', although such stock is not necessarily beyond the reach of change. For example, *The Times* editor clarified that their obituary for Thatcher has changed several times, being initially written while she was still Prime Minister, altered subsequently 'until it became like a patchwork', and then completely rewritten. Others are written by a journalist in-house, sometimes subject to the oppressive control of the few hours' deadline imposed by the editor in the case of important people:

> You hit the phones…, use *International Who's Who* …You hope against hope that you've commissioned the long ones, because you don't want to write about [Princess] Diana in five hours. (*The Times*)

Yet other obits will be commissioned from outside writers. Some of these will be regular contributors, such as the former Dean of Winchester who writes about the clergy for *The Daily Telegraph,* Emeritus Professor Douglas Johnson, who used to write the obits of anyone of French nationality in *The Guardian* (philosophers, historians, politicians...), or Alasdair Stephen, the London-based freelance obits writer for *The Scotsman,* already mentioned. Indeed, any of a newspaper's outlying correspondents, who knew the subject, may have to be persuaded on occasion to serve as obituarist, according to what else is going on and how important the deceased is.

Yet what finally gets in the obits page each day depends on a certain degree of chance — if two Latin American novelists die at a similar time, only one may be printed. If a major British death occurs this may elbow out — forever — a foreign dramatist.... As *The Telegraph* editor pointed out, the general public is unaware how many obits are never published. In other words, within the obituary world there is a huge discrepancy between the back stage and the front stage.

It should also be noted that many of these pieces are by journalists, chiefly concerned with news values. As such, they are aware that some of their choices may have more meaning and resonance within the narrow media and leisure worlds. 'We are guilty of amusing ourselves to death' comments *The Times*' editor, self-deprecatingly, hinting that such news values are impinging more on the obits than they used to, even in *The Telegraph* and *The Times.* In the same vein, the editor of *The Scotsman* observed: 'We are a celebrity society [...] page 3 models will have obits in 20 years' time'.

Secondly, after public sources of information, people also telephone to inform the newspaper about a death, sometimes offering to write obituaries. '[We] are enormously dependent on people ringing up [...] We have the great advantage that people want their friends and relatives to be in *The Times* obit page' (*The Times*' editor).

The other side of this coin is that people can put pressure on the editor: 'The family may say 'You're the only paper which hasn't done one'. You can respond in either way, depending on their manner' (*Daily Telegraph*).

As the editor of *The Herald* pointed out, there are limits to such pressures, especially since he is unprepared to give an obit to a 'boring individual' simply to heighten the 'profile' of a given organisation or institution. Moreover, those who request obits lack all sanctions. In this sense the obituary editor is totally autonomous, or at least answerable only to the newspaper's chief editor.

The *New York Times* editor was very clear about this:

> Friends and relatives often pressure the obits editor or the obits department. It happens all the time. Some are relentless. For example, we are often solicited to put in professors beloved for 40 years (Mr. Chips obits). I could fill the paper every day with these, but *we don't do them.* Similarly with partners for law firms — their news value is very limited. They are whoever they are, whatever the race or sex. I don't

have the *space* …. Our decisions are made on news value, admittedly a subjective judgement, but still far more equitable for our readers. We are not an equal opportunities section; that is, we're not looking to have a certain number of women, or African-Americans or lawyers or oddballs. We're looking for people whose lives and careers, well-known to the public or not, left a significant lasting imprint, for good or ill on those of us who remain among the living.

Many obit editors expressed matters similarly.

Thirdly, there are unpredicted overtures, which include the offer of obituaries by writers without professional skills in this area. The *New York Times* held an equally firm line on this: 'Relatives, friends or outsiders who feel they want to write obits are expressly forbidden.'

For others, things are less clearcut. The criteria used in deciding whether or not to include a contributed obit are partly their significance, partly stylistic — they are covered succinctly in the following formulation:

(1) expertise, (2) familiarity with the subject, (3) acquaintance and (4) ability to write — sometimes, not always, ability to deliver soon. (*The Times*' editor)

There are various responses to the non-professional obits. The former obits editor of *The Scotsman* explains why some are excluded:

There are times when we get offered obits […]which are written out of a kind of release of grief, if you like, and when you examine them closely there's nothing there other than "This was a very fine chap or a very fine lady, who held nice parties" […]. We take them in but we don't generally publish them.

He expects instead 'significant achievements' in the public sphere, so that the five hundred words should tell you why the person merits attention: 'If you're picking up someone useless, it's a waste of space'.

The unsolicited, one-off, obituary, as has been seen, accounts for as many as 20 per cent of the obituaries in *The Herald*, a newspaper that, like *The Scotsman*, has more space for figures in its landscape with a mainly Scottish significance. *The Herald*'s obits editor commented poignantly on this non-traditional cache of subjects, in tones very different from *The Independent*:

They don't usually disappoint me: there are few obituaries that people volunteer to write that are about lives that are really prosaic. […]. Some people whom I have never heard of have produced fascinating obits: they have had fascinating lives. For someone to bother to write, that person has done something special to touch several lives.

Finally, it should be noted that certain obituaries are included not so much because they commemorate a great person but because they allow reflections on a changing society. All the editors have obituaries for people who were one of the first or last in a given field. Thus *The Herald* editor referred to Gerry Thomas, the pioneer of the TV dinner, another to the last working ploughman (*The Independent*), the *New York Times* to the declining performers of extraordinary feats in carnivals, and *The Times*' editor to the last butler.[10] To some degree also, they look for 'characters', a hard-drinking Cumbrian hill-farmer, a New York lingerie shopkeeper who could tell women's bra sizes at a glance, or a professional burglar, given to debating points of law with the Bench.

The issues to which we now turn specify in more detail the papers' practices. These also serve to pinpoint some residual dilemmas.

RULES OF OBIT SELECTION

1. 'Going to the top'

Following the death notice, certain papers such as *The Times* go directly to institutions with which the deceased was associated — 'Oxford and Cambridge', the 'Royal Society', the 'National Portrait Gallery', the 'British Library' and 'to the companies and, within them, to their top people. Not just their Press Department' (*The Times*). Alternatively, via 'ringing in', the top comes to you.

This procedure encapsulates obliquely what *The Herald* obits editor says more straightforwardly. The obit is about *status*, about drawing the perimeter around *elites*, even if such elites also have their colourful exceptions.

2. Exclusion of the tendentious obituary in the interests of balance

The editor of *The Guardian* stated the paper's rule of resistance to the purely tendentious: everything suggests that the others would agree. Elaborating the point, he argued that no obit should be too one-sided[11] — that is, express only, say, a Zionist or a pro-Arab point of view.

Despite the editors' silence on this deviation, the present study shows that actual practice is not always in keeping with this rule. Indeed, in certain cases — admittedly, rare — the obituarist uses a harsh and critical language, unbalanced by any sympathetic observations. The two obituaries for Sadaam Hussain's sons, Uday and Hussay in *The Financial Times* (23 July 2003) exemplify this, both sons being depicted in terms devoid of any favourable interpretation — as 'ruthless, 'dictatorial' 'philanderers'. This suggests that where a consensus is sufficiently powerful and the collective consciousness sufficiently outraged, the 'tendentiousness' rule is ignored.

The editors, nevertheless, spoke only about the importance of rigour in the attributions of factual assertions, which should be based on the same level of evidence as required in a courtroom. There might be critical or negative obituaries, they accepted, including obituaries of their own nationals, but these had to be well-founded: 'We can be pretty tough on our own. But some of those you mentioned (Agnelli excepted)[12] for the most part weren't very nice fellows' (the *New York Times* editor).

3. Exclusion of the private and the routinised

Certain categories of people are routinely passed over: 'private' women, working-class or petit bourgeois individuals — even businessmen. Yet this limitation is not justified by editors in terms of class, still less in terms of gender. Rather it is on quite different grounds: that these groups are '*boring*' — in the *New York Times*' editor's terms, they have little news value or in *Le Monde*'s language, insufficient 'national or international notoriety'. Nevertheless, precise assessments of the horizon of the *boring* vary: the editor of *The Telegraph*, for example, believed that good war stories invariably go down well, a belief questioned by other editors, such as *The Scotsman* and the *Washington Post*.

Nor does the definition of 'boring' forestall some debates *at the margins* over whether certain 'standard' categories still deserve the privilege of inclusion, and if so, whether they deserve the traditional privilege of great length. Difficult individual cases then emerge which can indeed become the source of agonising self-monitoring. Thus the journalist from *The Times*' — with all the freedom of a *deputy* editor's perspective — would have preferred to cut the length of the *Times*' very long obit for Princess Margaret. He also commented, with some relief, that — barring the Archbishop of Canterbury and a few others — *The Times* now included only very few ex officio obits. In similar terms, the editor of *The Guardian* reported that he reviewed carefully all traditional areas such as the obits of diplomats. The rules that had formerly entitled everyone to an obit who had served for at least two regular tours of office are now subject to reassessment.

Individuals, it has been seen, need to 'make a difference' — ie, to have distinction — to be awarded an obituary. Yet in choosing between different categories of distinction, rules of thumb are again necessary, since only these operate to reveal who are the really 'interesting' (or meritorious) in current terms. *The Guardian* editor revealed how he had been approached to include an exemplary teacher, who had inspired generations of pupils, yet

> There are comprehensive teachers you feel you cannot justify including. Then, when we reject them, people can come back and say 'But you included such and such a pop star!' We also have a young readership [...] so it was suggested that I include a young pop star, Aliyah, who

died recently. If three or four people say they know that person, then I will say "yes".

Implicitly there is a clash here between two practical logics, one of fame and one of education: 'X is interesting, mainly because you have heard of her already'. This might be called the celebrity pole (Rojek, 2001: 9–20, 181–98). In contrast 'X is interesting, you will learn from his or her life' might be called the education pole. These are seen as competing principles, existing in a state of tension. At least for *The Guardian*, they produce a paradox, the paper's obits editor identifying this with evident unease:

> We can only print about four a day. We have a particular constituency — these maybe councillors or people who work in social services […]. But when some obituaries of these people are offered to you, you have to say 'I don't feel I can do this.

The Times editor, too, noted a secular trend to more celebrity obits, his discussion expressing realism and regret simultaneously:

> The most forgotten popular band drummer — who was abandoned after six months because his first record bombed — is going to get an obit, whereas the managing director wouldn't.

The Herald, however, operates quite differently in response to this, encouraging precisely the contributor-written obit of the good teacher or backbench MP whom *The Guardian*'s rules screen out: 'If people have bothered to write out a piece about someone's life, it usually turns out to be very interesting, even if it's someone I never heard of before'.

Is this the luxury of a newspaper editor within a much smaller nation? Or, alternatively, does it indicate the greater democratisation of the West of Scottish society? More research is required, but the second is more likely.

A further point, with the exception of the *Washington Post* deputy editor, all the editors accepted that there continued to be a marked disparity between the numbers of obituaries for men and those for women. The latter — younger than most of the others — cited the names of many women who had recently received obits, arguing that if three individuals died in any one day and two were women, both the latter would have obits written. Another conceded that there was a discrepancy to the disfavour of women, adding, revealingly, that certain women gained entry because their lives could be illustrated by compelling photographs of their dancing or acting days.

There is also general agreement that up to now the women who have died belonged to those generations of women typically neither active in the public sphere nor in higher positions within the labour-market. Hence, for the majority of these editors, their currently insignificant showing was still explicable in terms of the rule excluding 'private women'. As the *New York Times* editor remarked: 'Demographically, this will change as more women enter the workforce'.

Such a link between women's formal entry into the public sphere and their subsequent award of obits is not implausible. However, this belief brings the advantage that nothing needs to be done very differently from the past. The argument has a further implication. With the exception of the Royal family, public achievement — typically within a bureaucratised ladder of advancement — has been understood as the sole legitimate means of gaining an obit. Despite the editors' earlier inclusiveness in asking simply 'Do they deserve to be remembered?', their everyday procedures operated to exclude women (and men) who had made a significant impact *outside the conventional elite careers* of the Establishment/ State Nobility or beyond the *celebrity-strewn world of the arts, media and sport.*[13] Hence the highly exceptional appearance of figures like Michael Akintaro (see introduction). I shall return to this point in the conclusion.

A similar question was raised about the proportion of obituaries allocated to migrants and minority ethnic groups. This question was asked in a context in which contemporary British newspapers vary between 89 per cent and 92 per cent of their obituaries for white, 'majority' ethnic group subjects, as will be shown in the following chapter.

Certainly, the editors showed, in some cases, an active awareness that many asylum-seekers of the past have made a major contribution to British society: '[They] have had extraordinary achievements', to use the words of *The Independent's* editor. This contribution was sometimes linked to certain group characteristics, such as the prizing of great erudition within Jewish culture (editor, *The Times*). These perceptions of the past fuelled the view of the British journalists that more recent ethnic minorities would eventually gain obits when they had achieved in the 'public sphere' or the work force.

They also acknowledged that the increased proportion of obits from groups such as African-Americans is due to a new popular expansiveness, an extended reach of obits to cover areas such as jazz or football, whose legendary players would never before have featured. But there are clearly tensions here. *The Scotsman's* editor, arguing that wider, non-Eurocentric traditions already existed ('There is probably an affinity for black people in Scotland'), yet also told a story indicating that an 'eccentric fringe' of their readers object to obits for non-whites, even in the case of those as reputable as Dizzie Gillespie. It is worth considering whether the views of such an 'eccentric fringe' do not still tacitly influence selection, despite the editors' own openness.

Such a new cultural expansiveness to African-Americans is particularly striking in the case of the younger, *Washington Post* deputy editor. Indeed, he identified a whole category of subjects in the population who have been historically marginalised in the obits:

In America, everything seems to be viewed through the prism of race. Black lives tend to be dismissed, both everyday and in the obits. Historically, the black readers didn't realise that they could have obits, but they might realise now that they could have them in the *Washington Post*.

In his view, the *Post*'s regular inclusion of obits for its local readership meant that African-American churches might increasingly gain access for their own community.

Two comments are in order here: first, that the *Washington Post*'s unusual coverage of both local and national obituaries makes it in some respects more like the Scottish papers, which have opened up criteria for admission as *The Herald* editor described. (More precisely, in this respect, it occupies a middle place between *The Herald* and the *Guardian* or *Independent*.) Secondly, the view of 'race' as the key site of contradictions within American society provoked a markedly different use of the *genres* of the obituary, most noticeably in the case of this newspaper. Thus this editor spoke satirically: 'I love the Southern segregationist governors who said and did the most horrible things to distance the races' citing as an exemplar Hermann Talmadge, Governor of Georgia. His own obit for Talmadge, written without deadline pressure, dealt with his 'race-bating' whilst also shedding light on 'what drove him'. This critical obit was carefully structured to gain authority, particularly by quoting a well-known and reputable liberal, Ralph McGill, on Talmadge. This editor concluded 'If the truth demands it, we would be severe in our assessment of a person'.

4. The symbolic bauble: 'It's an accolade!' (*The Times*)

Journalists see the obituary as largely a mark of status or professional recognition. As the *New York Times* editor put it: 'To have an obit in the *New York Times* is to put the final nail in the coffin: it's a kind of award.'

Making this calculation, they also see difficulties or even conflict over who might deserve one in moral terms. This provokes questions about the internal self-censorship of journalists. This is far more important than explicit rules, as Durkheim acknowledged, in discussing the trust that provided the normative basis for everyday life (1984). Moreover, just as Durkheim referred to the decline of many religious or negative prohibitions that existed in traditional societies, so the obituary world also presents a similar picture of the declining traces of the pre-modern, with continued, marginal, turmoil about surviving relics.

One question: should obits be written about those viewed negatively, the 'villains', as opposed to the 'heroes' of our time, whose death provokes widespread mourning?[14] A variety of replies emerged in relation to this. The debate was focused on the inclusion of those 'who were not good people', such as Ian Brady and Myra Hindley, the Moors murderers, or Ronald

Biggs, the train robber. Here the papers were split. *The Times* would not give any of these figures obituary space: 'we don't cover murderers'. But the *New York Times* had covered figures like John Gotti (the Mafia leader). The editor of *The Guardian* would and *had* indeed done so in the past: he had included Arkan ('the Tiger'), of the Bosnian War. Yet *The Guardian* was also consistently concerned about the need to guard against 'glamorization'.

Some of the *rules about prohibition* were commonly agreed to have changed, at least amongst these British editors. Unlike the past, the subject is no longer excluded if he or she commits suicide. Yet variations emerged over whether this ought to be stated or not, and in what terms. In this context, for example, *The Independent* tends to use the phrase: 'he died by his own hand'.

An extramarital affair may now be mentioned: indeed it can no longer be assumed that the legal wife, as opposed to a mistress, is the one who will be most affected by the death.[15] Further, certain subjects are no longer rigorously excluded by their homosexuality, although equally, all the editors stated firmly that there is no pressing requirement to identify a person in these terms. Several editors commented spontaneously that, in contrast with the very recent past, a person is now no longer inadmissible if death had occurred through certain illnesses, such as HIV/AIDS. In all these cases, the older requirements were felt to be relics from the much wider range of consensus operating within earlier, pre-capitalist societies (see Durkheim 1984 on mechanical solidarity). These rules in capitalist modernity have now become denigrated as mere *taboos*. In turn, the world of British obits has become irrevocably separated from the world of traditional religions.[16]

Similarly, there has also been a transformation in the codes of the earlier obits. The editor of *The Independent* had earlier pointed out the confusing use of the code phrase to imply someone was gay: 'he never married...', which might mean just that. Similarly *The Times* — according to its representative — has abandoned 'he did not suffer fools gladly', a bizarre relic of an earlier period, where readers from the elite were trained how to read it. These and other phrases have now become ludicrous caricatures of reality to most editors. Yet, contrarily, they still occasionally amused themselves as journalists, playing the game of conventions in a small way.[17]

Finally, despite the exclusion of killers, murder on a very large scale does not deprive a subject of an obit. Thus all the editors pointed out that they had or would have carried obits for Hitler and Goebbels. Stalin would have appeared, although all agreed that 'he was not a very nice person'.[18] In other words, world/historical figures are included for their intrinsic sociological interest.[19] The editors alluded here to the ongoing process, in the present, of moulding collective memory, even if this was not the concept that they chose to use.

5. Honest testimonies or a positive celebration of a life?

Certain further dilemmas were the topics of questions in the interviews. On the one hand, there was a remarkable consensus amongst all the editors that an institution might be openly criticised in the course of an individual's obituary if the subject had suffered from its treatment. On the other hand, the most disturbing question was undoubtedly the clash between the journalists' commitment to unveiling reality, as against the old rule of 'not speaking ill of the dead'. Here — in line with their self-perception as bearers of the truth — all the editors stated that they would insist on certain points, even if the family were outraged. Yet, in somewhat contradictory terms, they also all stated that *they think of the widow* when they choose what to say.[20]

In this context, the editor of *The Herald* pinpointed the greater frankness of today's obits:

> [W]hen you come to write obits of people who have enjoyed a place in the public profile, they are more objective than they once might have been. Compare for example, those for the Duke of Windsor and Winston Churchill. They were not dishonest, but they did not tell the whole story. Nowadays you are more likely to get a fuller sense of their failings and flaws than before. Here I like the knowledge and insight of a good political journalist [...] *I want an obituarist to shed light on the dark corners.* (my emphasis)

Yet he also notes that certain shielding mechanisms still remain. A prime minister might have been 'a bastard', but the obits will all carefully avoid this fact.

This maxim about not speaking ill of the dead also raised the question as to whether specific obituaries for individuals are largely subjective, value-laden assessments. Indeed the interpretation of obits put forward by educated readers often highlights this subjective aspect. *The Guardian*'s editor alluded to this when he asserted that although *every* newspaper might carry a particular person's obit 'there are different shades depending on the readers'. In contrast, the editor of *The Herald* emphasised the objectivity that is the goal of obituary assessments. For him, it is not the different perspectives of readers but certain types of professional jealousy or antagonism that are a danger to objectivity. This affects the choice of whom to write the obituary:

> I'd have the same attitude to politics [as to film production]. I am not sure that politicians can bring the required objectivity to it. From both sides: they can be either overly critical or unduly sycophantic.

The Scotsman's editor elucidated further that where there was deep disagreement over such evaluations, a neutral language like 'successful', might be chosen instead. This eradicated clashes over the moral or political validity of the success or of the means taken to acquire it.[21]

These conflicting comments were sometimes underpinned by another sharp divergence, over whether obituaries *can ever really be objective*. Some editors hinted at *certain conditions for objectivity* by arguing that the more geographically distant the writer is from the subject, the more the 'darker side' can be shown. Others, the vast majority, were reluctant to portray any specific differences of judgement or to reveal any contested appraisal. In summary, these different views about objectivity, and its place, represent a profound gulf over the editors' vision and negotiation of the obituary world. They are closely bound up with the debate introduced in chapter 1, on the nature of collective memory.

JUDGEMENTS OF TASTE

Good writing is a source of pride for all obits editors. One editor, however — influenced by the Kantian philosopher of aesthetics, Eva Schaper — saw the obituaries as potentially being artistic in character: 'I have one, modest ambition. I want my obituaries page to be a work of art' (*The Daily Telegraph*). Thus he had disagreed with Andreas Whittam-Smith, the first editor of *The Independent*, that it is easy to get 'good writers' around an obit table, and that if some go, others will replace them. Yet he ought not to be interpreted as an aesthetic formalist: the artistic qualities of obituaries are far from being his sole or even main concern about their production.

If rarely chosen simply because of the brilliance of their writing, all obituaries have to meet certain literary standards. Every editor interviewed emphasised the need to avoid a 'run of dry facts', in a way that contrasted very sharply with the nature of the 1900 obits. Here *The Guardian*'s obits editor expressed most clearly the general structure of feeling, as he describes academics writing about their recently-dead colleagues:

> They may well be able to write an academic paper but not an obituary. Quite a lot of academics make it a ritual piece, about their c.v. and their honours, not so much what they actually did. Academics can also be a little too erudite. We don't want things dumbed down, but we do want to hear exactly what they have done. We don't want it to be over-simplified, but we are intelligent lay-readers and therefore they have to take us step by step through the argument.

Another put it more tersely:

There is a pedestrian, chronological approach, X born at a certain time, went to school at such and such a place... You, by contrast, must grab them by the lapel! (*The Independent*)

The *Washington Post* assistant editor has a similar, bohemian recoil from the 'dry' and polite discourse of owners of business:

Fortune 100, 200, 300: they are not very forthcoming about what they say, for public relations reasons. They can be horribly dry and guarded about the major decisions in their lives.

To this end, there is a constant fear of euphemistic codes simply because they kill good writing. *The Times*' editor expressed this ever-present danger of blandness: 'I personally would like us to be more judgemental [...]I would like less euphemism...' For all the editors, greater honesty and a good obit go together. One revealed cherished hopes: that some presentations of obits can actually get *young people* reading them, as is the case with the Swedish *Sveska Daggvardeit* (*The Independent*).

In brief, for the editors, language and style can make a major difference, but are ultimately inseparable from their specific set of moral/political concerns. It is the latter difference, of course, that leads to the major gulfs between the newspapers. The hostile or playful stereotypes about the other newspapers have already been indicated; but these in turn produced different modes of action — and these are ultimately what are at stake. As the former editor of *The Scotsman* points out

Some said of the obits that I've written — because I am an experienced writer — that they were very moving. And this is because I was moved by the person and moved by writing that would represent the person. I think that if you achieve that, then that's quite a powerful thing to do. To affect people's emotions in print.

FRAGMENTATION CREATED BY THE DIVISION OF LABOUR

Finally, it is a common theme of social theorists — from the classical sociologists to Bourdieu — that modernity fragments cognitive skills and creates a historically-unparalleled specialisation. The obituary editors, also, were aware of these little islands of knowledge and the separated, hermetically-sealed fields of professional and economic production they engendered. They spoke, however, of the potential an obituary had to momentarily open up these sealed universes and thus to counter the trend to estranging fragmentation. Reversing Weber, we might regard this vision as that of a 're-enchantment of the world' in which the obituaries featured as spaces of meaning and hope (Weber 1991: 139–40; 281–82[22]; Harvey 2000).[23] Hence one editor: 'Take academia: we want to find a peer who can attract people to the subject as much as to the person. In the case of science pieces, for example, people can briefly think that they understand' (*The Independent*). Again, as with the opening up of the dark corners with the obit of the political leader, the ambition can be to 'shine a light on something people didn't know much about at all' (*The Times*).

Could we argue here that there is a desire on the part of the editors to undo the 'structural transformation of the public sphere' which has narrowed and distorted communication (Habermas, 1989)? They envisage this as being an area of transparent discussion and debate, free from strategic action, where editors leave the judgement of importance to their fellow-specialists. It is important for them all that the obituary columns are sprinkled with the names as authors of philosophers or scientists, who, for a brief moment of sympathy with their dead colleague, take on the mantle of populariser more often left disdainfully to others.

CONCLUSION

In the eyes of the newspaper editors, the obits are in the grip of a long revolution, prompted by democratisation and the end of patriarchy. Yet the present research reveals that the obituaries continue to feature more prominently members of a largely masculine elite who themselves come from privileged social origins. Is the commitment to openness and yet the recurrent choice of these subjects from the dominant 'race', class and gender therefore contradictory?

There *is* a greater comprehensiveness now than there was in the 1900s and even the 1948 period. However, beyond the sphere of popular sport and the arts, those outside the power bloc are comparatively rare. Indeed, there were many hints that the traditional circuits and ex officio obituaries survive beneath the meritocratic mask. Thus although the *Washington Post* editor was unusual in actively challenged approaches to 'race', the operation of the editors' rules of thumb tends to lead to precisely the result shown in the next chapter, based on quantitative analysis. This is not due simply to their own choices; it may be explained by their assumptions about readers' demands. Nevertheless, the elaborating of so many elite lives takes place at the cost of *presuming*, unexamined, the *uniformity* of others. The social frameworks that produce this are a fascinating and under-researched element of collective memory.

This is not to argue that the obituaries should just be about 'average lives', whatever these might be. Nor is it to deny that the obits editors are profoundly preoccupied by the professional or deontological ethics regulating their actions. 'Is this obit too euphemistic?' they ask, or 'Is it boring?' 'Should we exclude so many businessmen in order to present the arts, sciences and academics?' The editors weighed their social responsibilities; on occasion, they became highly reflexive about certain decisions taken ('did we glamourise Arkan the Tiger too much?')... Such doubts reveal fascinating conflicts within the obit world. Yet they rarely seemed to be concerned about choosing their *categories* of subjects more imaginatively or *interrogating* dismissive terms, such as 'boring'. [24] Moreover, despite the talk of an 'obituary revolution', they seemed happier to play a purely gate-keeping role in relation to the artistic canon, where the key choices were defined elsewhere, by prestigious critics or juries' designation of academicians. Their own accounts, I would suggest, underestimate the tensions involved in being consistent with their rhetoric, and of recasting the obits to cover all 'those who make a difference'. In Britain, particularly, this would imply moving beyond the scope of the Southern English elite and its predictable love of pastoral figures from a rural landscape[25] (Green, 1990; Bourdieu, 2002c 249–59).

We are compelled to argue – outside certain clear-cut lines of universalistic achievement such as sport — that the editors are still *unconsciously* affected by the common patterns of action, speech and lifestyle by which an elite recognises itself. It is elite membership — and the cultural capital that accompanies it — that preserves the subject from the judgement of being 'boring'. In other words, studying obits is one route into today's status classifications, the ordering of symbolic capital. Such social classifications are still profoundly determined by the accidents of great wealth, or negatively, by forms of class racism. They disqualify from serious consideration those who have not been educated at great schools or the higher-ranking universities and those who do not work at the most esteemed of national institutions.

6 The lives we choose to remember
A quantative analysis

with Esperanza Bielsa

An analysis of whom we choose to remember reveals the underlying social determinants for the celebration of individual distinction or symbolic capital. Thus the question of who is selected for certain key national newspapers is considered systematically in this chapter, with particular reference to their social origins, educational backgrounds and nationality. Our starting point for this analysis is influenced particularly by Bourdieu's work on closure (or class ossification) over generations. Like him, we accept that sociology 'obliges' the truths of power relations to come into the open (Bourdieu and Passeron 1990: xxi). Like him, we find obituaries socially illuminating and share his acute perception of the seductions of such accolades, those 'symbolic baubles', as Napoleon called them (Bourdieu 2000a).

A rigorous assessment of Bourdieu's value for a contemporary theory of class stratification has recently been put forward by Savage, Warde and Devine (2005). Bourdieu, these writers argue, possesses a theory of capitals, assets and resources (CARs) which avoids the crude determinism of the base-superstructure model. This theory nevertheless acts in the spirit of Marx, in that industrial capitalism is distinguished specifically as a mode of production from commercial capitalism:

> [Bourdieu] had need neither of hanging on to a base-superstructure model nor of turning almost entirely to the study of representations' (2005: 43) but 'developed a theory of "the potential of certain CARs to be accumulated and converted over time and space".' (2005: 45)

Not least in his detailed explanation of how cultural capital is converted into economic capital — and how such capital also requires social capital in order to be fully utilised — Bourdieu's model is held to be conceptually and empirically richer than alternative accounts.

Agreeing with this approach,[1] this study aims to follow on Bourdieu's own fragments of obituary analysis to produce the first sociological 'objectivation' of obituaries (Bourdieu 1988a: 216–25, 1996b:0–53). It is based on samples of at least one hundred such obits from, respectively, *The Times* in 1900, 1948 and 2000–2001, as well as three other British newspapers for 2000–2001, *The Daily Telegraph, The Independent* and *The Guardian*.[2] In the latest period, one of the leading newspapers from France (*Le Monde*) and one of the three leading newspapers in America (the *New York Times*) is sampled as well, in an initial cross-national approach intended to heighten the comparison with the British papers.

It will be argued that although obituaries have become more democratised and now include figures significant for popular and counter-memory, they still reveal the influence of dominant Western elites, groups bound together especially by common origins and educational patterns (see Table 6.1). In this respect a Bourdieusian analysis of reproduction aids the theoretical assessment of obituaries, along with other sociological studies that emphasise the continued strategies of closure on the part of privileged classes. Of these, we might mention especially John Scott, with his historical sociology of the British power elite. He focuses extensively on those occupants of position of authority within the state elite who come from the power bloc, that is social groups aligned together by their similar background and experience, notably of public school (1991: 118–19, 120–21.)

OCCUPATIONAL BACKGROUNDS

Newspaper obituaries chiefly celebrate the lives of distinguished individuals from the service or 'dominant class', as conceptualised in Bourdieu's broad terms. Although his is a definition that is strikingly close to recent British categorisation of the 'service class', it should be noted that the strata many other studies classify as "middle class", or "bourgeoisie" are here categorised as "dominant class".[3]

Adding the last three right hand columns, as many as 95 per cent of the total figures featured in the obituaries belong to this class, whilst the middle classes, again using Bourdieu's terminology, are represented with a mere 4 per cent. The working classes and farmers are conspicuously absent, with just over 1 per cent in all. Taking the whole sample of 883 individuals whose occupation is known, there are only six working-class people and six farmers.

Throughout the twentieth century, a remarkable change can be observed in the representation of the different dominant class fractions. In *The Times*, 1900, obituaries were predominantly (56%) about those figures with *temporal power*, that is, from the dominant fraction of the dominant class — owners of great businesses, financiers, landowners, generals and politicians. Members of the *dominated fraction* (the liberal professions, scientists and cultural producers) were represented to a much lesser extent (30%). Additionally, obituaries in both *The Times* 1900 and *The Times* 1948 reserved a significant space for leisured aristocratic figures without work (10% and 11%).[4] By 1948, the proportion from the dominant fraction had already slightly diminished (from 56% to 49%), while that of the

Table 6.1 Changes in occupational class and class fraction over the twentieth century (in different newspapers)

	Farmers	Working classes	Middle classes	Dominant fraction	Cultural producers and professionals	Aristocratic other	Total
The Times 1900	1 .7%	1 .7%	3 2.1%	79 56.4%	42 30.0%	14 10.0%	140 100.0%
The Times 1948		1 1.0%		51 48.6%	41 39.0%	12 11.4%	105 100.0%
The Times 2000	1 .9%		5 4.7%	48 44.9%	51 47.7%	2 1.9%	107 100.0%
The Guardian	1 .8%	3 2.3%	9 6.8%	30 22.6%	90 67.7%		133 100.0%
The Independent	1 1.0%		5 5.1%	19 19.4%	71 72.4%	2 2.0%	98 100.0%
Daily Telegraph	2 2.0%		6 6.0%	48 48.0%	42 42.0%	2 2.0%	100 100.0%
Le Monde			2 2.0%	26 26.0%	70 70.0%	2 2.0%	100 100.0%
New York Times		1 1.0%	7 7.0%	38 38.0%	54 54.0%		100 100.0%
Total	6 .7%	6 .7%	37 4.2%	339 38.4%	461 52.2%	34 3.9%	883 100.0%

Note: This table is based on Bourdieu's occupational class categories, in which the dominant class is divided into two fractions, the dominant fraction and the dominated fraction (cultural producers and symbolic professionals) (1984: 526) dominated fraction (with more symbolic power) decisively increased (from 30% to 39%).[5]

This modern pattern culminated in the 2000–2001 obituaries, where obituaries for members of the dominated fraction — especially artists, actors, musicians and professionals — overtake those of the dominant fraction, particularly in *The Independent*, where they form 72 per cent, *Le Monde* (70%) and *The Guardian* (68%). The *Daily Telegraph* is now the only newspaper where the dominants with temporal power feature more prominently than the members of the dominated fraction (48% vs 42%): *The Times* is not very different from this, but inverts the figures in favour of the dominated fraction. The *New York Times* occupies a median point on this aspect between the two British newspaper poles (*The Times* and *The Daily Telegraph* at one pole, and *The Guardian* and *The Independent* on the other), dedicating 54 per cent of its obituaries to members of the dominated fraction and 38 per cent to the dominants. Another way of looking at this (not shown here) is to say that *The Times* (1900, 1948 and 2000–2001) and *The Daily Telegraph* (2000–2001) featured predominantly the aristocracy, as well as those consecrated through knighthoods or through the most official channels, through which they acquired academic, medical or military titles. In contrast, over 70 per cent of the figures featured in the 2000—2001 *Guardian*, *The Independent*, *Le Monde* and the *New York Times* lacked such titles.

These broad categories can be unravelled to reveal the specific occupations within which distinguished individuals cluster (see Table 6.4). As might be expected, these individuals have experienced remarkable specialisation. Despite occasional exceptions such as the composer Xenakis, equally celebrated for music and architecture (*The Independent*, 5 February 2001), the contemporary obituaries are the expression of a division of labour much finer than earlier periods. Current newspaper obituaries feature especially academics (7%) and a range of cultural producers, that is, the dominated fraction with symbolic power. Of these, strikingly, 8 per cent were musicians, 8 per cent writers (including popular writers), 5 per cent were actors and 5 per cent media personnel. The traditional higher professionals are represented by doctors (4%) and the clergy (4%); these can be categorised under the 'dominated fraction' since they possess *symbolic* power. The *dominant* fraction, possessing direct access to this-worldly power, are represented by army or navy officers (10%), who are especially numerous in *The Times* (1900 and 1948) and *The Daily Telegraph*. They are also represented by politicians (9%), industrialists or entrepreneurs (7%), civil servants or diplomats (5%) and judges or lawyers (2%).

It is perhaps predictable that manual workers are virtually unseen in obituaries, save those who later become leaders of great trade unions. Yet it may also surprise many sociologists that we find almost no trace of lower professional or middle-class occupations such as teachers[6] or nurses. Here we can begin to detect a self-reinforcing circle between the British masculine elite's membership of an occupation (eg, the higher ranks of the Army or the diplomatic corps) and the likelihood that such an occupation will be considered the terrain for distinguished action in the 'public sphere'.

GENDER DIVISIONS IN OBITUARIES

Indeed, obituaries, it is acknowledged, are written for those who have served within the public sphere in an exemplary fashion. Bizarrely — as discussed in chapter 4 — the last breath of feudalism was felt in the obituary column as recently as 1900 (*The Times*). In these entries, a genealogical principle operated in which those closest to the monarch were offered an obituary on grounds of blood,[7] rather than for achievement or service. Women in 1900 only appeared on the criteria of their blood connections. Their formal but systematic exclusion from the public sphere was the principle which simultaneously ensured their absence in the obituaries.

We would have expected the number of women who acquired obituaries to have increased with time[8]. There *are* certainly more women who are featured in *The Times* 2000–2001 (17%) than in *The Times* 1900, (11%).[9] Yet this difference is clearly not enormous: indeed, on closer inspection, there turns out to be no simple incremental increase or automatic evolutionary advance. There is a considerable jump between 1900 and 1948 (from 11% to 17%) but the number remains the same between *The Times* 1948 and the British newspapers in 2000–2001, with 19 per cent women on average. Indeed, the *New York Times* had fewer than *The Times* 1948 total.

This invites us to explore the possibility that women's obituary 'survival-value' might vary with a number of interwoven factors. Chief of these is the degree to which they gain access to the activities which conventionally attract high esteem. Important, too, is their freedom to engage single-mindedly in making their mark within a specific field (Bourdieu 2000a: 111–14). Whilst both genders may lack the capacity to persist in more autonomous areas (like the arts) for *economic* reasons, women in early adulthood — who often have the ultimate life and death responsibility for children — may lack the capacity to be as *seriously* engaged as men, at least under the present division of domestic labour.

Given such figures, which reveal the relatively low proportion of women in current obituaries, the recent sociological assumption about the imminent death of patriarchy (MacInnes 1998; Castells 2000) appears more questionable. Now, one plinth of this prophetic construction is the premise that American women are the most 'liberated' in terms of rates of divorce, single parenthood and other demographic features (Castells: 137–56). Despite this, it is noted that contemporary British newspapers have a higher proportion of women in the obituaries (19%) than the *New York Times* (14%) carries. Nor can the analysis sustain any hypothetical contrast between the more 'progressive' American press, vis à vis that of the more 'traditional' Old Europe: indeed, within this sample, the *New York Times* has exactly the same proportion of women with obituaries as *Le Monde*.

Further, it might be conjectured that obituaries, a measure of distinction, would be awarded more often to the individual who has ploughed his or her own solitary furrow, rather than to men and women who are supported by companions. Yet here again there are significant gender differences. In fact, most obits' subjects turn out to have been married. Yet fewer women given obituaries had this status at the end of their lives than men (69% women versus 88% men; not shown here). Not only were the obituaries' women more likely to be single, they were also more likely than men to be in the category of 'formerly married': the divorced, separated or widowed.

Most spectacularly, in Table 6.2, whereas 72 per cent of the male subjects of obituaries had either two or more children, this was true of only 45 per cent of the women. Indeed, a noticeably higher number of the women (36%) had not had children at all: well over twice the number of men. Thus (see Table 6.3) in the case of *The Independent* — the most accentuated in this respect — as many as 75 per cent of its female obituary subjects had had either only one or no children. This finding is partly a function of an earlier marriage bar. It is also an indication of the complex difficulties facing women once they become mothers, which are linked, in turn, to their continued segregation in the labour market, both vertical and horizontal (Bradley 1989, Crompton 1999 and 2000:165–83, and Walby 1997).[10]

From the pre-capitalist period, women have been more frequent representatives of certain crafts or occupational areas and these have changed only slowly (Bradley 1989). These traditional correlations also emerge in the obituaries. In this context, the increasing prominence of the arts as one stream of the obituaries over the course of the last century also favours the increased appearance of women.

Forty-six per cent of the female obituary subjects, but only 31 per cent of the male subjects, turn out to be from a field which has artistic or media importance.[11] Here they feature especially (see Table 6.4) as writers (including the popular writers next in the table) (11% of all the women and 7%

Table 6.2 Gender and children: Entire sample

	One child	Two or more children	No children	Step-children	Total
Male	63	333	65	4	465
	13.5%	71.6%	14.0%	.9%	100.0%
Female	18	45	36	2	101
	17.8%	44.6%	35.6%	2.0%	100.0%
Total	81	378	101	6	566
	14.3%	66.8%	17.8%	1.1%	100.0%

Table 6.3 Gender and Children: Changes Over Time (different newspapers)

Newspaper		One child		Two or more children		No children		Stepchildren		Total*
The Times 1900	male	8	40.0%	8	40.0%	4	20.0%			20
	female	3	50.0%	2	33.3%	1	16.7%			6
	both	11	42.3%	10	38.5%	5	19.2%			26
The Times 1948	male	6	15.0%	24	60.0%	10	25.0%			40
	female	2	33.3%	1	16.7%	3	50.0%			6
	both	8	17.4%	25	54.3%	13	28.3%			46
The Times 2000	male	11	13.8%	61	76.3%	8	10.0%			80
	female	2	12.5%	5	31.3%	7	43.8%	2	12.5%	16
	both	13	13.5%	66	68.8%	15	15.6%	2	2.1%	96
The Guardian	male	12	13.3%	67	74.4%	8	8.9%	3	3.3%	90
	female	3	12.0%	18	72.0%	4	16.0%			25
	both	15	13.0%	85	73.9%	12	10.4%	3	2.6%	115
The Independent	male	11	16.2%	46	67.6%	11	16.2%			68
	female	2	12.5%	4	25.0%	10	62.5%			16
	both	13	15.5%	50	59.5%	21	25.0%			84
The Daily Telegraph	male	6	8.2%	60	82.2%	6	8.2%	1		73
	female	2	14.3%	8	57.1%	4	28.6%			14
	both	8	9.2%	68	78.2%	10	11.5%	1		87
Le Monde	male	1	9.1%	10	90.9%					11
	female	2	40.0%	3	60.0%					5
	both	3	18.8%	13	81.3%					16
New York Times	male	8	9.6%	57	68.7%	18	21.7%			83
	female	2	15.4%	4	30.8%	7	53.8%			13
	both	10	10.4%	61	63.5%	25	26.0%			96

* All figures in the 'Total' column represent 100 percent.

Table 6.4. Occupations: Total sample, by gender

	Male		Female		Total	
Artists	24	3.2%	3	2.1%	27	3.1%
Popular artists	4	.5%			4	.5%
Writers	41	5.5%	10	7.1%	51	5.8%
Popular writers	10	1.3%	5	3.5%	15	1.7%
Musicians — Jazz	14	1.9%	3	2.1%	17	1.9%
Musicians — Classical	27	3.6%	6	4.3%	33	3.7%
Musicians — Rock/popular	12	1.6%	2	1.4%	14	1.6%
Musicians — Folk	6	.8%	1	.7%	7	.8%
Actors	27	3.6%	19	13.5%	46	5.2%
Dancers	3	.4%	2	1.4%	5	.6%
Popular dancers	2	.3%			2	.2%
Film/theatre directors/ cameramen/choreographers	12	1.6%	2	1.4%	14	1.6%
Artistic designers	2	.3%	4	2.8%	6	.7%
Architects	8	1.1%			8	.9%
Scientists	32	4.3%	4	2.8%	36	4.1%
Media	36	4.9%	8	5.7%	44	5.0%
Industrialists/entrepreneurs	54	7.3%	3	2.1%	57	6.5%
Bankers/financiers	18	2.4%			18	2.0%
Politicians	73	9.8%	3	2.1%	76	8.6%
Clergy	35	4.7%			35	4.0%
Academics	52	7.0%	6	4.3%	58	6.6%
Engineers	15	2.0%			15	1.7%
Sportsmen	22	3.0%	2	1.4%	24	2.7%
Army/Navy	89	12.0%	3	2.1%	92	10.4%
Doctors/Surgeons	33	4.4%			33	3.7%
Judges/lawyers/solicitors	15	2.0%	3	2.1%	18	2.0%
Civil servants/diplomats	41	5.5%	6	4.3%	47	5.3%
Farmers	5	.7%			5	.6%
Librarians/curators/teachers	13	1.8%	3	2.1%	16	1.8%
Sales assistants/managers	1	.1%	1	.7%	2	.2%
Manual	6	.8%	1	.7%	7	.8%
No paid work	2	.3%	32	22.7%	34	3.9%
Charity organisers/campaigners	1	.1%	5	3.5%	6	.7%
Other	7	.9%	4	2.8%	11	1.2%
Total	742	100%	141	100%	883	100%

of all the men) and as actors (14% of all women and only 4% of all men). Hardly surprisingly, they also appear more often in the category with 'no paid work', particularly amongst the aristocracy (23% of the women: only 0.3% of the men). On the bourgeois model (but not the aristocratic), they would therefore be thought to be without any individual achievement.

It follows that there is also a wide discrepancy between men and women in terms of class fraction: 43 per cent of men are in the *dominant* fraction of the dominant class but only 16 per cent of women. Let us consider the class that Bourdieu entitles the 'State Nobility'[12], the equivalent of the British 'Establishment'. Table 6.4 also shows that a large number of the men with obituaries were politicians (10%) — but only a tiny minority of the women (2%). Gender inequalities of this sort were equally conspicuous in the less visible field of economic power: for example, 2 per cent of men were bankers or financiers and 7 per cent entrepreneurs and industrialists, yet there were no women with obits in banking or finance and only three women (2%) in the industrial capital fraction. The traditional 'higher professions'[13] were another crucial source of obituaries for men (12%) but only for an amazingly low 2 per cent of the women (all in the legal profession). Conversely, in academia and science women seem to be catching up: 7 per cent of the women as against 11 per cent of the men were in these areas.

SOCIAL MOBILITY

Compared with the age of death or numbers of children, our knowledge about the social and economic trajectories of our obituary figures is both more uneven and more difficult to code. For example, in some traditions — especially the newspaper obituaries from the *New York Times* and *Le Monde* — there are frequently no details at all about the material and cultural capital of either the father or the mother. Our sample is thus reduced to a much smaller number of known cases. Not only this, parental occupations may be given in a form which makes classification problematic.

Consequently, the raw figures of mobility need to be interpreted quite subtly, with a recognition of various 'caveats'. On occasion, even assessing whether an individual's trajectory should be classified as 'social reproduction' or 'upward mobility' is difficult. For example, in quite a considerable number of cases, 'rising' occupational trajectories by no means always indicate access to the *material* experiences of wellbeing within the classic bourgeoisie.[14] Thus the logic of coding led us to place jazz musicians in the 'artistic producers' category, yet their economic rewards and symbolic capital are likely at their deaths to be much lower than, say, opera directors.

Nevertheless, qualifications accepted, social *reproduction* in intergenerational terms occurs in these obituaries much more frequently than we might have expected, standing at the total of over two-thirds of the subjects (71%; see bottom line Table 6.5). Of course, the 'constant flux' of a strand of upward mobility also appears, but in somewhat lower proportions than occurs in the general population. Only 28 per cent of obituary subjects had risen from middle or working-class origins, in terms of parental occupational position. This total figure of 28 per cent is in turn composed of 16 per cent who had experienced a major upward change and 12 per cent who

Table 6.5. Occupation, reproduction and mobility

	Reproduction		Upward mobility — major change		Upward mobility — minor change		Downward social mobility		Total*
Artists	12	70.6%	2	11.8%	2	11.8%	1	5.9%	17
Popular artists	2	66.7%	1	33.3%					3
Writers	21	67.7%	6	19.4%	4	12.9%			31
Popular writers	6	60.0%	2	20.0%	2	20.0%			10
Musicians — Jazz	3	100.0%							3
Musicians — Classical	10	100.0%							10
Musicians rock/pop	1	25.0%	2	50.0%	1	25.0%			4
Musicians — Folk	1	33.3%	1	33.3%	1	33.3%			3
Actors	20	64.5%	5	16.1%	5	16.1%	1	3.2%	31
Dancers	1	100.0%							1
Popular dancers	1	50.0%	1	50.0%					2
Film/theatre dir./Cameramen	3	75.0%	1	25.0%					4
Artistic designers	2	66.7%	1	33.3%					3
Architects	3	100.0%							3
Scientists	9	69.2%	1	7.7%	2	15.4%	1	7.7%	13
Media	14	70.0%	4	20.0%	2	10.0%			20
Industrialists/entrepreneurs	22	75.9%	7	24.1%					29

								Total
Bankers/ financiers	8	80.0%			2	20.0%		10
Politicians	36	70.6%	10	19.6%	5	9.8%		51
Clergy	7	50.0%	3	21.4%	4	28.6%		14
Academics	14	60.9%	7	30.4%	2	8.7%		23
Engineers	5	71.4%	1	14.3%	1	14.3%		7
Sportsmen	3	33.3%	2	22.2%	3	33.3%	1	11.1% → 9
Army/Navy	33	86.8%	1	2.6%	4	10.5%		38
Doctors	10	71.4%	1	7.1%	3	21.4%		14
Judges/lawyers	5	50.0%	1	10.0%	4	40.0%		10
Civil servants/ Diplomats	16	72.7%	3	13.6%	3	13.6%		22
Farmers	3	75.0%			1	25.0%		4
Librarians/curators/teachers	2	66.7%	1	33.3%				3
Sales assistants/managers	2	100.0%						2
Manual	1	100.0%						1
No paid work	16	88.9%	2	11.1%				18
Charity organizers	2	66.7%					1	33.3% → 3
Other	3	60.0%			1	20.0%	1	20.0% → 5
Total	297	70.5%	66	15.7%	52	12.4%	6	1.4% → 421

* All figures in the 'Total' column represent 100 percent.

had experienced a minor movement upward. Downwardly socially mobile individuals appear in negligible numbers — just over 1 per cent of the total obituaries. Since the obituaries largely celebrate lives that are evaluated positively, this is also entirely predictable.

Some figures on reproduction in other studies are in order, so as to situate these findings. For example, Bourdieu states that in France, 53 per cent of the professions with high incomes and high qualifications also had either professional or senior executive origins (1984: 114), while 42 per cent of the professions as a whole were recruited from the dominant class (1984: 121, also 128). This is a high proportion of reproduction, but not as high as our findings for the obituary subjects. Nevertheless, to reinforce the obituary findings, we note that Marshall and colleagues argue that Britain is *particularly* weak in terms of overall fluidity:

> Britain looks considerably less educationally meritocratic a society than do most of her industrialised counterparts ...the direct effect of class origins on class destinations is greater among individuals holding advanced and degree level qualifications in Britain than it is in any of the other eight advanced societies with which it has been compared. (Marshall, Swift and Roberts 1997: 95)[15]

Finally, Glass and Hall's 1954 study — useful because it featured subjects who were from the generation *immediately preceding* the current obituary subjects — shows only a marginally higher rate of upward mobility than that found in our sample (1954: 183). 64 per cent of their Status Group I sons had fathers from Status Groups I and II in comparison with our 71 per cent; 14 per cent of their Status Group I had experienced major upward mobility (from working-class origins), compared with our 16 per cent and 22 per cent minor upward mobility (from the middle classes), our figure being 12 per cent. In other words, the low proportion of upward mobility amongst those awarded the accolade of an obituary is only a slight accentuation of the low mobility reported in other studies.

Patterns of (class) reproduction are uneven, yet gender does not seem to exert a very significant causal force within it (table not shown here). Although dominant class women are slightly more likely to benefit from class reproduction than men, the difference is minimal (74% women versus 70% men). However, reproduction at the level of the dominants occurs within some occupations much more frequently than others. For example, it is notable that the three architects in Table 6.5 have all come from homes where there has been a similarly high volume of economic and/or cultural capital, having been the sons of, respectively, a colonel, a judge and an architect/surveyor. We might link this to the wider nineteenth and twentieth century history of architecture, which existed as a gentrified artistic profession, possessing its autonomous artistic field as well as an expanded, commercial sector. In similar terms, the sampled bankers and financiers have overwhelmingly (80%: eight) possessed social origins within the same class.

Some results are more unexpected; for example, of the ten judges and lawyers, only five came from the same social class. But we should not leap to extrapolate from such tiny figures the characteristics of the whole profession, especially given what we already know about the highly privileged social origins of judges (Wakefords 1974: 187). The clergy, too, have higher rates of fluidity or upward mobility than might have been predicted. Altogether 50 per cent (7) had moved up, three having experienced major change of class position, four a minor transition. This is a considerably greater rate of mobility than is found in the sample as a whole, yet here it may not be an oddity of the sample but ought to be linked to the declining popularity of the clergy as a career (Thompson 1974).

At the other extreme, the obituaries of members of the Armed Forces reveal the granite-like stability of these professions in class terms. Here reproduction is a commonplace: a much greater proportion than for the sample as a whole is composed of members from the dominant class (87%) and only one individual has had a major upwards trajectory. As is also to be expected, there were high rates of reproduction for those with 'no paid work' (89%), a group especially significant amongst the small sprinkling of female subjects who received obituaries in the earlier periods (*The Times* 1900 and 1948).

Turning now towards upward social mobility, the most striking groups emerge from those in the two classic avenues for social ascent: the popular arts and sport. If we combine the pop and rock musicians, the folk singers, the tap, tango and samba dancers and the popular writers or artists, then 32 per cent (7) have undergone a profound transformation in their structural position and 18 per cent (4) a slighter ascent (50% in total). Indeed, adding in the jazz musicians, 34 per cent of all the popular cultural producers have been upwardly mobile in a sample characterised as a whole by only 28 per cent upward mobility. The other major group from the point of view of upward mobility are from the sports: five out of the nine sportspeople had experienced a major material improvement. Qualitative research suggests that these findings would be even more clear-cut if we distinguished *between* different sports: football has a higher rate than rowing, for example.

TALES OF REPRODUCTION AND UPWARD MOBILITY IN THE DIFFERENT NEWSPAPERS' OBITUARIES

As their readers are well aware, different newspapers inhabit to some degree different social worlds, so that the obituaries of a single individual in each paper is subtly nuanced in relation to that paper's readership and perspective (see Table 6.6).

Table 6.6 Social mobility over time (different newspapers)

	Repro- duction	Upward mobility major change	Upward mobility minor change	Down- ward social mobility	Total
The Times 1900	39 92.9%	1 2.4%	2 4.8%		42 100.0%
The Times 1948	35 83.3%	3 7.1%	4 9.5%		42 100.0%
The Times 2000	45 61.6%	14 19.2%	10 13.7%	4 5.5%	73 100.0%
The Guardian	47 63.5%	13 17.6%	12 16.2%	2 2.7%	74 100.0%
The Independent	30 57.7%	14 26.9%	8 15.4%		52 100.0%
Daily Telegraph	54 78.3%	8 11.6%	7 10.1%		69 100.0%
Le Monde	30 83.3%	4 11.1%	2 5.6%		36 100.0%
New York Times	18 52.9%	9 26.5%	7 20.6%		34 100.0%
Total	298 70.6%	66 15.6%	52 12.3%	6 1.4%	422 100.0%

We have already noted the different class fractions' relation to repro-duction.[16] An extraordinarily high degree of self-recruitment (78%) and collective exclusion is represented within the *Telegraph*'s obituaries, which specialise in the dominant fraction (bankers, police chiefs, judges, Army officers). As many as 88 per cent of these had come from families within the same class.

Although similar to *The Telegraph* in some crucial ways, *The Times* 2000–2001 is in other respects different. It features much more upward mobility than the latter (33%), and is particularly prominent in the narra-tives of major upward mobility (19%). *The Guardian*, too, should be put on the same level as *The Times*, with 34 per cent upward mobility, includ-ing 18 per cent major upward mobility. But, compared with the high total sample overall of 71 per cent reproduction, it was *The Independent,* at only 58 per cent reproduction, which had dramatically less. Strikingly, it was the cultural producers and professionals within *The Independent* who were markedly more upwardly mobile overall, significantly higher than this group in all the British newspapers in 2000–2001.

The highest rate of social reproduction overall in the contemporary newspapers chosen was that of *Le Monde*, with 83 per cent, while the lowest was that of the *New York Times*, with 53 per cent. In brief, if we add a cross-national newspaper comparison, the *Daily Telegraph* loses its position as most likely to feature old money and *Le Monde* becomes more prominent. With *Le Monde*, often seen as a radical newspaper (Péan and Cohen 2003), we are again shocked into remembering not just Proust's depiction of the continued presence of the nobility in early twentieth century French circles, but also Bourdieu's designation of an 'aristocracy of culture' (1984: ch.1).

There are 'dynastic' patterns of stable generational replication. Yet the British obituaries also reveal certain telling inner movements or cross-currents.[17] An intergenerational flux occurred, in which sons or daughters shifted to another occupational group from that of their parents. Thus, the overall picture in the obituaries is not one of total petrification or stasis across the generations — far from it. In the case of our 2000–2001 obituaries, we notice an especially significant form of 'trading places' — a migration *from* positions within the economic and political elite *into* those in the cultural producers' and academic elite. Although already known in the nineteenth century, when groups like the Pre-Raphaelite artists came from the industrialist or merchant classes (Williams 1980: 158–59), this was a very minor current in the 1900 obituaries (7%) and remained so for some time later. Its significance now, in 2000–2001, is reinforced by the massive expansion of the service sector and especially of the media and arts infrastructures within late capitalist economies (Zukin 1988: 178–86). The result is that between one-fifth and one-third of all the recent 2000–2001 newspaper obituaries[18] are of figures who have personally made this shift, relinquishing the world of manufacturing production and direct surplus-value extraction for a world based on professional fees and public-sector salaries, in other words, a conversion of economic into cultural capital (Bourdieu 1984: 124–26).[19] The reverse passage, from origins in the dominated fraction to a destiny within the dominant fraction, goes much more against the grain of the period and has been made by a very much smaller group of subjects (6% in the British 2000–2001 newspapers, 3% in *Le Monde* and none in the *New York Times*).[20]

In summary, were we to take the obituaries as a proxy for the whole population, then some startling figures emerge in terms of the degree of upward mobility they disclose, with many fewer mobile individuals than most people would have expected. It is true that the *New York Times* obituary columns, with their considerably higher proportion of upward mobility, may be emblematic of a more open society, at least in this period. However, even in this case, an overall majority of the obituary subjects were people whose family backgrounds were also privileged.

Michèle Lamont has argued, against Bourdieu, that the French social patterns laid bare by him in *Distinction* cannot be taken as a general model for advanced capitalist societies (1992: 186). It seems from this obits study that she is vindicated, at least in part. If the newspaper obituaries can indeed serve as national proxies, there do seem to be significant differences between societies concerning the volume of social reproduction.[21] America appears to be more 'open', France least open and more traditional, and Britain in the middle. The structure of feeling in each of the British newspapers moreover, suggests a sharp distinction on this score: the *Daily Telegraph* is the most elitist in its choices, *The Independent* the most meritocratic of the four newspapers.

Yet there is also room here for some vindication of Bourdieu. Overall the amount of upward mobility found within these obituaries is perceptibly less than the hidden transfer of class *advantages* from one generation to the other (cf Scott 1986, 1991, 1997). Of course, this transfer is veiled by the rhetoric of career ascents. Such ascents are viewed from the perspective of the relative powerlessness of the young, thus highlighting the struggles necessary to achieve their possession of power in the senior generation. Moreover, such class transfer of advantages is, of course, impeded by certain genuine sources of contingency, from illness to alcoholism, to which the obituaries occasionally bear witness. But even such contingencies take their material toll less savagely on the dominants, with their substantial economic reserves, than on the working class, more exposed to the cold winds of material adversity.

EDUCATIONAL BACKGROUNDS

It has been asserted that the British elite is the outcome of an accommodatory process between the nobility of the feudal order and the rising industrial elites. In this process, education — especially the combination of public schools and Oxbridge — played a key role (Stanworth and Giddens 1974: 99; Scott 1991: 92, 111, 113–14). Given this context, it is remarkable that, in the entire sample, 77 per cent of the British subjects of obituaries have been to public schools (see Table 6.7).

Nor is this merely a relic of a past era: as late as 2000–2001, 80 per cent of the British obituaries' subjects in *The Times* and 78 per cent in *The Daily Telegraph* had experienced such private education, at a time when public schools collectively took 5 per cent of the total British school population (Scott, 1991: 113). The proportion in *The Guardian* and *The Independent* is significantly lower, but it is still around two-thirds of their total number of British subjects: 61 per cent and 67 per cent respectively. Thus although the proportion at public school today has gone down compared with *The Times* totals for 1900 and 1948 (approximately 90%), the fall is relatively minor. Indeed, it is a mere 10 per cent in the case of *The Times* over the whole twentieth century.

We could sketch this out in other terms. Only three individuals in the whole sample of British obituaries went either to elementary school or to secondary modern alone (a politician, an actress and a popular writer). This is, of course, related to the tiny number of manual workers in the

Table 6.7 Secondary education by citizenry (British subjects only in British newspapers, French subjects in *Le Monde* etc.)

	Public school	*Grammar school*	*Secondary modern/ council school*	*Total*
The Times 1900	8 88.9%	1 11.1%		9 100.0%
The Times 1948	37 90.2%	4 9.8%		41 100.0%
The Times 2000	36 80.0%	8 17.8%	1 2.2%	45 100.0%
The Guardian	25 61.0%	15 36.6%	1 2.4%	41 100.0%
The Independent	20 66.7%	9 30.0%	1 3.3%	30 100.0%
The Daily Telegraph	36 78.3%	10 21.7%		46 100.0%
Le Monde	1 100.0%			1 100.0%
New York Times	7 100.0%			7 100.0%
Total	170 77.3%	47 21.4%	3 1.4%	220 100.0%

obituaries. However, we suspect that many readers may be sharply disconcerted to discover that there are not more obituary portraits of figures who attended grammar school or free academies.

In terms of occupations, the traditional exclusive background of bankers, politicians, the armed services and the higher professions is revealed very clearly in the obituaries: almost all of these figures have been to public schools. However, much more unexpected are the obituaries of artists and writers, who have had equally as exclusive an education: all the artists (including popular artists), all the writers (except one popular writer) and seven of the eight actors have been to public schools.[22] The only occupational category strikingly more open to subjects with less exclusive educational backgrounds is that of scientist, of whom only 46 per cent went to public school.[23]

Secondly, Bourdieu writes on the 'esprit of the grandes écoles'[24] that their empowering effects on their former pupils can be compared with that of the Calvinist elect. It will be argued here, more generally, that the *higher education* of our obituary subjects has exerted a powerful effect on their habitus. Indeed our results entitle us to define higher education in the modern period as the principal pivot which shapes the rest of our subjects' careers, and perhaps their lives as a whole. The deep structure in the narratives of the year 2000 is that Oxbridge is at the heart of the British obituary (cf Kelsall, 1974: 177).

The occupational demand for higher education was much weaker in the nineteenth century than now, even for the dominant class. Consequently, the 1900 sample passed through these channels less frequently. Only thirty-six of the 142 *The Times* 1900 obituaries (all subjects) make any reference to university, and these are principally individuals who have gone into the Church or the Law, or who have a family tradition of going to Oxbridge.[25] In contrast, out of 133 *Guardian* (2000–2001) obituaries, 106 references occur (all subjects). Although in a proportion of cases (22 or 21%), these *Guardian* references indicate that the person had no higher education, the expectation that they would normally have gone through these channels has clearly become established, to a degree unimaginable a century earlier. Yet if, as a symbolic good, higher education was much rarer in the 1900 sample of *The Times*, Oxbridge exerted a more powerful influence when it did occur (see Table 6.8).

Taking now only British subjects (or more precisely, each paper's own nationals), this is etched out sharply, with 50 per cent of our 1900s subjects' higher education having been at Oxbridge (cf Scott 1991: 116). Given the survival of the gentrified and aristocratic elite, at the core of the 1900 cultural world of the obituary, the centrality of these colleges follows almost without saying.

The only serious alternative to Oxford and Cambridge, were the other old universities, such as King's College, London, Edinburgh, Glasgow, Belfast and Trinity College, Dublin. One-third (31%) had been to these, with a noticeable correlation between the medics and surgeons and attendance at these universities.[26] But other members of the dominant class dispensed with higher education. The 1900 subjects with a naval or military career learnt their arts of war in their regiments, often as little 'powder monkeys' stoking cannons. This was true even of baby aristocrats whose obituaries reveal that they started work at an early age, often only twelve to fourteen. Only one had been to a more formal training establishment, such as Sandhurst. In fact, what is most remarkable in 1900 is the narrowness of the channels through which British higher education was acquired at this time — no British subject had been to art school, no genteel young British women to finishing schools, no scientific or technical experts to technical institutes...

The 1948 *Times* shows the continued overwhelming importance of Oxbridge, with 44 per cent of the British subjects attending these colleges.[27] Such ancient universities tower in significance above all other forms — over three times as important, in numerical terms, as all the rest of the British universities put together (13%). The unrivalled primacy of Oxbridge is all the more remarkable in the light of the general ethos of reconstruction and planning that pervades many of these immediate post-war obituaries. Cer-

TABLE 6.8 Higher education: Own citizens (ie, British subjects only in British newspapers)

Newspaper	Oxford/ Cambridge/ Grande école/ Ivy League	Other British/ French/ American University	Art school, conserva- toire, etc	Military Academy, Naval Colleg	Foreign University	Polytechnic, Technical College	Finishing school	Seminary	No higher education	Total
The Times 1900	16 50.0 %	10 31.3 %		1 3.1 %	3 9.4 %				2 6.3 %	32 100.0 %
The Times 1948	20 43.5 %	6 13.0 %	5 10.9 %	5 10.9 %		2 4.3 %			8 17.4 %	46 100.0 %
The Times 2000	21 34.4 %	8 13.1 %	5 8.2 %	7 11.5 %	3 4.9 %	2 3.3 %	2 3.3 %		13 21.3 %	61 100.0 %
The Guardian	21 38.2 %	15 27.3 %	9 16.4 %			2 3.6 %			8 14.5 %	55 100.0 %
The Independent	18 35.3 %	14 27.5 %	7 13.7 %	1 2.0 %	2 3.9 %		1 2.0 %		8 15.7 %	51 100.0 %
Daily Telegraph	17 30.4 %	11 19.6 %	6 10.7 %	7 12.5 %	2 3.6 %	2 3.6 %	2 3.6 %		9 16.1 %	56 100.0 %
Le Monde	8 25.8 %	11 35.5 %	11 35.5 %	1 3.2 %						31 100.0 %
New York Times	21 31.3 %	33 49.3 %	6 9.0 %	2 3.0 %	1 1.5 %			1 1.5 %	3 4.5 %	67 100.0 %
Total	142 35.6 %	108 27.1 %	49 12.3 %	24 6.0 %	11 2.8 %	8 2.0 %	5 1.3 %	1 0.3 %	51 12.8 %	399 100.0 %

tainly, polytechnic studies appear for the first time on the obituary stage, but only two individuals had experienced this kind of training. Art schools (11%) and military academies (11%) both now begin to appear with equal, and not inconsiderable, frequency. All in all, despite the growing breadth of higher education, the 1948 *The Times* shows the 'eternal return' of certain key features, most notably, the prominence of Oxbridge.

If we turn to the very recent sample of British newspapers for 2000–2001, and again take only British subjects, the pattern is sharply different. The art school features prominently now, alongside drama colleges, and conservatories. There is, predictably, a much broader span of universities to which these subjects have gone, while the polytechnic also plays a role in their formation. There are many graduates of Sandhurst and the Dartmouth Naval College or their equivalents. But amidst this diversity there are still constant features, not least the continued privileged status of Oxford and Cambridge. This was the chosen establishment for as many as 35 per cent of all the known British subjects. The highest number came from *The Guardian* sample — 38 per cent having been to Oxbridge — but even the less intellectual *Daily Telegraph* had a solid 30 per cent whose academic experience was shaped by these colleges. If anything indicates more clearly the pre-eminence of old money within Britain — even in late modernity — it is hard to imagine it. Thus the world of the obituary in Britain turns out to be remarkably unified in one fundamental aspect, that is, the importance of public school and Oxbridge as a common starting point for many of those whose subsequent distinction guarantees them a place in its columns.

A key opposition now takes shape, one which we see as structuring much of what we note in our findings. Newspapers are read not solely because of the logic of their arguments but because of the pre-existing social contracts that they enjoy with their readers (Bourdieu and Passeron 1990: 25). There is a major division in the world of higher education between *The Times* and the *Daily Telegraph* on the one hand and *The Guardian* and *The Independent* on the other.[28] It shows up as a division over the number and type of creative actors included versus the representation of merchants, industrialists and financiers. This is mirrored, as Bourdieu explains (1984), in an opposition between the 'ascetic aristocratism' of the dominated fraction of the dominant class, more intellectual in its choices, and the dominant fraction of the dominant class, which specialises in the performance of control or authority functions. At the level of the obituary, it comes down to the newspapers whose obituary subjects had been trained either at university or at art school, versus those newspapers with a smaller proportion who had been at university and more with military school discipline. For example, *The Times* 2000–2001 only had 13 per cent at universities other than Oxbridge (half the number of *The Guardian* and *The Independent*), 48 per cent university-educated in total. But it is, of course, no surprise that it had more than *The Guardian* and *Independent* from military academies (12%) and that *The Daily Telegraph* had a remarkably similar pattern to *The Times*. In contrast, *The Guardian* and *The Independent* had respectively 66 per cent and 63 per cent of British obituary subjects overall who had been university-educated, a marked discrepancy with *The Times* 2000–2001 and its mere 48 per cent or the *Daily Telegraph* (50%).

Le Monde emerges as the extreme pole of the more "intellectual" *The Guardian* /*The Independent* axis, being conspicuous not only for having both the highest proportion of those who were arts school and conservatoire trained (together 36% of all their obits of French citizens) but also for the tiny proportion who had been to military academy (3%). However, those educated at the Grandes Écoles were a slightly smaller minority (26%) than the 35 per cent at Oxbridge in the British 2000–2001 papers.

Given both the greater number of American universities and their greater accessibility through 'night schools', the *New York Times* had the highest rate (81% of the obits of Americans) of those who had had university academic education. Interestingly, the Ivy League universities retained their hold: nearly one-third (31%) of the obituary articles concerned the alumni of Harvard, Yale, Cornell, Boston and the small East Coast liberal arts colleges.[29] The continuing prestige of their 'civilizing rituals', equivalent to the undiminished lustre of Oxbridge, is evident from the accolade bestowed by these obituaries.

NATIONALITY, ETHNICITY AND MIGRATION

Approximately two-thirds of obituaries in British newspapers are focused on British subjects. Adding together the first four columns of Table 6.9, *The Guardian* features the lowest number, 50 per cent, while *The Independent*, *The Times* 2000–2001 and *The Daily Telegraph* offer at least 60 per cent of obituaries of British subjects. A recent transformation in the obituary landscape is the increasing numbers of American nationals, who now rank second in the British newspapers. Indeed, in Britain, American obituaries are more numerous than those for all other European countries grouped together. *The Guardian* and *The Independent* have by far the greatest number of obituaries of U.S. nationals, with 29 per cent and 21 per cent, respectively. This reflects the importance that 'heroes of consumption' have in these newspapers, especially actors and popular musicians (Lowenthal 1961: ch. 4). Obituaries from Asia, the Middle East and Third World countries have a relatively marginal presence in all the British newspapers, ranging from 12 per cent (*The Times*) to 7 per cent (*The Independent*). The ones that do appear feature particularly politicians and, to a lesser extent, writers.

Yet the presence of *any* Third World figures in obituaries is a feature of newspapers only from the 2000–2001 sample. Neither *The Times* 1900 (with one exception), nor *The Times* 1948 include obituaries of colonised

Table 6.9 Nationality of obituary subjects

	Scottish	Welsh	British Irish*	English	Other European	U.S.	Canada	Latin America, Caribbean	Asia	Middle East	Africa	Australia and New Zealand	French (Le Monde)	Total
The Times 1900	1 .7%	1 .7%	7 5.2%	99 73.3%	23 17.0%	3 2.2%		1 .7%						135 100.0%
The Times 1948	2 2.0%	1 1.0%	3 3.0%	83 82.2%	5 5.0%	6 5.9%	1 1.0%					1 1.0%		101 100.0%
The Times 2000	5 4.8%	1 1.0%	2 1.9%	59 56.7%	10 9.6%	13 12.5%	1 1.0%	1 1.0%	4 3.8%	5 4.8%	2 1.9%	1 1.0%		104 100.0%
The Guardian	1 .8%	1 .8%	2 1.5%	62 47.0%	14 10.6%	38 28.8%	1 .8%	4 3.0%	4 3.0%		4 3.0%	1 .8%		132 100.0%
The Independent	6 6.3%	3 3.2%	1 1.1%	47 49.5%	10 10.5%	20 21.1%		1 1.1%	1 1.1%	3 3.2%	1 1.1%	2 2.1%		95 100.0%
Daily Telegraph	4 4.0%	1 1.0%	3 3.0%	61 61.0%	7 7.0%	12 12.0%		1 1.0%	3 3.0%	2 2.0%	4 4.0%	2 2.0%		100 100.0%
Le Monde				1 1.0%	13 13.0%	9 9.0%	1 1.0%	5 5.0%	6 6.0%	5 5.0%	1 1.0%	1 1.0%	58 58.0%	100 100.0%
New York Times	2 2.0%			6 6.0%	10 10.0%	71 71.0%	1 1.0%	3 3.0%	3 3.0%	2 2.0%	2 2.0%			100 100.0%
Total	21 2.4%	7 .8%	18 2.1%	418 48.2%	92 10.6%	172 19.8%	5 .6%	16 1.8%	21 2.4%	17 2.0%	14 1.6%	8 .9%	58 6.7%	867 100.0%

* Includes those born in what is now the Republic of Ireland when it was a British colony.

subjects or those from the Third World, thus reinforcing the claims made by Said about the prevalence of Orientalist/imperialist discourses. *The Times* 1900 is characterised by its very high proportion of obituaries of British subjects (80%) but also by the significant number of European figures (17%), members of a surviving cross-national aristocratic elite. By contrast, at this time, Americans accounted for only 2 per cent. *The Times* 1948 is characterised by its markedly national character (87% of obituaries are of British nationals), and also by the rising proportion of American obituaries (6%), which begin to displace the other European countries collectively (5%) as the second most important category.

The *New York Times*, with as many as 71 per cent of its obituaries dedicated to U.S. citizens, is as inward-looking as *The Daily Telegraph*, the most nationally-orientated of the British newspapers. In contrast, in *Le Monde*, the obituaries of its own French citizens amount only to 58 per cent. In other words, it is turned outwards to the world, so that this paper is more globally-inclusive than any other except *The Guardian*. More importantly perhaps, *Le Monde* is the newspaper which offers the best distribution of obituaries between different nationalities, for while it features non-French, EU nationals and Americans in second and third place (13% and 9%, respectively), 17 per cent of its obituaries are also representations of figures from Asia, the Middle East and the Third World countries, more than any other newspaper by a considerable degree.

As already hinted, significant differences in occupational categories in relation to nationality also emerge in the sample as a whole. Obituaries from American and European citizens tend to be overwhelmingly of cultural producers (67%) and professionals (63%) (not shown here), whilst nationals from Third World countries are predominantly politicians (between 29% and 44%, depending on the area). Interestingly, across newspapers, a high/low cultural division tends to be reproduced along national lines, with a large proportion of American subjects active in the popular arts and a large proportion of Europeans active in the older, consecrated arts.

For the first time in the 2000–2001 obituaries, relative to the earlier years in Britain, there appears a small proportion of people from ethnic minorities, in particular those stated explicitly in the obituary to be Jewish, or those defined as African, African-American, Afro-Caribbean and Asian, whom we have categorised as simply 'black'[30] (see Table 6.10).

Although, overall, 5 per cent of the obituaries' subjects for the British 2000–2001 newspapers are black and 5 per cent are Jewish — 4 per cent each of the total sample — two different patterns emerge. *The Guardian* (9%) — and to a lesser degree *The Independent* (5%) — dedicated more attention to black people on the one hand but less to explicitly-noted Jewish subjects (2% and 3%, respectively), while *The Times* and to a lesser degree *The Daily Telegraph* reversed these terms (thus *The Times* featured 2% black and 9% Jewish subjects). *Le Monde* shows a similar pattern to that of *The Guardian*: 8 per cent of its obituary subjects are black, but only

Table 6.10 Ethnicity of obituary subjects

	Black	Explicitly Jewish	White (non-Jewish)	Total
The Times 1900			142 100.0%	142 100.0%
The Times 1948	1 .9%		105 99.1%	106 100.0%
The Times 2000	2 1.9%	10 9.3%	95 88.8%	107 100.0%
The Guardian	12 9.0%	3 2.3%	118 88.7%	113 100.0%
The Independent	5 5.1%	3 3.1%	90 91.8%	98 100.0%
Daily Telegraph	2 2.0%	6 5.9%	93 92.1%	101 100.0%
Le Monde	8 8.0%	2 2.0%	90 90.0%	100 100.0%
New York Times	4 4.0%	11 11.0%	85 85.0%	100 100.0%
Total	34 3.8%	35 3.9%	818 92.2%	887 100.0%

2 per cent are explicitly Jewish. Strikingly, the *New York Times* dedicates only 4 per cent of its obituaries to black subjects, turning its back on the country's considerable African-American population. Explicitly-labelled Jewish obituary subjects featured more prominently than any other newspaper (11%).

On the other hand, an unexpectedly high proportion of individuals, or their parents, (38%) migrated to another country at some point, which identifies the obituary subjects as part of an internationally-mobile elite[31] (see Table 6.11). The current British newspapers with the highest proportion of migrating individuals are *The Times* 2000–2001 (45% in total; ie, extracting the 55% who have had 'no migration' from the other columns) and *The Daily Telegraph* (also 45%). *The Independent* has the lowest, but this still embraces nearly one-third of its obituaries. Yet overall it is the 1900 *Times* obituaries that show the highest number of migrating individuals: an extraordinary 48 per cent.

Turning now to causes of migration (Table 6.12) the vast majority (85%) were, of course, elite migrants, British Army and Colonial Officers, diplomats and judges, who were travelling to imperial destinations to stay as part of State governmental structures. By contrast, economic migration or voluntary career nomadism of those in certain highly skilled occupations, such as academics, musicians and architects, accounted in 1900 for only

Table 6.11 Migration (including non-migrants)

	Elite migration	Voluntary migration	Exile	Economic migration	Sent back to British school	Parents migration	No migration	Total
The Times 1900	52 41.3%	7 5.6%	1 .8%		1 .8%		65 51.6%	126 100.0%
The Times 1948	16 16.7%	8 8.3%	2 2.1%	4 4.2%		1 1.0%	65 67.7%	96 100.0%
The Times 2000	7 6.5%	25 23.4%	10 9.3%	1 .9%	3 2.8%	2 1.9%	59 55.1%	107 100.0%
The Guardian	3 2.3%	18 13.6%	12 9.1%	5 3.8%	5 3.8%	6 4.5%	83 62.9%	132 100.0%
The Independent	2 2.0%	13 13.3%	5 5.1%	2 2.0%	4 4.1%	5 5.1%	67 68.4%	98 100.0%
Daily Telegraph	13 12.9%	27 26.7%	2 2.0%			3 3.0%	56 55.4%	101 100.0%
Le Monde	5 5.0%	21 21.0%	5 5.0%		1 1.0%	4 4.0%	64 64.0%	100 100.0%
New York Times	2 2.0%	14 14.0%	4 4.0%			3 3.0%	77 77.0%	100 100.0%
Total	100 11.6%	133 15.5%	41 4.8%	12 1.4%	14 1.6%	24 2.8%	536 62.3%	860 100.0%

12 per cent of the cases. A century later, such career nomadism has become the largest cause of migration (not shown here) an average of 53 per cent in the four British newspapers (of all who have migrated), and relates mainly to individuals who move to highly paid and skilled jobs. This phenomenon has been described by Castells in terms of the *globalisation of specialty labour*: not just high-level professional labour, but also artists, designers, performers, sports stars, spiritual gurus, political consultants and professional criminals (2000: 130). Finally, a further, far from insignificant cause of migration is exile, or the search for asylum: in these 2000–2001 obituaries, an average of 17 per cent of all migrants are exiles, particularly marked in *The Guardian* (25%) and *The Times* 2000 (21% for each).

Cross-nationally (Table 6.11), 36 per cent of the *Le Monde* portraits have experienced some kind of migration, a figure comparable to that of *The Guardian*. By contrast, in *The New York Times* only 23 per cent of the individuals featured have been migrants. In both the *New York Times* and *Le Monde*, voluntary migration or 'career nomadism' is the major source and accounts for respectively 60 per cent of those who have migrated (Table 6.12). Such long-term cross-national trajectories on the part of the dominant class are too easily forgotten when the question of globalisation is debated today.

CONCLUSION

Amidst this detailed analysis of the social backgrounds of figures depicted in newspaper obituaries, several consistently clear-cut patterns have been established. First, obituaries are overwhelmingly of men, with a maximum of only 20 per cent portraits of women (*The Independent*). Nationally, they are predominantly British, American and European; ethnically, they are over-represented by the majority group within the obituary form, with the exception of the representation of a significant minority: the Jewish community in *The Times*. The occupational array is dramatically skewed away from farming, manual work, even middle-class professions (such as teaching and nursing), and into the higher professions, artists and the military and political elites. Not just this, the obituary subjects also derive predominantly from privileged families, as witnessed by their educational provenance, 77 per cent of the British citizens having come from public schools and 36 per cent having attended two universities alone (Oxford and Cambridge), in the latest period only reduced slightly to 72 per cent and 35 per cent. Finally, despite a minority of 'rags to riches' careers, the underlying structure is that cultural and material advantages have been reproduced, with 71 per cent of sons and daughters issuing themselves from the dominant class. Here then, is evidence that despite the diversification of the obituary and the appearance of some individuals who figure chiefly in a landscape of popular and counter-memory the collective memory of

Table 6.12 Migration (omitting non-migrants)

	Elite migration	Voluntary migration	Exile	Economic migration	Sent back to British school	Parents' migration	Total
The Times 1900	52 85.2%	7 11.5%	1 1.6%		1 1.6%		61 100.0%
The Times 1948	16 51.6%	8 25.8%	2 6.5%	4 12.9%		1 3.2%	31 100.0%
The Times 2000	7 14.6%	25 52.1%	10 20.8%	1 2.1%	3 6.3%	2 4.2%	48 100.0%
The Guardian	3 6.1%	18 36.7%	12 24.5%	5 10.2%	5 10.2%	6 12.2%	49 100.0%
The Independent	2 6.5%	13 41.9%	5 16.1%	2 6.5%	4 12.9%	5 16.1%	31 100.0%
Daily Telegraph	13 28.9%	27 60.0%	2 4.4%			3 6.7%	45 100.0%
Le Monde	5 13.9%	21 58.3%	5 13.9%		1 2.8%	4 11.1%	36 100.0%
New York Times	2 8.7%	14 60.9%	4 17.4%			3 13.0%	23 100.0%
Total	100 30.9%	133 41.0%	41 12.7%	12 3.7%	14 4.3%	24 7.4%	324 100.0%

the dominants is still uppermost. In this sense, the obituary testifies to the power of class, curiously, now 'the problem that dares not say its name' (Sayer 2005: 224).

Distinction, then, is preserved through a variety of mechanisms. We would not deny that the ascetic action of the elite (notable, for example, in the grandes écoles) plays some role among these. Yet the frequent family transmission of privilege is still overshadowed by the 'mountain climb' image of the individual's biographical trajectory dominant in these obituaries (Bourdieu 1986). It is not our intention here to underestimate the originality, merit or service of many of the obituary subjects. Rather it is to argue for the emergence of those conditions under which similar William Whytes, Gielguds and Wollheims[32] might bloom from very different strata, as well as for an expansion of the fields from which those bestowed obituaries might come.

PART II

Memories burnished at the shock of death

Discourse analysis of newspaper obituaries

7   The politicians' obituaries (1999–2006)

The qualitative analysis introduced here examines obituaries both for those who were professional politicians and those who influenced political opinion.[1] More broadly, these are the men and women who 'live off or for politics': those actors to whom Weber alluded when he spoke of people with 'a political vocation' (1991: 125–28). Many of these individuals are highly visible possessors of power — presidents, ministers of governing parties or mayors of capital cities; others operate in the great movements of politics as members of minority parties that never attained office, but may still have exerted a telling force. The analysis of such social movements ranges widely to include not just political activities engaged in party negotiations for government, but all those political activities which constitute the everyday stuff of politics — those 'individual or collective classification struggles aimed at transforming the categories of perception and appreciation of the social world, and, through this, the social world itself' (Bourdieu 1984: 483).[2] Such movements have to forge individuals together via a symbolic identification with the group, a unity which is based on a shared 'vision and division of the world' (Bourdieu 1984).

GENRES OF POLITICIANS' OBITS

Many obits focus on positive 'traditional' politicians in the sense that they and their families had been part of the hegemonic power bloc and made successful careers through the institutional channels of politics (see, for example, Hailsham, below). The greatest contrast is between the obits of such legitimate government ministers and those of oppositional political leaders, such as Abu Nidal, or authoritarian presidents, such as President Assad of Syria — men whose hold on power is stated to have brought torture and death to hundreds or thousands of their citizens (see, respectively, *The Guardian*, 20 August 2002 and *The Times*, 12 June 2000). Indeed, the highest proportion of all negative or critical obituaries in the early 2000s is for politicians. While *The Times*' obituary collections no longer label such men or women simply 'tyrants', current obituaries still characterise these figures as 'monstrous others', on whom the verdict of history — often understandably — will be implacably severe. Such pathologically dehumanised rulers are sharply differentiated from those politicians who merely use their office to enrich themselves.

Not all political obituaries can be fitted into these two initial types. There are also those that use a genre of heavy irony, especially notable for post-communist politicians, such as the Yugoslavian, Stipe Suvar, as we shall see. Tragic obituaries are notable here: individuals who had, in the obituarists' gaze, the potential for greatness, but who were destroyed by historical circumstances 'not of their own making'. Lastly, there are those for individuals who map out an *untraditional trajectory* yet receive profoundly *positive* portrayals. Ronald Reagan's obituaries exemplify this category, featuring as they did, his petit-bourgeois origins and his move from acting to politics via trade union organisation (see amongst others, *The Independent*, 7 June 2004; *The Guardian*, 7 June 2004). These analyses of different types of political obituary are complemented by a briefer section, inviting the reader to see them as contributions to different kinds of collective memory, official, popular and counter-memory. The last category featured especially political leaders from wider, non-party social movements.

If more negative obits have been written for politicians than for any other occupational category, this is no doubt because politicians are engaged more nakedly than the possessors of land or capital in conflicts between groups — those struggles which helped to forge the historical materialism of both Marx and Weber. On the whole, however, the obituaries neither dramatise issues in terms of the broader field of social power nor address specific questions using the language of class. For example, debates over whether the capitalist class continues to rules when a Labour Party (or social democratic party) governs are notably absent from the discourse of the obituaries (cf Scott 1991; Devine 1997). Instead, struggles in the contemporary political field are principally defined in terms of parties, or at most in terms of the conflicting forces of Left and Right, or nationalism and liberalism, which underlie them. Nevertheless, although lacking Weber's precise concepts, the political obituaries are broadly shaped by his categories: here we see modern rational-legal politicians set against traditional patrimonial leaders, charismatic Overmen pitching themselves against the machine politicians of bureaucratised parties. More acutely, these obituaries are underpinned by a philosophical anthropology which produces political-ethical critique in terms of the traditional notion of "freedom from" (Berlin's negative freedom) and other familiar substantive ends (equality, justice). In particular, the figures in the obits are caught up in the dilemmas provoked between an ethics of value-rational purity — undiluted commitment to one goal — and an ethics of responsibility. Figures such as Abu Nidal (beneath) have been fatally distorted by an 'ethic of ultimate ends' devoid of the ethic of responsibility. Ultimately, these portrayals tend to see the two ethics as 'not absolute contrasts but rather supplements' (Weber 1991: 127). The quiet — rather than the glorious — heroes of these modern obits are those who succeed in reconciling them (see for example, Jacek Kuron below).

TRADITIONAL POSITIVE OBITUARIES

The heartland of the obituary is found in the figures from the Establishment or State Nobility, figures who have played a protracted role in the theatre of state. Their scripts or political habitus are shaped not just through the close understanding by an elite of its interests, but by generations of their own families before them, occasionally in political dynasties. Whereas in many cases in the dominant class, the precise occupation does not follow that of the father, in the figure selected, Lord Hailsham (Quintin Hogg):

> the careers of father and son bear uncanny similarities. Both achieved remarkable success at the Bar; both became Lord Chancellor and both were drafted into the Conservative Party with the prospect of leadership. (Geoffrey Lewis, *The Independent,* 15 October 2001)

Moreover such specialised elite reproduction of temporal power continues. As another Hailsham obit notes, Lord Hailsham's daughter, Mary, herself became a High Court judge (Lord Roskill, *The Independent,* 15 October 2001).[3] Bourdieu, recalling Marx, writes of inheritance and social reproduction as 'the dead seizing the living', yet he rarely had quite such a precise inheritance in mind (Marx 1976 I: 91; Bourdieu 1981).

Hailsham's imposing whole-page obituaries offer a portrait of a leader who 'served his country' in an exemplary way: by implication, this was the traditional system of patrician candidates for important office working at its best. His great distinction was to have shone in both high legal offices in the judiciary and also in high political office, as Chairman of the Conservative Party, subsequently returning to the House of Lords, whose hereditary membership he had earlier renounced: 'He spoke often and to effect and almost always with great pungency and wit […] he *commanded great affection and respect* […]' (Roskill). His baronetcy and Knighthood of the Garter crown this roll of honour, in Lord Roskill's estimation, richly deserved. Similarly, *The Independent* main obituary, whilst admitting some personality flaws, ends resonantly in positive terms, demanding an appreciation of Hailsham's *grandeur*:

> History will not make that charge [that he might have achieved more]. Lord Hailsham was a patriot of honour and integrity, with a lifelong devotion to the public service and to the Christian faith in which he was nurtured. (Lewis, ibid)

Hailsham's well-placed position has already been noted. This prominence within the State Nobility is confirmed through his early promise. As Bourdieu points out, the mark of the State Nobility is not its earlier attendance at privileged schools, nor its examination success — that 'transubstantiation of privilege into achievement'— rather, it is the acquisition of honours and trophies *when young* (1996b: 20–21) Hailsham was precocious in this respect: he was awarded prizes and a scholarship at school (Eton), he gained a double First in classics at Oxford, entitling him to a fellowship at All Souls immediately after graduation; most spectacularly, he entered the Commons at the youthful age of thirty-one.

Obituaries rarely simply praise their subject and the two analysed for Hailsham are no exception; their praise acquires authenticity by the admission of countervailing weaknesses. Thus despite the magical aura given by his education and his illustrious career as Lord Chancellor, the obits are forced to note that 'he never held any of the great offices of State' (Lord Roskill, *The Independent*). In particular, Hailsham was passed over as Prime Minister, both because of ineligibility, as a peer, and 'apparent weaknesses of personality and judgement'. In this respect, both authors register miscalculations which had bought popularity, but at a price: an arrogant and melodramatic use of political theatre (ringing a hand-bell to announce the death of the Labour Party at one election), and a fateful clash with the Bar over barristers' fees. Even Hailsham's 'elegant' legal judgements are appraised as too individualistic. They did not permit straightforward generalisation within bureaucratised structures:

> His judgements were too lengthy and although always beautifully expressed, tended to seek after intellectual and logical perfection…Too often he did not give a practical lead to those who had daily to apply them. (Roskill)

He is acknowledged to have entered Parliament initially, in 1938, by fighting *against* the more progressive university candidate, A.D. Lindsay. Hailsham stood on a pro-Munich platform (that is — although this passes unanalysed — one of active appeasement of Fascist and Nazi power). The wider subjective meaning of his political philosophy appears only once, where his 1947 Penguin, *The Case for Conservatism* is quoted. This reveals his adroit combination of nineteenth century political economy and Burke. The 'embrace of tradition' is the leading phenomenon of his 1960s' *modern* conservatism:

> Its [the Conservative Party's] eternal and indispensable role [is]to criticise and mould the latest heresy of the moment in the name of tradition, as tradition itself has been enriched and moulded by all the transient theories of the past.

To reinforce the combination of Hailsham's time-honoured tradition with modernity, the central, dominating photograph presents him at his most anachronistic — in a bowler, buckled court shoes, tights, evening shirt and white tie (see Hobsbaum and Ranger 1983). As though to resonate with this stately effect, all the dissonant events of his life which might undermine his stature — his half-brother's tragic suicide, divorce from his first wife — are reduced to a few sentences. He thus represents the essence of the majestic Theatre of the Law.

Hailsham is shown in his obituary to have been a key member of the power elite. It might be added to this portrayal that he clearly derived his membership from the dominant power bloc. Scott has argued that ' [a] power bloc [...] is an alignment of social groups which have some similarity in social background and experience and which is able to monopolise positions of authority within the State elite over a sustained period' (Scott 1991, 118–19). Hailsham wielded his considerable 'temporal power' through his cultural capital, deploying it all the more effortlessly precisely because of his harmony of 'outlook and background' (Scott 1991: 120) with the dominant power bloc. Needless to say, many other obituaries are awarded to figures of this type, amongst them Lord Maclehose, *The Daily Telegraph*, 1 June 2000, *The Daily Telegraph*, 1 June 2000, Lord Onslow, *The Independent*, 17 March 2001 and Lord Belstead (*The Scotsman*, 8 December 2005).

Similar highly positive obituaries exist for the American equivalent of the 'State Nobility'. One such is for Kermit Roosevelt, whose distinction was to have been a leading figure in the CIA, and the 'mastermind' of various American interventions abroad (*Daily Telegraph*, 22 June 2000). Most notably, he substituted Nasser for King Farouk in Egypt, but then proceeding to oust the legitimate leader of the Iranian Government, Mossadeq, in a coup in 1953, co-ordinated with Christopher Woodhouse, the British soldier and MP (see also Woodhouse's obituary in *The Guardian* 20 February 2001). Roosevelt's obituary is extraordinary for two reasons: its *open acknowledgement* of the undemocratic and illegal power manoeuvres of those acting on behalf of the West, and the impeccable *elite credentials* of those doing the manoeuvring.

Indeed, *The Daily Telegraph*'s obituary is a bizarre account of the use of strong-arm tactics, popular carnival and the support of a local network of Iranian merchants — 'The Brothers' — to bring about the end of Mossadeq's premiership. Its readers are thus entrusted with the responsibility of knowing that America and Britain in the Cold War intervened authoritatively, against the Iranian parliamentary system, to ensure that Western geo-political interests were pursued. In this respect Roosevelt's obituary is entirely transparent that the CIA-British conspiracy, via The Brothers, had engineered the return of Anglo-Persian oil, newly-nationalised, to the private concessions originally operated by the Western oil corporations. The obituary's only justification for these extra-legal actions is to paint Mossadeq, the nationalist popular leader, as both eccentric and 'hysterical' in his orchestration of the descent of his country into chaos, committed as he was to various supposedly impractical schemes. It ends with a concession to balance, by admitting that, under the Shah's rule, many came to wish that Mossadeq had retained power.

A further remarkable feature of this obituary is its clarity that the coercion and manipulation used to pursue Western interests were perpetrated by the most well-educated minds of their generation: Kermit Roosevelt taught history at Harvard, from where he had graduated, Woodhouse had a double First in Classics from Oxford (*The Guardian*). More unexpectedly, for the naive, both politicians possessed an impeccable State 'pedigree': Roosevelt was the grandson of President Theodore Roosevelt and a distant cousin of President Franklin Roosevelt, Woodhouse's obit reveals that he was the son of the Liberal peer, Lord Terrington. Roosevelt's obit in particular unashamedly legitimates the West in terms of an enlightened *paternalism*.

There are Labour or social democratic variants of the trusted politician who achieves unusual respect. Despite a more upper-middle class ethos, they too, represent instances of class continuity, or 'reproduction', to use Bourdieu's terms. Donald Dewar (*The Times*, 12 October 2000) regarded as the 'Father of the [Scottish] Nation' at his untimely death, mirrored many of Hailsham's qualities, brilliance as a speaker, legal expertise, uncorruptibility and erudition. Like Hailsham, Dewar also came from a professional family, if one further from the power elite (his father was a dermatologist). He had also gone to an old university (Glasgow rather than Oxford). There were even the same distanced attempts to hold out hands to 'the people' — with, in his case, more than a trace of class racism, an assertion of anti-consumerist asceticism. By his death he had engineered a structural change — Scottish devolution — which was aimed at undercutting the turn of the disillusioned to popular nationalism. The final obituary tribute defines his claim on greatness:

> Few politicians can claim genuinely to have altered the course of constitutional history. Donald Dewar did... At the same time he won the affection of the Scottish people through a combination of modesty and self-deprecation which set him apart as that rarest of creatures — a trusted politician.

Each nation in the capitalist world has its political State Nobility.[4] From this elite came, in France, both Jacques Chaban-Delmas (*Le Monde*, 13 November 2000)[5] and Bernard Tricot, (*Le Monde*, 12 June 2000). In Germany, the obit for Gunter Rexrodt (*The Independent*, 24 August 2004) reveals similar elite membership: his own father had been leader of the German Liberal Democratic Party before Hitler's accession in 1933. In

America, the obituary of Mayor Lindsay, the son of a banker and Mayor of New York at thirty-seven years old, reveals the patrician East Coast elite to which he belonged as having an analogous cohesive 'nobility' in terms of both its relational position and functions (*The Guardian*, 21 December 2000). Not all such representatives of traditional careers, however, are given such an undilutedly positive appraisal as that of Dewar. Whilst never negatively portrayed as 'the other', they may be tragic or ironic.

The traditional State Nobility are given obituaries in which they are always portrayed as austerely set apart from the 'fun culture' and consumerism of the masses (Bauman 1998). In this respect, they incorporate the early bourgeois sense of individual containment and reflective tastes described by Ferguson (1990). Hailsham's life, we note, appears to be totally dedicated to his work and public duties. Dewar is an important variant of this: so ascetic that he did not even buy a new overcoat when his old one wore out, he nevertheless owned a collection of paintings by Scottish Colourists. Here is a form of artistic possession which, in this account, appears rigorously separated from other forms of consumption. The owner is in a sense possessed by his art and artistic reception takes place in a purely spiritual site (Bourdieu 1977: 197).

NEGATIVE POLITICAL OBITUARIES

In order to grasp the nature of the modern obituary, those lives high in the hierarchy of 'grievability' (Butler 2003: 32) need to be contrasted with a cluster of demonic figures. Represented in their columns with an archetypal otherness, the acts of these political influentials betray an inner degradation. For these leaders, a vocabulary is retained which is rarely or never used elsewhere: a rhetoric of 'ruthlessness', 'terror', 'warped drives', 'cruelty', 'philandering' and 'zealotry'. Such emotional terms resist any positive recuperation of their protagonists.[6] These were figures who perpetrated, often casually, widespread acts of violence, thus, in the obituarists' view, dishonouring any cause for which they pretended to stand. They are invariably portrayed in the obituaries as devoid of *any* altruistic or admirable qualities. In this sense the obits contribute less to a full historical or sociological comprehension than to simple moral dichotomies. Yet this process, too, may be useful for shaping collective memory.

Two negative political obituaries will demonstrate these points: the first, by David Hirst, remembers the life of Abu Nidal (pseudonym for Sabri Al-Banna), who committed suicide in 2002 (*The Guardian*, 20 August 2002), the second, by Ian Traynor, was written after the natural death of the Croatian leader, Franjo Tudjman (*Guardian*, 13 December 1999). The first, lengthy, obit retains a charismatic language of genius but fuses it with a disenchanted realism. It provides a historical context for Abu Nidal's moral career by comparing the State terrorism of the Israeli leader,

Menachem Begin, with the dissident terrorism of Nidal and his revolutionary Fatah and Black June movements. Within these irregulars' dissident
structures, Abu Nidal's 'special genius' emerged: he was 'the monstrous
king' who accepted favours in the Middle Eastern underworld for uniquely
'hideous crime', indeed, he was 'the ultimate mercenary.'

The obituary sketches an explanation for Abu Nidal's actions in terms of
the peculiarities of his birth — he was the twelfth son of a prosperous Palestinian orange-farmer who had married his servant after the death of his
first wife, the mother of the eleven older children. After his father's death,
this second wife was banished from the house, leaving Abu Nidal an unprotected child, spurned by his half-brothers. Within the turbulence already
created by this family drama, the Catastrophe occurred when Nidal was
eleven years old: the dispossession of the Palestinians in 1948 and their
collective downward mobility. The two together, the obituary argues, created the man who was to take 'disproportionate revenge' for the 'suffer-
ings of his infancy'. Rising from the refugee camps to become oil-rich in
Saudi Arabia, Nidal became a prominent critic of the two-state solution,
leading the struggle for the purity of the rejectionist stance, a politics of
absolute ends. When such rejectionists in rival movements — or in his own
— became weak or faltered, Nidal had them wiped out by his clandestine
organisations. Acts as everyday as going shopping with a member of the
mainstream Fatah movement merited instant execution. Undercover himself, Nidal inaugurated a 'reign of terror', orchestrating torture and deaths
on an unprecedented scale, on one occasion eliminating six hundred of his
own group.

The obituary thus identifies Nidal as a crucial contributor to the crises
over Palestinian legitimacy. However its own silences should be noted. The
obituary omits any reference to Israeli-American vetoing of UN motions
— passed by the whole of the rest of the world — for a two-state solution
within 1967 borders,[7] Its main argument is solely about Palestinian leadership — asserting that while Nidal claimed he was doing everything for
Palestine, he was in fact betraying it:

> the man who at the outset of his career so grandly styled himself Abu
> Nidal or "father of struggle" came by the end of it to be regarded by
> most of his compatriots as the antithesis of all the name stood for, the
> begetting of everything that was most treacherous and destructive of
> the cause that he had seemingly espoused more passionately than any-
> one else.

Nidal's obituary is an ideal type of the negative political genre. Others
critical obituaries adopt a similar structure: see, for example, that for Nas-
ution, the army general and politician complicit with the 'Great Repression', in which hundreds of thousands of Communists in Indonesia were
murdered (*Le Monde*, 8 October 2000), or that of Slobodan Milosevic

(*The Times*, 17 March 2006; the *New York Times*, 12 March 2006; *The Guardian*, 13 March 2006). This is the dark side of the dialectic with the celebratory, euphemistic obituary.

OTHER TYPES OF NEGATIVE OBITUARY

The political balance sheet may be unclear, so that different perspectives on a politician's practices vie for acceptance. Joe Modise, (*The Guardian*, 29 November 2001), who became defence Minister in the post-apartheid South Africa, was one such contentious figure. His obituary itself became a form of trial, with the case for him mounted by his friends and the case against him by South African sceptics (see Introduction). Where there has been better-founded, legal evidence of corruption, a negative obituary is particularly likely to appear, as in the cases of the Congolese leader, Laurent Kabila (*The Independent*, 18 January 2001), the Surinamese Henck Arron (*The Guardian*, 24 January 2001; *The Independent* 7 12. 00), and others. Even European leaders may occasionally be recipients of such uncompromising treatment. One such was Bettino Craxi, (*The Independent*, 21 January 2000) the former Italian Socialist Party leader, whose obituary, magnanimous in certain gestures, was all the more devastating for its overall harsh judgement. Craxi's distinction was to have pulled the Socialist Party up from near oblivion. But he did so, according to this obituary, at a terrible cost, proceeding to strip the party of 'all sense of ideological purpose, to bring himself, and it, to the very pinnacle of a rotten system.' Thus this author links the changed party iconography — the red carnation in place of the hammer and the sickle — to massive corruption, both for the benefit of the Party and for his own family. This included kickbacks from private companies acquiring public contracts, his facilitation of Berlusconi's rise through a change in the law on monopolies and a ubiquitous interpenetration of money and politics. Indeed, Craxi's career culminated in his exile and sentence, in absentia, to twenty-five years in prison.

It is symptomatic of an obituary where there has been established testimony of illegal procedures that the guilty person's subjective views are kept to a minimum. Thus Craxi's self-perception is simply presented as that of a man who possessed the virtue of decisiveness ('decisionismo!' in his own terms). Yet the reader is unlikely to sympathise with Craxi's own vision, not least because Craxi is described in a deprecatorily objectifying gaze as a 'little-known 'apparatchik' from Milan'. His Machiavellian self-defence, that of *necessary* realpolitik — is clearly not a perspective his obituarist shares: 'Throughout his career', he comments, 'Craxi was dogged by one fault that proved his undoing: while he was accomplished in the art of acquiring power, he was rather less distinguished in the exercise of it.'

Thus the conclusion is ultimately rebarbative:

The young Craxi may once have had visions of overhauling the Italian political system. In the end he merely came to embody the very worst of it.' (Andrew Gumbel, *The Independent*, 21 January 2000)

Not all 'negative' obits have subjects characterised as quite as amoral or as dedicated to quite such devastating realpolitik as Craxi, Modise and Nidal. Nevertheless, particularly in Eastern Europe, the imperatives of action found many politicians turning to a 'Janus-faced' nationalism. This left them guilty in the eyes of the West for failing to implement fundamental pro-market reform.[8] Many of the 2000–2001 obituaries, for example, feature Balkan politicians, and these shed new light on the wars in the former Yugoslavia.

One such politician was Stipe Suvar, a former sociology professor. His White Book, blacklisting dissident intellectuals, made him a: 'the Croatian Faust [...] who had sold his soul to engage in the wheeling and dealing associated with the Communist era politics of Federal Yugoslavia.' (*The Independent*, 1 July 2004). Suvar is condemned, on the one hand, for intellectual inflexibility: 'He was a classical Marxist who always thought in class terms and could not adjust to the national framework of politics that was established in Croatia…'

On the other hand, another Balkan obituary, for Franjo Tudjman (*The Guardian*, 13 December 1999) operates in almost reversed terms. In a language now *critical* of nationalism, this emphasises Tudjman's conversion from a tolerant Titoism to a more rabid, exclusivist political cult: its author's final judgement is a severe condemnation of his policies. This obituary recounts an underlying affinity with the extreme Right, despite the years of Titoism: Tudjman's active Holocaust denial, following on his exoneration of the Ustashe, his State-led persecutions, notably of Croatia's Serb minority, and his engagement in a nationalist war.

Everything is done within this narrative to distance the reader from him. It sets the scene with subtle forewarnings of his temperament — as in recounting Tudjman's over-investment in winning at tennis — and proceeds to a sombre, premonitory account of his childhood, in which both parents committed suicide. Details like the obituary writer's recollections of a dinner with Tudjman enhance these oppressive effects: heavy, cloying food had been all that was on offer. The author then introduces his organising motif — that of a leader suffering from a 'divided self'. Such a dualistic division serves a double purpose. It explains the contradictions within Tudjman himself; further, by figuratively making Tudjman stand for Yugoslavia, it signifies the schisms between fascists and Partisans, or, later, between Croatian separatists and Yugoslav federalists.

This unmitigatedly disapprobatory obituary has for its prime defence its subject's acknowledged anti-Semitism and racist anti-Serbianism. Thus, as an 'authoritarian leader', Tudjman is characterised finally as a 'nationalist zealot obsessed with his place in history'. Such zealotry brought him to purge the language of foreign elements and "Yugo-slavisms", to rename the currency, streets and football teams, to denounce the democratic opposition as traitors, even, finally, to preside over a creeping rehabilitation of the quisling Ustashe regime.

Note here that in Tudjman's obit, as in the much more numerous positive obits, the Second World War is always used as a touchstone to the moral standing of an individual. This is especially the case in *Le Monde* of this period, where the issue is when, rather than if, people joined the Resistance. Moreover, the Nazi period continues to have great resonance in *subsequent* historical conflicts, particularly affecting the Algerian War. One obit, for the radical, Georges Mattei, exemplifies this feature with great clarity. He is honoured for having spoken out, independently, to condemn the actions of the French Army in Algeria. In this conflict — 'the war without name' — he had testified that 'good little Frenchmen' were 'acting like Nazis' (*Le Monde*, 18 December 2000).

Yet, despite this international orthodoxy, a subject's pro-Nazi affini-ties can still be compatible, very occasionally, with a favourable portrayal. This is the case with Diana Mosley. The positive *Independent* obituary by an old family friend (3 August 2003) creates Diana as a Romantic muse. This extraordinary *appreciation* of a Nazi-sympathiser is justified by her virtuoso talents as a writer, the 'gift' of her beauty and — most important of all in the writer's eyes — her upper-class virtue of good taste. Diana Mosley appears as a seductive hostess within an aristocratic salon, whilst a carefully-posed photograph portrays her as a Madonna figure, with two Christ-like infants. Her second husband, Oswald Mosley, is described as a charismatic yet flawed figure. The flaw was his politics: 'Although I supported in a humble capacity Tom's [Oswald's] New Party' [states the author] 'I could not stand his brand of Fascism'. Yet this does not affect the allure of her remarriage to Mosley. This tone of admiration never falters, despite Diana's war-time imprisonment as a fascist.

The obituary situates Diana socially to some degree, but only so as to add lustre to her by distinguished connections. She was one of the six well-known Mitfords — the children of Lord and Lady Redesdale — all pos-sessing extensive cultural capital but little economic capital. They became part of a literary circle in rebellion against their 'unsophisticated, unintel-lectual' parents and the hunting/fishing aristocratic class fraction which they represented. Diana felt an affinity for the Bloomsbury group (see Wil-liams, 1980), and first married a poet, Bryan Guinness (Lord Moyne). She then gravitated to Mosley's company. After her imprisonment at the begin-ning of the War, she was later released into opulent exile in Vichy France, occupying a grand house, built for a Napoleonic Marshall, and free to resume her career as a literary critic for British little magazines.

In this obituary's romanticised portrayal the subjective view is given a privi-leged space. In Mosley she is said to have found her hero, 'the man of her dreams':

> Her cause became his cause and she subordinated everything, family and friends, to his dynamic interests. In 1936 she married him secretly, in Berlin, in the presence of Goebbels and Hitler.

Lest the reader is unclear about the 'dynamic interests' of Mosley, his personality is also depicted unambiguously positively: 'He seemed wise and farsighted. He had become a sort of sage.' Diana Mosley is portrayed in this obit as profoundly honourable, a sincerely 'compassion[ate] woman towards individuals' who believed to the end that Hitler could never have known about the camps.

This obituary aims, unusually, to *separate* the person from the political. Yet perhaps at no earlier period could such an aesthetic redemption of a member of the British Union Movement have been offered. Rarely has there been such a clear depiction of an 'aristocracy of culture' and, even more rarely, of the aura of its 'regressive modernist' wing (Carey 2002; Eagleton 1990: 369).

In sharp contrast, *The Herald* obit (14 August 2003) resists Diana Mosley's rehabilitation, stressing the collusion of some aristocrats with Nazism for political and ideological advantage. Its account of Diana's significance implicitly questions her formalist concerns with style and taste, adopting a moral-political perspective suspicious of her pursuit of money and of her self-blinding devices 'not to see' what the nature of social reality was. *The Herald* obituary, too, plays with the notion of Diana Mosley as a 'fairy-tale princess', but the cliché is rapidly deconstructed. Beautiful she might have been, but for all Mosley had been the 'wild man of British politics', it was Diana Mosley rather than her husband whom the intelligence services believed more dangerous.

It was argued in the last chapter that the political position of a newspaper can be linked to the genre of the obituary they carry. Thus *The Herald*'s Centre-Left position might have been *expected* to engender a negative obit for Diana Mosley, although, on this same basis, the relatively positive obituary in *The Independent* is much more unexpected. In general, there appears to be an obituary consensus that speaking *ill* of the dead, in the form of a critical obituary, is legitimate and necessary in the case of certain political figures. It is the just desert for those who arbitrarily dispense extra-legal violence, whether via State terrorism (Hafez al-Assad, President of Syria, *The Daily Telegraph*, 12 June 2000),[9] or via underground armies, like Abu Nidal or Arkan the Tiger, leader of the Serbian Unity Party (*The Guardian* 19 January 2000). It is the appropriate genre of obit for those who offered moral/political support to Nazism or for those who acted corruptly in public office. This is also — much more contentiously — the form of obituary for politicians who remained attached to a non-market based system of production when a market alternative became feasible.

Yet over and above these general 'rules', there is an area of political negotiation, depending not just on the acts of the deceased but on the positioning of the paper and *who gains access to authorship of an obituary.*[10] Thus socialists like Liber Seregni (Uruguay) or Tony Cliff (Britain) are honoured with positive obits in at least one paper, as is the Hamas leader, Aziz Rantisi. These relatively independent effects of authorship contribute inevitably to a certain perspectivism within the obituaries: variations in angle of vision and interpretation depending on one's situated point of view, as shown with Diana Mosley. Such disturbing perspectivism is particularly marked in the culture of late capitalist modernity.

IRONIC OBITUARIES

Obituaries on a recent death may seem like detached, almost bureaucratic, documents, impersonally recounting a c.v. of a recently-deceased leader, most notably in the objectivist style of the *New York Times.* But in the same measured tone of indirect reporting, they introduce on occasion unquestionably critical discourse. This change of gear invites a fresh reading of the whole obituary, which can then be seen as adopting an ironic perspective on the actor's entire life. One such obit was for Gunter Rexrodt, already mentioned, the former Economics Minister of the German Free Liberal Democrats, in their governing coalition with Herman Kohl's Christian Democrats. Of his period of office (1993–98), it is commented acerbically that unemployment statistics worsened, whilst of his lifelong habit of interlarding periods in private business (especially American banks) with public office we learn that

> He was criticised for his own heavy involvement with big business, leaving him little time to carry out his parliamentary and party responsibilities.

It is in this light that the obituary can be reread as a coded and subtly ironic analysis of a politician whose whole political agenda was geared to his narrow assessment of *instrumentally-rational* economic actions. Indeed, part of Rexrodt's own claim to distinction was his early espousal among politicians of an unregulated market. This account is careful to eschew any criticism of commercialism as such, but it does invite the analysis that those actively making money themselves are more likely to favour neoliberalism.

British political figures may occasionally reap the same ironic harvest but for different reasons. One such obituary, the second example, is for Viscount Whitelaw (*The Guardian*, 2 July 1999). This starts by recounting his distinction — his service as Deputy PM to Margaret Thatcher, the charm that converted those who had never met him into becoming supporters, the razor-sharp shrewdness — and more concretely — his farsighted prison-building programme. It recalls earlier jokes — from Mrs.

Thatcher's 'Every prime minister needs a Willie' to Whitelaw's own, non-sensical, body-swerve on Irish history ('I always think that it is entirely wrong to prejudge the past'). It outlines Whitelaw's background, identified as privileged: his education within an elite institution (Winchester), his service in the most patrician military corps, the Guards, and his landowner-ship. It culminates finally with the judgement that his 'thousands of acres in Lanarkshire' conferred on him an economic freedom that might have freed him for a truly autonomous statesmanlike role. Thus the ultimate irony is that Whitelaw's utter loyalty as a subordinate was also his most stigmatizing shame in the gaze of posterity. In the eyes of his obituarist, he had wasted his opportunities.

A last and curious example of the ironic political obit is Richard Gott's highly-coloured essay on Antonio Arguedas, a 'CIA agent, communist sympathiser, turncoat and opportunist' — a paradoxical figure, to say the least. Although failing to explain the structural constraints within which he operated, Gott's obituary reveals the politician as a supremely mercurial operator. Once a Left-wing lawyer and Bolivian politician, Arguedas became a 'turncoat' for the Right and, specifically, for the CIA, leading directly to internecine conflict, not least, the deaths of eighty miners. Yet bizarrely, despite this, Arguedas continued to keep a link with the Left, offering Castro, for example, Che Guevara's severed hands. Ultimately, having been released from a long prison sentence (for kidnapping children), Arguedas was himself killed, part of the 'collateral damage' from a home-made bomb he was carrying.

In general, even in its ironic subgenre, the obit form is judgemental and transparent — sometimes prosaically so. Yet with Arguedas's death, this author transforms the obituary into a tiny Dalshiel Hammett detective novel, a form in which reality is presented as ultimately unknowable.

TRAGIC OBITUARIES

Bourdieu has discussed a habitus that is unadapted to a transformed present as the 'Don Quixote' effect or 'hysteresis' (1968: 692, 1984: 142–43). Such a Don Quixote effect can possess tragic consequences. Amongst political actors are those who, having dispositions formed for a different set of social structures, are unfitted to the new circumstances. As the obits show, they are ultimately brought down by them.

This category of obituaries have elements of wider conceptions of tragic loss, but often depict their subject's fall with particular power. The difference between the tragic and the negative genre hinges on the crucial question of political responsibility. The tragic politician acts as he or she thinks best, in circumstances not of his own making and is brought down by them. The negative portrayal, in contrast, is written for one who might have chosen otherwise, but whose *own interests*, ideological as well as economic, blind him to the horrific consequences of his acts.

Very different types of political career can be destroyed by 'tragic' events — from a South African protagonist of apartheid, to an Establishment figure in Britain, like Lord Aldington, accused in court of knowingly sending Cossacks back, after the Second World War, to Stalinist gulags. The tragic obituary arises from an individual who is tacitly perceived as 'noble' but who encounters a predicament that destroys him. Each newspaper has its own conception of who is noble.

Thus Jaap Marais' (10 August 2000) adamant refusal to change from the old Vervoerd National Party positions represents such an anachronistic principle, even for the *Daily Telegraph*, but not an ignoble one. Recapitulating his Dutch ancestors' refusal as 'bitter enders' to accept the British victory in the Boer War, Marais' denial of the end of apartheid is recounted; it is described with all the pathos offered to the vanquished. Unlike other National Party politicians such as Coetsee (the former Justice Minister, who had died two weeks earlier), Marais had remained utterly faithful to his earlier position (on Coetsee, see *Daily Telegraph*, 31 July 2000). Indeed the two obituaries provide a hint as to why a lawyer like Coetsee possessed transferable skills useful in the new South Africa; Jaap Marais, on the other hand, living off the land like his Boer ancestors, had everything to fear from the ANC demanding back their property. Yet another detail helps to explain why his biography is tragic rather than that of an evil 'other' — a collaborationist with evil acts: this is the obituary writer's insistence on his cultivation. Marais was the man who had translated *Julius Caesar* into Afrikaans. Indeed, headlined a 'Diehard too Right Wing for National Party', the *Daily Telegraph's* obit mingles its tacit criticism ('Diehard' signifies 'flat-earther') with a respect for what it can still consider Vervoerdian 'ideals', in a manner unthinkable for other, more universalistic, anti-racist newspapers:

> a dour, unbending but oddly cultured figure, he clung tenaciously and with zeal to what he regarded as the Vervoerdian ideals, never wavering as the tide of South Africa's volatile politics left him and his dwindling group of followers isolated and derided.

One last type of tragic obituary is that for the political leader of Hamas, Dr. Abdel Aziz Rantisi, who was killed by the Israeli Defence Force (*The Independent*, 19 April 2004). This obituary — by Adel Darwish — suggests greatness, first, through its sustained presentation of Rantisi's own perspective and second, through its contention that Rantisi's early intransigence had shifted to a position labeled here as courageously 'moderate'— a ten-year truce with Israel if they withdrew from the Gaza strip and the Palestinian state was established in its place.

Here *the fall* has its origins in his family's dispossession of their house at the hands of Israeli terrorists when he was a baby: the most vivid scenes in the obit narrative are Rantisi's depiction of his former home, relayed to him through the collective memory of his family. But this is also a tragic obituary in the light of its protagonist's accomplishments and promising future — Rantisi, a brilliant student from the refugee camps, had been educated by the Muslim Brotherhood in Egypt and had become Chief Paediatrician in a Palestinian hospital. He was rerouted from his medical activities solely as a result of the conflict, and ended up exiled by Israel to a 'no man's land', 'the bare, snowy heights where the Israeli, Lebanese and Syrian borders meet'. The struggle finally swallowed him up, at only 57, leaving seven children fatherless. In this case as in others, the obituary prose gains some of its effects — consciously or not — from comparisons with earlier cultural models of a great and premature fall, like that of Othello.

DOMINANTS' MEMORY, POPULAR MEMORY, COUNTER-MEMORY

One grid which can usefully classify these obits separates out the plaited strands of 'national' collective memory to reveal the lives of very different kinds of subject. The *dominant class* are those who tend to have the normative obits which we have referred to above as the 'traditional positive' type. These upper-class figures, seen as naturally distinguished, have the capacity to have their own actions defined as public service. They thus usually hide from view the 'normal' privileges and the sectional interests which they champion. Firmly planted within the great political parties, they rarely have to articulate in detail their own symbolic visions and division.[11] However, in certain cases of 'fragmented habitus', the unusual conditions of the political field produce aberrations from the normative trajectory of politicians within the dominant power bloc, such as that of Hailsham (Bourdieu 2002a: 31–33).

One such is John Lindsay (*The Guardian*, 21 December 2000), a man who had been ideally socialised for the State Nobility — or even for the Presidency — with prep school, law at Yale and a job in a well placed firm of New York lawyers. His period in office as Mayor was the last period (1965–69) of a strongly unionised New York workforce: a workforce which created the American equivalent of the British 'winter of discontent' so that they might keep pace with escalating prices; at the same time one in five New York workers were on the dole. Lindsay was in effect confronted by 'urban crisis', with its roots in the flight of money to the outer suburbs. In the middle of this period he was re-elected, yet no longer by the 'silk stocking' Manhattan ward that had first supported him, but by Afro-Americans and Hispanics — a vivid indication of Bourdieu's Don Quixote effect or discordant habitus, and crystallised by his joining the

Democrats in place of his older paternalist Republicanism. Despite being described here as 'among the outstanding mayors of New York', Lindsay became in many respects an embattled figure — caught up in resisting corruption and enmeshed in religious and ethnic battles for positioning. At the end of his life, he was forced, humiliatingly, to turn to Beame, his successor as Mayor of New York, to ask him for pensionable and insured work. New York's subsequent bankruptcy as one facet of the contradictions of Keynesianism — and Lindsay's own broken health and wealth — testify to his involvement in a quite different and riskier battle than that of most of the dominants.[12]

POPULAR MEMORY AND COUNTER-MEMORY

Brief fragments of *popular memory* also appear and can be interpreted as part of a democratisation of the obituary. They can be linked to new principles of political vision of the world, lacking legitimation amongst all but the most unusual members of the ruling elite. However, although it was entirely unrepresented in the 1900 and 1948 obituaries, in the case of these obits such an underlying *general* vision and division was shared by many. These were obituaries for figures who had come via trade-union and/or local council to being MPs (Labour Party or Socialist Party, occasionally Communist Party, especially in *Le Monde*).

Now, although they often include research, many obits for these figures appear merely as a version of *Who's Who* for public presentation. However, the obits of certain MPs, such as those written by Tam Dalyell for *The Independent* (eg, Robert Parry, 11 March 2000, Edward Loyden, 30 April 2003, Maurice Miller, 1 November 2001, Richard Buchanan, 24 January 2003) are much more varied and innovative.[13] Indeed, these mark an important development of the political obituary. These mine published sources, such as Crossman's diaries, for information on the deceased, which supplement the writer's own personal memories. The obituary writer also draws on interviews with those who knew the subject well, quoted verbatim to give a more vivid flavour. Transcending the standard or coded euphemism, such obituaries develop new ways of broaching difficult issues, such as alcoholism. Underpinning all of these is affection, for the writing is only undertaken for those for whom the author feels an affinity. Interestingly, Dalyell's brief lives extend from a minority of Conservative MPs (for example, Sir Trevor Skeet, 18 August 2004, Bill Baker, 18 November 2000), to much larger group of Labour MPs: people who had possessed working-class origins, a recognizably autodidactic learning, and –alongside their regard for solidarity -an individually-shaped view of the world. They recall the subculture of Bourdieu's 'working-class reproduction' (1984: 32–34, 41–44, 251, 253; 1999, 6–8, 323–31), and make up a crucial component of obituary popular memory.

The obit has now begun to extend to those political actors whose social base has been most tenacious amongst the most misrepresented and stigmatised ethnic minorities, such as, Afro-Caribbeans. The Labour MP, Bernie Grant's obit — itself written by Tam Dalyell (*The Independent*, 10 April 2000) — is telling in that Grant might have become a comfortably-off higher professional (his father had been a Guianese headteacher and his mother a teacher, before becoming migrants to Britain). However, as a British student, he was denied an engineering scholarship to South Africa, its apartheid policies rendering him ineligible. He subsequently provided a voice for people subjected to poor treatment, sometimes at the hand of the police (which, in turn, made him appear in some quarters 'Number 1 public Ogre'). The obit's concern is to contradict that assumption, to offer a counter-memory and to provide a more profound rationale for its subject's actions. It argues that he was animated neither by resentment nor narrow ethnic exclusivism, but was:

> a champion not only of those who were black, but brown, yellow, white and all the colours of the proverbial rainbow.

This is another kind of fractured habitus, in which Grant's class position, in terms of a certain secure level of economic and cultural capital, is undermined by his social position in terms of ethnicity. This was an ethnicity which, in the 1960s, for all it brought social capital in the sense of social ties and potential favours — also brought social relations which were far from operating as capital: they offered only *dis*honoured names to drop and *dis*creditable, *noncreditworthy* connections (Bourdieu 1986b). As Stuart Hall remarks, such an experience of racism often *feels like* class subordination. In this context, an enduring — rather than temporary — radicalism developed in Bernie Grant, reinforced by memories of his family's slavery, his early religious hopes (Catholicism) and a later apprenticeship into socialism (Socialist Labour League).

Another obit offers an ideal-type of political counter-memory via the figure of Jacek Kuron, a critic of the Polish state socialist regime who was imprisoned three times and tortured. Kuron, one of the founding members of Solidarnosc in Poland, was also from working-class origins. He became a key figure both in the working-class and the intellectuals' resistance to Stalinism. Subsequent to the velvet revolution, with the return to capitalism, it was Kuron who tried to soften the economic shock therapy, consistently addressed the needs of the most disadvantaged with welfare measures. Indeed, one such welfare currency came to be christened with his own name: 'kuroniowkas'. The obituary defines him as unique as a politician in being able to speak for both workers and intellectuals (*The Independent*, 21 June 2004).

Exceptionally, there are memories too, of stigmatised minorities. These can only be defined as part of '*counter-memory*' since they remained distant from the mainstream of radicalism, in Britain associated with the Labour Party. Such counter-memories are at their most challenging when their authors inhabit the same universe as the subject depicted, as with the leader of the Socialist Workers' Party, Tony Cliff, whose obituary is written by a long-term member, Lindsey German (*The Independent*, 15 April 2000). Yet there are sometimes unexpected appearances of the obituaries that preserve counter-memory, although these may be restricted to those moments when an oppositional social movement is safely in decline. Thus we note, for example, that even the *Daily Telegraph* had an obituary for Bill Alexander (Assistant General Secretary of the Communist Party, 1965–69).

Strangely, in this obituary Alexander becomes a variant of the *Daily Telegraph* heroic form, the epic of the 'moustaches', those figures distinguished notably by their military service in the Second World War. On this occasion, Alexander and other fighting figures are recalled as members of the International Brigade, in their combat against Franco. Thus this obituary captures especially the physical ordeals of battle — as when in Spain the soldiers were so frozen that they had to warm their rifles under their armpits — just as, in *The Telegraph*'s and *The Times*' other obituaries, homage is paid frequently to the heroes of the war against Nazism. This obit ends climatically with Dolores Ibarruri's — La Pasionaria's — salute to Alexander and his fellow-Brigade members at their withdrawal in 1938. These words, repeated in eulogies for other International Brigade members, have themselves become etched into collective memory:

> You are history. You are legend. You are the heroic example of democracy's solidarity and universality. We shall not forget you, and when the olive tree of peace puts forth its leaves again, mingled with the laurels of the Spanish Republic's victory — come back!'

Alexander's own later conclusion — that *his* understanding of Marxism had had its day — was no doubt a consoling compensation for the papers' readers (*Daily Telegraph*, 20 July 2000).[14]

GENDER AND THE POLITICAL OBITUARY

Women begin to appear as independent political figures in this period, thus remembered in their own right: see, for example, the celebratory obituary for Maria Pintasilgo, the former Prime Minister of Portugal, 1979–80 (*The Independent*, 14 July 2004). She first became well-known in the public sphere as an engineer, subsequently making a name politically in the aftermath of the Portuguese Carnation Revolution. Having benefited from a middle-class background and considerable cultural capital, she initially gained the support of the Catholic Church — until her feminist intervention on the part of the Three Marias. Her premiership was marked by a major reorganisation of the Portuguese welfare state.

A similar pattern can be traced in Baroness Wootton,[15] Baroness Serota (*The Independent*, 22 October 2002) and Baroness Pike, the subject of the last obit being a Conservative neoliberal (*The Independent*, 16 January 2004). All the women politicians' obits show their entry into the public sphere premised on high cultural capital; in one case (Pike), with independent economic capital as an industrialist.

These women have been the pioneers, gaining important, even leading, national elected positions. Yet, occasionally, a different kind of representative figure appears in the obits page. Their voice has been important in the rank and file of significant movements but they themselves are often forgotten at death. However, these, too, have been distinguished figures, with unusual and memorable lives. Agnes Davy is a striking example (*The Herald*, 21 August 2003). She had been a revered primary headteacher for successive generations of children and a notable head of Ayr Council. The granddaughter of a miners' agent, she had a heritage similar to the Labour trade union backed MPs whose obits were written by Tam Dalyell. Another rare example is Dorothy Greenald, (*The Guardian*, 15 April 2002) a Yorkshire, millworker who left school at twelve years old, but who became, voraciously, self-educated. Following the radical tradition of her neighbourhood, she became the backbone of her local CND, a county councillor and a magistrate. Her friendship with E.P. Thompson, via his WEA evening classes, led to a circle of educated friends opening up for her and with this, work on the predecessors to *The New Left Review* (*The New Reasoner*, *The Universities and Left Review*).

Similarly, a number of papers carried an obituary for Mary Benson, a white South African exile. She had been visited by Mandela in her tiny London flat when he first toured as South African President, paying homage to a woman who herself suffered house arrest after he was imprisoned for treason, and who, 'more than anyone else kept his name and plight in the public eye' (*The Times*, 22 June 2000, the *New York Times*, 22 June 2000). Thus Benson, too, helped reshape the 'principles of vision and division' in South Africa. Indeed, by her death, an extraordinary transformation had occurred, since virtually 'no one' had ever supported apartheid![16] In brief, these latter two women were influential, both as exemplary figures in their own right but also through those whom they knew, as support personnel.

The obituary has now become extended to Third World women. Indeed, the lengthiest obit for a woman in this period is a figure — Mme Chiang Kai-Shek — associated with Chinese modernity, through her American university education, her family's wealth and her own autonomy. She also appears here as the traditional femme fatale and power behind the throne (*The Times*, 25 October 2003). Coming from a Methodist merchant family which encouraged the discipline conducive to riches, her father had acquired great wealth. Mme. Chiang is identified in this obituary with another form of fractured habitus, which produced a secularised, aristocratic, enjoyment of good taste made more uneasy by her family's earlier asceticism. Her 1930s political aim — the seduction of the American public to Chiang Kai-Shek's nationalism — was to some extent successful: indeed, she effectively won over American business figures and Theodore and Eleanor Roosevelt. But she was later rendered redundant, not just by the 1948 Maoist Revolution but, later, by Nixon's overtures to the Chinese in the 1970s. From then on 'it was far from clear that Chiang's survival was vital to US security interests.'

A distanced, ironic portrayal, Mme. Chiang's obit emphasises not just the contradictions already mentioned but also the inner kin drama which created her intensified focus on power in the traditional patrimonial mould. She is depicted as an exotic Eastern woman yet her sensuality is undermined by childlessness and veiled frigidity. The Revolution had brought down the Chiangs' nationalist regime yet Maoism was brought to power partly by her own stepson. Finally, she had gained Eleanor Roosevelt's respect, yet it was rapidly alienated by her imperiousness and excessive demand for luxury. Thus she is a figure of paradoxes — beautiful but too dangerously independent to be a Madonna figure; briefly powerful but later marginalised. This obit, far from glorifying, hints at Mme Chiang's long decline into powerless resentment.

I shall end with a very rare obituary and one which has quite different qualities to the traditional positive form for élites. The obituary itself appeared after a best-selling book and film had already appeared about its subject, under the melodramatic title of 'India's Bandit Queen'. Its protagonist was later killed by being gunned down outside her house in New Delhi, aged thirty-eight. She was Phoolan Devi, (*Guardian* 26 July 2001) whose trajectory appears at first typical of the most unprotected of India's uneducated workers. The daughter of lower-caste boatmen, married off when very young to a sadistic older man, she had fled her home only to be abducted and raped by an upper-caste criminal gang. Yet at this point, her moral career ceases to be that of the passive victim. Drawn no doubt by resentment, she practiced the only agency that appeared feasible, personal revenge via the death of her torturers. Killing twenty-two bandits, she turned herself in and was imprisoned for nine years. Prison turned out to be a turning-point, the apparently inhospitable scene of a rupture with her past. Yet a different kind of agency now opened out to her — as spokesperson for untouchables, the lower castes and for the rights of women. The electoral balance having been shifted by the quotas for untouchables, Phoolan Devi was elected a Socialist Party MP in Uttar Pradesh, where (despite a period out of office and a backlash from the radical Right BJP) she continued her unshakeable course. The obit's final words view her power now as paradoxically greater than during her life:

Phoolan Devi was the symbol of the struggle of the poorest of the poor and of the feminist crusade at its height.

CONCLUSION

Against the common-sense truism that the obituary is an accolade, in fact it has a variety of genres, or political/moral meanings. It may be as much a register of abysmal disgrace, like the judgement at Nuremburg, as a post-mortem accolade. At certain points the form can recuperate individuals socially who would once have been excluded, in this case by appealing to the distinction of their aesthetic taste (Diana Mosley). Indeed, in this respect, it is instructive that whereas the 1948 obits had only one critical obituary — that of the Nazi supporter, Unity Mitford, by this period another Nazi devotee, her sister Diana, receives, in at least one obituary, a singularly sympathetically assessment.

The obit stretches from the expression of disappointment at opportunities missed to the vindication of lives sustained trying to transform the opportunities of others, within a regional or a national political field. It recalls a minority who acted on fractured habituses (the very different cases of Bernie Grant or John Lindsay) as well as those — much more numerous — who have been members of the state nobility or Establishment and have acted in terms of the bureaucratic rationality of public service or a conservative raison d'Etat. These valedictory forms can be conceptualised as traditional positive, ironic, tragic and negative obituaries, but their exact content varies with each historical period.

In order to further register these contrasts — sociologically rooted in their volume and nature of capitals — we have introduced key typologies of collective memory. This has allowed us to shed light on the different types of political memory from the most hegemonic, which is that of the traditional leaders or the dominants, to popular memory and finally, to those who are remembered as part of counter-memory — a strand of outsiders, like Bill Alexander. By using these concepts, analysis of the obituaries as a new source of documents of life can illuminate how the stuff of individual biography can be integrated with history.

8 The writers' obituaries (1999–2006)

The obituaries given to those who have made a difference within literature are written by distinguished critics and writers, as well as by obit editors. Neither the editors nor the obituary writers are solely concerned with assessing the 'classics' of the future, although writers dying in their eighties have certainly had sufficient time for critical appraisal of their major works. Instead they delineate the entire literary field with all its intersecting relationships. A certain number of lesser writers appear, soon to become consigned only to historical interest. Thus the obituary editors' inclusion of a Nobel Prize winner such as Saul Bellow is undertaken with the full awareness that their pages also contain figures such as Barbara Cartland, who interests her obituary writers mainly for her popular success and confident transgression of literary rules. Cartland's prolific production of a formulaic series serves to make her a literary *monstre sacré* in the eyes of her obit authors: her caricatural writing heightens by reverse what literature should be like in our period.

Who appears in the obituaries' literary field and what position do they occupy in terms of aesthetic consecration? This section is mainly focussed on the 'components of the national culture', that is, the British field alone, ignoring obituaries of other nationalities. A short comparative analysis at the end of the section — on Bellow and on obituaries from national literatures in the global periphery — throws into relief the peculiarities of the British literary field in the early 2000s.

The obits clarify the main ideas of these writers, delineate the broader intellectual influences on them and establish their importance via their anticipated futures. This assessment of their distinction in literary terms is a key feature of the obituary. Further, they typically include details about the writers' backgrounds (social and economic capital) and education (cultural capital), allowing their social positions to be situated or objectivated. This illuminates the position-taking they adopted and stakes they possessed in the section of the literary field available to them. They were either closer to the expanded, heteronomous subfield or closer to the restricted, autonomous subfield, in which they were often guided by the 'Greenwich literary meridian' of Paris or London (see ch. 3; Casanova 2004: 87–88 and Bourdieu, 1993a, ch. 3). Occasionally, the authors' subjective assessment of their writing and their lives is contained within the obituaries, but this is exceptional. Consequently, the analysis below has had to be written largely without the material for a fuller, phenomenological dimension to writers' action, such as the impact of their own experience on their choice or language, genre or style. Nevertheless, it will become clear throughout that the transmission of hereditary privilege is still important in Britain in objectively determining who will acquire the honorific name of an author.

The deaths of the great priestly figures, at the most consecrated pole of the British literary field, provoke the longest obituaries and, by implication, the most vivid sense of social loss (see, in this period, Alan Pryce-Jones, Auberon Waugh, Anthony Powell, Peter Levi and Iris Murdoch). Predominantly male, these appointed representatives of Literature had developed powerful individual voices.[1] Their lives had been spent in circles with markedly interlocking memberships. Homogeneous in class terms, endowed with the good fortune of leisure and freed from material necessities, they emerged from Oxbridge and forged lifelong links with London literary groups or salons. Although more at home with the worldliness of Paris civilisation than the austere scholastic culture of the Kantian professorial ethos, these writers had only the most fleeting connections with a mass readership (Bourdieu 1984: 493–94). As writers, they supplemented their poetry or novels with journalism, yet at an early age they were distinguished by the dignity of their literary ambitions.

A second, less consecrated, group of British and Irish writers had been more buffeted by the conflicts and competitiveness of the contemporary literary field, swept as it is by Durkheim's 'cold winds of egoism' (Lukes 1973: 195). Although committed to living *for* literature and thus consumed by the 'illusio' of the literary 'game', these writers had nevertheless interrogated themselves constantly over whether they were making a mark. The obituaries for Gascoyne, Stuart, Brockway and Corke reveal periods of fertile production coupled with long intervals of writers' block or depression.

The British literary field can be contrasted with other national literary fields. In all these obituaries a great gulf can be detected between the literature of ideas and best-selling writing, even if very occasional works, such as Bellow's *Herzog*, managed to be both (see Bellow's obituary, *The Independent*, 6 April 2006). However, this contrast between the expanded and the restricted literary fields looms less large outside Western Europe and America, particularly for certain national-popular and post-colonial writers (Casanova 2004: 80–81). Such obituaries characterise writers who have a traditional 'prophetic' character, concerned with the fate of the whole nation and addressing themselves to a wide audience. They are thus sharply counterposed to the consecrated mandarin figures typified here by Pryce-Jones, Waugh, Powell and Levi, or at an earlier period, by Geoffrey Grigson or Robert Graves (Weber 1965: ch. 4; Bourdieu 1987a).[2]

THE BRITISH METROPOLITAN ELITE

The Magic of Consecration: Britain

In British obituaries, the most honoured authors are those who work in the most legitimate genres, such as poetry, or who have extended the novel to new subjects. They have typically held high offices such as the Oxford Professorship of Poetry or the Poet Laureateship. Appearing frequently in literary journals, they are published by the most prestigious publishers and receive reviews from well-placed professors.

Thus a magical aura of literary consecration radiated from the page-long obituaries in 2000, when Anthony Powell died, at age ninety-four. *The Guardian*'s obituary (30 March), by Norman Shrapnel, emphasises his 'huge achievement', selecting especially *The Dance to the Music of Time* series. This extended novel conveys the originality with which he came 'to have put such a stamp on his day and against the prevailing mood and style of the time'. Powell's work is then compared to currently highly-revered writers: Proust for example, or ancient Greek authors. This obit predicts that Powell will 'stand as essentially a comic writer in the English tradition — comic in the least uproarious way imaginable, reflective and often melancholic…':

> His vast army of characters, clubmen all (sic), pursue their power games through peace and war, marriage or divorce, in sickness and in health. War is for Powell-people an extension of ordinary life […] and rank is merely a crude token of what always existed in this elegantly-competitive world.'

The Guardian obituary also allows us to establish Powell's position *within the literary field* itself. Evelyn Waugh and the Sitwells were initial significant others. Further elective affinities are conveyed by his writing for *Punch* and the *Daily Telegraph*. An illuminating note reveals his occasional antipathies: the *Guardian* obituarist writes that, although he stayed in the same house as E.M. Forster, he chose never to meet him. From this, we can detect the careful distances that were preserved, especially from those whose Bloomsbury progressiveness might topple the stable social assumptions of his more aristocratic world.

Only brief hints of Powell's subjective vision as an author emerge in this obit. Powell is presented as seeking to construct a parallel literary universe, characterised by a unifying portrayal of the separate fields of modernity, notably the divergent occupations of the upper-middle class. He does so chiefly through his character, Widmerpool, who occupies positions in the Army, the City and the Labour Cabinet. Powell's underlying aesthetic and moral/political ideas emerge through these themes, notably his emphasis on experience being dominated by the role of chance, his celebration of wit, and his revulsion at sentiment.

A more analytical *Independent* obituary — by the writer, Hilary Spurling (29 March 2000) — is concerned with the link between Powell's choice of literary techniques and his conception of the social world. For this obituary, the achievement of the twelve-volume novel is 'formidable', and is again given the highest accolade, a comparison with Proust. The scale of this long view with its continuity of narrator allows unusual depth in the perception of the 'time' invoked, with its author's 'sense of flux and form', his need to find a temporal framework 'for a shapeless, rootless, fractured and perpetually shifting world'. It is this which establishes him as more than 'a satirist or comic lightweight':

> Few writers have explored the ravages of madness, despair, destruction, desolation and death more comprehensively than Powell.

This obituary sees his novels as organised around a Greek tragic vision, evident in the reigns of terror provoked by his characters' 'inner furies', the terrible fate of even the 'giddiest and most debonair' among them. His penetrating gaze undermines 'set views,' yet this way of seeing is a complex vision, linked to 'subtleties of feeling and psychological investigation'. This places him within a tradition of 'unprejudiced observers: from Lucretius to Shakespeare and Montaigne — a generous, capacious, 'humanistic' view'.

The Independent obituary provides similar resources to *The Guardian*'s for situating Powell. Referring obliquely only to his former 'school' — not explicitly to Eton as did *The Guardian* — it denotes his circle, which included the (ex-Etonians) Henry Green, Cyril Connolly, Graham Greene, as well as the Sitwells and Waugh. It categorises him as a modernist, fiercely critical of ideological uniformity and dandyism. Yet repelled by writing in a frivolous period, Powell turned away from the modern to centre on the Furies, who bring a train of destruction and war.

Powell's recourse to the Classical world is itself a recurrent element of modernity (Benjamin 1999: 15–16, Bourdieu 1993a: 58)). Yet a socioanalysis using elements of the obituary itself cannot fail to identify Powell's connections to the traditional gentry and, through that, to the 'persistence of the Ancien Regime' (Mayer 1981). Indeed, the 'elegantly competitive world' Powell evokes is his own upper-middle class milieu. His father, a Lieutenant-Colonel, and his grandfather were both 'distinguished soldiers': moreover, his life had been shaped through periodic uprootings for his father's postings. Yet his social position and disposition, as for many of the lesser aristocracy, was always undermined by inadequate financial means. Powell had indeed gone to Eton and Balliol (Oxford), but economic necessity meant that this was followed with mundane work in the anticommercial publishing company of Duckworth's, and as a scriptwriter in Hollywood.

Bourdieu and Moi have emphasised the distinctive turn to literature of producers with a declining trajectory, in the sense of a loss of family economic capital (Bourdieu 1996a: 84–87, Moi 1994: 35–42). In Powell's case this exists, too: indeed, the clash between his impoverished gentry world and the social relations of bourgeois modernity explains the underlying sources of his tragic vision better than his obituarists' accounts of his hostility to a frivolous period (see Goldmann 1964: 26, 34).

Two other literary figures command respect for their subjects' stature with lengthy obituaries, although their consecration is as critics rather than as producers. Alan Pryce-Jones — a novelist and biographer — is more distinguished for his gatekeeping role, as a reliable judge, selecting recipients for Ford Foundation grants, and particularly as Editor for over half a century, of the *Times Literary Supplement*. In Becker's terms, he provided professional rationales — reviews — for the creative actors within the literary art world (Becker 1982: 113); in Bourdieusian concepts, he procured influential access to the critical and journalistic fields for authors undergoing consecration (Bourdieu 1990b: 103; see also Brown 2001: 3–4, 29, 135). He introduced, in particular, the work of Musil to the British and parodied his British Council work as managing an 'import-export agency for modernists'. However, his obituary also stresses his enjoyment of luxury, not least his official Rolls-Royce (*The Independent*, 26 January 2000). It betrays traces of residual racism, describing his marriage — perhaps in his own words — into the 'international haute juiverie'.

If, on the one hand, Pryce-Jones represents the cosmopolitan aristocracy of culture, on the other hand there is the distinctively British iconoclast, Auberon Waugh. Waugh is vindicated as the ultimate 'Tory anarchist', an inveterate rebel against the Army, the academic Establishment and politicians, and 'one of the few great journalists of his generation'.[3] He is memorable, we learn, less for his novels, such as his early *The Foxglove Saga*, than for his editorship of *The Literary Review* or *Private Eye*. Now it might be conceded that *Private Eye* is hardly part of the *restricted* literary field, but it is still, nevertheless, remote from the expanded popular field of best-selling genre literature, as well as from middlebrow writing, like *Inspector Morse*. It stands on the margins of literary legitimacy.

The obituaries of Waugh depend, like their subject, on a biting irony. Both *The Guardian* and *The Independent* obits emphasise his love of excess — as when James Fergusson points out that he 'didn't mind playing the Fascist beast' (*The Independent*, 18 January 2001). They also distance themselves from this excess — as when he is recalled describing a wine as smelling of the 'dead chrysanthemums placed on the grave of a still-born West Indian baby' (*The Guardian*, 18 January 2001). Thus a paradoxical 'Tory anarchism' is revealed, not to be confused with any social transformation, since 'neither he nor any of the '[Private] Eye gang' were able 'to understand the basic principles of justice'. Waugh is interpreted as benignly elitist, a powerful satirist:

> His prolific journalism was pugnacious, opinionated, often outrageous, sometimes rabid and almost parodic in its displays of snobbishness and class hatred [yet] he could be very funny and agreeable company.

His obit suggests that he too suffered from the problems of being the son of a well-known father (see Bourdieu 1996a: 86–87 on the case of Flaubert).

Bourdieu argues that after 1850 there is a homology between position in the declining aristocracy and *modernist* production. This, of course, is far from meaning that writers from such origins were automatically consecrated, since they had to acquire the cultural capital to be acknowledged within the restricted field. Thus — no easy task — they had to use their intellectual resources to take up new positions within a competitive field already structured by the recognized literary movement of an older generation. In the case of these writers, three had roots in the aristocratic or gentrified elite: Powell, from the top Army hierarchy; Pryce-Jones, the son of a Colonel of the Guards and, on his mother's side, descended from Earl Grey ('Pryce-Jones came to terms with being born (sic) an aesthete in a military family'); Waugh, the son of the High Tory novelist, Evelyn Waugh, who had adopted a landowning existence with a country house and servants. In his son's case, the realisation that he was not the equal of his father as a writer undermined him: after the 'polite' reception of his novels, he deserted the genre in 1971.

Note that in this period, the most legitimate positions within the literary field presumed acquiring the ethos of a period at Oxbridge, although neither Waugh nor Pryce-Jones stayed to finish their degrees. Tellingly, none of these writers with the magic of full consecration had become recognised — as had Zola earlier — after a career of early success within the *commercial field*. On the contrary, they embodied and enacted in their whole way of being a high level of cultural capital, expressed more through a set of 'unaffected' manners and gestures rather than the product of a scholastic certification or training.

It is telling to compare these mandarin figures with Iris Murdoch, herself an Oxford Greats' graduate and a philosophy teacher. An obituary by another Oxford (Christchurch) academic, Peter Conradi, describes her as:

> One of the best and most influential writers of the twentieth century. Above all, she kept the traditional novel alive and in doing so, changed what it is capable of. [...]When asked by whom she was influenced, she was wont to reply she would have liked to have been influenced by Homer, Shakespeare, Tolstoy, Dostoevsky and Proust. This is not a modest list, and nor is her achievement a modest one. (*The Guardian*, 9 February 1999)

In particular, she is praised for exploring issues of desire in relation to morality, for her pioneering delineation of the Dionysian 1960s and for her sensitivity to men, and especially homosexual men, which few other women writers possess.

Iris Murdoch, too, was the child of the declining lesser aristocracy: her mother's family, part of the Protestant Ascendancy, had owned a large seventeenth-century estate. Although her father is described simply as a 'minor civil servant', who moved the family from Dublin to London, she was sent to a celebrated public school, Badminton. Unlike the other writers, Murdoch's migration and the fractured unity of a mixed Protestant-Catholic family gave her a profound understanding of being between two worlds (Bhabha 1994). Further, her position within literature has to be linked to a much deeper literary habitus: she was writing with a knowledge of a philosophical tradition in which issues relating to Scholasticism, Catholicism and Protestantism were still the subject of pressing debate. Moreover, in gender terms, her support from influential others, like John Bayley — who was himself to become the Oxford Warton Professor of English — and perhaps the absence of children, are telling details in accounting for the sustained volume and artistic stature of her novels and philosophical writing.

Less securely-consecrated writers

Obituaries also feature British writers who have been profoundly influenced by modernist movements, amongst whom we might cite James Brockway, the poet and translator (*The Guardian*, 2 January 2001), David Gascoyne (*The Times*, 28 November 2001) and Peter Redgrove (*The Independent*, 8 June 2003). The obituary of Redgrove, by his fellow-poet, Philip Hobsbaum, contained a persuasive call for his greater recognition. Unlike the first group, these figures have had no easy route to consecration. In sharp contrast to the more orthodox trajectories — even if wreathed in disappointed ambitions like an Auberon Waugh — their obituaries reveal a whole range of material and psychological obstacles, testaments to their crises of social worth and self-esteem. The obits also establish their importance — not just measured prosaically in various awards (like Redgrove's University Residencies and Brockway's Dutch knighthood) but in the reputation of other poets. Brockway's poetry in *The Poetry Review* is cited or Corke's early work praised:

> The poems were highly individual and very various, difficult to characterise: lyrical, satirical, elegiac, richly contrived, always well made. Several of them went into the anthologies of the time...' (Hilary Corke, *The Independent*, 11 October 2001)

David Gascoyne can serve as a typical figure in this respect (*The Times*, 28 November 2001). He was a poet and translator who eventually gained the title of Chevalier de l'Ordre des Arts et Lettres, but whose considerable distinction went unrecognised in Britain. Rather than going to university, Gascoyne had gone instead to the Regent St. Polytechnic, London. Here he began to forge ties with other writers. The anonymous obituarist links him to a loose group around Kathleen Raine. The inner circle — made up of George Barker and Dylan Thomas and Gascoyne — is described as having a different ethos — 'more spontaneity, a spirit completely free from cleverness' — than the better-known London group of the time. The latter were the more patrician, university-educated poets — Auden, Spender, MacNeice, Empson and Day Lewis— many of whom had also been to Eton.

In France, a collected edition of Gascoyne's poetry became a set text, while his translation of Breton's and Soupault's *Les Champs Magné-tiques* was particularly prized. Associating with the Surrealists in Paris, he wrote a very early and notable history of the movement for the editor of *New Masses*. However — the obituary adds 'like Chatterton' earlier — he became depressed and unable to write, still racked by a sense that his homosexuality had disappointed his father. His mental health returned after a conversion to Catholicism, but at the cost of formal excommunication from surrealism by Breton.

Gascoyne reveals the dilemmas and reverses of the avant-garde, especially for writers who lack sufficient certified cultural capital and whose family had a middle class economic position, without additional social connections. His father, a bank manager, was shocked by his bohemianism. Gascoyne was thus in a double bind: his life amongst the Surrealists allowed him to be openly gay but at the cost of wider marginalisation. When, in desperation, he chose greater social integration — Catholic conversion, even marriage — he was excluded from Surrealist circles and thus from the one group which he had prized artistically.

Perhaps unsurprisingly, in these obituaries, only two writers appear within the restricted literary field from the *subordinate classes*: Fred Archer, farmer, novelist and keeper of the Worcestershire collective memory and Ralph Bates. Bates, was one of the novelists of the Spanish Civil War (*The Olive Field*), and of the other major social conflicts of the interwar period.[4] Like Archer, Bates was a completely untrained writer, a working-class apprentice at the Swindon Railway works and student at the local Mechanics' Institute. He started writing about the failed revolt of the Asturian miners in 1934. An electrician and a fitter[5], he solved the material problems of subsistence by easily getting work as he wrote – more importantly, he had a network of support, spearheaded by the Communist Party's literary theorist, Ralph Fox. As a literary resource, his stake was that of the 'proletarian novel' which was aimed partly at demystifying capitalist social structures, partly at transforming its middle-class novel inheritance (Bourdieu 1993b:

41, Williams 1980). In the hands of Bates, as well as other untrained writers, like Robert Tressell, Patrick MacGill and Grassic Gibbon, this form offered a new set of narrative concerns and characters.

Indeed, Bates' novels about Spain earned him the title 'El Fantastico' and another kind of politically-based literary recognition, that of cultural commissar. He later left the Communist Party, becoming, a journalist for the American *The Nation*, then a Professor of English Literature at New York University. Nevertheless, Bates' trajectory, outlined in this obituary, recalls the very different context of the London Communist Party. The Communist Party was similarly experienced as a 'moral aristocracy' (Samuel 2006), not infrequently acting, it might be added, as an *escalator upwards* for its self-educated activists.

Within the restricted literary field, Francis Stuart, a British citizen by birth, has an unprecedentedly hostile obituary, offering a key counter-example to the celebratory form (*The Independent*, 3 February 2000). The adverse critical assessment is all the more remarkable in that such judgements for writers are much rarer than for politicians. His damaged reputation hinges not on his novels — admired for their psychological depth — but on his active collusion with Nazism. The negative evaluation in this case bears all the more weight in that its author is W.J. McCormack, a well-known scholar of the colonial Protestant Ascendancy in Ireland and in an unparalleled position to understand Stuart's place in both British/Irish relations and the Celtic Renaissance avant-garde. Part of a circle made up of Yeats, Liam O'Flaherty and Samuel Beckett, Stuart wrote fiction (*Women and God* 1931), *Pigeon Irish*, *The Coloured Dome* (both 1932), *Try the Sky* 1933). Invited to Germany to give readings, he stayed throughout the Second World War, writing scripts for German broadcasts. These praised both Hitler and Irish neutrality: Stuart's depth of complicity with Nazism is evident in his arrangements to send an SS German spy to Ireland.

McCormack's judgement of Stuart's work is scrupulously even-handed, noting Stuart's capacity, at his best, for 'disturbing, unrivalled novels of physical deprivation and religious intensity' but also noting his periods of artistic decline. Stuart ended his life converted to the Ulster Loyalists, arguably, from the point of view of artists, the ultimate outsider group. Yet the burning issue of this obituary is not this, but its subject's collaboration with Nazism. Stuart, his obituarist concludes:

> morally sleptwalked through the Reich', a feat made much easier since '[h]e was no democrat.

The obituarist is clear as to precisely what is at stake in Stuart's re-evaluation — it is also the re-evaluation of *Yeats'* flirtation with the Irish Fascist Blueshirts and the implication this might have for the Irish canon. The obituary-writer makes a crucial distinction between Yeats and Stuart. That is, he differentiates between the various tendencies within 'archaic avant-garde' of the Irish Celtic Renaissance and their relation to action (Eagleton 1995: 273, 299):

> As Yeats' extreme politics developed through an *arcane symbolism*, Stuart's complementary role became *active and direct*. He was to be conscripted as Yeat's posthumous anti-self [...] he worked at much of what his mentor had preached — the hard, yet bogus, aristocratic credo in an age of mass-murder and ideological hatred. At 37, he was either culpably ignorant of what had happened in Germany, or deliberately hostile to humane reasoning — or both (my italics).

This obituary judgement saves Yeats. In doing so, it effectively undermines the reader's belief in Stuart as a subject worthy of respect.

BRITISH POPULAR WRITERS — THE
EXPANDED LITERARY FIELD

The relationship between 'high and low' has changed in recent years. First, despite the exceptional poets' obituaries by Philip Hobsbaum, there has been a decline in close criticism of the type that appeared even as late as 1985 in *The Times*, at the death of Geoffrey Grigson.[6] In particular, there is an absence of the condensed yet rigorous analysis of structure and figurative language that was found in earlier obituaries.

Second, there is the parallel emergence in the twenty-first century of obits of writers in popular genres, writers who lack artistic recognition but who have been notoriously prolific. Here the obituaries portray authors who view their own writing as less prestigious than 'Literature', but as answering other needs, both for narrative pleasure and psychological defence (Forgacs and Nowell-Smith 1985: 349, Bourdieu 1984: 32–49). Such authors have divergent social origins. Whilst most of them come from the subordinate classes, the minority that does come from the dominant class typically lacks the highly-prestigious education that is possessed by the distinguished writers of the restricted field.

Third, a new discourse about successful writing has eroded the earlier distinction between 'exchange-value' and 'literary use-value'. Thus it is assumed by obit writers that certain *best-selling/ middlebrow writers have themselves contributed to the literary 'canon'*. We shall explore symptomatically the obituaries of two writers in this category, Patrick O'Brien and Winston Graham, but there are grounds for arguing that there is a contemporary clash over value and that the literary obituaries carry the traces with them of such a crisis (Guillory 1993).

It is clear, nevertheless, that the tone of obituary given in the 2000s to a popular writer such as Barbara Cartland is very different from that for, say, Iris Murdoch, Nathalie Sarraute or Peter Redgrove. When a figure like Cartland appears her obituary is interlarded with irony. There is no attempt to give such novels any literary value in aesthetic terms, least of all to claim that she is a producer of any singular texts:

> Her love stories, usually dictated in one sentence paragraphs, were — though stereotyped — brisk, researched with historical fervour and seldom cloying. Their popularity was genuine and long. (*The Guardian*, 22 May 2000)

The obits for Cartland seek to explain what interests readers might satisfy by reading her novels. In effect, the obituary writers have had to explore some of the sociological conditions for reception of the traditional romance, especially amongst women readers who have accommodated to patriarchal institutions, a readership now more often found in developing countries, or in the developed world, amongst the undereducated or very old (see Fowler 1991: 99). They also had to unravel the mystery as to how, as the author of more than six hundered 'big-selling romantic novels [and other works]', Cartland could reach such Stakhanovite heights of conspicuous production. In effect, in order to understand her 'deviant' action of prioritising quantity over quality, the obituaries all reinforced the image of Cartland as a *literary* pariah.

In her youth, Cartland had been deeply affected by the impact of a downturn in trade. The family collective memory later narrated that her grandfather, an industrialist in a Midlands brass factory, had blown his brains out after a bad investment; her mother had been impoverished by her father's death in the First World War. Threaded through these family insecurities was another clash which could be read as between agrarian capitalism and industrial capitalism. Her mother's family, of minor gentry, had been unable to agree upon a marriage settlement for their daughter with a factory-owner's son. Thus the brittleness of the twenties — described in her autobiography — hid the painful necessities of survival. This affected especially the female members of a family who had been doubly marginalised: lacking both solid material affluence and the gentry's secure social capital.

It was this marginality that drew her first to gossip column journalism and then after divorce, remarriage and widowhood, to novel writing. She started to write in what she jokingly called her 'factory' — novels produced at the rate of 10,000 words a day — dedicating herself and her assistants to a virtuoso work ethic. Her subjective vision revolved around a tough personal independence, but also to an absorption in the collective fantasies of aristocracy and monarchy.

Cartland's obituaries remain distanced yet dutifully supply a preliminary phenomenological understanding of her experience. Their authors present her as outrageously exaggerated: a comic, lonely and somewhat ridiculous figure. At the end of one, in a disenchanting act of subversion, even the Cartland social order of noble paternalism is challenged: the obituarist reveals that she did not even treat her servants well. She called all her maids by the same name, sometimes even slapping them. In other words, Cartland's death provided an engaging target for ironic obituarists.

However, not every best-selling writer is disadvantageously contrasted with literary writers. A much more celebratory tone emerges in the obituary for Patrick O'Brian (*The Independent*, 8 January 2000), a writer who had turned away from poorly-paid literary novels and biographies to a long series of Napoleonic War 'seafaring novels'. These are characterised by a 'recondite naval lingo' and 'authentic' details gathered from a reading of early nineteenth century editions of *The Times*. The readerly pleasures of O'Brian's recycled Jane Austen are emphasised, including his resort to well-tried literary conventions. In this obituary O'Brian's subjective experience of time is stressed: his writing, the readers are told, fed his passion for the old: he liked only 'old books, old wine, old friends, old houses...'. This obituary conceals a traditional repudiation of the modernist aesthetic, based on newness.

Crucially, O'Brian, like Cartland, had acquired little in the way of formal education: a term at the Sorbonne only. He nevertheless still benefited from considerable social capital: his father had been a Hampstead doctor, whilst he had links through marriage with the Russian, Count Tolstoy. His status is apparent in his permanently-reserved seat at Brooks', the London club. Such social power was coupled with the material ease of a house and smallholding at Collioure, in France. Yet such property and status relations — which might have drawn a better-educated writer to the restricted field (Baudelaire, Flaubert) — led in his case to rejection of the inconvenient experimental ethic. Illuminatingly, O'Brian ceased to recycle the consecrated texts into his own work at precisely that point, mid-way through the nineteenth century, at which writers developed the features of an autonomous modernism. O'Brian represents a typical instance of one of the three principles of legitimacy noted by Bourdieu — providing neither art for artists, nor art for an industrial or mass readership, he offered instead an art for a dominant class readership (Bourdieu 1993a: 51)

Unexpectedly, Winston Graham, another best-selling writer within the expanded field, is himself described as *canonised*:

> His creation of Ross Poldark, Cornish mineowner and saturnine adventurer, is what is likely to keep him in the literary canon (*The Guardian*, 14 July 2003).

With this obituary, we move into a new epoch, beyond the great cultural divide of High and Low, where the measure of reputation is that offered by significant fellow-writers. Obituary success is now defined in terms of wider public acclaim — an OBE, membership of the Royal Society of Literature, readers' affections and the sheer volume of novels sold: in Cornwall church services had to be retimed so as not to clash with the televising of his novels. Since the obit emphasises the link between the author and popular memory, it focuses on such instances of popularity: its writer is unaware that the legitimacy acquired through literary canonisation requires the recognition of the works by other artists (Bourdieu 1993a: 51, 69).

This new expanded canon — as defined by the obituary writers — is evident, too, in relation to the authors of genre fiction: horror literature, spy novels and science fiction. Writers once classified as unconsecrated, now find these genres suddenly no longer constitute a barrier to the production of 'brilliant' works: 'masterpieces'. Of course, as with Cartland, the more spectacularly vivid pulp writing is included purely for its exoticism as a trade. Indeed, the obit for Alan Boon stresses his view that Mills and Boon is 'escapism …We really ought to be subsidised by the NHS. We're much more effective than Valium.' (*Daily Telegraph*, 10 August 2000).

The obits clearly marginalise these formulaic extremes, yet the key change is that the obituary writers increasingly *equate commercial success with literary recognition*. In doing so, they wipe out the historical suspicion of the market as an *artistic* judgement of worth from Romanticism onwards, even if 'some [economic] successes may be recognised, at least in some sectors of the field, as genuine art'[7] (Bourdieu 1993a: 39). This key ambiguity around the idea of literary recognition is apparent in the obit for R.Chetwyn-Hayes:

> He was never able to break into the American market which would have ensured a modicum of *global recognition*, and more to the point, three or four times the amount of money he usually got from his British publishers. (*The Independent*, 31 March 2001; my italics)

Much the same can be said of the obituaries for M.M. Kaye, *The Times* (31 January 2004), Sheila Holland (the Mills and Boon writer, Charlotte Lamb: *The Times*, 12 October 2000) and Michael Elder (*The Independent* 16 August 2004), not to mention American writers such as Emil Petaja, (*The Independent* 23 August 2000) and Walter Wager (*The Independent* 20 July 2004). In brief, the writers' obituaries now begin to register popular taste, although arguably not popular memory, at least in the case of Graham and Cartland. Moreover, this is popular taste refracted through 'the power of the international publishing giants' (Casanova 2004: 169)

The literary periphery

In ending this chapter, I want to turn fleetingly from the obituaries in the British literary field to the obituaries of writers less well-known in the West, from the former East Europe, the Middle East and the post-colonial countries of Africa. In both the postcolonial setting and in Eastern Europe, a *prophetic type* of poet or novelist has been recurrent[8] (cf Lukács 1978; Casanova 2004). The writer in these areas, remote from the great or universal literary capitals — London, Paris, New York — continues to engage as a dissenter tied actively to social movements; he or she has had an impact on influential figures amongst the subordinate classes, and through them, on popular readers. Unlike those championed by a certain strand of post-colonial theory, however, such writers have not celebrated hybridity, rootlessness or a kind of cultural bricolage for its own sake (Bhabha 1994; Fisher 1995), nor do they valorise an 'insider-outsider' position as an epistemologically-privileged view[9] (Smith 2004). They should therefore be distinguished from those cultural producers who have migrated to the capitalist metropolises and stay there, retaining only a distanced, imaginary relation to their homeland (Spivak 1999).

They are however identified particularly with the defence of 'national-popular' concerns, renewed through decolonization movements, as Casanova has so brilliantly argued (2004: 80–81; 225–32). In particular, a strand of authors featured in these obituaries have been concerned to differentiate their writing from the conventions of the cultural 'universalism' characteristic of literary capitals like London (or Paris), cities which are also, for some writers, first known as imperial powers. Hence unlike, say, Naipaul, they rejected the alternative path of assimilation (Casanova 2004: 47–48, 205–12).

One such writer, still active, is Ngugi, who, in prison, turned away from the linguistic alienation of English in order to forge a new, Gikuyu novel, using this new literary space to communicate with his fellow-Kenyans (Ngugi 1986: 17, Ngugi 2002: xii, Casanova 2004: 275–76). Another was Holshang Golshiri (*The Guardian*, 20 June 2000, *The Independent*, 7 June 2000, *Le Monde*, 8 June 2000), an Iranian writer who, in his later years, was forced to use only a pseudonym, due to his dangerously-exposed position within Iran itself. His obituary marks the death of a writer who 'produced some of the finest novels and short stories in recent Iranian history'. Golshiri possessed great literary range — his first novel was concerned with the small-town lives of office-workers, his second, using Beckettian modernist devices, centred on the decline of the Iranian aristocracy (*The Prince*). Golshiri is particularly praised for his foresight: he characterised the nature of theocratic authoritarianism in his work, *The Shepherd and the Lost Sheep*, published a year before the 1979 Khomeini-led Revolution.

It was Golshiri who, having been criticised by both the Shah's and the Khomeini regimes, set up the Independent Writers' Association, an act which echoes with Zola's attack on the anti-Semitic persecutors of Dreyfus, in his 'J'Accuse!' After Khomeini's famous 'breaking of the pens' speech, which indicted those writers who did not express Islamic values, his fiction was banned. Indeed, it became forbidden even to write about the relations of men and women in novels. Golshiri's last novels were therefore published abroad and his formal literary recognition was non-Iranian, as in the case of his Remarque Prize.

This obituary is clearly at variance with the writers' careers of the West, none of whom have in this period experienced persecution. In these post-mortem assessments, the writers from the globally impoverished regions are shown, by necessity, to be more conspicuously and more often engaged in struggling towards political truths within their literary writing. They have been exiled, return, continue to criticise and are exiled or censored once more.

The same discomfort toward authorities and popularity with a mass readership as in the writing and action of Golshiri can be found in numerous other obituaries, including his fellow-Iranian Shamlou (*The Times*, 3 August 2000). In particular, the Palestinian poet, Fadwa Tuqan (*The Times*, 3 January 2004), was honoured by receiving the Palestinian Prize for Literature in 1996. Her poetry — secularist and feminist — made her, in the eyes of her obituarist, the spiritual mother of exiled and oppressed Palestinians. She developed, not unlike Golshiri, a capacity to discard the traditional 'forms of Arabic poetry which favoured rhetoric and dramatic phrases' for a modern poetry of solace

> assuaging the isolation of those exiled from their homeland. Tuqan articulated a national consciousness, celebrating a land and a people who felt they were denied liberty.

Once again, too, there is the crossing of restricted and expanded fields — in Tuqan's case 'phrases were taken up by dispossessed Palestinians'.

Not dissimilar types of writer can be found in China (Wang Ruowang, *The Guardian*, 9 January 2002)), Morocco (Mohamed Choukri, *The Independent*, 19 November 2003), Israel (Yehuda Amichai, *Le Monde*, 26 September 2000) and in the Ivory Coast (Ahmadou Karouma, *The Independent* 16 December 2003). Karouma, 'the African Voltaire' — forced into exile after jail — sold 100,000 copies of one of his books alone, yet gained also an array of well-regarded literary prizes.

In other words, we should not doubt that the conditions for 'literary prophecy' also exist, in which the individual writer can see herself as the spokesperson for the collectively disenfranchised and impoverished masses. Like other charismatic leaders, they are attributed the right to be such spokespersons only as long as they express the interests of the subordinate classes (Bourdieu, 1987a). No doubt writers such as Golshiri, Shamlou, Tuqan and the others suffered from the many inconsistencies — and interests — typical of membership of the dominated fraction of the dominant class, of which Bourdieu reminds us[10] (1996a: 251) Yet it would also be wrong to deny the social reality of prophetic and dissident writers in the contemporary obituaries, a current that is at variance with aspects of the Baudelairean bohemian, the *poète maudite*. For at least some of their writings are accessible to those rural and urban lower class agents who have gone without to acquire literacy, the precious key to understanding their own culture and changing their own social order.

This section of obits has shown that in the British literary field, the most consecrated writers have been London-oriented and nearest to the mandarin/academic pole. These have combined cultural capital with their families' considerable social capital and material ease. The obituaries also reveal the fraught recognition, by middle age, of poets, novelists and autobiographers caught up in a generational dialectic of recognised versus rupturing modernisms.[11] A smaller number of consecrated women writers also appears, like Dame Iris Murdoch, already legitimated in terms of academic cultural capital: prolific producers who have emerged from the most well-endowed literary spaces. Yet with the exception of Fred Archer and Ralph Bates, none of these writers in this sample are from the subordinate classes.

Without wanting to apply a reductive materialism, the obituary and Nobel Prize for Saul Bellow — beyond Britain — might then make him appear as a 'miraculous survivor', in Bourdieu's terms (*The Independent*, 6 April 2006). For his parents were 'poor immigrants', first to Canada then Chicago. Yet the aberration is not as striking as it initially appears. Bellow's nuclear family might have been penniless, but they came from a cultivated merchant class in Russia, whose cultural capital was evident from the rabbis in his extended family (Atlas 2000: 6–7). Moreover, his parents paid for a university education that was to give their son his grasp of literature and anthropological techniques. Like Henry Roth in New York, Bellow then applied these to his native, 'unliterary' Chicago (Atlas 2000: 48).

Finally, it has been argued that a different type of *prophetic* writer has emerged in the uneven development of the global periphery. The African and Middle Eastern writers described here have sometimes been empowered by the sudden and unexpected access of the dispossessed social strata to universities, at times devoid of any formal education, as in the case of Golshiri, whose personal cultural ties with his partner and wider literary circle compensated for his lack of certified cultural capital. Where they confront corrupt, authoritarian and racist ruling-classes and governments, the obituaries delineate the writers breaking into different literary groups. Amongst them are discovered certain authors who acquired a readership wider than in the West and yet who retained their innovativeness in literary terms.[12] A further analysis of such writers, through obituaries and other means, is necessary to reveal what are the determinants of each group.

9 The artists' obituaries (1999–2006)

If the visual is the dominant sense in modernity, as many have claimed, which ways of seeing enter collective memory in this period? This chapter explores the visual arts in today's newspaper obituaries,[1] emphasizing the greater variety of forms and the greater number of national and foreign artists represented than ever before. The range of obituaries now includes not just Academicians and modernists, but the iconic artistic producers of everyday life, such as William Hanna and Charles Schultz. Thus, the first point is that work in the terrain of the technologically-based arts, such as the animated comic strip, is no longer a barrier to the award of an obituary. Second, the obituaries now offer insights into the *conflicts* over the nature of art: mining them carefully sheds light on cultural producers' interests in their field: material as well as artistic (Bourdieu 1993a: 79). Third, a qualitative analysis of the obituaries reveals not only that different amounts of cultural and economic capital operate as the entry rate for membership and reputation in different parts of the field, more surprisingly, such variations occur even within the expanded field itself. Fewer capitals, it appears, are needed for comic strip cartoons than for political cartoons. Finally, just as the institution of art serves to incorporate once-transgressive artists in a dialectic of social ageing, so too, do the obits reflect this process (Poggioli 1968). At present, even 'outsider artists' — who blithely disregarded critics and curators — can be represented in the obits as artists and are significant to us also as a strand of counter-memory. Yet, at the outer limits, there are still political affiliations — especially Nazism — that remain obstacles to full artistic acceptance; artistic identities, spoiled in this way, cannot be renegotiated for a celebratory obituary.

I begin by situating the artistic obits in terms of nation and migration. The chapter then explores how contemporary distinction is evaluated for significant cultural producers, moving from the restricted to the expanded (commercial) fields, with photography as a newly-canonised art. In each obit we show how the artist's achievements are assessed, how each figure might be objectified sociologically, using the information about his trajectory supplied in the obit itself, and finally how the artist's subjective perspective (hopes, tensions etc.) might be understood. Certain major types of artist can be isolated, which illustrate in this period the variety of routes to consecration. This is demonstrated firstly for the restricted field, through figures selected to typify such different avenues, now all seen as legitimate: Franta Belsky (Academic), Terry Frost (abstract expressionist), Josef Herman (also modernist, but an expressionist), and Ken Kiff, who combined elements of abstraction with figuration.

Reading the obituaries reveals a profound relationship between the artists' degree of symbolic esteem and their national origin (Casanova 2004). This finding further extends the paradox of the contemporary art market, noted by many observers: that while there has been an internationalization of the artistic field in contemporary societies, the market is still very much more receptive to artists from the West than from Latin America or Asia (see, on this, the meticulous empirical work by Moulin 1992: 24–25, 48). More precisely, taking the British newspaper obituaries, the older artforms, which are considered the most noble, feature mainly British or naturalised British artists.[2] In contrast, in the popular or 'minor' arts, a large and diverse group of cultural producers from Europe and America appear, including Carl Barks, William Hanna, Darrow Whitney and William Hurtz, as well as the photographers Herb Ritts, Francesco Scavullo, Gisèle Freund, Denise Colomb, Roger Pic and Jean-Philippe Charbonnier. Indeed, specific national symbolic traditions can be detected running through the obituaries: news photography is linked to the French, cartoons or film animation to the Americans.

Yet, in contrast with the literary field, there are virtually no obituaries for visual artists from the global South. There are, however, a considerable number of migrant artists, whether forced into exile or voluntarily moving; indeed 35 per cent of all the artists in the systematic sample were migrant in some way. Although a feature of modernity right from the start, artistic 'nomadism' has evidently gained more ground recently, and became a notable feature of the period around the Second World War.

The obituaries disclose a large group of highly-esteemed artists who were forced to migrate — or whose parents were forced to move — most notably in the period of the rise of Fascism. To these are added other artists who have been cross-nationally mobile for voluntary economic or professional reasons. Taking only the recent obituaries of sculptors, painters or theatre designers gathered for qualitative analysis, we find that a significant group (Nicholas Georgiadis, Josef Herman, Alfred Cohen, Witold Kawalec, George Rickey, Franta Belsky, and Felix de Weldon) had all been long-term migrants to Britain, whilst Yann Goulet had moved from Brittany to exile in Ireland. In addition, the photographers, Francesco Scavullo, Gisèle Freund and Harry Watson, had all been migrant within Europe or to America[3].These obituaries indicate that the influence of migrant artists on the post-World War II art world may well have been unprecedented, and needs much greater analysis than has so far been given it.

MAPPING THE RESTRICTED FIELD

The language of artistic 'genius' and divine inspiration now appears to have lost its force (despite the obituaries of Felix de Weldon (*The Guardian*, 20 June 2003) and William Boyd Harte (*The Daily Telegraph*, 18 December 2003), which *do* still use this discourse). The ideology of individual 'gifts', however, is still important, even though the formation of modernist producers is now discussed in terms of their respective artistic groups. Talents still continue to be perceived in the contemporary obits as purely an individual attribute: these artists are treated as though segregated from the collective historical conquests of avant-gardes earlier. In line with this, the cooperative aspects of artistic production remain neglected and the focus is uniquely on singularity, rather than on the acquisition of artisanal, craft skills (Bourdieu 1993a: 258–61, Becker 1982, Harrington 2004).

Beyond the charismatic ideology of the artist that underpins so many obits, there is an increasing fragmentation and multiplicity of the types of artist represented: Academic artists rub shoulders with modernists, figurative with abstract expressionists. Leaning on Bourdieu and art historians, the obits can be best explored qualitatively in terms of these historic types.

In the sixteenth to eighteenth centuries, the system established in Academies, on a national basis, meant a professional regulation of the arts represented within each including authorizing training. Each national academy operated as a centre for artistic commissioning, and for selecting and judging works within the annual Academic exhibitions (Blunt 1981). (This evaluation of art on a competitive basis by peers was a crucial early prefiguring of modernity.) Some important medieval arts, such as pottery, had been excluded altogether in the Academic structures, on the grounds that they were utilitarian and therefore not fine arts (Heinich 1987). By the mid-nineteenth century, the first rupture with Academic art had already been made by means of the heroic modern movements. Yet even today, the *contest* between the Academic eye and the modernist 'fresh eye' still remains evident in the artists' obituaries[4] (Bourdieu 1993a: 238–53), as does the counter-struggle to regain legitimate status in the art potters' obits.

In Britain, the Academy had a less formative impact on art than in other European societies and the struggles around modernism were correspondingly less intense (Bourdieu and Dixon 1995). Even here, however, Academic artists have been linked progressively through the last century to the celebration of order. It is hardly surprising that Academic artists achieved at least a hallowed niche in these contemporary obituaries.

The sculptor, Franta Belsky, most clearly embodied the orthodox academic tradition of monumental public art (*The Guardian*, 6 June 2000). Belsky died adorned in medals and prizes, including the Czech gold medal of merit. Yet it is a paradox (although an expected outcome of modernism) that it should have been an *adopted* British artist, originally from

Czechoslovakia, who completed the public sculptural works in Britain most clearly dedicated both to the national memory of the War and to the country's traditional leadership. 'Born in Brno, Czechoslovakia', argues his obit, 'Belsky is claimed to have become by his death a major force in British sculpture', indeed he repaid his new homeland with 'sculptural busts representing the Queen, four generations of Royalty, Lord Mountbatten, Winston Churchill (twice), Admiral Cunningham'. *The Guardian* obituary does not substantially undermine the importance of this project, bar a ritualistic challenge to the elite's self-image. Belsky's monumental casts, it glosses, are of the 'great and *occasionally* good of the nation' (my italics). Despite this minor irreverence, Belsky is celebrated as the artist who made the most memorable sculptures of Winston Churchill, those that most capture 'the spirit of wartime Britain'.

Yet this obituary reveals that within the illusio (commitment) to the professionalism of Academic art, there is still room for intense conflicts over *who should be selected* for Royal Academy exhibitions. Belsky, despite interventions on his behalf by his patron, the Queen, had sometimes been passed over. The subjective view of the artist is quoted to show that such relegation had served to 'slow down his progress'. Indeed, everything in this *Guardian* obituary suggests that Belsky had become too academic even for the Academy. Belsky emerges from it as an artist who took on the prized and orthodox social role of honouring temporal power. Moreover, although artists' interests are usually decorously hidden behind disinterestedness, an objectifying reading (of his house in Oxfordshire and holidays spent skiing) reveals that Belsky was not without considerable benefit from this position-taking, both in terms of money and status.

Belsky's adopted British nationalism is situated in the obit chiefly in terms of World War II and his own perilous survival as a soldier: he had been in the remnant of the Czech army that arrived in Britain in 1940. But the sculptor's position-taking needs further objectification — Belsky was a member of a threatened Czech Jewish minority, one that had itself been split in the first part of the twentieth century between Zionism and socialist assimilation (Casanova 2004: 271–3). Moreover, his father, a well-known economist, had opposed his son becoming an artist. This made his conversion from one type of cultural capital into another an act of rebellion, exposing his vulnerability and explaining one possible source of his artistic conservatism. The strength of his regard for Britain and Churchill needs also to be related to this same vulnerability: Belsky suffered the loss of his entire family in the war, twenty-two members in all.[5] These experiences, we suggest, elucidate why Belsky became an Academic sculptor.

In stark contrast to Belsky as an artistic traditionalist, an unusually large, whole-page obituary is bestowed on the modernist, Sir Terry Frost (*The Times*, 3 September 2003). A prophetic figure of British abstraction when it was still an experimental art-form, Frost moved between totally abstract images and more expressive and accessible subjects (see for example his painting of fish laid out at the fishmongers, illustrated in the obit). Nevertheless, Frost's consecration as an individual painter was a somewhat unlikely process, partly because of the contemporary obstacles — within modernism especially — to painters finding enough to live on, and inter-linked with this, because of his lack of extended family support.

According to the obituary writer, Frost early acquired an innovative style, characterized as a variant of romanticism. His painting is interpreted as a celebration of joy and memory, not least, in humans' relation to the awe-inspiring nature of Yorkshire, where he worked. Abstraction in this obit is seen neither as 'effac[ing] the social in itself' (Clark 1999:310) nor as the distinctive formal expression of an empty modernity (Clark 1999: 10–13, 369; Guilbart 1983; Zukin 1988). More positively, Frost's abstract language is read as a variant of *heroic modernism* — his 'intensity of vision' and singularity of style is compared with maverick artists like Blake. Frost's retreat from realism was thus rooted in his quest for a new painterly means of encoding emotion:

> Combining strict formal discipline with great expressive freedom and a natural sureness of touch, he sought objective visual equivalents for the sensations, the memories, the sense of wonder that experience brings. (*The Times,* 3 September 2003)

Behind these aesthetic achievements — encoded at their core as 'natural' — there is a wider praise for his mode of being, his invigorating of others, generosity, '*faith*':

> One of the best-loved of British artists, Terry Frost enriched the lives of all those who came into his orbit of ebullience and generosity...He came quite late to painting, but his faith in the adventure of abstract art remained undimmed for more than half a century ...

Frost's trajectory sets in relief the difference of his background from that of his fellow-painters. His family home was with his grandparents. Classified more romantically in the obit as 'working class', they were 'bath-chair proprietors', thus part of a declining commercial petty-bourgeoisie. Frost had first painted prisoners with homemade brushes in his prisoner of war camp ('Prison camp was my university'), and was given a free educa-tion at Camberwell School of Arts and Crafts after being demobbed. No doubt his childhood experience of austerity helped him to endure the nor-mal poverty of an artist without a market: he and his wife lived with six children in a caravan at St. Ives. He survived also because of the peculiar strength and multiplicity of his social circles, which this obituary is unusual in acknowledging. After the war, protected by the shields against anomie offered by his wife and children, he was a member of successive artistic groups which acted as accumulators of collective artistic capital and laboratories of experimental technique (Poggioli 1968; Bourdieu 1996a). Frost was initially a member of 'The Circle', the St. Ives Penwith group of Ben Nicholson, Barbara Hepworth, Naum Gabo, Wilhelmina Barns-Graham, John Wells (*Daily Telegraph*, 3 August 2000)[6] among others, and was later part of the pioneering abstractionism of the Camberwell group (Lawrence Gowing, Victor Pasmore, William Coldstream and Claude Rogers). This was the launching-pad from which, as early as 1954, he was accepted for Lawrence Alloway's exhibition of Nine Abstract Artists. Later, in 1960, he travelled to New York for a residency, where again he moved in an abstract expressionist circle, that of Frankenthaler, de Kooning and Pollock.

Recollections within this obituary are underpinned by the ethos of gift exchange in such artistic circles, which is evident in Ben Nicholson's generous comment on Frost's art: 'You've got on to something that can last you the rest of your life'. Indeed, Frost's nostalgic subjective view of this early movement to abstraction — 'a happy time, when no reputations had been made and we shared everything' — recalls Simmel's stress on the adventure as a source of breakouts from the calculative instrumental rationality of late capitalism (Frisby and Featherstone 1997: 221–32).

The obituary description of the rigours of artistic experiment, as Frost progressively flattened space and used colour for structure, is legitimated by an underlying modernist model, its ethos that of preserving threatened values within the aesthetic sphere (Weber 1991: 347–54). Yet this obituary, read against the grain, also yields materials for an understanding of artists' more mundane interests. It is noteworthy, for example, that as Frost gains more recognition, he uses cheaper materials such as paper, thus expanding the market for his work. Nor did he ever *refuse* temporal artistic honours — Bourdieu's 'symbolic baubles' — Royal Academy election, ultimately, a knighthood.

Such an 'enchanted' portrayal, in Bourdieusian terms, of a mutually-supportive, cohesive bohemia is by no means universal for obituaries in the visual arts. In sharp contrast with Frost's harmonious progress, unresolved stylistic struggles and artistic dilettantism provoke a harshly critical assessment of Alfred Cohen (*The Guardian*, 7 March 2001). This artist — 'resolutely representational', even in the 1960s — ostensibly dedicated himself to art. However, he dissipated his time for work, became seduced by celebrities and was 'as likely to be found at the wheel of a Bugatti as painting'. In highlighting Cohen's orthodox style, *The Guardian*'s obituary is implicitly questioning the route of an artistic conservative. It and others like it, have as their ideological opposite *The Daily Telegraph*'s polemical critique of 'angst' in painters. This is the overt subtext within its obituary of William Harte (18 December 2003), a painter celebrated — *against* the orthodoxy of modernism — for his 'serene' and accessible painting.

Like Cohen, the obit for Patrick Procktor (*The Times*, 3 September 2003), also notes acerbically his failure to realize the early promise rewarded by his array of art prizes at the Slade, recording instead his diversion into 'enjoying frightening the horses with hints of chic depravity, delivered with theatrical flair'. In presenting his work as merely 'charming', the obituary critique of Proctor's excessively 'worldly' attitude is contrasted implicitly with a more scholarly perspective, privileging inner depth (Bourdieu 1984: 486– 88).

The 'economic world reversed' of bohemia becomes on occasion in these obits a territory of disputes and bitter enmities (Bourdieu 1993: 29–73). The Penwith Society, the group to which Frost had belonged, reappears in Sven Berlin's ironic obituary as the scene for protracted battles over what art should really be about (*The Guardian*, 4 January 2000). Nicholson, Hepworth and Frost had defended and practiced an aesthetic of total abstraction, but there was a resistance to this logic on the part of members such as Berlin. After failure to win his case for a minimal representational element in the new art, Berlin retreated from St. Ives — a desertion leading, we read, to his permanent 'exclusion from the mainstream of British art'. The effect of this bleak and uncontested judgement in Berlin's obituary thus serves only to enhance further the aura of the Nicholson/Hepworth group.

....

Obituaries also appear for less experimental painters and sculptors, amongst them those who offer a critical vision of manual work and its alternating cyclical rhythms with unemployment. The Expressionist Josef Herman (*The Independent*, 22 February 2000) is a typical figure in this respect, unseduced by abstraction (see also, *The Guardian* obituary for George Segal). Herman, a Jewish artist, left Poland in 1938 to escape anti-Semitism and the increasingly oppressive government of the extreme Right. He settled in Glasgow, where he was sheltered by fellow Jewish artists and a Scottish whiskey heiress, Catriona MacLeod, whom he eventually married. His paintings were preoccupied by the qualities of community and solidarity: he was drawn to close-knit villages in Suffolk and Andalusia, and especially to Ystradgynlais in Wales, whose miners he sketched and painted with an unusual monumentalism. The artistic qualities of Herman are thus somewhat stereotypically presented as *anti-modernist* — a realism underpinned by a penetrating philosophical humanism.

> These are pictures composed with rigorous classicism, lit by a coppery light from a sun half-eclipsed by cloud and smoke, and inhabited with miners who move with predestined pace like some tragic chorus.

As with Frost, Herman's personal qualities are also praised:

> As an artist he was immensely respected, as a man he was greatly loved. In his progress from ghetto urchin to venerable sage[,] Herman had amassed a vast experience of humanity that was always available to the comfort or enlightenment of the perplexed.

Herman's struggle was not merely to live without his family but to survive economically. The buyers of his paintings were not his subjects, the farmers and Welsh miners, but the post-war middle-class London Labour movement, especially from Jewish intellectual circles. Paradoxically, within their perspective, Herman's realism was allied too closely to a fatalistic stoicism. John Berger is introduced as the bearer of these more critical ideas within the obituary assessment. Noting the tension between Herman's stoical humanism and a proletarian realism, Berger points critically to the *passivity* of Herman's figures and their iconic physical labour. Thus from a socioanalytical point of view, the obituary reveals certain developing tensions between a public and its chosen artist, despite the initial elective affinity between his production and their taste (Bourdieu 1984: 232–34; 317). Herman,in other words, ultimately disappointed many of his buyers and sponsors because his paintings did not embody the same rationalist activism that they themselves possessed.[7]

A greater interpretative effort occurs when an artist appears to inhabit several incompatible categories at once, such as the Academic and modernist art worlds. This fits the more eclectic position-taking of a figure like Derek Hill (*Daily Telegraph*, 13 July 2000), who is presented in the *Daily Telegraph* as *both* a court artist — the familiar painter of Royalty — and a figure in the tradition of rural romanticism. Entitled by the writer a 'maverick', yet '*one of the greatest*' Irish landscape painters, Hill is explicitly characterized as an 'unclassifiable' painter. Unusually, the *Telegraph* obit itself objectifies the artist's peculiarities, explaining Hill's heterogeneous styles as deriving from his unprecedented material freedom. The son of a wealthy cloth-mill family, with private means, Hill had been permitted to leave his public school early and to travel and work abroad. This left him remarkably free from constraints, both to sell and to sink his identity into one specific artistic circle. Hills' legitimation as a modernist depended on a 1961 retrospective at the Whitechapel, organized under the auspices of the 'avantgardist' Brian Robertson, indeed, the obit claims that he was always 'too modernist' in both his landscape and portrait subjects to be an acceptable Academic painter. For this reason, the obituary elevates his canvases of the Mountbatten and Royal families to 'paintings of people', rather than mere portraits.

Yet if the obituary-writer strives to subsume Hill's work under the now-esteemed categories of modernism, a socioanalysis reveals incongruities. Despite having been a visitor to the Soviet Union in its avant-garde constructivist and productivist period, Hill had indeed spent much of his time on Academic Society portrait painting. Moreover, Hill had pursued highly-ambiguous connections, including a friendship with Unity Mitford, whom he had escorted to see Hitler in Berlin. The obit itself is aligned with a specific type of regressive modernism, a modernism that has developed from an initial anti-commercial focus on 'a world-in-reverse' and pure painting, to betray instead a close entwinement with aristocracy and with wealth (Gablik 1984; Crane 1987; Burger 1992).

Yet the obituaries of this period reveal that the restricted artistic field — the location of experimentation — never remains static. Its conventions perpetually change as wider historical experience changes (Bourdieu 1996a, postscript). If the history of modern art is in part the pursuit of 'truth to media' — the initial eradication of narrative content from paintings — by the 1970s metaphysical painters such as Ken Kiff (*The Independent*, 17 February 2001) had broken through the 'arid' alternatives of figuration or abstraction. His obituary praises a divergent transgressiveness: 'He was always pushing past the battlelines: the question of abstraction versus figuration....'

The obituaries in this period cover an exceptionally wide gamut of legitimate styles and clashes in artistic ethos. Yet there have also been certain *outer limits* to this freedom. Political interests exceptionally disqualify the actor from classification as a legitimate sculptor, as is shown by the sole negative obituary for an artist in this sample, that for Yann Goulet (*The Guardian*, 6 September 1999). Goulet's Breton nationalism, coupled with his German allegiances — Nazi uniforms, Nazi demonstrations — understandably rendered him impossible to recuperate.

THE PHOTOGRAPHIC FIELD

In the twenty-first century, obituaries include photographers of both sexes, from portraitists and advertising artists to photojournalists. These are men and women who did not simply 'live off' photography, but lived 'for it': possessing a view of photography as a mission. The phrase 'wedded to a photographic mission' is used of Denise Colomb (obit, *The Times*, 14 February 2004), a French post-war photographer, but it also captures the demands that the genre makes for all the photographers who receive obits in this period. The subjective angle of vision of Gisèle Freund, the photographer and photographic historian, also conveys vividly this sense of photography's mission, a consequence of its status as a 'universal language':

'To reveal man to man, to be a universal language, accessible to all — that for me, is the prime task of photography' (quoted in Freund's obit, *The Independent*, 20 May 2000).

There are certain main historical points to clarify in a sociology of photography, drawing on obituaries. The first is the change of the artistic status of photography, which is now accepted as a legitimate branch of the visual arts. Bourdieu and his fellow writers, astute about many things, failed to predict this degree of dynamism within artistic taste, regarding photography as perpetually doomed to be 'a middlebrow art' (1990). Yet there are enough indicators, both in the obituaries and elsewhere, to suggest that they were mistaken about this (Moulin 1992: 94; Fowler 2005a). Nevertheless, as in other parts of the restricted field, there are also profound difficulties for photographers in maintaining a material base for their more innovative work. These recurrent difficulties appear, for example, in the obituaries of Helen Muspratt (*The Guardian*, 11 August 2001) and James Ravilious (*The Independent*, 1 October 1999).

Yet if there is an art world of photography, in the sense of a restricted field, the obits also show that photographers and their historians tend to present an anti-aesthetic aesthetic, as will be shown. What is particularly new, featuring importantly in these obituary columns is photojournalism, a genre unmentioned by Bourdieu. It is this that has produced many of the notable photographers of modernity. In other words, aligned with the character of modernity in general, many of the most pregnant, even iconic, images of our time originated in news-photography — the sphere most concerned with the 'transitory, fleeting and fortuitous' (Frisby 1984: 4). There are certain qualities of subjective experience, in conjunction with the peculiarities of external reality, which preserve some of these pictures as 'decisive moments' (Cartier-Bresson 2004: 22). These images enter the collective memory as a form of witness to historical events.

The language of 'beauty' and 'art' is not entirely missing from these obits but it is deployed only by a certain group of photographers, duly appearing in their last notices. Paradoxically, many photographers reject these terms precisely because such concepts are linked, in their eyes, to a discourse of self-referential formalism. Consequently, in these obituaries it is only the lowest-status photographers, working in the most heteronomous areas of the artistic field, who are likely to have added an aura to their work by making this claim. Picturesque 'beauty' has been expelled from the sphere of painting but has taken refuge in the world of publicity artists. For example, the obit for the advertising artist and portrait photographer, Francesco Scavullo concludes 'He made plain people look beautiful and beautiful people look magnificent.' (*The Independent*, 13 January 2004) This love of aesthetic harmony is so dominant that it is reinforced in the obituary by the subjective avowal of Scavullo himself: 'I'm impressed by beauty [...]'.We shall develop these points below.

Against Bourdieu's conclusion in *Photography, A Middlebrow Art*, some of these photographers are remembered precisely because of their skill in using the photographic medium in an experimental manner. Helen Muspratt (born 1907) is a symptomatic figure in this respect. The daughter of an Anglo-Indian colonel, she trained at the Regent St. Polytechnic, and, at the suggestion of a former Principle of the Glasgow School of Art, Fra Newbery, became part of an artistic circle based on Purbeck in Dorset. Here she experimented with the solarisation techniques, pioneered by Man Ray. She developed, partly through this means, a series of exceptional portraits which revolutionized the genre:

> [Her] achievements [...] were widely recognized. She specialised in por-
> traiture, experimented with solarisation [...] and ranged into documen-
> tary work. Innovative [...] composition gave her pictures strong visual
> rhythms [...] Her work was at once understated and compelling.

Her importance is measured in the obit by her appeal to clients with
high cultural and social capital, not least to artists (Paul Nash) and influential Cambridge figures (Guy Burgess, Donald MacLean, Anthony Blunt
amongst them). Yet even *these* subjects were not sufficient to guarantee
secure recognition. Her later artistic obscurity can be defined as having
had various origins, not least, the conflicting demands of her autonomous
and pioneering photography vis à vis her necessarily less adventurous
commercial studio portraits. From such bread and butter work Muspratt
had to support her husband — a Communist Party organizer — and her
children.

A similar bearer of new photographic ideas was Ellen Auerbach, part
of a worker-photographer group which met initially at the Bauhaus (*The
Independent*, 13 August 2004). Auerbach, deeply committed to the avant-
garde, flourished less well as an immigrant in the coteries of post-war
American documentary realism: 'Women were no longer so welcome in
the world of photography as they had been in the liberal interwar years.'
Nevertheless, she produced enough work for a 'major retrospective' in Berlin in 1998. Thus in both these cases, women who might otherwise have
had the cultural capital to survive were *marginalised* — Muspratt by her
family's need for commercial photography and Auerbach by her flight from
the Nazis into an unhospitable environment, forcing a change of career.

The obituary of another photographer, James Ravilious, also makes
claims for his body of works as an unrecognised constituent of the
avant-garde:

> He will be remembered for his tireless efforts to capture the quintes-
> sential features of a tiny area of England [in] North Devon. Yet his
> pictures of the people, land, animals and buildings of this region are of
> far more than local interest. [...].
>
> [H]e produced images whose documentary purpose was never a
> limit on his artistic expression. Beautifully-composed, often lyrical [...]
> his photographs appeal as much to their subjects as they do to those
> who love good photography [...][He seized on] *miraculous fractions of
> a second* [...] to permit a surreal insight into what he saw as the 'odd-
> ness' of everyday life (my italics).

The veiled reference to the 'decisive moments' of Cartier-Bresson raises
the stakes in Ravilious's otherwise apparently anachronistic search for rural
England. Thus the obituary refuses to read Ravilious as a 'minor artist as

a minor genre' — however much that might fit Bourdieu's poignant sociological analysis of the fate of photography.

Yet it is clear that in certain respects Bourdieu was right: photographers
at the time he was writing, and Ravilious in particular were deprived of
recognition and were often very poor. Interestingly, if Ravilious's position
is addressed with an objectivating gaze, he belongs to a place in the artistic
field which is often associated with artistic innovations, or with a position-
taking that allows him or her later to be consecrated. The son of two artists
himself, his wife, Robin, was also the daughter of the engraver, Lawrence
Whistler (see, for his obituaries , *The Independent*, 23 December 2000 and
The Guardian, 6 January 2001). Her family had held property in this area
and it was to this that they went to live. Other friends lent them rooms —
sometimes in exchange for agricultural labour. In other words, Ravilious
had access to social connections — artistic and otherwise — and through
these, to a modicum of inherited economic capital. From this background,
he could add to the skills he had acquired from St. Martins' School of Art
and his sustaining social network. Even so, he had prolonged difficulty
in later career with his photographic patrons. No doubt stressing romantic conventions, the obit portrays him as struggling to retain a precarious living: without family and patrons this would have been realistically
unthinkable.

Other photographers whose obituaries appear here belong to the conflu-
ence of the documentary realist and avant-garde traditions. For example,
Roger Pic, the Parisian photographer, had been a powerful newsphotogra-
pher — specialising in portraits of anti-colonialist leaders like Ben Bella
and Ho chi Min — but he had also worked on the Brechtian Berliner
Ensembler, as well as Barrault's and Regnaut's *Les Enfants du Paradis*
(*The Guardian*, 15 December 2001). One particularly striking aspect of
the work of Pic himself, as well as that of Freund and Colomb (*The Times*,
14 February 2004) was their portrayal of contemporary writers and artists,
often bohemians. Freund's subjects, including Woolf, Joyce and Colette, are
said to give something of their charisma to her portrayals. Equally Colomb
'excelled as a photographer' portraying sculptors, painters and dramatists
such as Giacometti, Picasso and Artaud, to whom she was introduced by
her brother, a Parisian gallery owner:

'Like her contemporaries, Robert Doisneau, Henri Cartier-Bresson and
Willy Ronis, Colomb looked for the quirky, the affectionate and the ener-
getic in everyday life' (*The Times*, 14 February 2004). Her later collaboration with the photographers, Kertesz, Lartigue and Kollar saw her operating in a protective artistic group, again typical of the restricted field.

Colomb's obituary appraisal consecrates the deceased photographer
within an ancestry of other photographers, reaffirming recognized names.
In similar vein, the obit for Jean- Philippe Charbonnier begins:

In the middle of the 20th Century, France turned out a stream of photographers- Cartier-Bresson, Doisneau, Sieff, Boudin, Ronis — not to mention adoptive Frenchmen such as Brassai and the two Capas. The least-known of their number but with an eye as fresh as any was Jean-Philippe Charbonnier.

Such obituaries of photojournalists, then, serve to reaffirm a belated canon. But they also give a graphic sketch of the pressures of the mode of production in the field: news photographers, for example, often had to work under intense speed, frequently only having a single day for each country they visited. Charbonnier is depicted in terms that deliberately counter this heteronomous effect: he is described, despite these rigours, as retaining an 'aristocrat's temperament' (*The Times*, 5 June 2004), in this context, a highly consecrating move.

When today's obituarists of photographers look backwards, the bitterness of past struggles over form are eliminated. This is no doubt partly because in photography it is difficult to avoid an element of realism, now no longer so questionable. But it is also because of the nature of the period at which photography's importance was recognized and became theorized. These debates had lost the savagery they once possessed and the obituaries of photographers are as a consequence remarkably benign.

THE EXPANDED FIELD

Commercial and Popular Arts

Bourdieu's *Distinction* has two major components of the expanded field, respectively 'bourgeois art' and industrial art: it is to this latter that I now turn. The 'industrial' field is in fact made up of artisan or mass-produced work (Moulin 1967: 409–17). For the first time, cartoonists, comic artists and illustrators have been given obituaries, irrespective of their work's commodity status, and even devoid of the signature which has become so important in the bourgeois tradition of legitimating artists (see Don Lawrence, a sci fi and horror magazine artist (*The Daily Telegraph*, January 3 2004, *The Independent*, January 15 2004) and Denis McLoughlin, a popular magazine illustrator (*The Guardian*, October 5 2002) (cf Benjamin, 1979: 384; Canclini, 1993). Others signed their work: amongst the cartoonists, for example, Victoria Davidson (*The Independent*, 13 March 2000), Abu Abraham (*The Guardian*, 7 December 2002) William Papas (*The Guardian*, 26 June 2000) and Whitney Darrow (*The Independent*, 22 November 1999).

Varnedoe and Gopnik have distinguished between artists who are part of an overlord culture of advertising and pornography, and artists who are part of an underdog culture (1990). There has not yet, to my knowledge, been a news obituary for a commercial pornographer, nor for an advertising artist of the overlord culture. On the other hand there is a thriving field of the underdog cultural producers — not graffiti artists, who are still too transgressive to receive obituaries — but comic strip writers, popular cartoonists and magazine illustrators.[8] Their obits, like the news photographers, are of cultural producers who have made a mark on *popular memory*.

We could speculate that these developments, partly springing from new technology, take time before they acquire critics from within the consecrated genres. These winnow out the most powerful and daring practitioners and embrace them within the fold of the legitimate arts. Beyond this, there is a complex dialectic of innovation between the expanded culture and the consecrated professional artists' culture, as Varnedoe and Gopnik (1990) have also pointed out. This has extended from the Delaunays' and Picasso's depiction of adverts and newspapers within their paintings (1990: 36) to Schwitters' adoption of the new sans serif print in his Dadaist collages (1990: 52). In the beginning of the twenty-first century, we might similarly note advertisers' hijacking of Gillian Wearing's video techniques. Such crossovers in technique and subject imply that the boundaries between the restricted and expanded fields vary historically and cannot be regarded as totally fixed or reified.

The cartoon, the form where art is used most openly in the interests of social and political comment, is noted by the obit writers as the space for the critique of illegitimate power — censured or uncensured. Abu Abraham acquired a national reputation in India for his fearless cartoons of Indira Ghandi's authoritarianism and was given a state funeral in Kerala; Stanley Franklin's comment on the British Government's handling of the Falklands War was so powerful that it was withheld from the *Sun* as 'inappropriate' (*The Independent*, 6 February 2004), William Papas's 'fine pen for pricking egos' included memorable images of Rhodesia's unilateral declaration of independence.[9] These single images belong, in turn, to a wider cartoon world of social types. Some are claimed in the obituaries to possess a satirical force equivalent to the creations of Swift or Dickens: the Franklin images of Alf Garnett as a chauvinist Little Englander are good examples. Another cartoon genre with its roots in an older popular culture creates folk images. These reaffirm ethical rules or ideals, often in the form of a defamiliarising, yet still safe, animal world, as argued in the obituaries of William Hanna, the cartoonist of Tom and Jerry (*The Guardian*, 24 March 2001) or Marc Davis, the draughtsman of Chanticleer and Bambi (*The Guardian,* 11 February 2000).

Typically, the obituary evaluation of the cartoonist is framed in terms of the unexpected political consequences of their work, as in the comment that one of Papas' drawings was 'the worst blow *The Guardian* struck against the Labour Party'. In some cases, stylistic techniques are also addressed– for example, Abraham's:

> style of drawing was astonishing and singular. It was utterly contemporary, but lithe as the decorative linearity of the 16th and16th century Mughal courts of Akhbar and Jehangir, hinting without excess at arabesque and curlicue....

Again, William Hurtz's film cartoons are praised as '[s]pare, elegant, highly stylized [...] contemporary drawings' (*The Guardian*, 1 November 2000).

Yet the artistic habitus of the cartoonists is very often left obscure in these typically short obituaries. Hurtz's trajectory was no doubt facilitated by the cultural capital he acquired from his mother, an artist, as well as that gained from the Chicago Art Institute and the Californian Institute of Arts where he had been a student. But Abrahams appears to have had no cultural capital — he emerged from nowhere, lacked any higher education and first submitted cartoons simply as a reporter.

In industrial art as a whole, the economic and cultural capital of the artists is often very small, especially for film animation, in companies like Disney where a Taylorist division of labour applied, with different workers specialising on faces or arms or backgrounds. Thus whereas only three painters have origins in the subordinate class in these obituaries,[10] the industrial world of the magazine illustrator and comic strip animator is typically unadorned by any certified cultural capital from education. It is very much closer to material urgencies. These figures all have working-class or poor farming backgrounds: see for example, William Hanna (son of a sewage construction superintendent, *The Guardian*, 24 March 2001); Carl Barks (a poor chicken-farmer's son, *The Guardian* 30 August 2000; *Washington Post*, 26 August 2000; the *New York Times* 26 August 2000, *Le Monde*, 28 August 2000); Charles Schulz (a barber's son, *The Guardian*, 14 February 2000) and Stanley Franklin (an East End coppersmith's son, *The Independent* 6 February 2004). They have no higher education or at most an art school on the periphery: Minneapolis (Schulz), Kansas (Davis).

In contrast to the comic strip and magazine illustrators, political cartoonists are more often from middle or dominant class families, in which the subject has been able to acquire considerable *artistic* capital: see, amongst others, Gardosch (cultural milieu in Budapest, later Sorbonne, *The Guardian* 23 March 2000), Herblock (father a chemist; Lake Forest College, Chicago, *The Independent*, 21 November 2001), Emmwood (father a painter of landscapes; Leeds College of Art, *The Independent*, 24 September 1999); Ron Ullyet (father, a manager, Slazenger, *The Guardian* 25 October 2001), Victoria Davidson (father, an artist, mother, the daughter of a professor of Oriental languages, *The Independent*, 13 March 2000). More precisely, artistic capital varies according to the newspaper or magazine's typical readership — the tabloids employed a figure like Stanley Franklin (Working Man's College only),whereas the *New Yorker* cartoonist, Witney Darrow, had been to Princeton University, where his father had founded the Princeton University Press.

As with the painters, so too with comic strip artists and cartoonists: the obituaries offer a space where the interests, dilemmas and disappointments of the visual artist are laid bare. Some reveal the agency of the cartoonists themselves in struggling against their poor material life-chances. For example, it was Hurtz (*The Guardian*, 1 November 2000), unusually symbolically armed with *two* art-school qualifications, who demanded a rise, taking on Disney in the middle of the War. Even in these 'industrial arts', some draw aside a veil to reveal conflicts over artistic autonomy. Marc Davis, it is noted, regretted that his best work had been censored. Hurtz and others fought for more creative independence than Disney allowed. Indeed, against Disney's rule, they felt that they had founded, through their breakaway United Productions of America (UPA), a structure permitting greater originality, even in an unaltered commercial environment.

Schulz's very long obit, a homage to the 'world's most popular cartoonist', illustrates the guiding features of this 'underdog culture' (*The Guardian*, 14 February 2000). It is immediately apparent that this obit avoids any language of *aesthetic consecration*. Instead, the popular success of Charlie Brown and other Peanuts characters is accounted for partly by appealing to their distinctiveness, partly by appealing to the world they inhabited, where mishaps and disasters are ever-present. Thus phlegmatic resilience, escape tactics, common sense realism and disdain for the ultra-conformist are what is important. The obituary attributes this structure of feeling to Schultz's own lived experience — '"My whole life has been one of rejection. Women. Dogs. Comic strips"'. Such a sense of rejection allowed him to express in the comic a wider consciousness of bad fortune. As summed up in his obituaries, Schulz is a figure who stands for a debunking realism within the 'national popular' tradition — derived partly from the powerless world of childhood, partly from the world of the 'little man' (Forgacs and Nowell-Smith, 1985).

Unsurprisingly, comic strip artists' obituaries link art and money in ways which would be considered profane in the world of many of the consecrated artists. The market value of a Frost painting or a Belsky sculpture is never mentioned in these artists' obits, which serves to heighten the modernist doxa of the disinterested artist. In contrast, in the Schulz obit the opening line starts by *opposing* popularity to riches but then immediately proceeds to measure popularity precisely in terms of exchange-value ('a recent estimate paid him $1 million a month.'). Indeed, one of the attractions of the comic strip obituary may well be that it contains a narrative of upward social mobility, even if one punctuated, as in Schulz's case, by the artist's own subjective feeling of continuing to be 'a loser'. Yet it should not be forgotten that this commercial logic of success is invariably reinforced by something else — not *legitimate* symbolic capital, but symbolic capital nonetheless, in Schulz's case, a 1955, Reuben Award. Unlike the artists' knighthoods, these are genre-specific honours, yet, interestingly, they are selected by the newspaper artists themselves.

Folk Art

Traditionally, folk art, such as quilt making or non-religious embroidery, was anonymous work by 'non-artists', which might be collectively undertaken. Basic symbolism of colour and pattern were shared by everyone within a given locality, although regional variations might flourish and individually-talented quilters be singled out. Quilts and other folk products were typically made for family use, not sold on the market (Becker 1982).

Contemporary obituaries have now expanded to include folk artists. Yet increasingly the collective inheritance of their art is neglected and they are consecrated simply as individuals, on the model of the canonized modernists. One such is Johnny Warrangkula Tjupurrula, whose obit is written by the owner of a gallery dedicated to Aboriginal art, the gallery itself being a development of the late twentieth century (Rebecca Hossack, (*The Independent*, 17 February 2001). Tjupurrula, in this account, was in the 1960s an anomic aboriginal who became the seedbed of an artistic revolution. Encouraged by an Australian teacher to paint his traditional designs on murals, he went on to become one of the 'founding fathers of the modern aboriginal painting movement', using acrylic paints for the tribal designs. His paintings are differentiated from others by his 'fluidity of execution' and 'daring'— marking a distinctive style.

This obituary certainly alludes to a hitherto unnoticed aboriginal collective memory. Yet what is also striking is the defense of Tjupurrula's artistic status in terms of the commercial value of his paintings. In his obituary writer's eyes, his highest claim to importance is the sale of one of his early paintings for A$206,000 (£75,000), three years later, A$486,500. 'For the first time', she remarks, 'an aboriginal artist was achieving prices comparable with — indeed higher than — the established figures of modern Australian painting'. The obit ends by quoting the very high price for *Water Dreaming at Kalipinypa*, even speculating that it had been this kind of money that led him to return to painting after a break in the early 1990s.

High prices, of course, ensure independence from patronage. Yet such financial assessments diametrically differentiate this field of art from that of the heroic avant-gardes. Indeed, the newly commercial character of aboriginal style may have been one of the factors that led to a scandal associated with another Australian artist, Elizabeth Durack, the daughter of a large station owner (*The Guardian*, 5 June 2000). Having exhibited with Nolan and other modernists, she adopted the persona of a fictitious male aboriginal artist, Eddy Burrup, producing a body of works under that name. She only chose to unveil herself in *Art Monthly* in her nineties, causing a debate about whether or not she had calculatively purloined an identity, thus adopting an aboriginal style divorced from its iconography.

Yet, in this saga of an artist who appears to be entirely transgressive within the official art-institution, her obituary omits the *nature of the public for aboriginal style*. In Bourdieu's socioanalysis of the artworld it is less easy to ignore the 'interest in disinterestedness' of the consumers of these symbolic goods. Indeed, buying the once-despised work of the exotic Other — originally so dehumanized that they were not even counted in the 1961 Census in Australia — proves simultaneously that the owners of such paintings are both anti-racist and art-lovers: symbolic profits indeed. Thus a (profane) objectification of the taste for art — omitted from the obit — reveals the complex motives interacting within the 'spiritual soul of the bourgeoisie' (compare Bourdieu 1984: 19).

Outsider Artists

The present is marked by the increasingly rapid recuperation of transgressive and outsider artists into the 'inside' (Heinich 1998b). The definition of the 'inside' itself becomes a moveable boundary, linked to the artist's location and hence perspective (Finney, 1997: 82). The obituaries are part of this process, too, moving into the area of counter-memory. They even record the biography of a convicted forger of Dalis and Chagalls, Konrad Kujau, a trained artist who always signed paintings twice, once with his own name and once with that of the supposed artist (*Le Monde* 15 September 2000).

Yet with such outsider artists, the measure of artistic value is not simply their originality but their sales figures. This creates a little war inside both the art-world and the obituary world as a result. Perhaps the strangest piece is in *The Independent*, the work of a Primitive Baptist, who writes the biography of a Baptist artist, his friend, Howard Finster (*The Independent*, 29 October 2001).This goes to pains to stress Finster's hatred of 'the world' — not least, the fetishistic measurement of value in exchange values. It was this hatred which also fuelled his choice of sculpture from waste objects. If a found object for his sculptural works seemed to have value, such as gold, he at once destroyed it. The tension added to this obit is that Finster himself succumbed to the ethos from which he had once been so intransigeantly distanced. Gallery dealers — initially, in this scenario, seen as 'tempters' and Biblical 'art-snakes' — slowly embraced him in their commodified world, which the obit writer 'just to be ornery' calls the 'New Improved Garden of Eden'. Finster's initial view is that of a naive:

> I'd go to the dump and find some of the prettiest things you've ever seen [...] Most of the stuff [there] is junk and not worth anything, and, if it is

worth anything, I damage it to where it ain't worth anything. […]The
longer I live on this planet the less I can adapt to it.

Yet even his obituary-writer has to acknowledge that Finster later became
a knowing inhabitant of the artistic field: 'Now, boys' [Finster is quoted as
saying on one work] ' that's a piece of what your art expert fellers call your
genuine folk art.' Here, the obit-writer wittily tells his friend's story, but
only in order to cast a disenchanted eye on 'art'. His concluding assessment
is deeply ironic and stands profoundly at odds with Rachel Hossack's com-
mercially-validating comments on Tjupurrula:

> Nowadays one hears of aesthetic jungles in which Finsters fetch over
> $30,000. Genuine folk art, one guesses.

CONCLUSION: ART, MONEY AND VALUE

The recent rapid commercial successes of a section of the youngest avant-
garde indicate that the old boundaries between art and the market are
increasingly being eroded (Bourdieu 1996a, 344–47; Zolberg and Cherbo
1997; Cook 2000: 168–78; Stallabrass 1999). Additionally, the framing
of art is being increasingly shaped by corporate power (Wu, 2000) and in
some Western cultures, by an anti-artistic moral/religious agenda antagonistic to modernism (Bourdieu and Haacke, 1995; Heinich, 2000).

How does this relate to the artists' obits? The Enlightenment-derived
dichotomy, between art (or aesthetic use-value) and money (or exchange
value) does not appear in its classic form in the obituaries (on this, see
Guillory, 1993). This is partly because their authors want to rehabilitate
once-marginalized forms of popular art. It is perhaps also because they are
concerned less with making aesthetic judgements and more with renewing
collective memory of these works. Thus on the one hand, William Hanna
is praised for having a genuinely comic tempo, a good team and strong
draughtsmanship, or William Hurtz admired for embodying in his popular
cartoons a variant of an expressionist, metropolitan style. On the other
hand such obituaries for the artists in popular genres often conflate market
success with artistic power. The comic strip artist, Don Lawrence's obit in
The Independent is one such:

> [T]he ever-reliable Lodewijk took charge of the plots again […]. The
> results speak for themselves with sales of over two million albums
> and Lawrence himself acquiring a mantelpiece of European cartoon-
> ing awards…. (*The Independent* 15 January 2004, see also *The Daily
> Telegraph*, 3 January 2004).

Here the emphasis on Lawrence's *sales* provides supplementary justification of his works' claimed aesthetic value.

10 The sports' obituaries (1999–2006)

A minority of the contemporary obituaries within the broadsheets have now taken on a role that was once distant from them — preserving popular memory. This is unprecedented for news obits. In the earlier samples, of 1900 or 1948, the producers of theatre, opera or 'well-made novel' were featured, but the obit columns were silent about popular figures such as music hall artistes or footballers.

Popular memory is defined here as those recollections of the past which are conserved in the minds of the subordinate classes. It is used in the sense in which Luisa Passerini wrote about the popular memory of factory, artisan and domestic life under Fascism in Turin (1987). It is essential to be alert to her warning that where a period has been very painful, as in Italy at this time, people could not speak about their experiences in the course of everyday life. In the face of constant necessity or fear of repression, they recalled openly only areas of humour or joking relationships (Passerini 1987: 68, 74–80; Passerini 1992: 7).

Whereas Passerini and her fellow historians have tapped such popular memory by oral history interviews, my approach is to use the written biographies encapsulated in obituaries to cast light on popular recollection. However, it has to be borne firmly in mind that this current of memory is filtered by the frames of journalists or other obituary writers, who have themselves been through a long process of formal education. As spokespersons for others, they combine popular memory with a cultivated style and sometimes an aesthetic gaze — and in that sense cannot be confused with the popular culture of the subordinate class.[1]

The newspaper obituaries' memories of those who have made their names in sport tap in also to their social existence outside this field. Such obituaries may reveal, sometimes with great vividness, collective actions in which a sense of injustice smoulders into an explosion of unguarded emotions. These may on occasion take a form of group revenge, as is told in relation to the early life of Drobny, the tennis player, in his obituary (*The Guardian*, 15 September 2001). Drobny, in the Second World War a young factory-worker, lived in Prague, which had been occupied with great brutality by the Nazis. His obituary recounts how, immediately after the war, he saw women surrounding a German soldier, whom they had stripped naked and were roasting on a spit, sticking swastika badges in him as they turned him. Such experiences of coercive power shape the subjects' lives. Similarly defining moments appear in the obituary accounts of several Afro-American touring jazz bands, whose players' early experiences of being turned away from hotels simply because of their 'race' is reported to have marked them for life. Yet although such obits serve in crucial ways to counteract a wider historical amnesia, in this chapter the focus will be narrowly on the field of sport and what impinges on it. [2]

Sports and other leisure activities vary in terms of their position in social space over time and society. In particular, they can change their position in the hierarchical order of social relationships, as happened most evidently in the case of driving for pleasure (Bourdieu 1984, Hobsbaum and Ranger 1983: 297, 300). Equally, riding — in the 1940s an elite activity — had, by the late twentieth century undergone a process of democratisation; riding lessons had become a cheap luxury (Bourdieu 1998a: 4). Boxing, once enjoyed by aristocrats (end of the nineteenth century) was abandoned by them when lower social classes adopted it (Bourdieu 1998a: 4). Conversely, the structural position and meaning of a single sport, such as golf, may vary as between different countries, for example Scotland and England. Cricket — apparently homogeneous — is markedly different in different parts of Britain, being played in the South mainly by the dominant and middle class, but in the North by the dominant class *and* working-class Lancastrians and Yorkshiremen. Equally, cricket was taken up by the masses — as well as the elites — in the West Indies, for example, and became a particularly important post-colonial crucible for the emergence of the Jamaican and other islands' identities (Smith 2006). These striking differences in the structure of feeling in relation to cricket also surface in the obits of cricketers.

The *visibility* of different sports varies massively in the obits, taking both the rigorously selected sample and the wider sample for the qualitative analysis. Biased as this selection is to the British papers, we note that football — currently losing its exclusively working-class, masculine association — is the most numerous of the 152 obits[3] dedicated to sports. It is followed after a considerable gap by cricket, and after another gap, by boxing and rugby union. Climbing, racing and athletics are a little less in evidence and there is a slightly lower representation for swimming, baseball and cycling. Certain activities — weight-lifting, riding, skiing, canoeing, fencing, American football, basketball — have only a tiny sprinkling of representative figures, while some sports are absent altogether from the obituaries. Pigeon racing, for example, is followed intensely — occasionally murderously — in some parts of Britain, such as Easterhouse and Maryhill, in Glasgow, but there are no obits for prize pigeon ('doo')-fanciers (Quinn 2004). 'Doo-racing' has not emerged from folk activities as a form of 'sporting art for art's sake'. It is not yet seen as a form of free play, devoid of utilitarian objective, which is regulated by a rationalised set of rules and adjudicated by disinterested umpires (Bourdieu, 1993b:120).

Popular memory recalls individuals whose activities expressed the sense of honour of the subordinate classes. One mark of favour in return is that such players attracted large crowds to watch them. In the twentieth century, of course, these audiences have become commercialised and the sporting activities they have always patronised have gone through various mutations to become spectator activities. Note that, unlike Lukács, the term 'popular' is not here restricted to those activities that foster the rational interests of the class, thus helping the collectivity to become a class for itself. The present, less essentialist, use covers any activity that is part of the collective memory of the subordinate classes, even if it has no obvious political function. Such forms deserve the title 'popular memory' when they preserve a folk memory of popular experiences and actions which are in danger of being forgotten. Of these, some memories are still familiar, like the techniques for coping with poverty in the 1930s Depression, but others are less so, including the active discouragement by the dominants of working class literacy or the whipping of pregnant single women.

Occasionally obituaries reveal figures who have gone on to lose the support of the mass audience. This may happen even if they had successfully transferred to becoming national rather than local icons. Indeed, after their death, it may even be an obituary that rescues them from obscurity and from the dramatic fall from grace. Such fluctuations in the ebb and flow of collective consciousness — in relation to the action of the hero — are important conditions for popular memory.

Certain general points ought initially to be made. First, unlike the memory of the dominants, popular memory tends to be demystifying. Whilst freely acknowledging individual talents or 'magical' accomplishments, popular memory operates with a specific emphasis on the social, or on mutual aid. In football, for example, we can identify a consistent stress in the obituaries on the collective aspects of individual goal-scoring, so that each player appears to a large degree as *interdependent with the others.* This sense of collective endeavour is less likely to emerge in the obits of players of elite sports (for example, in the late twentieth century, tennis, riding, golf and sailing). Even where a team is vital to an elite activity (as in rugby union), collective memory tends to emphasise the distinctiveness of each player's contribution and to downplay the collaborative element (see below on John Matthews).

Second, the obits show widespread traces of Elias's 'civilizing process' (2000: 161–71). For this reason, as Hadas argues, the sports of the feudal aristocracy, such as duelling, foxhunting or fencing — itself the more 'civilised' form of duelling — play a very small part compared to those more peaceful activities associated with the bourgeoisie and with the city (Hadas 2003). That the feudal sporting forms were crucial to a combative sense of honour was reinforced in Central Europe precisely by the prohibition of such feats of masculine prowess to Jews, in a stigmatizing inversion of the usual process of forming a noble male habitus (Bourdieu 2001b:51n).[4] In the 2000s obits, more naked aristocratic violence, such as duelling, has been replaced by regulated and competitive forms of violence. Horse racing and, to a lesser degree, its technological equivalent, motor-racing, has largely replaced the predatory chase of hunting[5]; boxing replaces both popular and aristocratic fighting.

The emergence of athletics and cycling represents at first a historical extension of this area of competitive masculinity to less well-placed classes: these activities then became broadened to embrace women's competitive activities, especially in swimming and cycling (Hadas 2003). Similarly, whilst the 1900 and 1948 obits portrayed only cricketers, racehorse-owners and hunters,[6] the 2000s obits included the less patrician activities of boxers, swimmers and cyclists, whilst extending their orbit to include notable sportswomen.[7]

Third, the early nineteenth century Romantic identification of mountains with the sublime — as in Kant or Ruskin — expresses theoretically the close affinity between the peaceful activity of climbing and the asceticism of the dominated fraction of the dominant class. Here again, the obituaries register the democratisation of this once patrician form of leisure (see Bourdieu 1996b: 40–53). Yet, forever hovering on the edge of a transformation into a regulated competitive sport, the popular memory of climbing also retains this individualistic and artistic ethos, concerned more with the *style* of the climb than the crude numbers of peaks mastered. It therefore appeals to its devotees by recalling forms of productive activity and effort that are marginalised in the everyday work controlled by the instrumental reason of modern large-scale industry (see, for example, the obit for Jammy Cross, the Cumbrian woman climber; *The Times* 13 March 2004).

Finally the rise of *cooperative and competitive masculinity* in the form of *football* is the most noticeable development of the nineteenth century and later. The obits cannot fail to indicate the strong collective identifications associated with the game, at the level of workplace, region and religion. Nevertheless, the obituary form lends itself especially to an individuating treatment of each notable player, focussing especially on the given footballer's style. Even if understood as popular memory, the publication of obituaries for footballers is in itself a telling sign of the sport's gentrification, alongside its greatly increased economic investment.

Taste in sport offers few exceptions to Bourdieu's famous generalisation 'Tastes classify and they classify the classifier' (1984: 6). Here we shall explore how the actor's positioning in the field of power shapes the choice of (taste for) different sports, not least the choice of popular versus distinguished sports.[8] Such socio-historical positioning profoundly affects experiences of play within the game as well as the particular obstacles the players may face in pursuing it. Yet the sports themselves are relatively autonomous fields and, as such, experience their own rhythms and tensions. At the end of this chapter, the obituaries will illuminate the distinctive or specific conflicts within the sporting field itself:

Even when marked by the major events of economic and social conditions [the history of each sport] has its own tempo, its ...own crises, in
short, its specific chronology. (Bourdieu 1993b:118)

Such crises are mirrored in the controversies over flouting rules and even
on the status of various rules within the national game. In the reassessment
of these conflicts, we could argue that the obituary operates as a form of
final arbitration on the justice of the various damaging claims circulating
against certain obituary subjects.

POPULAR MEMORY, CLASS HABITUS
AND TASTE FOR THE GAME

Many of today's obits in the area of sports are for footballers who played
the game from the late 1930s on, gaining caps for the national team and
titles such as 'Footballer of the Year'. Some have had careers which are
particularly memorable: Tam Dalyell points out in an obit note that when
Ronnie Simpson died, a Parliamentary petition to commemorate his name
was passed by the House of Commons, an honour only handed out to one
other player in forty-two years (*The Independent*, 22 April 2004).

These players are typically working-class men who are often described in
their obituary as 'diminutive', just as Diego Maradona was, in his rise from
the slums of Buenos Aires (see, for example, John Bonnar (*The Herald*,
17 January 2004) and Henry Cockburn (*The Independent*, 17 February,
2004)). The obituaries invariably describe how they have compensated for
their lack of inches with their fitness and skills, not least by aerial leaps and
ball control. Even if unmentioned in the actual text, the photographs of this
generation often revealingly display their lesser height.[9] Clearly football is
one of a small number of games where a body shape based on generations
of poor nutrition can produce wiry agility and precision ('mazy action'),
offsetting the absence of other means of physically dominating the field.[10]
In contrast — and *outside* the sphere of popular memory — the obituary
of the public school and Cambridge tennis player, Bunny Austin, recounts
a starkly different physical style ('elegant, [...] his long, fluent forehand and
backhand ground strokes [gave] him an almost languid air') (*The Times*,
28 August 2000).

Most footballing obituaries are centred on players from the poorest districts of Northern or Scottish industrial cities, more occasionally from the
deprived districts of Southern towns, as in the case of the Norwich City
player, Ron Ashman (*The Independent*, 24 June 2004). They may explicitly reveal the affinity between the demands of the game and the habitus of
the players. Dalyell, for example, in his obit for George Farm, the Scottish
goalkeeper, emphasises the social structure which had made him — not just

the fact that he came from a family of foundry workers, but that these men had produced the armour for the Dreadnoughts in the Second World War, working at the Atlas steel plant in Armadale, West Lothian (*The Independent*, 30 July 2004). Drawing on the recollections of a fellow Scottish International player who saw Farm as the bravest goalkeeper with whom he had played, Dalyell implies that the tough resilience of the foundrymen themselves went into the game.

Oddly, accolades for players typically repeat a raft of ostentatiously feudal compliments — 'the prince of centre-halves', 'Prince of Wales', 'Gentlemen George' — and so on. These dramatise the regard in which they were held, not unlike the 'nature's gentlemen' who were the heroes of popular 1880s' dime novels (Denning 1998). Tellingly, the subjective perceptions of the individual footballer — and even of his friends who commemorate him — are more restrained than these effusive crowd distinctions. These comments again tend to fit broadly the experience they have had of working-class life. Of Henry Cockburn, a fellow-player remarked 'He was totally reliable, both as a player and a comrade.' (*The Independent*, 17 February 2004). Wilf Mannion, who played for Britain against the Rest of Europe in an epic match in 1947, was hailed, in the time-honoured way, as 'the man of the match'. He himself referred to his performance more modestly, stressing the cooperative division of labour and that he was 'just a useful cog in a well-oiled machine' (*The Independent*, 15 April 2000). His obituarist comments: 'the diminutive blond inside forward omitted' that *he* was the compound permitting 'the smooth running of the big wheels', Stanley Matthews and Tommy Lawton.

Football was a game particularly suitable for poor working-class players because it was not colonised by the cult of amateurism that existed in other sports, such as tennis (Bourdieu 1993b, 121–23). This division (amateur-professional) in many ways parallels the high culture-low culture division within the wider field of cultural production, a point to be developed later. Whether because of the players' greater poverty or because of the connotations of football with 'low culture', material rewards also feature much more prominently in the popular sporting obits, especially in comparison with those for, say, science or politics, where the assumption of 'disinterestedness' is overwhelmingly prevalent. It is common to see references to the amount of money for which the player was sold, whilst there are also comments on the historical transition in the 1960s from very modest amounts per player to the much greater amounts for today's players. The obituaries for footballers who experienced the old regime of payments often relay their open resentment about their wages, especially when the players' poor pay was coupled with the clubs starting to do well, in the greater affluence of the post-war period. Thus Mannion refused to re-sign one year for Middlesborough (1948), in what might be called a 'one-man strike', his return having to be quickly renegotiated when the club became desperate. Although unmentioned by the writer, this obit shows also the impact of a trade union culture of solidarity: Mannion criticised the illegal payments of extra cash to certain players, yet rejected individualistic gain by refusing resolutely to name the players involved.

If the material parameters of football are revealed in these obituaries as very different from those of elite sports, it is also clear that becoming a premier league and national player in this generation did not necessarily mean major upward social mobility. Whether due to their lower rewards or their own lack of an ethos of saving, the footballers rarely ended their playing lives enriched. Mannion, who again serves as an ideal type, had 'cherubic looks' and a 'splendid achievement', and was, moreover, perceived as chiefly responsible for helping Great Britain to the 6–1 'annihilation' of the rest of Europe in 1947. Yet he never acquired sufficient money or commanding presence to be upwardly mobile. After his playing years, not 'cut out for administration', he subsequently became a manual worker:

> Thereafter he experienced cruelly lean and harrowing times, being reduced to working on building sites and for the railway.

Perhaps these footballers' obits can be regarded as marking 'the end of a world', not dissimilar to the end of the peasant ethic in Kabylia (Bourdieu 2003a) or the end of a collectivist ethos of working-class ('Red') reproduction (Bourdieu et al, *The Weight of the World* 1999: 317– 20). Mannion's experience mirrors that period. As everyone knows, the objective situation of the player in the contemporary game has since been materially transformed.

AMATEURISM AND CLASS

Certain participants in sports that had the traditional amateur status lacked, themselves, the proper affinity for this in terms of class origins — in other words, they suffered from the material urgencies of life in a sporting world where it was assumed that participants were wealthy. These sportspeople often suffered a mismatch of habitus (Bourdieu 2000a: 159–63). On the one hand, the mismatch merely demanded greater effort and ingenuity – thus Alice 'Jammy' Cross, a rock climber, 'co-equal' with her husband in pioneering many climbs in the Cumberland area, would cycle twenty miles to a mountain, climb all day, cycle twenty miles back and get up early for work on Mondays (*The Times*, 13 March 2004). Her climbing partner — later her husband — was a factory shoemaker, so the most vital parts of their equipment, the boots, were homemade. For her, the greatest obstacle was not their poverty but the older male climbers' view that women were 'shackles on achievement' — they defiantly named their next route 'The Shackle'.

On the other hand, the rules might trap participants in a double bind. Neither the tennis player Donald Budge (*The Guardian*, 28 January 2000)

nor Jack Holden, 'arguably the greatest marathon runner Britain has produced' (*The Herald*, 13 March 2004), could survive on the tiny daily allow-
ances given to amateurs for expenses. But Holden was also criticised by his
fellow athletes — the Oxbridge students then dominant — when he took
a job as a groundsman to support himself. Even with his earnings, he had
insufficient to buy new running shoes. His most dramatic confrontation
was in the Auckland Empire Games in 1950. His old shoes having fallen to
bits in the course of the Marathon, he continued, barefoot, the blood from
his feet provoking his pursuit by a Great Dane, who snapped at his heels.
The tension in this obit is less between the man and the dog than between
the man and the other runners, all amateurs.[11] Nevertheless, an epic victory
such as Holden's has something of the old battle sequences of the earlier,
1900 obituaries: it reveals heroic agency as well as constraints.

To understand the theory and practice of amateurism within which these
subjects were struggling, it is instructive to read the contrasting portrait of
the rugby union player, John Matthews. Matthews, a minor public school-
boy and Guys' Hospital student, was Captain at the time when the British
team successfully confronted the Springboks. He was 'a solid scrummager,
though not the most athletic of lineout jumpers' (*The Times*, 22 February 2004). The obituary refers to his modesty and conviviality. Yet it also
reveals that membership of the touring team required as many as 'four
months away': in other words, it presupposed a considerable material freedom and affluence. It is not surprising, then, that Matthews subsequently
became a dentist with practices at Wimpole St. and Harley St. — the
private pinnacle of the profession. The obit also reveals, with unusually
barbed comments, this player's tricks of advancement, which we might see
as an inconspicuous yet effectively 'natural' pursuit of distinction. These
included his addition of Clive to his full name, that is, the careful inclusion
of an auratic ancestor to add lustre to his family, the turning of his back
to the selectors — thus showing his shirt number when he accomplished a
good move — and the invention of a later date of birth, so as to impress the
selectors with his youth. Is it too much to see these various strategies as the
part and parcel of the structural underpinnings of amateurism?[12]

Of course, some of the footballers, boxers and rugby league players did
use sport as *a way out of poverty*, frequently ending up owning pubs, bed
and breakfast houses, or small hotels. Alice Cross, for example, for many
years kept an inexpensive hotel in the Lakes, where she became the de
facto guardian of young climbers. For other such players, money suddenly
materialised and players got caught up in a dizzying round of consumption,
for which they lacked all community controls. Many ended their lives once
more in poverty. Such tales of upward and downward mobility are a minor
but persistent strand of these sporting obituaries and recall dramatically
the 'anomic' experiences of declassification depicted in Durkheim's classic
1897 account (1968). It is precisely this sense of delusory weightlessness
which is expressed most clearly in the life of Bubi Scholz, the 'puny' boxer

from a working class area of Berlin, who went on to become a world champion (*The Independent*, 23 August 2000). Scholz's roller-coaster trajectory is all the more absorbing in that in his heyday, he interpreted his own success as political: a mirror of the rise of post-War Germany from the ashes. Thrust into prominence by his boxing wins, he invested his money in business in perfumery, regaling himself with the comforting view (or sociodicy) that his riches epitomised the healthy vitality of West German society:

> I am in business now, the archetype of a successful man. There are hundreds of thousands like me in the Federal Republic. If I had the courage of megalomania, I would say: *we* are the republic.

Yet Scholz's sudden prosperity evaporated quickly — he began to drink excessively, became an alcoholic and shot his wife in a fit of jealousy. He went to prison for her death and returned, bloated and Alzeimer's-ridden, to end his days in an ugly and cheap Council flat.

THE RACIALISED FIELD OF SPORT

The sporting life as *either* salvation *or* a poisonous gift is even more prominent in the obits of African-Americans or Afro-Caribbeans. We note first that the development of the sport may be quite different from that initially consecrated by the 'aristocratic' Olympic committees (Bourdieu 1993b:121). Weightlifting is a good example of this: it represents a control over the body that is associated increasingly over time with an external transformation of bodily physique. The problem has been that the ensuing competence has often been perceived neither as the possession of a significant skill nor a talent. It is also no accident that many weight-lifters started the activity for precisely the utilitarian desire to strengthen their bodies and thus protect themselves more adequately.

In these violent street struggles, the racialised minority is particularly vulnerable. Only one obituary for a weightlifter appears here, yet, interestingly, it is for the Jewish East Ender, Hymie Binder, who developed his skill in London's Whitechapel between the Wars (*The Times*, 13 March 2004). After the War Binder started his own weightlifting gym and, with two Jewish friends, one of whom had been in a concentration camp, formed a famous equivalent to the Marx brothers in this East End sport. His obituary commemorates him more as a great trainer of legendary weightlifters than as a distinguished participant himself.

Illuminatingly, in this tiny fragment of memory, Hymie Binder appears as a *classless individual*, who, as a young private in the war, had to explain his weightlifting to General Montgomery, while his cheery familiarity later extended to his encounter with the Royal family. Yet, even in *The Times*, his obituary cannot be told without a key defining moment of his past —

his active engagement in the Battle of Cable Street, where Mosley's fascist Blackshirts were confronted by Jewish and Irish opponents. In this sense, Jewish collective memory, at stake in this obituary, marks out a different historical terrain from that figured in the narratives of the elite.

The sporting obituaries often replicate this pattern of initial commitment for the sake of protection, or as compensation against violent discrimination, especially in the case of African-American boxers. Blackness and sport are interwoven with misfortune in these narratives. Such tragic obituaries — except for Bubi Scholz, the only unambiguously tragic sporting obits — have certain common dimensions. They reveal, first, the same pattern as the footballers' trajectory — success and prosperity, followed later by drink and nomadic isolation. Second, they reveal, a distinctive sporting apprenticeship, in which the young black boxer has to take part in various ceremonies of degradation. These are the heritage of slavery in the sporting field — where, as with Beau Jack, a young black boxer will be required to fight blindfolded with four or five other boxers, the winning couple matched against each other in the regulated way (*The Guardian*, 28 February 2000). These 'brutal Battle Royals' are never mentioned in the case of white boxers. Third, even if the African-American achieves recognition and develops a subtle sense of the feel for the wider social game — as did Beau Jack when he gave up his earnings for war bonds — the long-term success and elevation that accompanies success in the American Dream is always absent for these sportsmen. Beau Jack ended his glorious career doing the menial work of a hotel shoeshine boy; equally, Cleveland Williams became a boxing success but, for all that, was nearly killed by a Texan policeman's bullet (*The Guardian*, 28 September 1999). And even those whites who flouted the formal or informal segregation of the 'races' could find themselves made redundant, as in the case of Jack Scott, a sociologist of sport and sports director at Oberlin University (*The Guardian*, 11 February 2000). Having appointed two African-Americans to prominent positions in the university training team, he was pushed out of his job by conservatives.

In terms of the field of sport itself, racialised structures penetrated in this period to the deepest levels, including the separation of 'Negro Leagues' for baseball distinct from the white league. A descending circle of recognition occurs here, in which the Negro Leagues were structurally subordinate. Yet when, after the Second World War, the baseball league was desegregated, the black leagues became creamed of all their best players.

The obituary for Henry Kimbro returns vividly to these systematic injuries of 'race' (*The Independent*, 24 August 1999, and *The Guardian*, 13 July 1999). Kimbro lost key team-mates when the desegregation era started and they gravitated to the more affluent white teams. Moreover, due to the inferior status of the Negro Leagues, he never gained the recognition of the Baseball Hall of Fame, the ultimate sporting accolade. Rather the reverse, he was scapegoated in the white press. In a direct quotation (*The*

Guardian), Krimbro protests that he was being demonised as a 'bad man' and explains this in terms of his lack of education and hence of the capacity to express himself. Here the subjective voice of the dead man serves to underline his cultural dispossession, in sharp opposition to the benign assurance about having overcome bad fortune that is implicit in the Hymie Binder obit.

A final tragic obituary is that for Moacir Barbosa, the goalkeeper, who was scapegoated for having let in a goal at an epic Brazil-Uruguay World Cup match of 1950 (*The Guardian*, 13 April 2000). Again the obituarist frames this in terms of racialised inequality. Barbosa, the only black Brazilian player, was unable to stop an ingenious goal from Uruguay, who went on to win the game. Barbosa was then stigmatised for the failure by the Brazilian fans and fell pathetically from grace. Twenty years later, the former goalkeeper overheard a woman in a shop telling her son 'Look at him, son. He is the man that made all of Brazil cry'. Many years later, impoverished and the incessant object of hate, Barbosa's obit recounts that he still sought to vindicate himself — 'I'm not guilty. There were eleven of us.'

NATIONAL ICONS

Many of the sportsmen who are commemorated in the obits — particularly footballers and cyclists — became 'folk heroes', and are remembered with extraordinary affection. Some of these, however, made a transformation from folk hero to national or international icons. These play a key figure in popular memory, associated in our period with very long obits. They suggest once again the significance of certain mass events in the sporting calendar for the creation of modern national ceremonies: the football Cup Final, for example has played, since 1871, a key role in cementing both a cross-regional class identity and a national identity (Hobsbaum and Ranger 1983: 299–300). Moreover, it is a feature of these individuals, that they had already undergone a metamorphosis into national figures well before their death. In contrast, Abraham Lincoln was first mourned at his death in 1865 as a compassionate or even comic folk hero. It was only after a generation (1909) that he had gained the epic grandeur of stature appropriate for a national icon (Schwartz 1990).

Only a minority of individuals in this sample might be said to have had this national or international stature with a general public, notably Emil Zatopek in athletics and Stanley Matthews and George Best in football.[13] Chris Brasher, also a national icon, never quite had the same easy and familiar links with a popular public and is a more detached, Olympian figure. In contrast with the other cases, as will be argued, the obituary for the West Indies' cricketer, Roy Gilchrist, underlines the unorchestrated and unpredictable aspects of such national prominence, where iconic status is not proof against downfall.

Stanley Matthew's page-long tributes hail his unique footballing triumphs, both in terms of his longevity as a player and in relation to the subtlety of his play. *The Guardian* starts with a classic obituary judgement:

> Nicknamed the wizard of dribble in Britain, known abroad as der Zauberer, Stanley Matthew who has died aged 85 was the first ever European footballer of the year and arguably the outstanding British player of his generation. (24 April 2000)

The obituarist's technique is to emphasise the critical assessments of Matthew's early playing — 'Too individualistic! Too unpredictable! Too slow to release the ball!' But this only serves to enhance the extraordinary nature of his mature achievement, not just in the elegance of his ball control, but in his repudiation of fouls.

He is presented in *The Independent's* obituary as from working-class origins — although also from a sporting family: his father was a boxer — the 'fighting barber of Hanley'. Further, like Mannion, he had his conflicts over money with the manager of his first club, Stoke City, Bob McGrory, yet neither he (nor Mannion) are presented as having been diminished by these wage disputes. The main point in this obit is that Matthews' achievements might have been bought at the cost of an anti-social asceticism (going to bed at 9.30 p.m.) — an asceticism from which the obituarist distanced himself, yet he played at the height of his capacities for longer than anyone else, until well past fifty. Nor is it just as an old and brilliant 'Methusaleh' that he is honoured: the obituary describes the intervention of Stoke businessmen early in his career to get Matthews' tussle with his manager, McGrory, resolved because his affectionate local supporters' low morale had so dramatically *affected production*. It is in this sense that we can talk of Matthews as representing popular memory.

Brasher, by contrast, represents the tradition of public school, Oxbridge athletics and the Olympics' disinterested amateurism (*The Guardian*, 1 March 2003). His obituary is unstinting in praise of his long-distance running distinction, not least his Olympics Gold medal. It emphasises too, his co-operative spirit — he was one of the three athletes who, running together, allowed Bannister to beat the four-minute mile record. Later he is said to have extraordinary vision in establishing the London Marathon, which he advocated, in terms symptomatic of the 1980s, as unifying participants and spectators beyond 'racial' differences. His background and education guaranteed him the power to translate his competences into a new context: he subsequently had all the marks of a distinguished career as administrator of general programmes for the BBC. However, this is a life emblematic of the distanced grace of an elite iconic figure, rather than that of folk heroism.

Zatopek's obituaries are the least ambivalent for all the national heroes, for in these he combines in a way that the others do not quite manage, exceptional performance as a runner with exemplary personal or political/moral qualities (see *The Independent*, 23 November 2000, *The Guardian,* 23 November 2000). He shares with Abraham Lincoln and Stanley Matthews the same poor origins (he was a carpenter's son who became a Bata factory worker, in Moravia) and it is the world of immediate material necessity which perhaps instilled into him the extraordinary asceticism to which all the obits testify — a struggle for mastery involving running in Army boots (or barefoot) through the snow, or constant breathing exercises, which occasionally induced fainting. The asceticism however was in the interests of the sport — testimony to the growing strength for him of the sporting illusio, not in the interests of any kind of religious salvation. He had extraordinary victories or rather epic successes, the three gold medals of the 1952 Helsinki Olympics having been his most sustained achievement. It is perhaps worth pointing out that the habitus of running was different in Finland from Czechoslovakia, because, in the generation earlier, Finns had already become national icons and running had acquired the character of a secular 'second religion' (*Guardian*, 23 November 2000). This connection with the Finnish tradition seems to have appealed to Zatopek and spurred him on. In his dizzying set of successes at Helsinki, he won two golds, then, encouraged perhaps by his wife's gold, he triumphed in a further long-distance run.

Zatopek's national athletic reputation could not protect him from political sanctions. Despite having a Czech Army career which reached the heights of a Colonel, his early support of the Prague Spring in 1968 was sufficient for him to be demoted, post-Dubcek, to menial work and to 'ritual humiliation' in the seven years subsequently.[14] The same qualities that had ensured his earlier individual mastery over bodily weaknesses, had clearly now emerged as a preparedness to speak out against the grain of complicity with Soviet power. The implication of both obituaries is that it was precisely through this lack of collusion that he remained an unfading representative of popular consciousness.

This independent courage is also enhanced by his popularity — the obits are full of little stories of his joking with other athletes to encourage them to run their best and they tell, finally, of his act of generosity when he gave a fellow-Australian runner one of his gold medals. By the 1980s he had become an international star, but when he visited London and was put up in a luxury hotel he rejected it as 'too aristocratic'.

What comes through, particularly in the *Independent* obituary, is a strong 'self' that has attained a degree of unity. In other words, the obituary is not just an arid list of achievements nor even an analysis of the causal mechanisms producing this distinguished series of performances. Its tacit appeal also, perhaps, is that it offers an image of how one should live one's life (Taylor 1989) or what Williams called 'resources of hope' (Williams 1989).

Occasionally, the terrain of sport becomes a site of unexpected struggles, perhaps most notably in the case of 'cultural intermediaries' who have none of the aura of the contending players. Thus while some individuals are celebrated as innovative rule-makers, responsible for the further rationalisation of the sport (see, for example, Sir Peter Johnson, the chairman of the world authority on yachting (*The Guardian*, 30 July 2003)), others have been given negative obituaries. The most instructive instance of this was the uniquely critical obit for the Italian, Primo Nebiolo, President of the International Amateur Athletics Federation for eighteen years (*The Guardian*, 8 November 1999). Having dropped innuendoes of Mafia connections, the obituary implies that the Italian President was unacceptable in every single action of his career. In a curious form of British chauvinism, he is castigated as much for his attempts to equalize the Northern European nations' voting strength with that of the South as he was for his blatant efforts to use the Kuwaiti Royal family into demanding the withdrawal of an opponent to his own rule. Coupling these acts with Nebiolo's transfer of the Federation to Monte Carlo to escape 'the severity of English law', his 'loss' of certain drug tests and his blatant rigging of event results to favour his own country, the obituary in effect depicts the field of sport as a terrain of the Michelsian 'iron law of oligarchy'. At this point, sport ceases to be defined as an autonomous space at all. In the bitterly disillusioned obituary of Nebiolo, winning becomes simply the outcome of nationality, money and influence, not of independent sporting determinants.

A little more should be said, in this context, precisely about the sporting field as one that can be understood by the logic of practice, and the particular model of individual agency that this model offers. The sporting habitus in these obits is one where the players have developed a 'feel for the game', in which their minds operate like a *pense-bête* or memory-pad for their well-practiced moves. The co-operative game is one that is based, of course, on a highly social mechanism, where the striker, for example can only make the spectacular goals if he is fed the ball by other players. The obit writer understands, for example, the importance of other runners in providing the arena in which an individual can go ahead of the field and make a famous new record. In this sense the obit writer has a connoisseur's gaze — he admires the orchestrated action in football or American football, rather than possessing the lay gaze which is enthralled by the visible surface of virtuosity (Bourdieu 1993b: 124).

Of course, the obit writer also celebrates great and arduous individual feats, sometimes insisting that they amount to 'genius'. For example, Earl Wiggins' technique of 'jamming' was one whereby he used his clenched fist to lever himself up mountains, ('a form of Russian roulette few chose to pursue [...] [he] wagered his salvation on raw ability and madness', *The Independent*, 24 January 2003). But in most of these cases the obituary writer also reveals that the innovator is the one who has the whole history of the field at his fingertips. The development of new techniques shows that the virtuoso assumes and then goes beyond what is already known, just as a virtuoso artist is saturated with the history of the field (Bourdieu 1988b, 1996a, Goode 1978: 233).

It is also noticeable in the current obituaries that the language of art is used to legitimate or validate a sportsperson's distinguished feel for the game. There appears to be only one cultural field, so that terms developed in one area, such as the term 'auteur' in film theory, are applied to the area of sport. Thus an individual who pioneers a new route is said by fellow rockclimbing obituarists to be like an auteur (see Alice Cross, op. cit., John Sumner (*The Independent* 13 March 2004 — but not *The Times*, 10 April 2004) and Patrick Berhault, (*The Independent*, 7 May 2004). Indeed, sometimes such an individual breakthrough is named for ever after the person who first did the route or who first accomplished the manoeuvre. However, as another obituary writer reveals, such a stamp of individual identity is itself unevenly distributed according to the sportsperson's access to wider power. Thus a woman endowed with negligible amounts of social power, such as the black figure-skater, Mabel Fairbanks, failed to get her name stamped on the skating future despite a string of fertile innovations (*The Guardian*, 8 October 2001).

The 'auteur' label of virtuoso sportsmen is part of a wider phenomenon of complimenting good players by an honorific comparison of sport with the terrain — art — which is par excellence that of divine gifts and transcendent genius (against this, see Bourdieu, 1993a). Thus note the frequent use of the phraseology of high culture — a footballer can be described as a 'cultured player' or he/she will be praised for their 'cultivation of distribution', in a move which implicitly hijacks the language of high art to upgrade the standing of something feared to be or unfairly labelled as popular culture. Equally a 'legbreak bowler' appears here as an 'artist' and a 'philosopher'. If the appeal of art becomes too formulaic, the obituary borrows another language, that of magical techniques. Schiaffino is described by Brian Glanville as 'almost clairvoyant' in his understanding or as 'almost magically' slipping past the defender. In this more limited sense, too, the obit re-enchants the modern world.

CONCLUSION

We have focussed particularly on the sporting obituaries as part of popular memory, showing how the most distinguished sportspersons may retain a powerful local base of supporters whilst also becoming national icons. Such players may also, of course, end in a fall from grace. This was the case with Roy Gilchrist, a dispossessed Jamaican, and one for whom cricket was the only legitimate cultural investment for their tumultuous passions (Smith 2006). It was for his powerful bowling that Gilchrist was selected to play an Indian/Pakistan tour, yet precisely what made his bowling powerful was the undertow of aggression behind its speed. Such play is understood in his obit as a product of material urgencies. Gilchrist, born on a plantation, living in 'grinding poverty', was 'a difficult man to control'. Charged with ridding the touring team of indiscipline, Gilchrist's captain sent him home for bowling too many 'beamers', balls aimed at the players' heads. Thus aged only 24, his international career was summarily ended.

In this obituary Michael Manley, the former Jamaican Premier, describes the Gilchrist case as

> a tragedy born of an interaction between a flawed individual and a malformed society, an almost Greek inevitability as man and system proceeded to their inevitable and final conclusion. (*The Guardian*, 24 July 2001)

Here cricket remained an autonomous field, regulated by its own laws. Yet the social crisis it triggered reveals how its rules operate, with all the harshness of necessity, on actors whose practices are profoundly shaped by the wider field of power.

11 The trade unionists' obituaries (1999–2006)

A brief note is in order on the small number of the obituaries of trade unionists — classified under manual workers or 'other': 1 per cent of the formal sample. The thin folder of the trade-unionist cuttings for the qualitative sample contrasts with the luxuriating sheaves of the obituaries in the actors', musicians', academics' and politicians' files.[1] Their absence from newspaper collective memory is informative, not least given their effectiveness in aiding the removal of absolute poverty for four-fifths of the Western working class in the twenty-year period, 1950–70. For within the turbulence of the global economy of capitalism, this period was the 'golden age of the worker' in West Europe and America (Brenner 1998). Yet, by the 1970s, the reforms of those years came to seem to an influential section of the population, so many 'barriers to accumulation' (Panitch and Gindin 2005: 110). Moreover, by the time of the sample at the end of the century the Foucauldian 'care of the self' was fast becoming a more attractive ethos, eclipsing the traditional ethical basis for labour discipline.

By 1997 in Britain, trade union membership had declined dramatically, due in no little part to the contraction of manufacturing industry.[2] The greater unionisation of the hugely-expanded service sector has not compensated for this loss. Moreover, the new professional and technical sector of the labour-market began to imprint its distinctive cultural stamp on the TUC, diluting its earlier pithy speech and avoiding its antagonistic images of management (Sampson 2004: 63). Simultaneously, the relations between the trade unions and the parties changed. Most dramatically — by the 1990s, the union influence on Labour had sharply declined, due in part to the lessened scope for the bloc vote.

The catalyst of anti-trade union legislation of the 1980s, added to the structural decline of union membership, accelerated social inequalities.[3] Yet — perhaps more than at other periods — such objective widening of differences in economic, cultural and social capitals was more often interpreted as due to the absence of 'economic realism' — or in the periphery, to national oppression, rather than to class antagonisms (Bourdieu 1987b). Even where a language of class *has* been deployed in public discourse, the two wings of the working-class movement — industrial and political — often failed to beat in harmony, as Raymond Williams once noted. Undoubtedly this was in large part because of disillusionment with earlier Labour governments (see Scott 1991: 139, Devine 1997: 132). Finally the vision of trade unionism itself changed throughout Europe and America, particularly from the late 1960s, with the rise of a fresh debate about France as a 'blocked' society, or, in Britain, trade unions as 'dinosaurs'. This shift in language favoured a new, flexible and non-bureaucratic image of the enterprise, surprisingly projecting onto it that ethos of independent creativity and visionary thinking that ultimately derived from the newly-canonised authority of the avant-garde. Boltanski and Chiapello called this, in 1999, 'the new spirit of capitalism'.

As early as 1976, Boltanski along with Bourdieu had made a prescient reading of this French discourse, distinguished as it is by its recognition of the application to ordinary production of the vocabulary of the modernist avant-garde and especially of the avant-gardes' resonating politics of time (Bourdieu and Boltanski, 1976, Bourdieu, 2002b: 138–9). What was at stake was the ability of the technocratic strata to transcend the old classifications and especially old political polarisations, by an invitation to a new bet on the future (Bourdieu 2002b: 211, see also Nora, I, 1996: 6, III, 1992: 1009). This future was depicted as one that had only a single possible direction. Its direction was not just towards *the end of ideology* but *the end of history*, thus bestowing on contemporary accomplishments the upper limit of all *potential achievements* of humankind.

The inevitable converse of seeing the 'present as pregnant with a necessary future' is that all the old oppositional language becomes outdated or archaic, and with it all the accomplishments of trade unionists, including the Welfare State (Bourdieu and Boltanski 1976). The leading management theorists of the 1970s identified an ill-assorted collection of *outmoded groups* — from peasants and trade unionists to insignificant civil servant officials (Bourdieu 2002b: 138).[4] In this new politics of modernist time, some actors are adapted to the 'shock of the new': they accept, with it, a new social Darwinianism. Only those who have 'a fear of the future' insist on a resistance to change: these are the outdated remnant, stuck in the mud of their local bases, unable to experience the breadth of vision open to the true cosmopolitan (Boltanski and Chiapello 1999). The universe of possible modes of domination is therefore complete and the only serious contenders for the foreseeable future are the technocratic strata with their 'uniquely reasonable' hopes (Bourdieu 2002b: 131–46).

As a consequence of these divisions, trade unionists became increasingly seen in an aesthetic optic, as profoundly conservative, not unlike the Academic painters who had to be swept away in the first period of experimentation by the painters of modern life. Moreover, having been situated at the sharp end of social conflict, the trade union officials' lives are depicted as having been unusually fraught. The traces left in the few obituaries that have been published for trade unionists often convey unease. Criticised stringently by the Left as well as by those with temporal power, these actors lacked both the assured serenity of the traditional dominant class and the honour given to those who create consecrated cultural goods.

THE OBITUARIES OF TRADE UNIONISM

All the union leaders who are awarded obituaries had their roots in the subordinate classes and in this sense they represent, like many subjects of the sports obits, popular and counter-memory.[5] Materially very poor in their youth, these men — for there are in this sample no women amongst them — came from the 'Red Belt' (industrial villages and towns, especially from single- industry localities such as Partick, in Glasgow or the East Ends of great cities, including Paris) (Bourdieu, 1984; Goldthorpe et al, 1968; Nora, I, 1996: 205–40).

Obituaries, in Goffman's words, are 'the last theatre of the world'. Given the culture of ambiguity around trade unionism, it is hardly surprising that the obits of trade-union leaders are often calculated to subtly discredit their subject, nor that the most critical obits of trade unionists have appeared in papers that have historically favoured the perspective of the Right. Here I address how these four types of obituary portrayal incorporate popular memory and thus how, seen through this prism, the dignity of such posts is shaped in the future.

1. Traditional working-class: positive trade union obituaries

One category of such obits is of trade union officials whose lives were spent struggling abstemiously for the interests of their occupational group or class. In these traditional obits, the subject's roots within the working-class are unquestioned, so that the later demands of action — such as an effective strike — arise out of the interaction between his leadership and the rank and file's trust (compare Vincent 1981; Holyoake 1892). An underlying pattern runs through them: it narrates the story of a radical home, with its canon of dissenting authors, attendance at a Socialist Sunday School, early school-leaving and the first, manual job (however good their school work). The subject is typically tested or challenged in early adulthood: in the obituaries of older trade unionists, they choose to go to the Spanish Civil War or (in France), fight early in the Resistance. Returning from war, the obituary's protagonist throws himself into trade union action as part of his apprenticeship. Here the ways within the obituary start to markedly diverge.

On the one hand, the unpaid trade unionists remain at the grass roots, as shop-steward or committee member, often galvanised into action by a particularly dramatic experience: an accident or a strike. These are rare amongst obituaries at the British level, although somewhat more often found in Scottish national newspapers, such as *The Herald*.⁶ On the other hand, the trade-union portraits depict men who are elected as national general secretaries or other full-time officials whilst still remaining dedicated, disciplined figures.⁷

The obituary for John Foster, a national organiser, is a memorable example of this traditional type (*The Guardian*, 9 July 1999). Its author is Ken Gill, who, as a fellow Communist trade union leader, shared the same habitus and had an intimate understanding of this field of industrial power. The obit emphasises Foster's achievement as a member of a team of union officials at the UAEW (Engineering Workers) and particularly as the national organiser, from 1962–81. His work, the constantly extended conversion of non-unionised men and women to union membership demanded intensive periods of travelling and living amongst strangers. Foster's remarkable achievement, Gill claims, contributed to his union, the UAEW (together with the Transport and General Workers) peaking at twelve million members in this period.

The son of a greengrocer who had hawked his produce from a horse and cart in East London, Foster turned early into a 'consummate lecturer, who illustrated theory with anecdotal evidence'. He achieved this as a result of becoming a 'working-class intellectual', greatly influenced by the mass unemployment and the Spanish Civil War. Reading widely and closely, Foster nevertheless insisted — in time honoured fashion — that theory should never be separated from practice. He was also quick at detecting future trends and was one of the first to advocate keeping workers' pensions separate from employers' investments. Foster was also well-known as a man of integrity, whom employers knew would keep his word. This trustworthiness in turn accumulated *symbolic capital* for the group.

In a rare obituary insight into his subjective vision, we learn that Foster, as an older man, was disappointed in the decision of a trade union fellow engineer to take a peerage. In other words, this trade unionist remained faithful to a worldview with a dichotomic vision of classes, a vision inhospitable to accepting privilege within the imagined unity of the nation. Hence Gill's final accolade: Foster

> epitomised the honourable trade union leader of his time — skilled, respectable and respected.

This portrayal typifies the positive appraisal of trade unionists. However, trade-union obituaries may, on occasion, defy the usual canons of 'balance' and pronounce unreservedly critical judgements.

2. The negative radical trade unionist obituary — illegitimate power

Certain union activists — notably in the *Daily Telegraph* obits — 'morph' into figures of dogmatic and truculent intransigeance. Such hostile obit delineation might be purely the consequence of the different angle of vision of the *Telegraph*, whose editorial politics oscillate between the realist denial of utopian goals and the conservative desire to reinstate a lost organic society. However — like the leaders of any progressive party — the fraught trajectory of the socialist trade unionist provokes dilemmas which cannot be easily solved without danger to the other values for which she or he stands: in the case of socialists, those of democracy and civil liberties. It is the structural clashes between both remaining consistently radical and also acting by all means possible to maintain a power base that produces the symptomatic perversions of corruption and elitist isolation. The spokesperson thus becomes detached from those in whose name they claim a voice, as Bourdieu describes in his account of political fetishism and the self-consecration of the delegate (Bourdieu 1991: 208–9). In turn, it is this tangled ball of underlying structural forces which allows such caricatural portrayals to acquire the semblance of plausibility.

Reprinted in our sample period, *The Daily Telegraph* has three obits from the late 1980s or 1990s: those featuring Frank Haxell,[8] Reg Briginshaw, and Jack Dash. Whilst appearing to provide fairness by proffering compliments, the tributes in these obits merely serve as traps, to strengthen the critique already made. Their portrayals are unambiguously negative, although the union-leaders' offences vary from forms of deviance which would be recognised as unacceptable by their own union grass roots — such as Briginshaw's repeated sale of his own union premises — to forms which might be praiseworthy to their own members (such as the same leader's 'enthusiastic support ... of the application of union power for political ends'). All three were associated with the Communist Party and all three were trade-union leaders who were skilled in their mobilisation of their members for collective ends. These, of course, included wage-struggles, represented here as exorbitant and spiralling out of control. Yet, over and above their implied authorship over inflation, they are also presented as corrupt, either via vote-rigging, or via financial manoeuvres (one such leader, Briginshaw, had bizarrely invested the proceeds in South African apartheid-period krugerrands). In each case they were attributed with extraordinary ability to destroy the industry they represented. As though by a perverse individual genius, they wreaked havoc, by means of a 'naturally' docile and innocent rank and file.

The obituary writers operate here as avenging angels finally unmasking power. Refusing the allure of a figure who in old age might be regarded as a 'character' (Jack Dash, the dockworkers' leader), or who even became ennobled (Reg Briginshaw, the printers' leader), the obit authors stubbornly insist on a deeper and more dangerous reality: responsibility for the closure of the London docks for the former, disruption of one industry after another for the latter. Yet what makes these portrayals so effectively destructive is that they imperceptibly elide traditional working-class values of mutual aid or self-sacrificial activism with certain narrowly-instrumental practices, especially those that have trampled roughshod over democracy. The obit for Frank Haxell is the most clear-cut and persuasive in this respect: its claim is that even his own allies repudiated him for bringing the Communist Party into disrepute by 'condoning illegal and undemocratic methods'.

It is not without significance that that these men are denied any presentation of their subjective views. Devoid of all attractive saving graces, they lack even gravitas — Briginshaw is stated to be, physically, an 'ageing Tarzan', with a 'froggish face'. His personality, like Haxell's above, is quintessentially dangerous 'unstable, with a marked tendency to megalomania'

The adverse judgements in this category of obits are exemplified in the case of Haxell:

> Frank Haxell … was a ruthless Communist whose control of the Electrical Trades Union wreaked havoc throughout British industry for a decade before his power was broken by the High courts in 1961 [...] Haxell was a brilliant, dedicated organiser … he invented the 'guerrilla' strike to maximise disruption at the least cost to his union, legitimised the unofficial strike and in 1955 managed to halt the national press for 26 days. He was also a singularly unattractive personality, an arid and humourless zealot and a rigidly orthodox Stalinist. (Massingberd 1998: 26–8)

3. The 'labourist' conciliatory official.

Although often a youthful militant, like the first type, this typical figure is a model trade unionist who is committed both to his members' interests and to the *national interest*, perceived as an essential reality beyond the simple play of immediate class interests. This subject opposes a strong class standpoint viewed from the standpoint of the proletariat, with its 'wertrationalitat' or ultimate evaluative commitment to emancipation. Instead, s/he seeks to reconcile certain conflicting interests, such as that between vigorous trade union action and staying within the law. Ultimately a 'moderate' leader, she or he is guided by the collectivist ethic, but refuses to pursue this with single-minded tenacity. In other words she or he has relinquished the 'ethic of an absolute end' for devotion to several possibly-conflicting ends and to the rational techniques to achieve them. Weber calls this search the 'ethic of responsibility' (Weber 1991: 127).

By far the largest category of the trade unionists is of this type: Len Murray can stand for them all. Characterised as a tragic figure when leader of the Trades Union Congress, he was finally broken by the effects of the 1970s' anti-trade union legislation, retiring early (*The Times*, 22 May 2004; *The Independent*, 22 May 2004).

The objectification of Murray makes it clear why he was so torn. His principles of vision (and division) were those of a man who was a 'miraculous survivor' (Bourdieu 1996b: 104–5): a farm labourer's son, he had become a scholarship boy and burseried student at New College, Oxford. From here, he went direct to the TUC economics dept — possessing a strong and intense vision of social change. Most unusually at this time, he was a bureaucrat, who had had no direct experience of manual work. A Methodist lay preacher, there was a profound homology between Murray's church-inspired beliefs in reconciliation and his union philosophy of 'partnership' within an individualistically-based 'social contract' (Thompson 1968: 350–440).

Murray's obituaries portray him as a good man, caught in a situation not of his own choosing. His life had in itself exemplified the more advanced, meritocratic elements of British society and seemed to point to a slow Bernsteinian evolution. Nevertheless, he was forced instead into social disillusionment. All his earlier optimism and work ethic (the burning of midnight oil, the days out on the stump) were now put in question. In the obituaries, the breakdown of the post-war class compromise is given in miniature, through Murray as its protagonist.

The Times' obit is written from a perspective that reinforces the legitimacy of Murray's own pluralist position. Murray accepted the framework of a market-based capitalism and also the reality of industrial disputes. Yet he was caught in commitment to a mode of institutionalised trade union conflicts which were now being undermined. The destruction of his own beliefs physically damaged him:

> By the time the second General Election had confirmed the Conservatives in power, the TUC was a broken reed, with Murray finding it difficult to control its warring elements. It was never again to recover its former influence and Murray , by this time suffering from ill-health, left office early … he had seen his cherished belief in consensus in the conduct of economic life utterly vanquished.

4. The new bureaucratic union official or the new Bernsteinianism

The fourth and final type represents a late modern 'consumerist unionism' rather than the older politics of Marxist or Protestant asceticism (see Bauman, 1998). One such typical official was Clive Jenkins, the Association of Scientific, Technical and Managerial Staffs leader, whose obituary is profoundly ironic in tone (*The Independent*, 23 September 1999). Whilst acknowledging his success in unionisation rates, the obituary subtly denigrates his highly instrumental rationality. Jenkins' entire significance lay in the deal between him and his members — he acted rationally to secure his members' material improvements, they, in turn, allowed him to enrich himself. Union leadership here became merely another kind of cash nexus between official and rank and file, increasingly reduced to purely monetary advantage.

In terms of realpolitik, Jenkins's *Independent* obit defines him as hugely successful. ASTMS was brilliantly built up in 1970 from a minnow to a 'large fish' as it merged with other strong unions, the membership increasing in the period from 11,000 to 650,000. Jenkins' own power base was remarkable: he was a supreme industrial strategist and, in Tony Benn's words, quoted in the obituary, he built up the Union like a Tammany Hall political machine. He was equally strategic in building up his own economic capital, the first union official to become a millionaire. He did so by astute — and entirely legal — property deals and a golden handshake of £213,000. Like a Brett Easton novel, there is a great deal of money mentioned in this obit.

Yet if in mentioning money so often, the obit seems to break with the rules of gentrified bourgeois anti-capitalism, deeply laid in the nineteenth century novel (Lovell, 1987), it also adopts a condescending language never used of the Great and the Good (Lord Maclehose, say, or Lord Hailsham):

> He [Jenkins] was an eccentric but charming little man, who was the original millionaire 'champagne socialist'.

Overwhelmingly, his weaknesses are summed up in his fatal arrogance:

> 'The word 'arrogant' could have been invented for him'… 'he always appeared to be involved in a permanent love affair with himself'..

The obituary's coup de grace is the light shone over his dubious friendships, which, even in his lifetime, might not quite have ranked as social capital:

> Clive the Mouth, as TUC colleagues fondly dubbed him, was born to enjoy the good things of life, but like many wealthy socialists of his generation he wanted everybody to aspire to similar good fortune… it was little surprise to anyone that he was a friend of the late, disgraced tycoon, Robert Maxwell.

Jenkins subjectively perceived himself as a man of vision and foresight. Yet the obit undercuts such a classification, casting him instead as one who had power but little judgement, accommodating himself effortlessly to a world he claimed to criticise.

CONCLUSION

The figures evaluated most positively in this very small qualitative sample of trade unionists are those whose obituaries are written by writers who share their own viewpoint, whether a radical vision of social transformation or a partnership model of industrial relations. Len Murray receives a highly positive appraisal, but he represents most clearly a corporatist trade-union-ism, attractive to Keynesian business employers, which offered a partner-ship with the latter rather than a promise of usurping them. Murray was therefore Weber's 'responsible politician' par excellence. As in the case of other, more radical trade unionists, this kind of power-broking role takes a personal toll which, in this period, not infrequently became unendurable (Weber, 1991). Finally a new, bureaucratic trade unionism is depicted, typi-fied by Clive Jenkins, who turns to embrace the unstable consumer desires earlier denied both union leaders and rank and file. Here the earlier goal of a transformative change gradually loses its urgency, at least in the eyes of his obituary-writer.

We have seen also that these trade-union obits, although embedded in popular memory, represent various genres. Positive and negative are con-trasted typically by Foster and Jack Dash. Murray in this period has much of the resonance of a tragic hero, whilst Jenkins' otherwise disturbing suc-cess is met with the familiar critique of personal embourgeoisement, an attack meted out in a colloquial, trenchant and highly ironic style.

12 Conclusion

Late capitalism undoubtedly has its own cultural logic: one which is still profoundly marked by the 'transgressions to the power of two' stemming from high modernism (Heinich 1998b). Partly as a reaction to this esoteric art, there has emerged, throughout the West, societies in which easily-accessible auto/biographical musings are found everywhere (Plummer 2001). And just as auto/biographies are fashionably proliferating and luxuriating in length, so also obituaries are flourishing as *miniature* documents of life. These authoritative observations on the self have burst out of the narrow conventions of their nineteenth century chrysalis and are increasingly available, like the biography, to a wider and glistening range of voices. In relation to life-stories, this extraordinary phenomenon has led to auto/biographies being written by professional thieves (The Jack-Roller), by native Indian villagers in Guatemala (*I Rigoberta Menchu*) as well as by late Parisian surrealists (Anais Nin) and the ghost-narrators of Prime Ministers and rock stars. As Plummer has powerfully argued:

> In a society such as ours, flooded with biographical musings, here is a rich mine for the researcher. [....] Right now, at the start of a twenty-first century, the telling of life-stories has become such a voluminous business that we could start talking of something like an auto/biographical society. (Plummer 2001: 28, 78)

Similarly, obituaries take up greater newspaper space and are high on the list of readers' priorities; they spill out of the most legitimate channels (London-based broadsheet newspapers) into professional journals such as the *British Medical Journal*[1] (*BMJ*) or *Network* (British Sociological Association) and even into parish magazines. They are part of a wider need to pay homage to the dead but perhaps also part of a lingering desire for community, gemeinschaft. 'Britain', remarked one sociologist 'must be the most highly-obituarised society in the world' (Martins, 2004).[2]

Obituaries may yield research material for sociologists, just as they are standardly used for contemporary appraisals by architectural and art historians. However, in this study my intention has rather been to explore who nas been given an appreciative obituary, in order to engender a new way of understanding the death of the great, which we call collective remembering. Now this collective memory is itself made up of fragments or shards of memory, which deal with the 'epiphanies' or 'turning-points' in a life: those defamiliarising experiences or crises that provoke status passages in a moral career (Plummer 246: 81, 83). However, in the case of the obituary, the revelation of the different stages of the self is subordinated to the interests of stratification: the prime social objective is that of honouring the distinguished. And surprisingly — as Bourdieu and Bauman have remarked — the most poignant aspects of redrawing of the boundaries of those who have 'distinguished Being' as against those consigned to Nothingness, is that the rejected now feel 'nobodies', where once they were secure in their status (Bourdieu 1991: 126; Bauman 1992).

This fascination with the biography is not confined to the early twenty-first century. Kracauer, that perceptive observer of modernity, had already drawn attention in the interwar years to the 'pas-de deux' between modernist forms and popular culture (Frisby 1985: ch. 3). He observed that biography had once been an erudite form but that now it was a familiar aspect of everyday life. Indeed, Kracauer makes the essential point about this – that the biography is important at a time when there is a search for an authenticated and meaningful life, especially when the experimental novel no longer offers this. So 'the gist of a prose work which used to be provided by the invented narrative is now regained through an authenticated fate' (1995: 103). In the literary world of the novel, things have become blurred and ungraspable. However, the bourgeoisie can 'escape' via the biography — a form which places in a *museum* great individuals:

> history is condensed into the lives of its highly visible heroes. These heroes become the subjects of biographies not because there is a cult of hero-worship but because there is a need for a legitimate literary form…' (1995: 103)

Kracauer understood the main source of the production of biographies. Admittedly, he failed to predict the future heroes of the modern biography and obituary, for he sees the key passage in his time as a transition *from* erudite early artists' biographies, *to* the First World War generals and politicians and diplomats (like those of my 1900 obituary sample). He never anticipated the potential morphing of the obit/biography again, into its contemporary form — where it has as its subjects singers, actors and artists, not just the temporally-powerful class fraction. But he is right about the redemptive urge that the biography serves in its drive to pantheonisation:

> If there is a confirmation of the end of individualism, it can be grasped in the museum of great individuals that today's life puts on a pedestal. And the indiscriminate manner in which this literature seizes on any

and all statesmen is evident both of an inability to make correct period-specific selections, and, equally, of the redeemer's hurry. (1995: 105)[3]

THE REDEEMER'S HURRY: CHANGES IN THE CONTEMPORARY OBITUARY

The obituary editors — as we have seen in chapter 5 — believe that we stand at the brink of a new era of diminished obligation and unprecedented freedom. Could they have their fingers more closely on the pulse of obituary production than occasional commentators on these columns, such as Butler (2004)? Yes and no. Yes, in the sense that the obituaries are throwing off the old 'carapace of the [aristocratic or] bourgeois ego' (Ferguson 2004: 27). As has been shown via study of the 1900s, the obits were once linked to the use of a 'restricted code' within its columns, drawing on highly-for-mularised structures, much as liturgical chants fall within strict bounds. There has been a genuine change here. In another sense 'no' — the obituaries have only started to fully exploit the possible changes envisaged in the perspective of a long cultural revolution. This is so, despite the vehement protestations to the contrary of most obits editors.

To summarise, the obituaries have indeed been transformed to a degree. They can now incorporate a Gospel singer like Pop Staples (*The Independent*, 21 December 2000), a heterodox theatre director like Joan Littlewood or an academic like Jan Karski, made a 'righteous Gentile' after the War.[4] It is true that some newspapers — especially *The Times* and *Daily Telegraph* — still pride themselves on their military heroes, whom they label 'the moustaches'. But even these are changing; there are fewer individuals for whom the general's or admiral's appointment sits on the shoulders like an assured destiny and who gain their recognition essentially from their birth.[5] Instead, the obituaries feature stories of extraordinary bravery on the part of *untraditional heroes* — as in the case of the Gurkha Ganju Lama VC (*Daily Telegraph*, 3 July 2000) or Agansing Rai, VC, ' a man of great wisdom and stature' who led his men to take Japanese bunkers on a vital supply line under fire, sometimes on his own,[6] but who could not be promoted because he was a native soldier (*The Guardian*, 10 June 2000). They stress not hierarchy and subordination, discipline and unquestioned obedience, but the moments of altruistic risk, of dedicated valour — like the naval midshipman who led others in throwing out his boat's unex-ploded shells, stored in an ammunition-locker which had become engulfed in flames (Archie Cameron, *The Daily Telegraph*, 10 July 2000). The reader — however anti-militarist– is gripped by curiosity at such altruistic risk-taking rather than individual flight. Nor are the war obituaries just tales of men. There are woman, such as Freddy Bloom, who spent two years in a Japanese prisoner of war camp — five months in a room (17 ft. × 10 ft.) with fifteen men, forced to sit immobile all day (*The Times*, 19 June 2000)

— or the Frenchwomen who led teams of Resistance fighters, like Henriette Gilles- Cristiani (*Le Monde*, 2 May 2000); perhaps most poignant, there is the nurse, Vivian Bullwinkel (*Telegraph*, 17 July 2000), whose boat, full of nurses fleeing from occupied Singapore, was captured by the Japanese. (All the nurses were told to walk into the sea and were then strafed from behind by the machine guns of the Japanese army.)[7]

In brief, the end of the feudal ancien regime, with its aristocratic military heroes has come very late to these war obituaries —no doubt because these funeral tales have continued to bind a retrospective gemeinschaft, or community, through conflict, rekindling memories of a united social defense against the enemy in the two World Wars (Simmel 1964). It could not be said that the obituaries' account of mass warfare frames combat as a loss of ego-depth (cf Ferguson 2004), but rather — especially in *The Times* and *Telegraph* — of inspirational leadership, selflessness and generosity.

However in the systematic samples, the military are slowly declining in proportion. Gone, too, are the days when the obituaries simply portrayed an old aristocratic elite whose genealogy could itself be nakedly admired. If the obituaries of the year 1900 were about kinship and affinity, even by 1948 this had changed. These are the heroes of the 1930s 'utopia of planning' instead (Samuel, 1985).

All societies have honoured the great and the good. Bauman demystifies the obituary and other 'immortality strategies'. If the ruling ideas of each epoch have been those of the ruling class, so also, he writes, the dominants bind future generations so that their class and its ideas are thought immortal. This creates inequalities in survival in memory after death (Bauman 1992: 58). Some are honoured; others become mere rubbish, objects to be removed as fast as decently possible from view, like waste (Scanlan 2005: 98, 131). In modernity, argues Bauman, immortality strategies change. They used to be based on the claims of the prosperity achieved under the dominants' rule or on their extraordinary longevity. In modernity, instead, a secular society honours those who make durable forms for consumption — eternally-lasting goods. And, in his view, this creates a more poignant rubbishing of others who lack such distinction — he quotes Bourdieu: "Cultural consecration does indeed confer on the objects, persons and situations it touches a sort of ontological promotion akin to transubstantiation" (Bauman, 1992: 65–66).

It could be agreed that with the casting off of the old aristocratic carapace (the old Establishment), a dilemma about the nature of distinction has been prevalent. There has, first of all, been a break expressed with the past and a rethinking of the categories of distinction. The old public sphere — as in Ancient Greece — with its systematic exclusion of women and slaves from the polis — has been seen as in need of extension, as having been drawn too narrowly. At the same time, the public sphere of achievement is still the most 'objective' news guide to selection (remember what the *New York Times* obit editor said, 'We are not an equal opps area'). To enter into the world of the obit at all, some public achievement is necessary.

The quantitative chapter fuels an argument that that since 77 per cent of the obituaries featuring their own nationals represent people who have been to public school, there is still a great potential for charting *other* types of distinction. The obituary editors may be unaware of the extent to which their gift of an obituary — uncommodified, free, not to be bought — is still unconsciously donated to an elite privileged from birth. This derives especially from the institutions from which they take their subjects ('the Army, the old universities, the Church...'). The editors realise that they are in danger of overemphasising the media world, but they may be unaware of ignoring other social realities outside these boundaries.

Fifty-five per cent of the 2000 obituaries are of those in the arts (together with media); a further significant fraction is of scientists. There *has* been an embrace of highly autonomous occupational fields within the obits. Thus while we have written of the obituaries beginning to span dominants' memory, popular memory and counter-memory, Halbwachs' influence should also not be forgotten in his concern for *occupational* memory. This is shown brilliantly in his *The Collective Memory of Musicians*. Here he emphasises that musicians, rather than having a particular sensitivity to the sounds of nature, are peculiar in belonging to their own society, with its own laws, which is distinct in its interest in 'pure music' from the rest of the society. He adds

> It is not that an individual finds in himself — and in himself alone — a new theme, a combination of sounds that his mind creates from nothing. But he discovers it in the world of sounds which the society of musicians is alone in exploring: it is because he accepts its conventions [....] that he comes to do so. (Halbwachs 1997: 39, my translation)

The musician's obit, because it is often written by a fellow-musician, can open up this social world. Similarly, the long obituaries for the Nobel scientists, Francis Crick (*The Independent* 3 August 2004) and David Blow (*The Times* 1 July 2004) opened up fleetingly the lab worlds of America and Britain (especially the group working at the Cavendish in Cambridge), where the work discovering the coding of genetic information into molecules and the X-ray crystallography of proteins was undertaken. The rational, Enlightenment aspect of the obituary, then, is its reduction of the bewildering elements of the division of labour — those aspects which made for anomic lack of understanding in the midst of the interdependencies of modern society, or contribute to disenchantment in the midst of progress. Within this *re-enchantment* of life the obits act to break down fragmentation. In this sense they contribute to death as a 'sacred time' — evident most strikingly when the whole society is engaged with grieving for a loss, as with the death of Victor Hugo in the French Third Republic. Even dissidents, we have suggested, have to acknowledge the general structure of feeling within their own 'schismatic theatre'.

However, these categories of distinction are *still* too narrow. Could the obits become further democratised without entirely losing their emphasis on distinction? There are two possibilities here, the *rise of the celebrity* to replace the military-aristocratic elite or alternative *expansions of the public sphere*. The current obits can be linked to differential chances of recognition in life. Certain groups, as we have seen in the quantitative study, are very largely excluded in this politics of recognition — immigrant leaders, labour leaders, women without paid work.

In relation to the rise of the celebrity, the emergence of the 'hero of consumption' (popular entertainers or sportspeople) was already noted in America by Lowenthal as early as 1946–47, although his category of 'consumption' was notoriously blunt. At that point, 67 per cent of the biographies in *The Saturday Evening Post* and 78 per cent of those in *Colliers* featured such heroes or heroines (1961: ch. 4). In Britain, as we have seen from the obituaries editors, the phenomenon is now accelerating — my file of musicians' obits bulges abundantly, not just with current icons but with the past icons of all the proliferating cults discernable on the musical scene. This inclusion of the celebrity will have realised its logical extreme when obituaries appear for, say, the residents of the Big Brother series. Increasingly, celebrities appear less because of the esteem of their musical or artistic peers than because of their fame. Such an aura of fame is, of course, notoriously evanescent, yet its fleeting qualities are not insuperable obstacles for the subsequent award of obituaries.

I turn now to the future and the cultural politics (as opposed to the empirical arguments) of this study. If celebrity populism is rejected as an abdication from any adequate basis for extending the obits, what remains? The answer lies around the notion of a re-examination of the public sphere so that it might better include a counter-public sphere or proletarian public sphere. Nancy Fraser has argued for both a politics of 'recognition' (status) and a politics of 'redistribution' (class) as twin elements inherent in any notion of justice (Fraser and Honneth 2003: 60). Inescapably, part of this 'politics of recognition' is the continued expansion of the obituaries into previously neglected regions. The surprising aspect of this study is that those neglected territories were shown to be middle class as well as working-class regions.

Studies by historians have revealed archival materials which sustain our belief that there is a whole category of actors — at present largely bereft of obituaries — who might potentially be awarded them. Take, for example, the authors of secular, working-class autobiographies, a type of writing which was distilled in the nineteenth century from the older model of spiritual autobiography. From one masterly study of 142 such autobiographies by David Vincent (1981), it is clear that their authors were partly seeking to reconstruct their past selves by writing memoirs, partly refuting stereotyped conceptions of their class.[8] But it is also obvious that these were men and women who took part in transforming the social order — often at great risk — through political activity, trade unions or simply mutual aid. It was no accident, argues Vincent, that one such autobiographer, Thomas Hardy, was also founder of the London Corresponding Society; another was founder of the first London Cooperative movement (William Lovett) and yet another, Joseph Arch, forged a national farm labourers' union. Their historian writes:

> It is clear that the self-improving working-men made an essential contribution to the developing ideology and organisation of the working class, and that in the context of an intensification of class hostility, the most sober and rational men could find themselves in conflict with the law, as the careers of many autobiographers demonstrate. (1981: 195)

These men and women acquired valuable skills which enhanced their own lives but also 'were indispensable to the emerging working class' (1981: 194). Certainly they saw themselves as more prey to contingency than members of other classes — their lives, they wrote, were a 'lottery' so constrained by social and other determinants that they were like corks floating directionless in water — yet for all this one could write:

> the struggles of many of the working men of this country, if placed on paper, would read as well, and be as interesting as the lives of many a coronetted lord. (William Aitken, quoted Vincent, 1981: 29)

Most of these autobiographies suggest men who were unusual[9] and yet who could surely be considered 'distinguished'. The cultural analysis given us by Raphael Samuel of self-educated, organised workers in the 1940s and 1950s (2006) suggests similar sources of distinction. Many of them also wrote memoirs or were the object of pamphlets.[10] Strangely, with the exception of the obituaries by Tam Dalyell, their equivalent today are largely missing from past and contemporary obituaries, as was discussed in chapter 6. Yet this emphasis on justice from below has been historically crucial, as Barrington Moore classically pointed out, and as Kracauer acknowledged earlier, in the inter-war years, 'Only with the mass itself can a sense of justice rise up that is really just' (Kracauer, quoted Frisby, 1985: 147).

Bauman, in his work on 'immortality strategies', powerfully unmasks the ways in which stratification in life is reiterated in death. Yet he surely erects a false binary division when he offers us *either* the inequalities of the contemporary individualist West *or* a totalitarian Eastern European-type politics. In the latter, any appeals to the 'immortality of a group' operate as a dangerous practise of modernist 'gardening' — flagrantly ignoring the finitude of lives (Bauman 1992: 127) and ushering in Orwell's Room 101. Yet all these largely uneducated leaders whose memory, we have suggested, might be honoured with obituaries, claimed authority through representing a group's immortal needs, and appealing to a different, but rational, future, imprudently risking everything in the pursuit of higher ideals (Samuel 1985: 41).

We could put this more broadly in terms of Taylor's *Sources of the Self*. It could be said – as we argued with the obit of Zatopek — that the search for such 'sources of the self', or moral-political insights, is one of the motivations for readers to read obituaries. Such a low-key search goes hand in hand with the obituary's business of making critical or appreciative judgements on individuals. It is therefore important that against a seductive nihilism and relativism, Taylor has recently argued for a 'retrieval of buried goods'. There is, in modernity, he suggests, a search not just for *respect* for others but for the post-Romantic dignity of unalienated *self expression* and *autonomy*. So far so good — this fits with the obituaries' welcome increase in the arts and sciences. However, Taylor goes on to argue for a retrieval of the 'constitutive goods' of the self — particularly those that appear in the search for justice, universalism and benevolence. Certain social frameworks are necessary for this — such self expression has to involve others, groups with their own horizons — and also conversations with others— even if only dead significant others. In other words, whilst acknowledging not unified *but situated* selves — actors in 'anthropologies of situated freedom' (Taylor 1989: 515) — he reasserts the concern for justice, as opposed simply to the narrow conception of personal identity as self-expression.

In conclusion, we could see the obits not just as prizing so many individual instances of the 'State Nobility' — Bourdieu's 'symbolic baubles' in the social mechanisms of success and class reproduction. They might act instead as instruments of a wider social recognition and become in this way a culture for the whole society, much as the whole population watched Greek drama (Arendt 1958, Goode 1978).[11] Further, the obits columns might continue to yield access to a rich mine of narratives which feature significant individuals, but in an even more objective and penetrating manner than is often offered at present. Obit editors in a highly individualistic society rightly prize those signs of dedicated pioneering, transformation and transgression (the utopia of conservative or liberal philosophies). But such an ethos also underestimates the degree to which the highest achievement of autonomy is dependent on collective inventions — the corporation of scientists or the heroic bohemia of artists, with their multiple cooperative ties (Bourdieu, 2004). Conversely, such conditions for autonomy are threatened by the 'university in ruins': the demand for the rapid commercialisation of knowledge in science, or utilitarianism in social science and the humanities (Martins 2004). It is the collective social institution of science and art which permits critical refutation and symbolic revolution. It is to be hoped that the obituaries will become more attuned to such social realities.

Notes

INTRODUCTION

1. Robert Graves' ménage à trois, John Gielgud's homosexuality and Elizabeth Young's heavy investment in drugs are all recalled in the British obituaries. *Le Monde*'s pages include the artist, Bernard LaMarche-Vadel, who committed suicide. These are not isolated instances.

2. An obituary as 'a notice or announcement of death or deaths, especially in a newspaper; usually comprising a brief biography of the deceased' is dated from 1738 in the 1972 *Shorter O.E.D.*

3. Given the headings under which he classifies his subjects Aubrey is most absorbed by poets, prose writers (including political philosophers like Hobbes) and artists (38%), but also by mathematicians (16%) and in scientists or inventors (another 10%). Moreover, like the most recent obituaries in *The Guardian*, *The Independent*, the *New York Times* and *Le Monde*, his pages rarely show men who were dominant in the feudal period, that is, soldiers and priests (respectively 2% and 3%). He shows 'goodwill' towards women by asserting that the life portrayed might be that of a woman or a man, since souls have no sex (1898: 118). Nevertheless, his allusions to women as muses and to a 'great mistress' who was the 'inventress of a new science — the art of obliging' (1898: 119) — suggest the familiar separation of gender spheres. Indeed, the representation of women in his *Lives* is tiny — 3 per cent, a smaller proportion even than the 19 per cent of current obit biographies. It might also be noted that whereas some of Aubrey's men have been socially mobile, like Sir John Birkenhead, the son of a saddler, all the women are from the aristocracy. Yet like the flamboyant Massingberd later, Aubrey does honour a patrician concubine, in *Brief Lives*, Venetia Digby (1898: 231).

4. An exception was Antonio Arguedas, the Bolivian politician (*The Guardian*, 29 February 2000).

5. Le Goff mentions memorial or Obituary Books at the Abbey of Cluny, which included for the first time in the twelfth century the aristocracy, and not just the clergy (1984: 291). However, the present study is focused solely on the ephemeral modern obituary which was initially first produced in the eighteenth-century magazines.

6. It should be noted that *The Times* was sold initially to coffee houses alone; only fifty years after its start as the *Daily Universal Register* was the paper available by individual subscription (Anon 1935: 36).

7. However, *The Times* acknowledged its dependence on advertising (Anon 1935:20), which set strict limits to its claims to 'disinterestedness'. Moreover,

in the nineteenth century, Hazlitt, in *The Edinburgh Review*, and others, saw
the paper as representing the 'mercantile interest' (Anon 1935: 492, 496).
Note that its editor, John Walter II, was not slow to prosecute its printers for
trade union action when twenty-eight of them went on strike (Anon 1935:
86).

8. In chapter 4, it is argued, following Mayer, that by the end of the century,
this was undermined by fear of greater democratisation and levelling (1981:
321).

9. On the invention of tradition — omitting the obituary — see Hobsbaum and
Ranger (1983).

10. Similarly Davidoff, reported by Scott, traced the decline of the open public
sphere of sociability of the eighteenth century and the rise within the ruling
class of private hospitality, in which women played a key role as hostesses
(Scott 1991:100–101).

11. Personal interview.

12. Personal interview with the current the *New York Times* obits editor.

13. Marilyn Johnson also asserts that "Historians tell us that we are living in the
Golden Age of the obituary" (2006: 10). Unfortunately, Johnson's book was
received after the present study had been written. It is a lively and interesting
example of the "radical democratization" thesis, which this book aims to
seriously question.

14. See also the replication of Sudnow's study which reasserts his conclusions,
stressing especially the social rationing operating to the disadvantage of the
elderly and the disabled (Timmermans 2000: 143, 145).

15. In terms of one recent writer in the influential *Le Monde Diplomatique*, the
turn to collective memory should be repudiated: it is a theoretical shift away
from the contextualisation and situating of individuals within groups that is
the crucial to the historians' craft, in favour of a 'moralisation' and 'individualisation' of the past (Bickerton 2006). This is not a position that we share:
see chapter 1.

16. Against Hutton's historical relativism, it is worth noting that other historians
do not draw the same conclusion: Fentress and Wickham compare dominants' and popular memories of the General Strike, concluding on one crucial
issue that although neither was precisely right, nevertheless, local working-
class memory was closer to the truth than alternative memories (1992: 117).

17. *The Guardian* obituary omitted the wider reassertion of Latin American
authoritarianism in Reagan's governmental support for Salvadorean repression, provided no contextualisation for his consistently anti-democratic
support for the 'contras' against the democratically-elected Nicaraguan government and was silent about the widening inequalities that have been the
consequence of Reagan's monetarist neo-liberalism.

18. The obit by Tam Dalyell for William Wade, the scholar of constitutional law,
for example, reiterated the importance of the jury's finding of 'not guilty' in
the case against Clive Ponting, despite the judge's summing-up against the
defendant. Wade had acted as witness for Ponting, against the Crown.

19. Compare here Marx's analysis of this 'imaginary universality' in his critique
of Hegel's analysis of the Prussian bureaucracy (O'Malley 1970: 45–53, especially 46) and note here also his praise of Feuerbach's *socio-genesis* of works
(O'Malley 1970: xxix), a term which Bourdieu also deploys.

20. Compare this with Bloch's theory of artistic value (cultural surplus), in his
analysis of art's fructifying of myth, 'significant realism', and 'aesthetically-
attempted' Utopian images (1986: I, 210–17).

21. Contrast the study of Gordon and Nair, which elucidates the multiplicity of activities that were actually being undertaken by women in public and concludes that they were, at the very least, present in a 'feminine public sphere' (2003: 3–6). However, they also acknowledge the strategic importance of definitions of the public realm (2003: 243, n. 20). Arguably, activities such as religious evangelism, philanthropy and even the social imperialist mission were then excluded from the public sphere.

22. Only about 5 per cent of the age-group at present attend public school (Scott 1991: 113).

23. In Britain, in 2005, the proportion of migrants of Asian and Afro-Caribbean origin is combined at 7 per cent.

24. A dissection of the various structures of meaning recurrent within the different plot-structures or genres of writing can be found in Frye's *Anatomy of Criticism* (1957). Frye's analysis of the tragic and ironic forms helps to elucidate the links between the obituary and certain fundamental Western principles of symbolic vision and division (especially tragedy and irony or satire, 1957: 206–23, 223–39). However, for the present analysis, Frye's three tragic characters, the tyrant and the Machiavellian villain on the one hand and the submissive heroine on the other have been analytically categorised into two obituary types, the 'negative' and the 'tragic'.

25. The positive type in turn has echoes of the romance myth, especially Frye's realist romance. It typically views the hero's actions, the family and the society as loosely integrated despite the division of labour ('In every age the ruling social or intellectual class tends to project its ideals in some form of romance, where the virtuous heroes and beautiful heroines represent the ideals and the villains the threats to their ascendancy' p. 186) (Frye 1957: 186–206).

26. Again, as a Bourdieusian analysis would anticipate, the mode of obituary differs in different newspapers. Agnelli's obituary in the *New York Times* was studiously neutral.

27. The newspaper context is also significant. In newspapers other than *The Guardian*, a passage detailing practices such as this might be considered simply a necessary part of the competitive success ethic on the part of skilful brokers.

28. Nobody could mistake the obit for John DeLorean for entirely neutral news ('Almost everyone who had business dealings with car maker John DeLorean [...] suffered either money losses in the millions, public vilification for the vanished cash or both. Through all this turbulence, DeLorean remained unscathed: even if he did lose a fortune, he had not been entitled to it in the first place' *The Guardian*, 21 March 2005).

29. The obituary is silent about the precariousness and poverty of this industry for its workers prior to Dash's organization.

30. The memory of the 'dominateds' here, especially in Latin America, could be said to be reduced to 'a memory outside memory' (Halbwachs, cited in Namer 1987: 73). The *Guardian* obituary attests to the roots of Reagan's success in being able to use a Brechtian popular language to praise ordinary soldiers and workers whilst supporting big business interests. Thus it ultimately sets greater store on his jargon of sincerity than on the consequences of his politics, not least the increased U.S. incarceration rates and the largest deficit in American history. It thus adopts here a benign obituary model.

31. This is why — with reservations — the mounting of a new formula for *Other Lives* in the *Guardian* is to be welcome. This is a step towards opening up these columns to a wider — and more democratised — basis of distinction.

CHAPTER 1

1. I take the theme of 'la querelle de mémoire' from Bickerton (2006: 14).
2. Bourdieu glosses this later by stating that collective representations are transmitted to the body — `written on the body' as the sentence is scored onto the body of the prisoner in Kafka's Penal Colony — in contrast, individual representations are restricted to each person's own memories, hopes, and dreams (Bourdieu 2000: 141–42).
3. 'Memory is the epic faculty par excellence' Benjamin argues — a comprehensive memory stores events and understands their importance (Eiland and Jennings, 2002: 153).
4. Eiland and Jennings also point out that Benjamin produced a shorter version of these for radio, also in 1931–32 (2002: 220–21). Here again Benjamin's adventurous approach in abandoning the old antagonism between art and technology and in using popular technology to communicate the inventiveness of these German thinkers shows his difference from the other members of the Frankfurt School (Jay 1996). This difference may have been underpinned by his own dependence on work in the popular media given his lack of an academic job (Buck-Morss 1991).
5. For example the peasants in the Cevannes had a long popular memory of being Protestant and thus having been opposed to the Edict of Nantes, fervent partisans of the French Revolution, supporters of Dreyfus and early activists in the Resistance (Fentress and Wickham 1992: 92–93).
6. I use this phrase to mean his increasing focus on texts alone·
7. Such amnesia is at stake, for example, in East Germany's post-1945 highlighting of the regional Resistance in World War II, to the exclusion of Jewish wartime suffering (Misztal 2003: 59).
8. The very long obit for Madame Chiang Kai-Shek (*The Times*, 25 October 2003) does at this time mention that Chiang purged his party of Communists, whilst it has a highly-disenchanted angle of vision on the Chiangs' enthrallment of the Americans (the magazines, *Time* and *Fortune*, had declared them 'Man and wife of 1937'). Yet there is still no reference in this obituary to Chiang's cruelty.
9. See especially in *Realms of Memory*, Nora on Gaullists and Communists, Alain Corbin on *Divisions of Time and Space* (the dialectic of provincialisation and Parisianisation) Antoine Prost's *Monuments to the Dead*, Marcel Gauchet on *Right and Left* and, on the decline of the peasantry, Armand Frémont's *The Land*.
10. In certain cases the judgement ceases to be authoritative, as in instances of miscarriage of justice or where judgement has been based on excessively narrow interpretation of the terms of reference.
11. Ricoeur sees funerals and memorial services for those near us as 'halfway between private memory and social memory' (2000: 53n). Obituaries are classifiable in such terms depending on where they appear - parish magazine obits are closer to private family memories or to local community memory, national broadsheets to social memory.
12. As a young Russian academic remarked (Irina Sirotkina, personal communication), the widespread inclusion of obituaries in Russian newspapers would have been impossible before Gorbachev. Stalinism meant that otherwise admirable people had either too many skeletons in their cupboard, as a result of forced complicity with the regime, or they were cut off from their professions for long periods, as were prisoners in the gulags.

13. It would be wrong to assume that this is invariably so: as Cynthia Koonz points out, in 1992, the French high court trial of Paul Touvier found him innocent despite general recognition that he facilitated the murder of hundreds (1994: 260).

CHAPTER 2

1. The heraldic funeral (fifteenth century to the eighteenth century) was one in which a herald from the College of Arms, dressed in the arms of the dead nobleman, 'declare[d] the deeds of this noble prince', and presented the arms to the heir (Gittings 1984: 37).
2. This is an early instance of what Bagheot was to famously describe, in the Victorian period, in terms of the ceremonial function being four-fifths' of the monarchy, while the executive function was stripped to a mere fifth.
3. This highly-coded form was preponderant in *The Times* 1900 and still prevalent in 1948. It is now characteristic of only a minority of obits, especially in the British newspapers.
4. Note that Ariès's theory of the tame death has not gone unquestioned — not least because his evidence is based particularly on the idealizing literature with which noble warriors' deaths were depicted (Elias 1985). Despite this criticism, the overall argument is convincing.
5. Such presents were a relic of the need for gifts to Charon, the boat-keeper of the Lethe (Ragon 1983: 69–70).
6. I am grateful to Harvie Ferguson for showing this connection, which has its origins in Montaigne's (sixteenth century) Essays.
7. Brenner emphasises in the case of England in the late twelfth and thirteenth century, the absence of legal protection for unfree peasants from arbitrary exactions by their lords: moreover, the legal arena was one in which any resistance offered was ended by the peasant being thrown out of court (1985: 241, 249).
8. Note, however, that Brenner's powerful analysis of the seigneurial crisis attributes this mainly to the Western European peasant communities' capacity for resistance and flight (1987: 284–95).
9. Somewhat later, Ariès, on the seventeenth century, describes this process of the emancipation of the soul and of its prudent lifetime search for salvation, or as he brilliantly summarised it 'The fate of his soul tomorrow depends on his works today, on his consciousness, self-control and foresight ....The soul has become the advance guard of the self' (1981: 286).
10. A call to the traditional order was also implicit in Balzac's critique of the bureaucratically over-regulated death of post-Revolutionary Paris, in his *History of the Thirteen* (1974 (1833–35):139–147). This indictment of excessive administrative regulation in the handling of the decisions about death, has been surprisingly ignored by sociological historians.
11. An alternative route to satisfying the anatomists' demand for dead bodies was the institutionalisation of voluntary donation of bodies for research, as of organs now.
12. In the case of mourning, the decency of a regulated, upper-class death depended particularly on women, who represented the family honour in this sphere just as they represented it in matters of sexual purity. Indeed, the laying out of the dead and provision of the food and hospitality associated with the funeral had always been the domain of women, who were, of course,

designated closer to natural and material reality than to the world of reason or ideas.

13. The notion of a simple division in practices disappears with new research on the late nineteenth century showing the significant ceremonials and expenses of mourning for the respectable working- class (Strange 2005).

14. Gittings comments "funeral sermons were printed and sold as popular pamphlets; they were therefore the forerunners of modern obituaries" (1984: 138).

15. The initial celebration of excellence and glory was in Ancient Greece and Rome. Note that here too the status of slaves and women debarred them from such honours, in a process not irrelevent to today's obits (Arendt 1958: 44; Hopkins 1983).

16. This is in evidence on numerous occasions recently: the death of Paul Foot is one example alone.

17. The collapse of collective frameworks for experiencing death is most clear-cut in the decline of belief in the after-life. Survey responses on such an issue are a highly imperfect indicator and should not be reified. Nevertheless, the numbers denying any kind of afterlife are significant, ranging from 74 per cent (in Sweden) in 1968 to 40 per cent and 37 per cent (in France), in 1973 and 1977 respectively (cited, Vovelle 1983: 714).

18. Moreover, in an already individualised social order, the dying are caught in the embarrassment of those around them. Paradoxically, their control over their passions — unprecedented in relation to less developed societies — offers great barriers to revealing their affections (Elias 1985: 27).

19. An analytical understanding would have to refer to the highly determined nature of such catastrophic social crises, crises being the consequence of a series of interlocked structuring contradictions (Bourdieu 1988a: 161–62).

20. Although women often take the role of caregivers, their historic entry into the labour market may itself have had a part to play. It was women who traditionally nursed the sick and dying, whilst mourning was signalled by their staying within the home (Strange 2005).

21. Weber argued in his famous essay on Religious Rejections of the World (1991) that the peasant died sated with life.

CHAPTER 3

1. Bourdieu lays out his theory of the subject at greatest length and with greatest qualifications, in *The Logic of Practice* (1990a): any interested reader should turn to this text.

2. An important criticism of this account of biography has been made by Passeron (1991) who claims that for Bourdieu, lives are structured too much by a fixed and determined past, as though one's choice of journey were to be simply explained by those available on the route map of a given Underground network. Passeron's preferred image is of a bus on a given route, in which passengers can get on or off at different points. One might further emphasise, as against both these — as Bourdieu indeed does with his notion of sociogenesis and collective invention — the ways in which underground journeys can be changed as the *network itself changes* (for example, with the building of a new line). Analogously, social death or symbolic dishonour can be *altered* by voices of resistance: the legal emancipation of homosexuals in the 1960s allowed them to choose occupations such as academia or politics which would previously have been closed or, at least, dangerous for them. In his later work,

as a response to Passeron and other critics, Bourdieu examines the capacities of groups to transform their own conditions of existence, whilst also stressing unconscious continuities through the preliminary action of the habitus (2001b). In particular, he sees certain oppressed groups — such as women and homosexuals — as possessing *more* capacities to change the 'route map', and thus their underlying pattern of exclusion, than other degraded groups possess. This is precisely because they possess the cultural capital to do so (2001b: 118–24).

3. This is entitled the *Annuaires des Ancièns Elèves de l'Ecole Normale Supérieure*.

4. Students are more likely to accept their weaknesses if they are informed that they are 'not talented at philosophy' or their essay is 'dull'. If a teacher were to tell them that they are weak because they come from the subordinate classes, both students and other teachers would find the judgement shockingly unacceptable.

5. Research has demonstrated more recently the presence of similar *gendered* evaluations: essays judged good but over-conscientious tend to be by women.

6. Bourdieu continued to be concerned with such euphemistic codes, notably those discovered and demystified by the microsociologists of laboratory life. However, instead of seeing the euphemisms as simply an idealising mask over the more brutal reality as they do, he argues for the truth of both accounts, which operate as a dual consciousness in the minds of scientists, *regularising* their activities in terms of scientific rules (2004: 24–25).

7. Toril Moi emphasises — as has been seen — the 'spiteful obituaries' for Simone de Beauvoir (1990): the critical form is documented further in the Introduction and Part II. However, the newspaper obituary does not yet yield the totally uncensored and overtly biased criticisms found in internet obituaries. Such vituperative obits followed, for example, the death of Edward Said. His *Orientalism* was stated in one such Internet outburst to be 'the intellectual equivalent of 9/11'.

8. This term, shared with Lacanian psychoanalysis, is applied systematically in Bourdieu's 'socioanalysis'.

9. Such criticisms of mechanistic determinism come from various sources, as we shall argue beneath.

10. I take Bourdieu to mean by this that certain possibilities are only possible at certain periods, not least, *after* the 'revolution from below' that instituted capitalism. See Bloch's earlier use in *The Principle of Hope*, which Bourdieu cited when he was the recipient of the Bloch Prize (1998c).

11. But see also in Bourdieu's earliest empirical work with Sayad, his sense of the 'end of a [traditional] world', with the 'social surgery' undertaken by the French Army in Algeria, not least through the imposition on Kabyleans of strategic hamlets (1964: 17, 19, 55)

12. In *Homo Academicus*, adapting *Capital*, Bourdieu points out that this is, in certain historical situations, particularly striking. The first is where a specific contradiction emerges in the usual pattern of class reproduction. In the post- Second World War period, this means that educational certificates fail to guarantee the expected jobs. The second, added to this, is where a high-intensity fusion of various underlying crises occurs. A successful revolution requires — either temporarily or more long-term — the orchestration together of a series of specific contradictions (1988a: 156–66).

13. In Bhaskar's terms, Bourdieu increasingly made a distinction between epistemic and judgemental relativism, proposing the methodological view that, in sociology, knowledges are analysed regardless of their truth (epistemic

relativism) while holding (against judgemental relativism) that not all knowledge is equally well-founded (see Knorr-Cetina and Mulkay 1983: 6, 14)

14. Bourdieu later (1994) adopts the phrase 'the imperialism of the universal' to describe a phenomenon in which the context-bound nature of a particular cosmopolitan literature, dealing, for example, only with humanist issues in Europe, is mistaken for a transcendently universal literature (Bourdieu 1998a: 89–90, 2002b: 289; see also Casanova 2004: 34)

15. For his criticism of such short-circuited analyses, see 1990b: 140–49.

16. Attacks on Bourdieu's method of objectivation are strange, especially given his impeccable concern to understand practices in a manner authorised by the founding fathers of sociology. Thus note that his late work on peasant marriage strategies rests on two fundamental insights: Marx's view of peasant heirs in his *Sketch of a Critique of Political Economy* that 'the earth inherits the inheritor', and Weber's view in *Ancient Judaism* (1952) that the rise of the prejudice against the peasantry can be dated to the emergence of the urban commercial classes. Bourdieu's process of 'objectivation' aims throughout to understand such material and symbolic interests (see 2002c: 169)

17. Against the standard critique that Bourdieu's approach has been over-reductive (see, for example, Sayer 2005), the most illuminating positive evaluations are arguably still those of Taylor (1999), and Pinto (1999).

18. He makes an interesting point, in *Science of Science and Reflexivity* that Merton's over-integrated model of the norms of science — far from being the product of a Wasp 'enchanted universe' — was actually the work of a Jewish scholar. Put more poignantly, Merton's idealizing 1942 article was making a 'hypercorrect' contrast, typical of a new immigrant, between the conditions of the barbarism from which he was fleeing and what he hoped was normal scientific autonomy (2004: 13).

19. Bourdieu points out that in highly autonomous fields, such as poetry or science the only link with the social world is the combination of social conditions that come into being that permits 'the people who benefit from them [to] do things of this kind.' (2004: 15)

20. This is at stake in works such as Lodge's *Small World*, with its 'falsely lucid', 'truly narcissistic' 'self-satisfied representation' (1999: 617).

21. Thus, for example, Kafka is understood not just as influenced profoundly by the national popular movement in the literary periphery against the Hapsburgs, but also by the Prague anti-Zionist Yiddish theatre.

23. 'Against the old distinction made by Wilhelm Dilthey, we must posit that *understanding and explaining are one*' (Bourdieu et al. 1999: 613).

24. There remains a certain tension between Ricoeur as a theorist of phenomenology and Bourdieu as a theorist of practice. It is important to note that I am not claiming here that the two sets of concepts are interchangeable: indeed Ricoeur is notably more spiritualist in certain textual analyses than I would advocate. However, it is my view that Ricoeur does have an approach which permits us to fill out or supplement aspects of Bourdieusian theory, and this is at its most illuminating in his theory of the imagination.

CHAPTER 4

1. Note however, that the gentrified lives of the aristocracy described here occasionally include ennobled industrialists (see Conclusion below).

2. Excluding the foreigners, this selection of 1900 obituaries includes only twenty-eight whose death occurred beyond the South-East or South-West of England.

3. The General's grandson, Julian, like his grandfather, an eminent anthropologist, also bought a country estate in Spain to study the surrounding village (see his obituary, *The Guardian*, 14 September 2001)
4. Crowther and Dupree (1996) note that 20 per cent of all United Kingdom medical students who began their studies in 1871 trained at Glasgow or Edinburgh. Obituaries reveal that a considerable number of the Edinburgh-trained GPs were from England (31 per cent) (1996:395).
5. Crowther and Dupree note that — despite national mythology — Scottish medical students in the late 1860s and 70s were from families with 'at least a modest degree of property': only 14 per cent of those subsequently GPs had working-class fathers (1996: 397) I am grateful to Ann Crowther for advice about religion and the choice of medical education (private communication).
6. Sara Mills has written an insightful chapter on the ambiguities of Kingsley's gendered discourse in the context of African social relations, see 1991: 153–74.
7. A well-documented study of Mary Kingsley emphasises that her membership of a subordinate gender facilitated a break with the overall imperialist or Africanist view of natives as 'monstrous others'. She did pioneer, before Malinowski, a functionalist conception of social structures and stressed methodological relativism, whilst her awareness of the significance of fetishes in native cultures preceded high modernists, like Picasso. Yet at the same time, she retained elements of evolutionary assumptions and was thus ambivalent about imperialism:

    She cannot detach herself from the instrumental reason of empire (progress and industrialisation), but neither can she embrace its [current] ethical and cultural values. [...] Africa [for her] was that space in which European civilization might be able to grasp its originating values....' (Gikandi, 1996: 155)
8. In this respect, they depart from the biography of E.T. Cook (1911), which emphasises his estrangement from his wife, Effie, and his devotion to the young Rosa La Touche, whose mentor he became.
9. Bourdieu would ask us to question how far this actually happened as opposed to being a mode of address to an implied worker-reader. The evidence is mixed but Ruskin College, at least, was run by trade unionists for the education of ordinary workers.
10. This entry into the legal theatre requires revision of mechanistically determinist theories of the law, in which the law, eternally and uniquely, merely endorses and reinforces the entire economically dominant class.
11. That is to say that he sees the aesthetic and other experience of warfare and combat as based upon 'a socially constituted phenomenon: a constructed reality'(Ferguson 2004: 10).
12. See, however, the earlier nineteenth century struggles between the peaceful bourgeoisie and the military elites in France (Ben-Amos 2000), chapter 2 above.
13. See, for example, Canon Myers, 18 February 1948: 'It was in these parishes that his great work was done, unobtrusively and wholeheartedly...His goodness seemed to spring without effort from a sheer love of goodness.'
14. He could therefore be said to represent the perfect limit case for the Bourdieusian theory of reproduction.
15. Writing in 2005, amidst the unfolding disasters of the Iraq War, a parallel set of interests can be identified on the part of a capitalist minority which has never been prepared to take Iraqui independence seriously, from 1920 on.
16. Unity Mitford was shot in the head at a pro-Nazi rally in 1939 and died exceptionally young.

CHAPTER 5

1. The British popular tabloids do not have obituary pages as such, presumably because obits have been linked historically with a social elite. Their editorial staff were unavailable for comment about this.
2. This is an early synonym for 'amateur'.
3. The *Daily Telegraph* in 2000–2001 featured obituaries which were by far the most open of the newspapers about the actions of those brokers and procurers of power, the CIA and MI5, no doubt secure in the knowledge that their readers were unlikely to lead any popular movement of revolt (for one instance, see chapter 7 on Kermit Roosevelt, 22 June 2000).
4. For example, at the University of Benin (Nigeria) it is a policy that there must be an obit when someone dies: the university pays the cost. This is an aspect of modernity. 'It's not just family and friends. The workplace also recognizes great value in the services that the person put in...'. This 'modern trend' in Nigeria is also creating a new social division — 'If you are middle class or high class, many pages of the newspaper will reflect your work [...] . But if you are from the lower class it is really quite difficult, because of the financial implications' (personal communication, Sylvester Odiagbe, Government researcher/PhD student, 30 January 2006).
5. This rate is lower in the Scottish newspapers — *The Scotsman* pays £200 for a large obit (2004 prices).
6. Telephone interview with Tam Dalyell, August 2005. He has also written a range of obituaries of footballers, mainly Scottish. Dalyell might be seen as a 'gatekeeper' opening up the obituary into wider British cultures just as John Lehmann in the 1930s had opened up the novel for working-class novelists or E.P. Thompson expanded history to embrace narratives of the working class.
7. Personal communication: telephone interview.
8. Anonymity was particularly valued by *The Times*, not least for permitting editorial intervention with contributors' obituaries. Sir Walter Scott once made the case for anonymity:

    '[T]here will always be a greater authority ascribed by the generality of readers to an oracular opinion issued from a cloudy sanctuary of an invisible body than to a mere dictum of a man with a Christian name or a sirname (sic), which may not sound much better than those of the author over whom he predominates.' Quoted in Anon., 1836–1837 (October-January): 302.
9. The American editors spoke of the wide reading of obituaries online from all over the world — a globalization of resources which is unprecedented in its implications. This affected their own choices — throwing up potential new subjects whom nobody else in America had chosen, such as a political prisoner in Paraguay, imprisoned under Stroessner, who died in jail after twenty-five years. Yet it also operated as a sanction against doing your own, if it could not be as good in the time as — say — *The Independent*'s obit (*Washington Post*).
10. A similar set of criteria is used in tourism where tourists may go sightseeing to visit the 'last wild man in America' (MacCannell 1989: 88).
11. The tendentious assessment and an honest, critical assessment may not always be distinguished at the higher editorial levels. Prof. Gavin Stamp wrote a critical indictment of the work of one architect for his obituary, which appeared on the day of the funeral. The family protested vehemently and the editor 'carpeted him in his office', warning him never to repeat the offense (Stamp, personal communication).

12. My question gave examples of critical obits, exemplifying these by reference to a heterogeneous collection including Laurent Kabila (Zaire), Franco Tudjman (Croatia), Hadid Hélou (Lebanon), Gianfranco Agnelli (Italy).
13. I am not suggesting here that everyone, however 'private' their achievement deserves an obit. I am challenging whether there is not a persistently masculinist and elite-influenced choice of the *arenas* of the public sphere from which an obit follows, just as the high-ranking genres of the visual arts in which men have been most dominant in modernity (oil painting and sculpture rather than, say, embroidery) are also the ones which have yielded more consecrated figures.
14. We use these terms loosely, all too aware of the divergence of perspectives about the value of different people's lives. It should also be noted that the terminology of 'heroism' and 'villainy' was repudiated by the obituary editors themselves.
15. Symptomatically, this was usually discussed in terms of the 'widow'. This may be purely a linguistic convention or it may revealingly betray these obit editors' default position, ie, that the subject will be male.
16. However, certain taboos persist in many newspapers, usually via silences. The obituaries for Elizabeth Young (*Guardian*, 23 March 2001 and *The Independent* 22 March 2001) obliquely revealed these by their infraction, for these were the first in Britain to refer to pioneering writing produced from a range of experiences in which taking heroin, hash and cocaine were salient elements. The writer, Wilf Self, who wrote a subtle and understated obit of Elizabeth Young in the *Independent*, concluded: 'She was waspish, wrong and worldly'.
17. Note occasional playing with the old obits codes, as in the acerbic comment for the architect, Roderick Gradidge 'With him it was not just a matter of not suffering fools gladly, he was reluctant to suffer *anyone* gladly' (*The Guardian* 25 January 2001).
18. *The Times did* run an obituary for Stalin. It appeared initially in their obituary collections, under the title 'Villains' A further republication appears in Brunskill 2005: 131–46.
19. In carefully framing these acts, an evaluative light is cast on them, although some obits remain studiously factual and neutral (see Goffman 1975).
20. See footnote 15.
21. This editor had written an obit of a politician he had subjectively responded to as 'an arrogant, drunken Tory'. In the final obit there was no hint of his own evaluation, and an emphasis instead on the MP's eccentric stories and public sayings. Ironically, this had been reprinted in a book of obits.
22. Weber's disenchantment of the world sprung from the growth of an ever-transforming culture, alongside the receding of all magical or irrational sources of salvation, both of which provoked the sense of the lack of meaning in modernity.
23. I am grateful to Sasha Weitzman (University of Tel Aviv) who offered the suggestive concept of 're-enchantment' in this context.
24. For example, it is conspicuous that while they referred to potato growers and farriers, they never referred at all to any individuals who might come from and actively represent the working-class.
25. Williams' 'known' and 'knowable communities' as opposed to its 'deeply unknown community' still provides the vast bulk of British obit portraits (1985).

CHAPTER 6

1. We would take issue, however, with their view that Bourdieu falls into the trap of (left) functionalism by emphasising instead his Bachelard-derived 'realist rationalism', his analyses of resentment rather than eternal love of one's fate (*amor fati*; in Bourdieu and Wacquant 1992), and his specific inclusion of a 'margin of liberty' in which transformation rather than reproduction may be played out.

2. These four newspapers were chosen because they were the only papers covering the entire U.K. which carried obituaries on a regular basis.

3. Bourdieu's boundary between the dominant class and the middle class is different from those of many other theorists. Thus, for him — excluding primary teachers, whom he places within the middle class — all professionals and cultural producers are classified as possessing the high levels of economic and cultural capital of the dominant class.

4. The proportion of obituaries dedicated to figures from the working and the middle classes is negligible in both *The Times* 1900 and *The Times* 1948. In the obituaries from *The Times* 1900, there is only one working class figure, three middle class individuals, and one farmer. In *The Times* 1948 all the obituaries depict individuals from the dominant and the aristocratic classes, except one working class figure (1%).

5. The distinction between temporal and symbolic power follows Bourdieu's discussion (1996b: 263–72).

6. There were a significant number of teachers in *The Times* 1948, but principally from the large public schools.

7. As Bourdieu recognises, paradoxically, even 'blood' is a pre-eminently social classification and a genealogical analysis of genealogies would show that the family tree is prone to fuzzy logic (1990a: 35). It erases from vision, for example, illegitimate offspring, those large numbers of the gentry's 'fly-blows', of whom Catherine Cookson irreverently writes.

8. A greater proportion of those women — now in their sixties — who first moved full-time into the labour market in unprecedented numbers may subsequently receive obituaries. It is noted in this connection that at present the average age of death, as detailed for those people given obituaries, is seventy-seven.

9. Due to constraints on length, the tables printed in this chapter only represent a tiny proportion of our tables overall. The percentages at this point, together with others in the chapter, come from additional unprinted tables.

10. Crompton has recently drawn attention to women's strategic search for niches where family-friendly careers could be pursued — within the professions, general practice rather than brain-surgery, for example. She also links women's number of children to their occupation: in banking (1998), 63 per cent of women had one child or none, compared with only 32 per cent of the men; even as GPs women had fewer children than male GPs, although compared with banking, fewer had only one child or none (35% women vs 17% men) (2000: 169–74).

11. 'Cultural producers' in this definition include architects and media staff.

12. Bourdieu defines the State Nobility as an elite whose educational titles are guaranteed by the state, and who are found in the top echelon of both public and private sectors (professions, politicians, business executives and civil servants).

13. The term 'traditional professions' here excludes engineers: it denotes architects, doctors and surgeons, clergy and judges or lawyers.

14. Bourdieu's class categories decompose class in relation to economic and cultural capital, as in his diagrams using correspondence analysis in *Distinction* (eg, 1984: 128–29). They also recombine these two elements of capital within an occupational class model using a linear hierarchy (eg, 1984: 526)

15. As Savage comments, Marshall et al's study (1997) also reveals that, if education is kept constant, class origins now (in 1989) played a somewhat less strong a role in Britain that they did in1972: at that point the odds ratio for the son of an unskilled labourer attaining a service-class position, as against the son of a higher service-class father, was 6:1, later it improved to 2.2:1 (2000: 90). On Bourdieu's analysis of the combination of social capital and cultural capital needed to get a job in the State Nobility, see 1996b.

16. It should be noted that these obituaries are not just related to British subjects.

17. Further qualitative analysis is needed to deepen our knowledge of the links between the subjects' material experiences, their groups and their cultural ideas or tastes. The authors of many British obituaries are colleagues who have been active in the same field and who provide details about the genesis of cultural production within certain groups: to stay only with *The Independent*, see Richard Wollheim's obituary for Bernard Williams (17 June 2003), John Richardson's comments on the art historians, philosophers and historians who met in Wollheim's Chelsea house (17 November 2003) or Alan Ryan's account of 'the game of [university] musical chairs' between the most consecrated philosophers in Britain and America, in his obituary for Stuart Hampshire (17 June 2004). In contrast, memories of class can be those of poverty — see the obituary for Clive Jenkins, in which the subject recollects his ear being bitten by a rat as a baby (23 September 1999)

18. This varies between 22 per cent of the *Telegraph* obits to 34 per cent of *The Guardian* obits, with the other British newspapers in between.

19. Another conversion takes place, of course, when those with cultural capital enter the labour market; here, high educational qualifications, that possess a rarity not yet devalued, can be appropriately cashed in for high salaries.

20. *The Times* 1948 is divergent in this respect, with as high a number as 24 per cent having transferred from the dominateds to the dominants.

21. This is a crucial assumption, and it may well be ill-founded. We are aware that *Le Monde* has a particularly marked circulation amongst the intelligentsia and that using obituaries from *Le Figaro*, for example, could have produced different results. (On newspaper readership and possession of capitals, see Bourdieu 1984:452.)

22. Britain may be more exclusive in its recruitment of writers than elsewhere, at least as mediated via the obituaries. Although we have no comparable figures for school, Sapiro shows that, in the 1940s in France, 27 per cent of professional writers (including best-selling genres) came from the 'classes populaires' and petty-bourgeoisie (1996: 23); 24 per cent had the bac only; 11 per cent an inferior qualification (1996: 28).

23. The scientists were followed — after a gap — by the civil service, of whom 63 per cent went to public school, academia (67%) and the media (69%).

24. The most elite of the grandes écoles have a place similar to Oxbridge in Britain and to the Ivy League universities in the United States.

25. In this paragraph and the last one of this section on higher education, we have included all subjects. In the other paragraphs we have used as a base only the national citizens of the respective newspapers: British citizens for British newspapers, French for *Le Monde* and American for the *New York Times*.

26. Medical education at Oxbridge throughout the nineteenth century required clinical training elsewhere: hence universities such as Edinburgh were the obvious resort for these middle-class professionals.

27. Gordon Marshall and his colleagues usefully cite the British figures on the percentages of various twentieth century cohorts who have degree-level education, though they do not further specify Oxbridge degrees. Thus of the pre-1920s cohort, 4 per cent overall had degrees (males 6% and females 2%); 1920s — 6 per cent (males 9%; females 4%) 1930s — 8 per cent (males 11%; females 5%); 1940s — 11 per cent (males 15%; females 6%) 1950s — 14 per cent (males 17%; females 10%), post-1960 — 13 per cent (males 17%; females 8%), from Table 6.1 (1997:108).

28. In this respect, our findings amplify Bourdieu's conclusion about the elective affinities between newspapers, their journalists and their readers (1984: 240).

29. Wacquant points out that the 'tightly integrated network of Ivy League Universities and private boarding schools functions as a close, if partial, analogue to the French devices of grandes écoles and their associated classes préparatoires' (Bourdieu, 1996b: Foreword; Wacquant) xiv).

30. We follow UNESCO and Miles in arguing that any classification of 'race' from phenotypes or genotypes is arbitrary, and that the continued use of physical differences depends upon attributes that are the consequence of social recognition and interactive negotiation (Miles 1982: 9–21, especially 20; Miles 1993: 2–9). Nevertheless such social realities continue to be significant and we have therefore, on the basis of their photographs, included some subjects as 'black', even in the absence of any verbal signifiers of ethnicity. On the other hand, we have classified subjects as Jewish only if they are defined as such in the obituary or if they (or their parents) came from Germany or Eastern Europe in the Nazi period or at the time of anti-Semitic pogroms.

31. Despite opposition, we have adopted a theoretical construct rather than a common-sense notion of migration. More precisely, whilst we have included in our term 'migrant' the sons and daughters of immigrant settlers, we have also included all subjects who have crossed national boundaries to spend a substantial period in another country. This embraces, controversially, some not often classified as migrants, such as those 'career nomads' of whom architects, staying overseas for prolonged periods with major international projects, represent a typical case. This construct has the advantage of categorising as 'migrants' imperial colonialists and settlers who left, say, France, to live in Algeria, some returning at the end of their lives, some staying on.

32. This highly-schematic characterisation of the obituary subjects omits those figures such as Giovanni Agnelli, the heir of the Fiat company, who received at least one negative or critical obit, in his case as a 'playboy' and a businessman who authorised his managers' bribing of judges (see Introduction).

CHAPTER 7

1. The wider sample includes 173 political actors.

2. Bourdieu adds that this constitutes 'a forgotten dimension of the class struggle' (1984: 483).

3. An obituary for Sir Malcolm Hogg (*The Times* 18 February 1948), Hailsham's grandfather, clarifies that his great-great grandfather had been one of the last chairmen of the East India Company; Sir Malcolm himself (also Eton and Balliol) had been a politician in India sitting on various Vice-Regal bod-

ies from 1905–25 and was rewarded with a Bank directorship. Hailsham's ancestry reveals a further 'inheritance' in the legal field: Sir Malcolm's wife had been the daughter of a Bombay judge.

4. The nomenklatura of the Communist bloc in the period after the Second World War betrays many similar features (on the USSR, see especially Mawdsley and White 2000). As these authors point out and their own individual portrayals confirm, the members of the nomenklatura in the 1960s and 1970s was typically from lower social origins but increasingly well-educated.

5. *Le Monde*'s obit for Chaban-Delmas is an interesting case in that it uses the ironic mode. As this reveals, Chaban-Delmas, who served as a Gaullist Prime Minister, became part of the State Nobility but he lacked intergenerational links within it. The "galloping major" as he was satirized within this irreverent obituary, was a man who had risen from a 'simple and modest flat in Paris' — probably a coded reference to petit-bourgeois origins.

6. Moreover, the obituaries often only testify to what is — from alternative sources — historically indisputable.

7. These motions were backed by the rest of the world, save Micronesia and the Marshall Islands in 1976 (Philo and Berry 2004: 39, 52).

8. There are exceptions to this rule. See the favourable obits for the Macedonian and Bulgarian leaders, Boris Trajkovski (*The Times*, 28 February 2004) and Peter Mladenov (*The Times*, 2 June 2000), the former of whom implemented profound market reforms and the latter free elections.

9. All of Assad's obituaries acknowledge that he put down a rebellion against his rule in 1982 with unmitigated force, the *Telegraph*'s estimate being a death-toll of 10,000 civilians from the city of Hama.

10. In certain newspapers, such as the *Daily Telegraph*, the services of the foreign politician to the British state assume a great significance in the overall assessment of the political success of the leader — hence a politician such as Jack Lynch is given an accolade for his pragmatism.

11. This is not to deny that such figures have sometimes had a vital role in retaining public infrastructure: see, for example, Charles Joelson's amendment to retain school libraries and counselling services, 1969 (the *New York Times*, 21 August 1999).

12. See also the obituary for Abe Beame himself, *The Guardian*, 13 February 2001.

13. These observations were established with the help of an interview (by telephone) with Tam Dalyell, August, 2005.

14. Ibarurri herself appears in *The Daily Telegraph*'s *Book of Rogues* (1998: 62–66). She is found there for three reasons: her refusal to listen to Anarchist and P.O.U.M. criticisms of the Spanish Communist Party's policy, her 'slavish' adherence to the Soviet Central Committee in exile and her residual patriarchalism that denied women in the Civil War the right to fight on the frontline.

15. This obituary is earlier than the rest in the sample, *The Daily Telegraph*, 13 July 1988 (collected in *The Daily Telegraph*, 2004).

16. I am grateful to Prof. H. Ticktin for this observation.

CHAPTER 8

1. Female writers like Iris Murdoch (*The Guardian* 9 February 1999) or Sarah Kane (*Daily Telegraph* 24 February 1999) are still exceptions.

2. Bourdieu refers to writers high in terms of the hierarchy of consecration as 'mandarins' (1993a, ch. 1). He refers to two types of prophetic figures, the young and temporarily unrecognised avant-garde in post-1850s capitalist modernity (whose contemporary equivalents, at their death, we have called the 'insecurely consecrated') and writers who fill the more traditional role of the prophet in various religious movements, setting their personal revelation against the authorities' orthodoxy (Weber 1965: 54, Weber 1952; Bourdieu on academic proletarians, 1991: 12–13)

3. The Obituaries Editor of the *Daily Telegraph*, interview.

4. The term 'outsider writer,' adapted from Zolberg and Cherbo (1997) could be applied to Archer and Bates.

5. Bates' grandfather's trawler may suggest that he had middle-class roots. Be that as it may — as in all obituaries, we have limited information — Bates received the poor schooling and restricted training opportunities of the 1920s working-class and identified with the latter.

6. This lengthy obituary appeared on 30 November 1985.

7. This is evident in the obituary for M.M. Kaye, which discusses her epic romance *The Far Pavilions*: 'It was futile of some reviewers to complain of its overdone melodrama , and its uncritical acceptance of life under the Raj in terms of the men who ruled it [...] The public voted with its pockets and the book sold millions of copies over the next few years.' (*The Times*, 31 January 2004)

8. Bourdieu in his dialogue with Mammeri, uses the term 'prophetic' to refer to traditional poets in Kabylia who use their familiarity with popular thought and words to coin new terms, acting as spokespersons in crises such as war (Bourdieu and Mammeri 1978, Bourdieu 1990b: 96–7)

9. Andrew Smith has identified a renewal of romanticism, now linked with the syncretism of post-colonial diaspora, in the works of critics such as Homi Bhabha and writers such as Ben Okri. The writers whose obituaries are mentioned in this section should be differentiated from this strand of post-colonial discourse. (Smith 2004: 252–61, Ahmad 1992).

10. Such inconsistencies include a rhetorical alliance between cultural producers and working-class whilst maintaining social distances between them.

11. The obits remind us that writers such as Paul Bowles — and the small group of British surrealist poets, who stretched linguistic conventions to the limit — attained only accidental, late and fraught recognition.

12. We are not arguing that all writers located in authoritarian regimes acquire a broad readership: the Spanish metaphysical poet writing during and after Franco, Valente, is a highly autonomous writer, whose work never became popular — except among poets — and even then only those interested in the most difficult formalist or metaphysical thought (*The Times*, 27 July 2000).

CHAPTER 9

1. This chapter is based on a qualitative study of 148 obituaries of visual artists, drawn from various newspapers (forty-four painters, fifteen sculptors, three art dealers, twenty-three photographers, six potters, twelve designers, engravers and embroiderers, twelve illustrators and wood engravers and thirty-three cartoonists, animators and magazine or newspaper comic strip illustrators). It supplements the small number of artists found in the systematic sample.

2. The exceptions are the Australian painters Elizabeth Durack and Johnny Tjupurrula, the Egyptian, Prince Hassan and the American and naturalized American sculptors, George Segal and Felix de Weldon.
3. See also the painters, Dick Lee and Daphne Hardy Henrion and a series of cartoonists, such as the Indian-born Abu Abraham and the Greek-born William Papas.
4. Thus the author of Josef Herman's obituary comments sardonically: 'the late flower pieces he showed may be seen as dues which he felt able to pay the academy and his admirers.'
5. He was later to recreate his image of Churchill, this time for a Havel-led Czechoslovakia, to commemorate Gorbachev's declaration of the end of the Cold War.
6. The only article for a man who had acted as an assistant to a woman (Barbara Hepworth), Wells' obituary gives symbolic freight to his reputation by citing Naum Gabo's judgement that he was 'the Paul Klee of the Constructivist movement'.
7. Joseph Herman's obit is thrown into relief by another obituary of a painter of Welsh miners, Nicholas Evans (*The Times*, 14 February 2004; *The Independent*, 9 February 2004). Evans, a train driver, had been too poor to afford paints and paper at school and only exhibited for the first time in his seventies. In Bourdieu's concepts, Evans was an autodidact (Bourdieu 1984: 84–85), who lacked the immediate rapport with a public and the support from both fellow-artists and patrons that Herman obtained. Moreover he was a Pentecostalist sect member, interpreting disasters like the Aberfan landslip in terms of modern crucifixions, and the mines as pits of hell. In direct opposition to Herman, Evans, as recorded by his obituarist, was an unaccommodating painter: 'the men's faces are big because I want to overpower you. I'm shouting at you. Because I am angry' (*The Independent*). Evans might have taken the art world by storm, but he perhaps would not have had an obit had it not been for the critical influence in 1978 of the Camberwell Art School teacher, Lawrence Gowing. Gowing acted as 'support person' (Becker 1982) for Evans, who became regularly selected for the Royal Academy Summer Show.
8. Underdog culture is associated also with the literature and art for children. This also appears in the obits (see Kathleen Hale, the illustrator of the Orlando books, *The Guardian*, 28 January.2000), but a new indeterminacy characterizes this period as between children's and popular adult forms, such as film cartoons.
9. One Papas cartoon, had a caption 'In civilized hands' as a barefoot African woman pulls, single-handledy, a heavy garden roller, Ian Smith sitting nearby with a whip.
10. In the qualitative study, only Terry Frost, Nicholas Evans (*The Times*, 14 February 2004; *The Independent*, 9 February 2004) and Johnny Tjupurrula (*The Independent*, 17 February 2001) had origins in the subordinate classes.

CHAPTER 10

1. See Bourdieu on the naïve gaze (1984), and against standard accounts of popular culture (1993b, 1– 7).
2. It is not assumed here that every eyewitness account is true in terms of concrete details, but it is argued that they are intersubjectively valid at a deeper

level of recollection, that of 'structural-organisational' meanings (see Kovács 1992: 122)

3. This includes the obituaries for the qualitative analysis in addition to those appearing in the quantitative analysis.

4. In this respect it is noticeable that the *Daily Telegraph* features fewer footballers and more cricketers than *The Guardian* and *The Independent*. Perhaps too, it is not surprising that, along with the military and naval officers, the *Telegraph* also features a Master of Hounds and a woman deer-hunter who was a crack shot with her rifle.

5. This period, which covered the passing of the ban on fox-hunting, did not have a not a single obituary for those involved with this activity outside the pages of *The Daily Telegraph*.

6. The 1900 obituaries included some for aristocrats whose lives were wholly dedicated to leisure activities, typically hunting and point-to-point racing.

7. Obituaries for sportswomen were remarkably few and far between and were concentrated especially in swimming and cycling. The financial base tends to be particularly mentioned in these obits — as in the struggle of the women competitors to avoid sponsorship, which they thought would reduce their independence (see eg, Edie Atkins, the cyclist, *The Independent*, 1 October 1999). Indeed, dramatic confrontations over female autonomy appear as a recurrent and conspicuous feature of the women's obituaries. Here the ideal-type obit must be that of Eleanor Holm, who refused to leave a party at 9 p.m. the night before her swimming event in the Berlin 1936 Olympics and whose male Olympic official denied her the right to compete the day after: without her, America spectacularly lost the event (the *New York Times*, 2 February 2004) (see also the barriers to Aileen Soule's participation in the Antwerp 1920 Games after selection — she went on to win a gold medal in diving at 14 (*The Independent*, 22 October 2002)).

8. Sports — such as cricket or rugby — never went through the same rupture between the commercial expanded field and the restricted field as developed in the 1850s in music, literature and art. Nevertheless, the carefully-maintained gulf between those games with an amateur ethos and those without had the same consequence: that of the exclusion of the masses (Hobsbaum and Ranger 1983: 300). The sporting obituaries cast light on this.

9. Centre halves are the exception.

10. The working-class bodily hexis is perhaps shown most conspicuously in the little vignettes about Ronnie Simpson retold in his obituary (*The Independent*, 22 April 2004). As he became more successful he was presented with a dilemma between taking his dentures out for the game, which was safer, and being able to smile and talk at a winning presentation, also desirable. He — and another team member — solved the problem by keeping their dentures on the field in his goalie's cap. The obit lacks the space to mention that this is a direct indicator of the impact of poverty on the body: an entire generation of Glaswegian working-class youth were given, for their twenty-first birthday, the present of having their teeth removed — perfect or damaged — to save them the cost of later dentistry.

11. The antagonism over amateurism is linked explicitly in this obit to social clashes: 'Students, mainly from Oxbridge, formed the bulk of the British Olympics team in those days. Southern sticklers for Corinthian propriety saw a way to exclude the working-class Midlands upstart who was threatening to win everything.'

12. In this respect we would regard the "objectification" of Matthews' obituary as exemplifying features which apply more broadly in the cultural field. Mat-

thews had clearly learnt to use individualistically the ethos of the amateur, just as Bourdieu writes about the strategic 'interests in disinterestedness' that apply in the arts (1993a). (He illustrates this by citing the symbolic profits gained by Picasso through wearing workers' overalls.)

13. The obituaries for Best used the language of 'genius' of his playing and 'flawed genius' of his personality: yet only one emphasized that his constant practice as a child at single exercises might have formed his dispositions (see the full-length obituaries in the four British papers on 26 November 2005 and *The Scotsman*, 28 November 2005). The sporting obituaries as a whole testify to the importance of training in sport, implicitly demonstrating that the feel for each game becomes literally embodied. Such discipline, like military discipline, is in part — as Bourdieu comments — a form of social compliance. But in the most distinguished players, it becomes something else — a means of self-expression. C.L.R. James, despite his highly sociological view of cricket, still calls this 'genius', as do many of the obit writers (see Smith 2006). Perhaps the most difficult terrain for defending the argument that 'natural gifts' are *an ideology* is in sport. Yet all of Bourdieu's examples of strategic practice — and its bodily responses to various games — spring from this field. Indeed, rather than natural genius, the self-expression of the memorable player should be regarded as the paramount case for his theory of 'improvisation', regulated as it is by underlying social conventions (1990a). (I am grateful to Andrew Smith for the development of these ideas, although he may disagree with my conclusion.)

14. Compare the career of the Hungarian Olympic boxer, Laszlo Papp, which was ended internationally by his great difficulties in gaining permission to leave the country after the 1956 Uprising, sealed by a total ban after 1962 (*The Guardian*, 18 October 2003).

CHAPTER 11

1. There are no trade unionists in the formal sample for 1900 and 1948 and for *The Daily Telegraph*, *The Times* and *The Independent*, 2000–2001. In the formal sample of the *New York Times* there was one trade unionist and two each in *The Guardian* and *Le Monde*. There were no women trade unionists in the *Chin Up Girls* collection of *Telegraph* obits and only three trade unionists in the other *Telegraph* collections (notably two in the *Telegraph*'s *Obituaries of Rogues*). The qualitative sample yielded 15 trade unionists (compared, for example, with 148 for the visual artists and 152 for the sportspeople.)

2. In 1979 63 per cent men and 39 per cent women in Britain were union members, but this had sunk in 1997 to as low as 32 per cent men and 18 per cent women (Sampson 2004: 63–64)

3. The percentage of disposable income earned by the top 20 per cent increased from 35 per cent in 1979 to 41 per cent in 1991–92; even more dramatically, the bottom 20 per cent saw their proportion fall below the earlier meagre level of 10 per cent to a new low of 7 per cent (Devine 1997: 121–22, Panitch and Gindin 2005, 110). A similar pattern emerged in America in 1991, with the top 20 per cent owning 45 per cent and the lowest 20 per cent falling to an identical 7 per cent share (Devine 1997: 118).

4. The effects of this 'visionary' technocratic ideology are difficult to distinguish in Britain from those of Thatcherism and later Blairism. Nevertheless, studies such as Skeggs (1997) have shown convincingly that the women of Northern working-class origins whom she interviewed had decisively ceased

to define themselves in the language of class, thinking of themselves rather as respectable, 'ordinary' people. See also the powerful study of Charlesworth (2000), which similarly identifies social processes which create a strongly embodied working-class habitus, but without engendering a politics of class.

5. There is only one exception, George Walker, an adherent of the principles of the American Moral Rearmament movement and the editor of a successful moderate trade-union newspaper. He was the son of an Anglican vicar (*The Independent*, 26 August 2004).

6. Examples at this time include the poignant obit for Des Warren. Warren, an unskilled building labourer was active in the 1972 building-workers' strike, which was asking for a minimum wage of £1 and hour and the end of the notorious "lump" system of subcontracted labour. Having organised flying pickets, Warren was charged afterwards under the Conspiracy Act and was given three years: a sentence he regarded as political. Warren was given frequent forced medication in prison and to this 'liquid cosh' he attributed his later Parkinson's disease. Even the austere *The Financial Times* thought his charge was 'politically-motivated' on the part of the then Tory Home Secretary (*The Independent*, 28 April 2004). See also obits for the electrician and dedicated oil industry health and safety expert, Bob Ballantyne, *The Guardian*, 22 June 2004), and the miner and founder of the Claimants' Union, Joe Kenyon (*Independent*, 7 June 2000): in all these cases the obituaries recall individual voices that would normally be forgotten at the level of national memory.

7. See also the French Resistance leader, concentration camp prisoner, Renault worker and leader of the Confédération Générale du Travail (CGT), Henri Krasucki (*The Guardian*, 29 March 2003), the former Secretary-General of the French CGT and Central Committee member of the French Communist Party, Lucien Molino (*Le Monde*, 13 September 2000), and the American leader of the metal-workers' union and former Secretary-General of the Communist Party, Gus Hall (*Le Monde*, 19 October 2000).

8. Frank Haxell, originally 30 May 1988; Reg Briginshaw, originally 28 March 1992 (both included also in Massingberd 1998: 26–28; 173–76) and Jack Dash (9 June 1989) (Massingberd, 1999: 43–47 also 2001, 75–80).

CHAPTER 12

1. See for example, *BMJ* 2 March 2002, 549–50. One such medical obituary was written *in anticipation of his death* by the subject himself, which gives a whole new meaning to the obits' editors' term 'advancers'.

2. Personal communication.

3. Kracauer concedes that some examples of biography *sublate* the form, to 'stand outside the haze of ideology' (1995: 105). We would have to take issue with his view that the biography/obituary always incorporates only the memory of the dominants or of occupational groups like artists, thus testifying to an 'unarticulated rejection of the authority that arises out of the depth of the masses'. Nevertheless, in its current form, popular memory does emerge as a mediated construction, filtered, most significantly, through the sieve of educated journalists.

4. Karski's historic significance lies solely but importantly in his wartime actions — he had a photographic memory and was chosen by the Polish underground as an eyewitness in 1943 of events in the Warsaw Ghetto, including the extermination of Jews in cattle trucks, 150 at a time, and shootings in Belzec, an

extermination camp, where he masqueraded as a guard. In London, Victor Gollancz had a nervous breakdown at his news, but he failed to convince either Anthony Eden of his reliability, or, in America, Franklin Roosevelt and a *Jewish* Supreme Court judge. He thought he had failed — "I was a young man, a little guy, merely a courier, I had no leverage talking to the most powerful men' (*The Times*, 17 July 2000).

5. Fewer, they now are, but not absent — see eg, Lieutenant-Colonel Henry Howard, the son of an officer; Gresham's school and Sandhurst (*Daily Telegraph*, 24 July 2000). He was distinguished however by several acts of bravery — whatever might be thought of their context — as when he led action against an Arab rebellion in Palestine in 1936, holding a hill despite being shot through both thighs.

6. The obituary also notes that he was only given an honorary captaincy after retirement: as a native soldier he was denied promotion beyond senior native co-officer . Yet five thousand people attended his funeral.

7. The sole survivor, the obit's subject, was shot, but escaped by simulating death. Her subsequent career as the Matron of a large Australian hospital fitted perfectly the biographical ascent of the normative obituary story: it was not the long drawn-out anti-climax that is the obit writer's bane with so many of the Second World War military heroes.

8. Thus over and over again, political economy — with its alienated or reductive conception of human labour — was countered with a moral economy.

9. There were very few women autobiographers at this time. This might have been the product of the family rule — harsher for them — against 'washing dirty linen in public' or the consequence of a publishers' bias against women's memoirs.

10. See amongst them, Wal Hannington, Ruth and Eddie Frow, Lewis Jones, Peggy Duff and other members.

11. In this way I reiterate Goode's conclusion when he argues against the systematic *subversion* of prestige-allocation accomplished by the current 'class, sex role, ethnic, racial and religious patterns' (1978: 282). He ends his book on heroism:

Not only are the achievements [today] of men and women in the arts, sciences, invention, sports, in courage and in many other realms abundant; they are given more admiration by more people than in the past. Moreover I insist that there are thousands of unsung heroes as well people who achieve greatly in activities that are given only modest or local attention [...] if more people are encouraged to achieve greatly or well [...] we shall in fact honour more people for more kinds of contributions to human beings everywhere (1978: 393–94).

Bibliography

PRIMARY MATERIALS

The Daily Telegraph, 2000–2001
The Guardian, 2000–2001
The Independent, 2000–2001
The Times, 1900, 1948 and 2000–2001
Le Monde, 2000–2001
The New York Times, 2000–2001
BBC, Radio 4, *The Obituary Writers*, 3 February 2006.
Brunskill, I. (2005). *Great Lives*, London: Times Books, HarperCollins.
Massingberd, H., (1997). *The Third Book of Obituaries*, London: MacMillan.
Massingberd, H., ed. (1998). *The Daily Telegraph Fourth Book of Obituaries: Rogues*, London: Pan.
Massingberd, H., ed. (1999). The *Daily Telegraph Fifth Book of Obituaries*, Twentieth-Century Lives, London: MacMillan.
Massingberd, H., ed. (2001). *The Very Best of The Daily Telegraph Books of Obituaries*, London: Pan.
Osborne, P., ed. (2003). *The Guardian Book of Obituaries*, London: Atlantic Books.
Powell, G. and Ramsay, K., eds. (2004). *Chin Up, Girls! A Collection of Daily Telegraph Women's Obituaries*, London: John Murray.

SECONDARY MATERIALS

Ahmad, A. (1992). *In Theory*, London: Verso.
Alexander, J.C. (1995). *Fin de Siècle Social Theory*, London: Verso.
Anon, (1836 (Oct) –1837 (Jan.)) Sketches of Germany and the Germans *The Quarterly Review*, Vol. LVIII, no. CXVI: 302.
Anonymous (1935). *The History of The Times: The Thunderer in the Making, 1785–1841*, London: The Times.
Antal, F. (1947). *Florentine Painting and Its Social Background*, London: Routledge and Kegan Paul.
Arendt, H. (1958). *The Human Condition*, Chicago: Doubleday Anchor.
Ariès, P. (1981). *The Hour of our Death*, Oxford: Oxford University Press.
Ariès, P. (1994). *Western Attitudes to Death* London: Marion Boyars (1976).
Atlas, J. (2000). *Bellow: A Biography*, London: Faber and Faber.
Aubrey, J. (1898). *Brief Lives*, ed. A. Clark, Oxford: Clarendon.

Bakhtin, M. M. (1984). *Rabelais and his World*, Bloomington: Indiana University Press.

Balzac, H. (1974). *History of the Thirteen*, Harmondsworth: Penguin (1833–85).

Baudrillard, J. (1993). *Symbolic Exchange and Death*, London and Seven Oaks: Sage.

Bauman, Z. (1992). *Mortality, Immortality and Other Life Strategies*, Cambridge: Polity.

Bauman, Z. (1998). *Work, Consumerism and the New Poor*, Buckingham: Open University Press.

Beck, U. and Beck-Gernsheim, E. (1995). *The Normal Chaos of Love*, London: Routledge.

Becker, H. (1982). *Art Worlds*, Berkeley: Unversity of California Press.

Ben-Amos, A. (2000). *Funerals, Politics and Memory in Modern France*, 1789–1996, Oxford: Oxford: University Press.

Benjamin, W. (1973). *Understanding Brecht*, London: New Left Books.

Benjamin W (1979). *One Way Street*, London: New Left Books.

Benjamin, W. (1999). *The Arcades Project*, Cambridge, MA: Belknap Press of Harvard University Press.

Bennett, T. (2005). The Historical Universal: the role of cultural value in the historical sociology of Pierre Bourdieu, *British Journal of Sociology*, Vol. 56, no. 1, March, 141–162.

Bergson, H. (1991). *Matter and Memory*, New York: Zone Books (1896).

Bertaux, D., ed. (1981). *Biography and Society*, London: Sage.

Bhabha, H. (1994). *The Location of Culture*, London: Routledge.

Biau, V. (2000). *La Consécration en Architecture*, Thesis submitted to l'Ecole des Hautes Etudes, Paris.

Bickerton, C.J..(2006). France's History Wars, *Le Monde Diplomatique*, Feb. 14–15.

Bielsa, E. (2006). The Pivotal Role of News Agencies in the context of Globalization, *Global Networks*, forthcoming.

Bloch, E. (1986). *The Principle of Hope*, Vols. I to III, Oxford: Blackwell.

Bloor, M. (1991 [1976]). *Knowledge and Social Imagery*, Chicago: University of Chicago Press.

Blunt, A. (1981). *Art and Architecture in France 1500–1700*, Harmondsworth, Middlesex: Penguin.

Bohman, J. (1999). Practical Reason and Cultural Constraint, pp. 129–152 in ed. R. Shusterman, *Pierre Bourdieu. A Critical Reader*, Oxford: Blackwell.

Boltanski, L. and Chiapello, E. (1999). Le Nouvel Esprit de Capitalisme, Paris: Gallimard.

Bourdieu, P.(1964). *Travail et Travailleurs en Algérie*, Paris and Le Hague: Mouton.

Bourdieu, P. (1968). Structuralism and the Theory of Sociological Knowledge, *Social Research*, Vol. 35, no 4, 681–706.

Bourdieu, P. (1975). L'Invention de la Vie de l'Artiste, *Actes de la Recherche en Sciences Sociales*, 2, 67–94.

Bourdieu, P. (1977). *Outline of a Theory of Practice*, Cambridge: Cambridge University Press.

Bourdieu, P. (1981). Men and Machines, pp. 304–317 in eds. K. Knorr-Cetina and A. Cicourel, *Advances in Social Theory and Methodology*, London: Routledge and Kegan Paul.

Bourdieu, P. (1983). Erving Goffman: Discoverer of the Infinitely Small, *Theory, Culture and Society*, Vol. 2, no. 1, 112–13.

Bourdieu, P. (1984). *Distinction*, London: RKP.

Bourdieu, P. (1986a). L'Illusion Biographique, *Actes de la Recherche en Sciences Sociales*, 62/63, pp. 69–72.

Bourdieu, P. (1986b). The Forms of Capital in ed. J. Richardson, Handbook *of Theory and Research for the Sociology of Education*, New York and London: Greenwood Press.

Bourdieu, P. (1987a). Legitimation and Structured Interests in Weber's Sociology of Religion, pp. 119–36 in eds. S. Lash and S. Whimster, *Max Weber, Rationality and Modernity*, London: Allen and Unwin.

Bourdieu, P. (1987b). What Makes a Social Class? *Berkeley Journal of Sociology*, 32, pp. 1–18.

Bourdieu, P. (1988a). *Homo Academicus*, Cambridge: Polity.

Bourdieu, P. (1988b). L'Iconoclasme Spécifique Accompli par un Artiste suppose une Maîtrise virtuose du Champ artistique (Interview with Roger Chartier), *Sociotoile*, Part 5, pp. 117, 217, etc – 717 (7 pp.) (http://www.iwp.uni-linz.ac.uk.at/lxe/sektktf/bb/hb00.09.htm (Hyper-Bourdieu web site, accessed 16.4.06)

Bourdieu, P. (1990a). *The Logic of Practice*, Cambridge: Polity.

Bourdieu, P. (1990b). *In Other Words*, Cambridge: Polity.

Bourdieu, P. (1991). *Language and Symbolic Power*, Cambridge: Polity.

Bourdieu, P. (1993a). *Field of Cultural Production*, Cambridge: Polity.

Bourdieu, P. (1993b). *Sociology in Question*, Sage

Bourdieu, P. (1993c). Concluding Remarks, pp. 263–75 in Calhoun, C., Lipuma, E.and Postone, M., *Bourdieu: Critical Perspectives*, Cambridge: Polity.

Bourdieu, P. (1994). *Raisons Pratiques*, Paris: Seuil.

Bourdieu, P. (1996a). *The Rules of Art*, Cambridge: Polity.

Bourdieu, P. (1996b). *The State Nobility*, Cambridge: Polity.

Bourdieu, P. (1998a). *Practical Reason*, Cambridge: Polity.

Bourdieu, P. (1998b). Georges Canguilhem: an Obituary Notice: *Economy and Society*, Vol. 27, nos. 2 and 3, May 190–92.

Bourdieu P. (1998c). A Reasoned Utopia and Economic Fatalism, *New Left Review*, 227, Jan.-Feb .

Bourdieu, P. (1998d). *Acts of Resistance*, Cambridge: Polity.

Bourdieu P. et al (1999). *The Weight of the World*, Cambridge: Polity

Bourdieu, P. (2000a). *Pascalian Meditations*, Cambridge: Polity

Bourdieu, P. (2000b). *Les Structures Sociales de l'Economie*, Paris: Seuil.

Bourdieu, P. (2001a). *Contre-Feux 2: Pour un Mouvement Social Européene*, Paris: Raisons d'Agir Editions.

Bourdieu, P. (2001b). *Masculine Domination*, Cambridge: Polity.

Bourdieu, P. (2002a). Habitus pp. 27–4 in eds. Hillier, J. and Rooksby, E., *Habitus: A Sense of Place*, Aldershot: Ashgate.

Bourdieu, P. (2002b). *Interventions, 1961–2001*, Marseille: Agone.

Bourdieu, P (2002c). *Le Bal des Célibataires*, Paris: Seuil.

Bourdieu, P. (2003a). *Images d'Algérie*, Graz: Actes Sud.

Bourdieu, P. (2003b). Conference at the University of Athens, 14 Oct. 1996 in ed. I. Lambiki-Dimaki, *Social Sciences and the Avant Garde in Greece, 1850–1967*, Athens: National Centre for the Social Sciences.

Bourdieu, P. (2004). *Science of Science and Reflexivity*, Cambridge: Polity.

Bourdieu, P. (2005). *The Social Structures of the Economy*, Cambridge: Polity.

Bourdieu, P. and Boltanski, L. (1976). La production de l'Idéologie Dominante, *Actes de la Recherche en Sciences Sociales*, Juin, 2/3, 4–73 (also collected in Bourdieu, 2002b).

Bourdieu, P., with Boltanski, L., Castel, R., Chamboredon, J.-C., and Schnapper, D. (1990). *Photography: A Middlebrow Art*, Cambridge: Polity.

Bourdieu, P., Chartier, R. and Darnton, R. (1985). Dialogue A Propos de l'Histoire Culturelle, *Actes de la Recherche en Sciences Sociales*, 59, 86–93.

Bourdieu, P. and Dixon K. (1995). Une Double Cosmogonie nationale, *Liber*, Supplement to *Actes de la Recherche en Sciences Sociales*, 24, October, 2.

Bourdieu, P. and Haacke, H. (1995). *Free Exchange*, Cambridge: Polity.

Bourdieu, P. and Mammeri, M. (1978). Dialogue sur la poésie orale en Kabylie, *Actes de la Recherche en Sciences Sociales*, 23, 51–66.

Bourdieu, P. and Passeron, J.-P. (1990). *Reproduction in Society, Education and Culture*, London: Sage.

Bourdieu, P. and Sayad, A. (1964). *Le Déracinement*, Paris: Minuit.

Bourdieu, P. and Wacquant (1992). *An Invitation to Reflexive Sociology*, Chicago: University of Chicago Press.

Bouveresse, J. (1999). Rules, Dispositions and the Habitus, pp. 45-63 in eds. R. Shusterman, Bourdieu, *A Critical Reader*, Oxford: Blackwell.

Bowness, A., ed. (1985). *Barbara Hepworth: A Pictorial Autobiography*, London: Tate Gallery.

Boyer, M. Christine (1996). *The City of Collective Memory*, Cambridge, MA: M.I.T. Press.

Bradley, H. (1989). *Men's Work, Women's Work*, Cambridge: Polity.

Bradley, H. (1996). *Fractured Identities*, Cambridge: Polity.

Brenner, J. (2000). *Women and the Politics of Class*, New York: Monthly Review Press.

Brenner, R. (1985). Agrarian Class Structure and Economic development in Pre-Industrial Europe, in eds./ Aston, T.H. and Philpin, C.H.E. *The Brenner Debate*, Cambridge: Cambridge University Press.

Brenner, R. (1998). The Economics of Global Turbulence, *New Left Review*, No. 229, May-June.

Brinkley, D. (2000.) *The Life of Rosa Parks*, London: Phoenix.

Brockmeier, J. (2002). Introduction in *Culture and Psychology*, Vol. 8, no.1, March.

Brown, M. E. (2001). *William Motherwell's Cultural Politics*, Lexington: Kentucky University Press.

Brunskill, I. (2005). *Great Lives*, London: Times Books, HarperCollins.

Buck-Morss, S. (1991). *The Dialectics of Seeing: Walter Benjamin and the Arcades Project*, Cambridge, MA:

Burger, P. (1992). *The Decline of Modernism*, State College: Pennsylvania State University Press.

Butler, J. (1997). *Excitable Speech*, London: Routledge.

Butler, J. (2003). *Precarious Life*, London: Verso.

Bytheway, B. and Johnson, J. (1996). Valuing Lives? Obituaries and the Life Course, *Mortality*, July 219–34.

Canclini, G.N. (1993). *Transforming Modernity: Popular Culture in Mexico*, Austin: University of Texas Press.

Carey, J. (2002). *The Intellectuals and the Masses: Pride and Prejudice amongst the Literary Intelligentsia, 1880–1939*, Chicago, IL: Academy.

Cartier- Bresson, H. (2004). *The Mind's Eye*, New York: Aperture.

Casanova, P. (2004). *The World Republic of Letters*, Cambridge, MA: Harvard University Press.

Casey, E. (1987) *Remembering: A Phenomenological Study*, Bloomington: Indiana University Press.

Castells, M. (2000). *The Rise of the Network Society*, Volume 2. Oxford: Blackwell.

Charle, C. (2002). Intellectuels et Fin de Siècle en Europe, pp. 257–274, in eds. M. Einfalt and J. Jurt, *Le Texte et le Contexte*, Paris: Edition de la Maison de l' Homme.

Charlesworth, S.J. (2000). *A Phenomenology of Working-Class Experience*, Cambridge: Cambridge University Press.

Checkland, S. (2000). *Ben Nicolson*, London: John Murray.

Clark, A., ed. (1898). *Aubrey's Brief Lives*, Oxford: Clarendon.

Clark, T.J. (1999). *Farewell, to an Idea*, New Haven: Yale University Press.

Compagnon, A. (1997). Marcel Proust's Remembrance of Things Past pp. 211–248 in ed. P. Nora, *Realms of Memory*, Vol. 2, New York: Columbia University Press.

Connerton, P. (1989). *How Societies Remember*, Cambridge: Cambridge University Press.

Cook, E.T. (1911). *The Life of John Ruskin*, London: George Allen and Co.

Cook, R. (2000). The Mediated Manufacture of an Avant-Garde in ed. B. Fowler, *Reading Bourdieu on Society and Culture*, Oxford: Blackwell.

Corrigan, P. and Sayer, D. (1985). *The Great Arch*, Oxford: Blackwell.

Coser, L.A., ed. (1991). *Maurice Halbwachs' On Collective Memory*, Chicago: Chicago University Press.

Crane, D. (1987). *The Transformation of the Avant-Garde*, Chicago: University of Chicago Press.

Crompton, R., ed. (1999). *Restructuring Gender Relations and Employment*, Oxford: Oxford University Press

Crompton R. (2000). The Gendered Restructuring of the Middle Classes: Employment and Caring, pp. 165–183 in eds. R. Crompton, F. Devine, M. Savage and J. Scott, *Renewing Class Analysis*, Oxford: Blackwell.

Crowther, A. and Dupree, M. (1996). The Invisible General Practitioner: The Careers of Scottish Medical Students in the Late 19th Century, *Bulletin of the History of Medicine*, 70, 387–413.

Davidoff, E. and Hall, C. (1984). *Family Fortunes*, London: Hutchinson.

Davies, D.J. (2005). *A Brief History of Death*, Oxford: Blackwell.

Denning, M. (1998). *Mechanic Accents*, London: Verso.

Devine, F (1997). *Social Class in America and Britain*, Edinburgh: Edinburgh University Press.

Dickie, G. (1974). *Art and the Aesthetic*, Ithaca, NY: Cornell University Press.

Dixon, K. (1998). *Les Evangiles du Marché*, Paris: Raisons d'Agir.

Dollimore, J. (1998). *Death, Desire and Loss in Western Culture*, Harmondsworth (check): Allen Lane: The Penguin Press.

Douglas, J. (1967). *The Social Meanings of Suicide*, Princeton, NJ: Princeton University Press.

Dubois, J. (1997).*Pour Albertine*, Paris: Seuil (Collection Liber).

Durand, P. (1998). *Crises: Manet via Mallarmé*, Leuven: Peeters Vrin.

Durand, P. (2002). Ecriture et Systèmes de Prescription pp. 25–38 in eds. Einfalt, M.J. and Jurt, J., *Le Texte et le Contexte*, Paris: Edition de la Maison de l' Homme.

Durkheim, E. (1965). *Sociology and Philosophy*, London: Cohen and West.

Durkheim, E. (1968). *Suicide*, London: Routledge and Kegan Paul.

Durkheim, E. (1984) .*The Division of Labour in Society*, London: MacMillan.

Durkheim E (1992). *Professional Ethics and Civic Morals*, London: Routledge.

Eagleton, T. (1984). *The Function of Criticism*, London: Verso.

Eagleton, T. (1995). *Heathcliff and the Great Hunger*, London: Verso.

Eiland, H. and Jennings, M.W., eds. (2002). *Walter Benjamin: Selected Writings*, Vol. 3, Cambridge, MA. Belknap Press of Harvard University Press.

Einfalt, M.J. and Jurt, J., eds. (2002). *Le Texte et le Contexte*, Paris: Editions de la Maison de l'Homme.

Elias, N. (1985). *The Loneliness of the Dying*, Oxford: Blackwell.

Elias, N. (2000). *The Civilizing Process*, revised ed. Oxford: Blackwell.

Felski, R. (1989). *Beyond Feminist Aesthetics*, Cambridge, MA: Harvard University Press.

Fentress, J. and Wickham, C. (1992). *Social Memory*, Oxford: Blackwell.

Ferguson, H. (2000). *Modernity and Subjectivity: Body, Soul and Spirit*, Charlottesville: University of Virginia.

Ferguson, H. (2004). The Sublime and the Subliminal: Modern Identities and the Aesthetics of Combat, *Theory, Culture and Society*. Vol. 21, 3, June 2004, 1–33.

Fergusson, J. (1999). Death and the Press, in ed. S. Glover, *The Penguin Book of Journalism*, Harmondsworth: Penguin.

Feyerabend, P. (1993). *Against Method*, London: Verso.

Finney, H. C. (1997). Art Production and Artistic Careers pp 73–84 in eds. V.L. Zolberg and J.M. Cherbo, *Outsider Art*, Cambridge: Cambridge University Press.

Fisher, J. (1995). Editorial: Some Thoughts on 'Contaminations' pp. 3–7, *Third Text*, No 32, Autumn.

Forgacs, D. and Nowell-Smith, G., eds. (1985). *Antonio Gramsci: Selections from the Cultural Writings*, London: Lawrence and Wishart.

Foucault, M. (1976). *The Archaeology of Knowledge*, New York, 1976.

Foucault, M. (1977). *Language, Counter-Memory, Practice: Selected Essays and Interviews*, (ed. D, Bouchard), Oxford: Blackwell.

Foucault, M. (1978). *The History of Sexuality, Vol. I*, London: Allen Lane.

Fowler, B. (1991). *The Alienated Reader*, Brighton: Harvester Wheatsheaf.

Fowler, B. (1997). *Pierre Bourdieu and Cultural Theory : Critical Investigations*, London : Sage.

Fowler, B. (2005a). La Photographie et l'Esthetisme Aristocratique pp 53–63 in eds. J. Dubois, P. Durand and Y. Winkin, *Le Symbolique et le Social. La réception internationale de la pensée de Pierre Bourdieu*, Liège: Les Editions de l'Université de Liège.

Fowler, B. (2005b). Collective Memory and Forgetting: Components for a Study of Obituaries, *Theory, Culture and Society*, Vol. 22, 6, 53–72

Fraser, N. and Honneth A. (2003). *Redistribution or Recognition: A Political-Philosophical Exchange*, London: Verso.

Frisby, D. (1985). *Fragments of Modernity*, Cambridge: Polity.

Frisby, D. (2001). *Cityscapes of Modernity*, Cambridge: Polity.

Frisby, D. and Featherstone, M. (1997). *Simmel on Culture*, London: Sage.

Frye, N. (1957). *Anatomy of Criticism*, Princeton, NJ: Princeton University Press.

Gablik, S. (1984). *Has Modernism failed*? London: Thames and Hudson.

Gedi, N. and Elam, Y. (1996). Collective Memory, What is it? *History and Memory*, 8/1 30–50.

Gershuny, J. (2000). Social Position from Narrative Data, pp. 43–65 in eds. R. Crompton, F. Devine, M. Savage and J. Scott, *Renewing Class Analysis*, Oxford: Blackwell.

Gikandi, S. (1996). *Maps of Englishness*: Columbia: Columbia University Press.

Gittings, C. (1984). *Death, Burial and the Individual in Early Modern England*, London: Croom Helm.

Glass, D.V. and Hall, J.R. (1954). Social Mobility in Britain pp. 177–217 in D.V. Glass (ed.) *Social Mobility in Britain*, London: Routledge and Kegan Paul.

Goffman, E. (1975). *Frame Analysis*, Harmondsworth: Penguin.

Goldberg, C.A., (2003). Haunted by the Spectre of Communism, *Theory and Society* 32, nos. 5–6, 725–773.

Goldmann, L. (1964). *The Hidden God*, London: Routledge.

Goldthorpe, J.H. et al (1968). *The Affluent Worker: Industrial Attitudes*. Vol 1, Cambridge: Cambridge U.P.

Goode, W. J. (1978). *The Celebration of Heroes*, Berkeley, University of California Press.

Gordon, E. and Nair, G. (2003). *Public Lives*, New Haven, CT: Yale University Press.

Green, N. (1990). *The Spectacle of Nature*, Manchester: Manchester U.P.

Guilbaut, Serge (1983). *How New York Stole The idea of Modern Art*, Chicago: University of Chicago Press.

Guillory, J. (1993). *Cultural Capital: The Problem of Literary Canon Formation*, Chicago: University of Chicago Press.

Guillory, J. (1997). Bourdieu's Refusal, *Modern Language Quarterly*, December, 367–398.

Guttsman, W.L. (1963). *The British Political Elite*, London: McGibbon and Kee.

Haacke, H. (1995). *Framing and Being Framed*, New York: New York University Press.

Habermas, J. (1989). *The Structural Transformation of the Public Sphere*, Cambridge: Polity.

Hadas, M. (2005). *The Birth of Modern Man*, University of Corvinus, Budapest, translation of the Hungarian book of the same title, published in 2003 by Helikon Kiado.

Halbwachs, M. (1958) .*The Psychology of Social Class*, London: Heinemann (1955).

Halbwachs, M. (1980). *The Collective Memory*, London: Harper and Row.

Halbwachs, M. (1997). *La Mémoire Collective*, Paris: Albin Michel.

Harrington, A. (2004). *Art and Social Theory*, Cambridge: Polity.

Harvey, D. (2000). *Spaces of Hope*, Edinburgh: Edinburgh University Press.

Heinich, N. (1987). Arts et sciences à l'Age Classique: Professions et institutions culturelles, *Actes de la recherche en sciences sociales*, 66–67, 47–78.

Heinich, N. (1996) .*The Glory of Van Gogh*, Princeton, NJ: Princeton University Press.

Heinich, N. (1998a). *Ce Que L'Art Fait A La Sociologie*, Paris: Gallimard.

Heinich, N. (1998b). *Le Triple Jeu de l'Art Contemporain*, Paris: Minuit.

Heinich,N. (1999). *L'épreuve de la Grandeur*, Paris : La Découverte.

Heinich, N. (2000). From rejection of Contemporary art to Culture War, pp 170–217 in eds. M. Lamont and L. Thévenot, *Rethinking Comparative Cultural Sociology*, Cambridge: Cambridge University Press.

Hertz, R. (1960). *Death and the Right Hand*, London: Cohen and West [1907].

Hill, C. (1974). *Change and Continuity in 17th Century England*, London: Weidenfeld and Nicolson.

Hobsbaum, E.J. (1987). *The Age of Empire*, London: Abacus.

Hobsbaum, E.J. (1999). *Industry and Empire*, Harmondsworth: Penguin.

Hobsbaum, E.J. and Ranger, T. (1983). *The Invention of Tradition*, Cambridge: Cambridge University Press.

Holyoake, G. (1892). *Sixty Years of an Agitator's life*, London: T. Fisher Unwin.

Hopkins, K. (1983). *Death and Renewal: Sociological Studies of Roman History*, Vol. 2, Cambridge: Cambridge University Press.

Houlbrooke, R.A. R. (1998). *Death, Religion and the Family in England, 1480–1750*, Oxford: Clarendon Press.

Hume, J. (2000). *Obituaries in American Culture*, Jackson: University of Mississippi.

Hunter, J.P. (1990). *Before Novels*, New York: W.W.Norton.

Hutton, P. (1993). *History as an Art of Memory*, Hanover: University of Vermont Press.

Ingham, G. (2000). Class Inequality and the Social Production of Money in eds. R. Crompton, F. Devine, M. Savage and S. Scott, *Renewing Class Analysis*, Oxford: Blackwell.

Jameson, F. (1986). Third World Literature in the Era of Multinational Capital, *Social Text*, Fall.

Jamieson, L. (1998). *Intimacy*, Cambridge: Polity.

Jay, M. (1996). *The Dialectical Imagination*, Berkeley: University of California Press (1973).

Johnson, M. (2006). *The Dead Beat*, New York: HarperCollins.

Joyce, J. (1968). *Ulysses*, Harmondsworth: Penguin.

Kant, I.(1979). *The Conflict of the Faculties*, Lincoln, University of Nebraska Press.

Kantorowitz, E.H. (1957). *The King's Two Bodies*, Princeton, NJ: Princeton University Press.

Kelsall, R.K. (1974). The Higher Civil Service, pp. 170–184 in eds. P. Stanworth and A. Giddens, *Elites and Power in British Society*, Cambridge: Cambridge University Press.

Knorr-Cetina, K. (1983). The Ethnographic Study of Scientific Work, pp.115–140 in eds. K. Knorr-Cetina and M. Mulkay, *Science Observed*, London: Sage.

Knorr-Cetina, K. and Mulkay, M. (1983). Introduction, pp. 1–18 in *Science Observed*, London: Sage.

Koonz, C. (1994). Between Memory and Oblivion pp. 258–280 in ed. J.R. Gillis, *Commemorations: The Politics of National Identity*, Princeton, NJ: Princeton University Press.

Kovács, A. (1992). TheAbduction of Imre Nagy and his Group pp.117–124 in Passerini, L., ed. *Memory and Totalitarianism*, Oxford: Oxford University Press.

Kracauer, S. (1995). *The Mass Ornament*, Cambridge, MA: Harvard University Press.

Kundera, M. (1982). *The Book of Laughter and Forgetting*, London: Faber and Faber.

Lamont, M. (1992). *Money, Morals and Manners: The Culture of the French and American Upper Middle Class*; Chicago: Chicago University Press.

Landes, J. (1988). *Women and the Public Sphere*, Ithaca, NY: Cornell University Press.

Lara, M. P. (1998). *Moral Textures*, Cambridge: Polity.

Latour, B. (1983). Give me a Laboratory and I will Raise the World, pp. 141–170 in eds. K. Knorr-Cetina and M. Mulkay, *Science Observed*, London: Sage.

Lawlor, L. (2003). *The Challenge of Bergsonism*, New York: Continuum.

Le Goff, J. (1984). *The Birth of Purgatory*, London: Scolar Press.

Levine, L. (1988). *Highbrow/Lowbrow*, Cambridge, MA: Harvard University Press.

Lovell, T. (1987). *Consuming Fiction*, London: Verso.

Lovell, T. (2003). Resisting With Authority, *Theory, Culture and Society* 20, 1–17.

Lowenthal, L. (1961). *Literature, Popular Culture and Society*, Palo Alto, CA: Pacific Books.

Lukács, G (1978a). *The Theory of the Novel*, London: Merlin.

Lukács, G. (1978b). *Studies in European Realism*, London: Merlin.

MacCannell, D. (1989). *The Tourist*, New York: Schocken Books.

MacInnes, J. (1998). *The End of Masculinity*, Buckingham: Open University Press.

Maravall, J.A. (1986). *Culture of the Baroque*, Manchester: Manchester University Press.

Marcuse, H. (1972). *Negations*, Harmondsworth: Penguin.

Margolis, J. (1999). Pierre Bourdieu: Habitus and the Logic of Practice pp. 64–83 in ed. R. Shusterman, *Pierre Bourdieu: A Critical Reader*, Oxford: Blackwell.

Marshall, G. Swift, A. and Roberts, S. (1997). *Against the Odds*, Oxford: Oxford University Press.

Martins, H. (1993). Hegel, Texas, in ed. I. Velody , *Knowledge and Passion*, London: Tauris.

Martins, H. (2004). The Marketisation of Universities, *Metacritica, Revista de filosofia*, no 4.

Marx, K. (1973). *Grundrisse*, Harmondsworth: Penguin.

Marx, K. (1976). *Capital*, Volume I, Harmondsworth: Penguin.

Marx, K. (1995). The Eighteenth Brumaire of Louis Napoleon (1852), in ed. T. Carver, *Marx: Later Political Writings*, Cambridge, Cambridge University Press.

Matsuda, M. (1996). *The Memory of the Modern*, New York and Oxford: Oxford University Press.

Mawdsley, E.and White, S. (2000). *The Soviet Elite from Lenin to Gorbachev*, Oxford: Oxford University Press.

Maybury, K.K. (1995/1996). Invisible Lives: Women, Men and Obituaries, *Omega*, 32 no. 1, 27–37.

Mayer, A. (1981). *The Persistence of the Old Regime*, London: Croom Helm.

Maynes, M.J. (1989). Gender and Narrative Form in French and German Autobiographies in eds. J.W. Barbre and the Personal Narratives Group, *Interpreting Women's Lives*, Bloomington: Indiana University Press.

McGuigan, J. (1992). *Cultural Populism*, Routledge.

McNay, L. (2000). *Gender and Agency*, Cambridge: Polity.

Michels, R. (1962). *Political Parties*, London: Collier MacMillan.

Miles, R. (1982). *Racism and Migrant Labour*, London: Routledge and Kegan Paul.

Miles, R. (1993). *Racism after `Race Relations'*, London: Routledge.

Miller D. (1987). *Material Culture and Mass Consumption*, Oxford: Basil Blackwell.

Mills, S. (1991). *Discourses of Difference*, London: Routledge.

Misztal, B. (2003). *Theories of Social Remembering*, Maidenhead: Open University Press.

Moi, T. (1990). *Feminist Theory and Simone de Beauvoir*, Oxford: Blackwell.

Moi, T. (1994). *Simone de Beauvoir: The Making of an Intellectual Woman*, Oxford: Blackwell.

Mosse, G (1990). *Fallen Soldiers: Reshaping Public Memory of the World Wars*, Oxford: Oxford University Press.

Moulin, R. (1967). *Le Marché de la Peinture en France*, Paris: Minuit.

Moulin, R. (1992). *L'Artiste, L'Institution et le Marché*, Paris: Flammarion.

Muel-Dreyfus, F. (2001). *Vichy and the Eternal Feminine: A Contribution to the Political Sociology of Gender*, Durham, NC: Duke University Press.

Namer, G. (1987). *Mémoire et Société*, Paris: Meridiens Klincksieck.

Ngugi wa Thiongo (1986). *Decolonising the Mind*, Oxford: James Currey.

Ngugi wa Thiongo (2002). *Petals of Blood*, Harmondsworth: Penguin.

Nora, P. (1984). *Les Lieux de la Mémoire* (vol. 1), Paris: Gallimard.

Nora, P. (1989). Between Memory and History, *Representations*, 26, Spring, 7–24.

Nora, P. (1996). *Realms of Memory* (vol. 1), New York: Columbia University Press.

Nora, P. (1992). *Lieux de Mémoire* (vol. 3), Paris: Gallimard.

O'Malley, J. (1970). *Karl Marx. Critique of Hegel's `Philosophy of Right'* (1843), Cambridge: Cambridge University Press.

Ollman, B. (1976). *Alienation: Marx's Conception of Man in Capitalist society*, Cambridge: Cambridge University Press.

Orr, J. (1977). *Tragic Realism and Modern Society*, London: MacMillan.

Orwell, G. (1965). *Decline of the English Murder and Other Essays*, Harmondsworth: Penguin.

Osborne, P. (2003). Introduction to *The Guardian Book of Obituaries*, London: Atlantic Books.

Osiel, M. (1997). *Mass Atrocity, Collective Memory and the Law*, New Brunswick, NJ: Transaction Publishers.

Panitch, L. and Gindin, S. (2005). Superintending Global capital, *New Left Review*, 35 (second series), Sept.–Oct, 101–123.

Passerini, L. (1987). *Fascism in Popular Memory*, Cambridge: Cambridge University Press.

Passerini, L. (1992). Introduction to Passerini, L. (ed.), *Memory and Totalitarianism*, Oxford: Oxford University Press.

Passeron, J.-C. (1991). *Le Raisonnement Sociologique*, Paris: Nathan.

Passeron, J-C. (1989). Biographies, Flux, Itineraires, Trajectoires, *Revue Francaise de Sociologie*, Vol XXXI, 3–22.

Péan, P. and Cohen, P. (2003). *La Face Cachée du Monde : du Contre-Pouvoir aux Abus de Pouvoir*, Paris: Arthème Fayard.

Pinto, L. (1999) Theory in Practice, pp. 94–112, in ed. R. Shusterman, *Bourdieu: A Critical Reader*, Oxford: Blackwell.

Plummer, K. (2001). *Documents of Life*, 2, London: Sage.

Poggioli, R. (1968). *Theory of the Avant-Garde*, London: Belknap Press of Harvard.

Pollock, G. (1996). Agency and the Avant-Garde, pp.315–342 in eds. G. Pollock and F.Orton, *Avant-Gardes and Partisans Reviewed*, Manchester: Manchester University Press.

Popular Memory Group (1982). Popular Memory: Theory, Politics, Method, pp. 205–252 in eds. R. Johnson et al, *Making Histories*, London: Hutchinson.

Quinn, P. (2004). *Easterhouse 2004: An Ethnography of Men's Experience, Use and Refusal of Violence*, Unpublished PhD thesis, University of Glasgow.

Ragon, M. (1983). *The Space of Death*, Charlotteville: University of Virginia Press (1981)

Reed-Danahay, D. (2005). *Locating Bourdieu*, Bloomington: Indiana University Press.

Rex, J. (1974). Capitalism, Elites and the Ruling Class, pp. 208–219 in eds. P. Stanworth and A. Giddens, *Elites and Power in British Society*, Cambridge Cambridge University Press.

Richardson, R. (1989). *Death, Dissection and the Destitute*, London: Penguin.

Ricoeur, P. (1984, 1985 and 1988). *Time and Narrative*, Vols. I, II and III, Chicago: Chicago University PressI.

Ricoeur, P. (1991). *From Text to Action: Essays in Hermeneutics II*, London: The Athlone Press.

Ricoeur, P. (2000). *La Mémoire, L'Histoire, L'Oubli*, Paris: Seuil.

Rojek, C. (2001). *Celebrity*, London: Reaktion Books.

Rose, J. (2003). Out of the Ivory Tower, Suzy Mackenzie interviews Jacqueline Rose, *Guardian*, 4 January 2003, 20–23.

Rosenblum, B. (1978). *Photographers at Work*, London: Holmes and Meier.

Sampson, A. (2004). *Who Runs this Place?* London: John Murray.

Samuel, R. (2006). *The Lost World of British Communism*, London: Verso.

Sapiro, G. (1996). La Raison Littéraire, *Actes de la Recherche en Sciences Sociales*, 111–12, Mars, 3–36.

Sapiro, G.(2002). La Responsabilité de l'Ecrivain, pp. 219–240 in eds. Einfalt and Jurt, *Le Texte et le Contexte*, Paris: Edition de la Maison de l' Homme.

Sapiro, G. (2003). Forms of Politicisation in the French Literary Field, *Theory and Society*, 32, Dec. 633–652.

Savage, M. (2000). *Class Analysis and Social Transformation*, Milton Keynes: Open University Press.

Savage, J. and Frith S. (1993). Against Cultural Populism, *New Left Review*, 198, Mar.-April, 107–116.

Savage, M., Warde, A. and Devine, F. (2005). Capitals, Assets and Resources, Some Critical Issues, *British Journal of Sociology*, Vol. 56, no. 1, March, 31–48.

Sayer, A. (2005). *The Moral Significance of Class*, Cambridge: Cambridge University Press.

Scanlan, J. (2005). *On Garbage*, London: Reaktion Books.

Schwartz, B. (1982). The Social Context of Commemoration: a Study in Collective Memory, *Social Forces*, 61, no. 2 (Dec.) 374–97.

Schwartz, B. (1990). The Reconstruction of Abraham Lincoln in eds. D. Middleton and D. Edwards, *Collective Remembering*, London: Sage.

Schwarz, B. (1982). The "People" in history, pp. 44–95 in eds. R.Johnson et al, *Making Histories*, London: Hutchinson.

Scott, J. (1986). *Capitalist Property and Financial Power*, Brighton: Wheatsheaf Books.

Scott, J. (1991). *Who Rules Britain?* Cambridge: Polity.

Scott, J. (1997). *Corporate Business and Capitalist Classes*, Oxford: Oxford University Press.

Sennett, R. (1984). *The Fall of Public Man*, London: Faber.

Simmel, G. (1964). *Conflict*, Glencoe: Free Press.

Simmel, G. (1978). *The Philosophy of Money*, London: Routledge.

Skeggs, B. (1997). *Formations of Class and Gender: Becoming Respectable*, London: Sage.

Smith, A. (2003). Reading Wealth in Nigeria: Occult Capitalism and Marx's Vampires, *Historical Materialism*, 9, 39–61.

Smith, A. (2004). Migrancy, Hybridity and Postcolonial Literary Studies, pp. 241–261 in N. Lazarus, *The Cambridge Companion to Postcolonial Literary Studies*, Cambridge: Cambridge University Press.

Smith, A. (2006). *Beyond a Boundary* (of a *Field of Cultural Production*): reading C.L.R. James with Bourdieu, *Theory, Culture and Society*, 23, 4: 95–112.

Smith, J. and Watson, A. (1998). *Women, Autobiography, Theory*, Madison, London: University of Wisconsin Press.

Southern, R. W. (1970). *Western Society and the Church in the Middle Ages*, Pelican.

Spivak, G.C. (1999). *A Critique of Postcolonial Reason*, Cambridge, MA: Harvard University Press.

Stallabrass, J. (1999). *High Art Lite*, London: Verso.

Stanley, L. (1992). *The Auto/Biographical I*, Manchester: Manchester University Press.

Stanworth, P. and Giddens, A. (1974). *Elites and Power in British Society*, Cambridge: Cambridge University Press.

Stedman Jones, S. (2001). *Durkheim Reconsidered*, Cambridge: Polity.

Strange, J.-M., (2005). *Death, Grief and Poverty, 1870–1914*, Cambridge: Cambridge University Press.

Sudnow, D. (1967). *Passing On: The Social Organisation of Death*, Saddle River, NJ: Prentice Hall

Taylor, C. (1989). *Sources of the Self: The Making of the Modern Identity*, Cambridge: Cambridge University Press.

Taylor, C. (1999). To Follow a Rule... pp. 29–44 in ed. R. Shusterman, *Bourdieu: A Critical Reader*, Oxford: Blackwell.

Terdiman, R. (1993). *Present Past: Modernity and the Memory Crisis*, Ithaca, NY: Cornell University Press.

Thompson, E.P. (1968). *The Making of the English Working-Class*, Harmondsworth: Penguin.

Thompson, K. (1974). Church of England Bishops as an Elite pp. 198–207 in eds. P. Stanworth and A. Giddens, *Elites and Power in British Society*, Cambridge: Cambridge University Press.

Ticktin, H. (1994). The Nature of an Epoch of Declining Capitalism, *Critique*, 26, pp.69–94.

Timmermans, S. (2000). Social Death as Self-fulfilling Prophecy pp 132–148 in eds. L. McKie and N. Watson, *Organising Bodies*, London: MacMillan.

Trinity College, Dublin (n.d./1945?) *How to Write for T.C.D.: No. 5, The Obituary Notice*. Tralee, Ireland: The Kerryman Ltd.

Urbain, J.-D. (1989). *L'Archipel des Morts: Les Sentiments de la Mort et les Dérives de la Mémoire dans les Cimetières de l'Occident*, Paris: Payot.

Varnedoe, K and Gopnik, A, eds. (1990). *High and Low*, New York, Metropolitan Museum of Modern Art.

Vincent, D. (1981). *Bread, Knowledge and Freedom: A Study of 19th Century Working-Class Autobiography*, London: Europa.

Vovelle, M. (1983). *La Mort et L'Occident, de 1300 à nos Jours*, Paris: Gallimard.

Wakeford, F. and J. (1974) Universities and the Studies of Elites, pp. 185–197 in eds. P. Stanworth and A. Giddens, *Elites and Power in British Society*, Cambridge: Cambridge University Press.

Walby, S. (1990). *Theorizing Patriarchy*, Oxford: Blackwell.

Walby, S. (1997). *Gender Transformations*, London: Routledge.

Walter, A. (1994). *The Revival of Death*, London: Routledge.

Weber, M (1952). *Ancient Judaism*, Glencoe: Free Press.

Weber, M. (1962). *The Protestant Ethic and the Spirit of Capitalism*, London: Allen and Unwin.

Weber, M. (1964). *The Religion of China*, Glencoe: The Free Press.

Weber, M. (1965). *Sociology of Religion*, London: Methuen.

Weber, M. (1978). *Economy and Society*, Berkeley: University of California Press.

Weber, M. (1991). *From Max Weber*, eds. H. Gerth and C.W. Mills, London: Routledge.

Wiener, M. J. (1985). *English Culture and the Decline of the Industrial Spirit, 1850–1980*, Harmondsworth: Penguin.

Williams, G.A. (1976). *Goya and the Impossible Revolution*, London: Allen Lane.

Williams, R. (1966). *Modern Tragedy*, London: Chatto and Windus.

Williams, R. (1980). *Problems in Materialism and Culture*, London: Verso.

Williams, R. (1985). *The Country and the City*, London: Hogarth.

Williams, R. (1989). *Resources of Hope: Culture, Democracy, Socialism*, London: Verso.

Winter, J. (1995). *Sites of Memory, Sites of Mourning*, Cambridge: Cambridge University Press.

Wu, C.-T. (2000). *Privatising Culture*, London: Verso.

Zangwill, N. (2002). Against the Sociology of Art, *Philosophy of Social Sciences*, 32, 2, 206–18.

Zolberg, V.L. and Cherbo, J.M., eds. (1997). *Outsider Art: Contesting Boundaries in Contemporary Culture*, Cambridge: Cambridge University Press.

Zukin, S. (1988). *Loft Living: Culture and Capital in Urban Living*, New York: Radius.

Index

Page numbers in italics refer to figures or tables.

A

Aboriginal collective memory, 213
Abu Nidal Sabri Al-Banna, 165–167
Academic artists, 199
Academic cultural capital, 15
Aesthetic criteria, Kant, 67–68
Affirmative concept of culture, 31
African-Americans, 225, 226
  cultural producers, 100–101
Afro-Caribbeans, 176, 225, 226
Agnelli, Giovanni, 18
Akintaro, Michael, 3–4
Alexander, Bill, 177
Altruistic risk, 245–246
Amateurism
  class, 223–225
  sports' obituaries, 223–225
Ancient regime, Mayer's argument on
      persistence, 101–103
Anonymity, 114
Archer, Fred, 188
Archetypal otherness, 165
Archivising drive, 36–37
Arguedas, Antonio, 172
Aristocracy, 246
  capitalism, 102
  declining, 186
  feudal landscape, 83–84
  The Times obituaries 1900, 82–85
    civil servants, 84
    sacrificial figures, 84–85
    second or third sons, 84
  The Times obituaries 1948, critical
      obituary, 95–97
Art, 32, 61–62, 91–94, 247
  art for its own sake, 5
    vs. material insecurity, 5
  autonomy, 72–73
  Bourdieu, Pierre, 68–70, 72–73

critics of Bourdieu's theory of art,
      73–76
  determinism, 72–73
  difference in portrayal, 5
  World War I, 96–97
Artists' obituaries, 197–216
  cartoonists, 210–213
  commercial arts, 209–213
  expanded field, 209–215
  folk art, 213–214
  mapping restricted field, 199–205
  migration, 198
  national origin, 198
  outsider artists, 214–215
  photographic field, 205–209
  political cartoonists, 211–213
  popular arts, 209–213
  restricted artistic field, 199–205
Aubrey, John, 4–5
Auerbach, Ellen, 207
Author-attributed contributions, 6–7
Authoritative legal judgement, 38
Authorship, 114
Autobiographies, working class,
      248–249
Auto/biography, Bourdieu, Pierre, 60
Autonomy, 250
  art, 72–73
  Bourdieu, Pierre, 71–72
  literature, 72–73
  women, 9–10

B

Barbosa, Moacir, 227
Bates, Ralph, 188–189
Beautiful death, 49, 51–52
Bellow, Saul, 196
Belsky, Franta, 199–200
Benjamin, Walter, 30–33

Benson, Mary, 178
Bergson, Henri, 25–26
Binder, Hymie, 225–226
Biographical illusion, 14
  Bourdieu, Pierre, 60–61
Biographies, source of production,
      244–245
Black Death, 48
Bourdieu, Pierre, 13–17, 129
  artistic field, 68–70, 72–73
    critics of Bourdieu's theory of art,
        73–76
  auto/biography, 60
  autonomy, 71–72
  biographical illusion, 60–61
  canonisation, 80
  change, 66
  classification, 64
  culture, 68
    class, 68
  death, 59–60
  feminism, 76–80
  Guillory, John, 70
  habitus, 64, 65, 66, 67
  liberty, 66–67
  logic of practice, 59
  market, 70
  misappropriations of, 65–67
  phenomenology, 76–80
  social theory, 59–80
  sociology of science, 71–72
  study of obituaries, 62–64
    greater intellectual virtues, 64
    lesser virtues, 63–64
    linguistic codes, 62–63
    occupational ethics of academics,
        63
    ordered classifications of
        intellectual judgements, 62
    public sphere, 64
    women, 64
  theory of capitals, assets and
      resources, 129, 130
  theory of practice, 13–17
  time, 77–78
  transformation, 66–67
  universalism, critique, 67–71
Bourgeoisie
  Enlightenment values, 102
  The Times obituaries 1900, 85–88
  The Times obituaries 1948, 98–99
Brasher, Chris, 227, 228
Brief Lives (John Aubrey), 4–5

Briginshaw, Reg, 237–238

C
Canonisation, 31
  Bourdieu, Pierre, 80
Capitalism
  aristocracy, 102
  cultural logic, 243
Cartland, Barbara, 181, 191–192
Cartoonist, artists' obituaries,
      210–213
Casanova, Pascale, 75–76
Celebrity, 248
Ceremonial occasions, 22
Change, Bourdieu, Pierre, 66
Charbonnier, Jean-Philippe, 208–209
City, analysis of modern, 30–31,
      32–33
Civil memory, death, 52–55
Class
  amateurism, 223–225
  death, 51–52
  obituary, 6
  sports' obituaries, 223–225
  writers' obituaries, 182
Class habitus
  popular memory, 221–223
  taste, 221–223
Classification, Bourdieu, Pierre, 64
Class reproduction, 8
Clergy
  religious activism with political
      radicalism, 97
  The Times obituaries 1948, 97
Cockburn, Henry, 221, 222
Coercive power, sports' obituaries,
      217–218
Coffee-houses, 5
Cognitive machine of education, 14
Cohen, Alfred, 202
Collective awakening, 32
Collective memory, 25–40
  attenuation, 38
  collective imagination of past utopia,
      31
  cultural production, 10–11, 33
  declining, 37
  distortion, 11
  fragmentation, 38
  of groups, 28
  Halbwachs' concept, 27–30
  history
    Halbwachian antithesis, 28–29

relationship, 28
tension between, 11
impact of commodity on, 31
memory-clarification and distortion
at social level, 39
in nations, 28
newspapers, 30
obituary as repository for, 40
significance, 10
storytelling, 30, 32–33
Collective representations,
characterized, 26
Colomb, Denise, 205
Commemorative epoch, 35–36, 37
Commercial arts, artists' obituaries,
209–213
Commercial economy, gift economy,
obituaries as intersecting worlds,
111
Communist Party, 177
Competitive masculinity, 219–220
football, 220
Conspicuous consumption, funeral
rites, 52
Cooperative masculinity, football, 220
Counter-memory, 17, 30, 34
ethnicity, 175
marginalised others, 34–35
politicians' obituaries, 175
race, 175
reverse discourse, 35
stigmatised minorities, 176–177
trade unionists' obituaries, 235
Cowan, Joseph, 85–86
Craxi, Bettino, 167–168
Critical obituary, race, 121
Cross, Alice Jammy, 223, 224
Cultural capital, economic capital,
migration, 143
Cultural iconoclasm, 13
Cultural inheritance, 31
difficulties, 32
Cultural logic, capitalism, 243
Cultural politics, 248
Cultural production
collective memory, 10–11, 33
developing new techniques of
production, 33
The Times obituaries 1900, 91–94
tension with popular culture, 91
The Times obituaries 1948, 100–101
Culture
affirmative concept of culture, 31

Bourdieu, Pierre, 68
class, 68

D
*The Daily Universal Register, see The
Times*
Dash, Jack, 18–20, 237–238
Death, 12–13, *see also* Specific type
18th century philosophers, 49–50
19th century rationalists, 49–50
anguish of your death, 50–51
apparatus of civic commemoration,
52–55
Bourdieu, Pierre, 59–60
class, 51–52
different ideological visions, 43
early Christianity, 44–45
Enlightenment, 49–50
feared as remote yet imminent,
48–49
historical sociology, 41–58
individualisation, 55–56
invisible death of late modernity,
55–58
loss of self, 45–48
medicalisation, sequestration and
secularisation, 55, 57
narrative forms in Christianity, 42
new institutions, 49–50
new secular rituals, 12–13
pre-Christian, 44–45
progressive bourgeois thought, 49–50
rediscovery, 57
Romanticism, 50–51
social value, 105–127
symbolic processes, 41
taboo about, 57–58
tame death of 12th century, 44–45
Death notices, 114
Democratisation, 16
leisure, 219–220
newspapers, 8
Determinism, 65
art, 72–73
literature, 72–73
Devi, Phoolan, 179–180
Dewar, Donald, 164
Distortion
collective memory, 11
obituary, 11–12
Diversity, subject selection, 15, 22–23
Division of labour, obituary writers,
fragmentation, 125–126

Dominant class, 15
  bodily dispositions, 84, 86
  education, 61
  empowerment, 61
  memory, 174–175
Don Quixote effect, 172, 174–175
Dreams, memory, power of the social,
    27
Durack, Elizabeth, 213–214
Durkheim, Emile, 26, 27

E
Eccentricities, 21
Economic capital, cultural capital,
    migration, 143
Education, 15
  elite, 61
  empowerment, 61
  narrowness, 146
  occupation, 145–146
  subject selection, 15, 22–23, 144–
    149, *145*
  writers' obituaries, 182, 186
Effigy, 43
Empowerment
  education, 61
  elite, 61
Engineers, *The Times* obituaries 1900,
    87–88
Enlightenment
  death, 49–50
  universalism, 13–14
Epic wisdom, storytelling, 30, 32–33
Ethnicity
  counter-memory, 175
  sports' obituaries, 225–227
  subject selection, 15, 22–23, 120,
    151–152, *152*
Eulogies, 53
Extramarital affairs, 122

F
Feminism, Bourdieu, Pierre, 76–80
Feudal landscape, aristocracy, 83–84
Finster, Howard, 214–215
Folk art, artists' obituaries, 213–214
Football, 222–223
  competitive masculinity, 220
  cooperative masculinity, 220
Foster, John, 236
France
  memory struggle, 35–39
  state funerals, 52–55

gender, 53
Freund, Gisèle, 205
Frost, Sir Terry, 200–202
Funeral rites, conspicuous
    consumption, 52

G
Gascoyne, David, 188
Gender, 9, 245–246
  of obituary editors, 10
  politicians' obituaries, 177–180
  sports' obituaries, 223
  subject selection, 133–137, *134*, *135*,
    136
    with children, 134, *134*, *135*, *138*
    occupation, 134–137, *136*, *138*,
      140–141
    single *vs.* married, 134
  writers' obituaries, 186–187, 191–192
Genealogy, 42
Genius, Ruskin, John, 93
The Gentleman's Magazine, 4
Gift economy, commercial economy,
    obituaries as intersecting worlds,
    111
Globalisation, period, 81
Global South, subject selection, 15
Golshiri, Holshang, 194–195
Grant, Bernie, 176
Grave-robbery, 51–52
Greatness, different perspectives, 17
Greenald, Dorothy, 178
Grief, hierarchy, 3
Group cultural inversions, 30
The Guardian, subject selection, 113
Guillory, John, 70

H
Habitus
  Bourdieu, Pierre, 64, 65, 66, 67
  women, 77
Hailsham, Lord, 161–163
Halbwachs, Maurice, 27–30
Harlem Renaissance, 100–101
Haxell, Frank, 237–238
Heinich, Nathalie, 73
Hell, 45–48
Heraldic certificate, 42
Heraldic funeral, *The Times* obituaries
    1900, 83
Herman, Josef, 203–204
Hero of consumption, 248
Hill, Derek, 204–205

History
  collective memory
    Halbwachian antithesis, 28–29
    relationship, 28
    tension between, 11
  social memory, passage from, 36
  witness, 39
Holden, Jack, 224
Homosexuality, 122
Hostesses, public sphere, 89
Hurtz, William, 211–213, 215
Hysteresis, 172, 174–175

I
Ideology of natural talent, obituary
    editor and writer interviews, 16
Inclusiveness, 8
The Independent, 6–7
  subject selection, 112–113
Individual agency, sports, 230
Individualisation, death, 55–56
Indulgences, purgatory, 47–48
Industrial capitalism, 129
Industrial capitalists, *The Times*
    obituaries 1900, 85–88
Internalisation of external necessity,
    65–66
Involuntary memory, 32
Ironic obituary, 20–21
  politicians' obituaries, 160, 171–172

J
Jenkins, Clive, 239–240
Judiciary, *The Times* obituaries 1948,
    97–98

K
Kai-Shek, Mme Chiank, 178–179
Keynesianism, 103
Kimbro, Henry, 226–227
Kingsley, Mary, 90
Kinship memories of elite, *The Times*
    obituaries 1900, 81
Kuron, Jacek, 176

L
Lambert, Eugène, 91
Lane-Fox-Pitt-Rivers, Lieutenant-
    General Augustus Henry, 87
Lawrence, Don, 215
Leisure
  democratisation, 219–220
  popular memory, 34

Le Monde, subject selection, 112
Liberal professionals
  The Times obituaries 1900, 85–88
  The Times obituaries 1948, 98–99
Liberty, Bourdieu, Pierre, 66–67
Life history approach, 61
Lindsay, John, 174–175
Linguistic codes, 62–63
Linguistic representations, 38
Literature, *see also* Writers' obituaries
  autonomy, 72–73
  determinism, 72–73
Littlewood, Joan, 22
Logic of practice
  Bourdieu, Pierre, 59
  sports, 230
Loss of self, death, 45–48

M
Mannion, Wilf, 222–223
Marais, Jaap, 173
Market, Bourdieu, Pierre, 70
Matthew, Stanley, 227, 228
Matthews, John, 224
Mayer, Arno, 101–103
Media, 61–62
Memory, *see also* Specific type
  Bergson's model, 25–26
  celebratory forms, 35
  conflict with dominant memory,
    29–30
  dominateds' recollections, 29–30
  dreams, power of the social, 27
  kinds, 26
  politicisations, 37
  power, 25
  significance, 25
  social frameworks for capitalism, 33
  sources, 16–17
Memory struggle, France, 35–39
Migration, artists' obituaries, 198
Military, 245–246
  The Times obituaries 1900
    imperial service, 83–84
    pattern of ritualised ascent, 83
  The Times obituaries 1948, 95–96
Mitford sisters, 169–170
Modernist forms, popular culture, 244
Modise, Joe, 18–19, 167
Montgomery-Massingberd, Hugh, 6–7,
    107
  licensed idiosyncracies, 107–108
  stylistic change, 107, 108–109

Moral terms, subject selection, 121
Mosley, Diana, 169–170
Mosley, Oswald, 169–170
Munkácsy, M. de, 92
Murdoch, Iris, 186–187
Murray, Len, 239
Music, 91
Musicians' obituaries, 247, 248
Muspratt, Helen, 206–207

N
Narrative indeterminacy, 38
National collective memory, decline,
    36
National icons, sports' obituaries,
    227–231
Nationality
  artists' obituaries, 198
  subject selection, 149
    American obituaries in Britain,
      149–151, *150*
    Asia, the Middle East and Third
      World obituaries in Britain,
      149–151, *150*
    migration, 152–154, *153, 155*
National memory, 17
Nazism
  Nazi sympathisers, 169–170
  writers' obituaries, 189–190
Nebiolo, Primo, 230
Negative obituary, 18–20
  politicians' obituaries, 159–160,
    165–171
    demonic figures, 159–160,
      165–171
  trade unionists' obituaries
    illegitimate power, 237–238
    negative radical trade unionist,
      237–238
Negro Leagues, 226–227
Newry, Viscountess, 88
News euphemisms, 22
Newspapers
  collective memory, 30
  democratisation, 8
  political identities, 112–114
  reader demographics, 113
  readers' horizon of relevance, 22
Ngugi, 194
Nobility, 42–43, 61, 161–162
  acquisition of honours and trophies
    when young, 162
  American equivalent, 163–165

France, 165
Germany, 164–165
obituaries, 162–165
Nora, Pierre, 35–37

O
Obituary, *see also* Specific type
  authoritative accounts, 11
  benchmark of later consecration, 7
  Bourdieu's theory of practice, 13–17
  changes in contemporary, 245–250
  class, 6
  collective memory, *see also*
      Collective memory
    obituary as repository for, 40
  cost, 111
  cultural transition from spiritual to
      secular, 41
  dissident voice against State power,
      12
  distortion, 11–12
  early, standard form, 42
  as first drafts of history, 6
  first modern, 4
  focus, 3
  gendered exclusion, 9
  genres, 17–23
  great flowering at end of 20th, 7
  highly critical, 7
  honest testimonies *vs.* positive
      celebration, 123–124
  informality, 108
  interviewed subjects before they
      died, 7
  ironic, 20–21
  judgements of taste, 124–125
  Massingberd revolution, 7
  measure of value, 8
  metamorphosis, 107–109
  modern movement, 108
  nature of distinction, 246
  negative, 18–20
  newsly transformed, 245
  origins, 12, 41–42
  payment for, 111
  positive, 17
    untraditional, 21–23
  production, 15, 114–117
  readers' priorities, 243–244
  recapitulating past, 11
  revolution since 1970s, 3–4
  secular, 5
  sociogenesis, 4–10

sociological objectivation, 129–156
source of production, 244–245
subject selection, *see* Subject
  selection
symbolic revolution, 7
tragic, 20
transformation in codes, 122
Obituary editors, 16, 245
  characterized, 106
  gender, 10
  ideology of natural talent, 16
  interviews, 16, 106
  judgements of taste, 124–125
  newly transformed, 245
  subjective avowals of openness, 105,
    106
Obituary writers, 16
  anonymity, 114
  authorship, 114
  British *vs.* French and American,
    110, 111
  commissioning outside writers,
    114–115
  division of labour, 125–126
  freelance, 111, 114–115
  ideology of natural talent, 16
  interviews, 16
  judgements of taste, 124–125
  non-journalists, 111–112, 114–115
  non-professional obituaries, 116–117
  popular memory, 175
  semi-professionalised specialist,
    111–112, 114–115
  specialisation, 125–126
  sports' obituaries, 230–231
  who knew individual on personal
    basis, 112, 115
Objectivism, 65
Objectivist/subjectivist division, 66
Objects of exchange, women as, 81,
    88–89
O'Brian, Patrick, 192
Occupation
  education, 145–146
  public schools, 145
  subject selection, 151
Occupational background, subject
    selection, 130–133, *131*
  by gender, *136*
Olivier, Edith, 100
Organised forgetting, 35
Orwell, George, 35
Osiel, Mark J., 11, 38

Outsider artists, 197
  artists' obituaries, 214–215

P
Patriarchy, 9–10
Pearce, Edward, Lord Shore, 19
Performing arts, 91
Phenomenology, Bourdieu, Pierre,
    76–80
Photography
  artists' obituaries, 205–209
  sociology of, 205–206
Photojournalism, 206
Physicians, *The Times* obituaries 1900,
    87
Pintasilgo, Maria, 177–178
Place memory, 27
Political cartoonists, artists' obituaries,
    211–213
Politicians' obituaries, 159–180
  counter-memory, 175
  gender, 177–180
  genres, 159–174
  ironic obituary, 160, 171–172
  monstrous others, 159–160
  negative obituary, 159–160, 165–171
    demonic figures, 159–160,
      165–171
  popular memory, 175
  positive obituary, traditional,
    161–165
  tragic obituary, 160, 172–174
  Weber's categories, 160
  women, 177–180
Popular arts, artists' obituaries,
    209–213
Popular culture
  modernist forms, 244
  writers' obituaries, 190–193
Popular memory, 16, 217
  characterized, 33–34
  class habitus, 221–223
  defined, 217
  demystifying, 219
  leisure, 34
  obituary writers, 175
  politicians' obituaries, 175
  sports, 34
  taste, 221–223
  trade unionists' obituaries, 235
Positive obituary
  politicians' obituaries, traditional,
    161–165

Positive obituary (*continued*)
    trade unionists' obituaries,
        traditional working class,
        235–236
Post-colonial migrants, 15
Powell, Anthony, 183–185
Power
    memory, 25
    misuse, 18–20
Power bloc, 163
Private sphere, defined, 89–90
Privileged education, 15
Procktor, Patrick, 202–203
Professional engagement, women, 78
    necessary suspension of professional
        effort, 78
Pryce-Jones, Alan, 185, 186
Public memory, politics of spectacular
    fission, 34
Public schools, *see also* Education
    occupation, 145
    subject selection, 144–146, *145*
Public sphere, 5
    expansions, 248
    hostesses, 89
    salons, 89
Purgatory, 47–48
    indulgences, 47–48

R
Race
    counter-memory, 175
    critical obituary, 121
    sports, 225–227
    sports' obituaries, 225–227
    subject selection, 15, 22–23, 120–
        121, 151–152, *152*
Rantisi, Abdel Aziz, 173–174
Ravilious, James, 207–208
Realist rationalism, 67
Religion
    subject selection, 15, 22–23
    The Times obituaries 1900, 81
Reproduction, subject selection, by
    newspaper, 141–144, *142*
Reverse discourse, counter-memory, 35
Rexrodt, Gunter, 171
Rhetoric of equality, 8
Rhetoric of openness, 105, 106
Richardson, Sir Maurice, 18
Ricoeur, Paul, 39
Romanticism, death, 50–51
Roosevelt, Kermit, 163–164

Rural Arcadian, 109
Ruskin, John, 81–82, 92–94
    genius, 93
    social economy, 93–94

S
Sacred group landmarks, 27–28
Salons, public sphere, 89
Sankey, Lord, 98
Scholz, Bubi, 224–225
Schoolteachers, *The Times* obituaries
    1948, 97
Schulz, Charles, 212
Scientists, 247
    The Times obituaries 1948, 98–99
Secular republican culture, symbolic
    structures, 43–44
Segregation of the dying, 57
Seigneurial crisis, 45–48
Selective justification, 41
    history, 41
Self, fundamental contingency, 14
Self-censorship, subject selection, 121
Self expression, 250
Social capital, 61, 191, 192
Social economy, Ruskin, John, 93–94
Social imperialism, 84
Social memory, history, passage from, 36
Social mobility, 92
    subject selection, 137–141, *138–139*
        gender, 140–141
        by newspaper, 141–144, *142*
        occupation, 137–141, *138–139*
Social relations, modern metropolis, 31
Social reproduction, differences
    between societies, 141–144
Social theory, Bourdieu, Pierre, 59–80
Sociology of science, Bourdieu, Pierre,
    71–72
Specialisation, obituary writers,
    125–126
Spiritual biography, 42
Sports
    expressing sense of honour of
        subordinate classes, 219
    individual agency, 230
    logic of practice, 230
    popular memory, 34
    position in social space over time and
        society, 218
    visibility, 218
    race, 225–227
    taste, 220–221

Sports' obituaries, 217–232
  amateurism, 223–225
  class, 223–225
  coercive power, 217–218
  collective actions, 217–218
  demystifying, 219
  Elias's civilizing process, 219
  ethnicity, 225–227
  feudal compliments, 222
  gender, 223
  national icons, 227–231
  obituary writers, 230–231
  race, 225–227
  women, 223
State funerals, France, 52–55
  gender, 53
Status, subject selection, 117
Storytelling
  collective memory, 30, 32–33
  conditions, 30
  epic wisdom, 30, 32–33
Stuart, Francis, 189–190
Stylistic change, Montgomery-
      Massingberd, Hugh, 107,
      108–109
Subject selection, 105, 109, 243–244,
      247
  category of actors, 248–249
  characters, 117
  consistent variations by newspaper,
      15
  daily procedures, 16
  diversity, 15, 22–23
  doxic, 110
  editorial criteria for inclusion,
      105–106
  education, 15, 22–23, 144–149, *145*
  ethnicity, 15, 22–23, 120, 151–152,
      152
  exclusion
      acts of, 109–110
      of private, 118–121
      of routinised, 118–121
      tendentious in interests of balance,
          117–118
  gender, 133–137, *134*, *135*, *136*
      with children, 134, *134*, *135*, *138*
      occupation, 134–137, *136*, *138*,
          140–141
      single *vs.* married, 134
  global South, 15
  The Guardian, 113
  honest testimonies *vs.* positive

  celebration, 123–124
  The Independent, 112–113
  Le Monde, 112
  material base, 110–112
  migration across national
      boundaries, 15
  moral-political insights, 250
  moral terms, 121
  nationality, 149
      American obituaries in Britain,
          149–151, *150*
      Asia, the Middle East and Third
          World obituaries in Britain,
          149–151, *150*
      migration, 152–154, *153*, *155*
  newly transformed, 245
  newspapers' self-images, 112–114
  news values, 115
  obituary as award, 121–122
  obligatory, 110
  occupation, 130–133, *131*, 151
      by gender, *136*
  outside pressure to select, 115–116
  positivist fantasies, 105
  public schools, 144–146, *145*
  quantitative analysis, 129–156
  race, 15, 22–23, 120–121, 151–152,
      152
  readers' composition, 113
  religion, 15, 22–23
  reproduction, by newspaper, 141–
      144, *142*
  rules, 105, 117–124
  self-censorship, 121
  social mechanisms for inclusion,
      114–117
  social mobility, 137–141, *138–139*
      gender, 140–141
      by newspaper, 141–144, *142*
      occupation, 137–141, *138–139*
  sources of the self, 250
  status, 117
  stratification in life reiterated in
      death, 249–250
  The Telegraph, 113–114
  The Times, 112–113
  The Times obituaries 1948, 95
  universities, 146–149, *147*
  women, 119–120, 133–137, *134*,
      135, *136*
      with children, 134, *134*, *135*, *138*
      occupation, 134–137, *136*, *138*,
          140–141

Subject selection (*continued*)
　　single *vs.* married, 134
　working class, 248–249
Suicide, 122
Surgeons, *The Times* obituaries 1900,
　　87
Suvar, Stipe, 168
Symbolic structures, secular republican
　　culture, 43–44

T
Talent, 8
Tame death, 44–45
Taste
　class habitus, 221–223
　popular memory, 221–223
　sports, 220–221
The Telegraph, subject selection,
　　113–114
Theory of capitals, assets and resources,
　　Bourdieu, Pierre, 129, 130
Theory of reproduction, 14
Third World, women, 178–180
Time
　Bourdieu, Pierre, 77–78
　women, 77–78
The Times obituaries, *see also* by year
　commemorations, 6
　conventional and formulaic form, 6
　deaths in order of precedence, 6
　early obituaries, 6
　Establishment character, 6
　as first drafts of history, 6
　staff, 6
　subject selection, 112–113
The Times obituaries 1900
　aristocracy, 82–85
　　civil servants, 84
　　sacrificial figures, 84–85
　　second or third sons, 84
　bourgeoisie, 85–88
　cultural production, 91–94
　　tension with popular culture, 91
　doctors, 87
　as dominants' memory, 81
　engineers, 87–88
　heraldic funeral, 83
　industrial capitalists, 85–88
　kinship memories of elite, 81
　liberal professionals, 85–88
　military
　　imperial service, 83–84
　　pattern of ritualised ascent, 83
　religion, 81

　significance, 81
　surgeons, 87
　upwardly mobile individual, 88
　women, 81, 88–90, 94
　　defined by male relatives, 88–90
　working class, 86
The Times obituaries 1948, 95–101
　aristocracy, critical obituary, 95–97
　bourgeoisie, 98–99
　clergy, 97
　cultural production, 100–101
　elite, new structure of feeling about
　　war, 96
　judiciary, 97–98
　liberal professionals, 98–99
　military, 95–96
　schoolteachers, 97
　scientists, 98–99
　subject selection, 95
　women, 99–100
　　traditional family roles, 99–100
　　tragic obituary, 100
Time sovereignty, 9–10
Tjupurrula, Johnny Warrangkula, 213
Tomb sculpture, 42
Trade unionists' obituaries, 233–241
　counter-memory, 235
　labourist conciliatory official,
　　238–239
　negative obituaries
　　illegitimate power, 237–238
　　negative radical trade unionist,
　　237–238
　new Bernsteinianism, 239–240
　new bureaucratic union official,
　　239–240
　popular memory, 235
　positive obituaries, traditional
　　working class, 235–236
　sample size, 233
Trade unions, 19
　anti-trade union legislation, 233
　membership, 233
　old oppositional language, 234
　old political polarisations, 234
　profoundly conservative, 234
Tragic element, 20
　women, 20
Tragic obituary, politicians' obituaries,
　　160, 172–174
Transformation, Bourdieu, Pierre,
　　66–67
Transformative agency, 13
Tudjman, Franjo, 165, 168–169

Tuqan, Fadwa, 195
Tyranny of memory, 37

U
Universalism, 13–14
  Bourdieu, Pierre, critique, 67–71
Universities, subject selection, 146–
  149, *147*

V
Valour, 245–246
Vocational habitus, women, 77

W
War, 56–57
  new structure of feeling about war, 96
  phenomenology, 96
Warrior's death, 44–45
Waugh, Auberon, 185–186
Whitelaw, Viscount, 171–172
Will, 42
Witness, history, 39
Women, 9, 76–80, 245–246
  autonomous professional jobs, 9
  autonomy, 9–10
  domestic roles, 9
  greater caring responsibilities, 9
  habitus, 77
  investment in the game, 77
  lesser family values, 64
  objects of exchange, 81, 88–89
  politicians' obituaries, 177–180
  professional engagement, 78
    necessary suspension of
      professional effort, 78
  public *vs.* private world, 64
  sports' obituaries, 223
  subject selection, 119–120, 133–137,
    134, 135, 136
    with children, 134, *134, 135, 138*
    occupation, 134–137, *136, 138,*
      140–141
    single *vs.* married, 134
  Third World, 178–180
  time, 77–78
  The Times obituaries 1900, 81,
    88–90, 94

defined by male relatives, 88–90
The Times obituaries 1948, 99–100
  traditional family roles, 99–100
  tragic obituary, 100
tragic element, 20
vocational habitus, 77
writers' obituaries, 186–187,
  191–192
Working class, 95
  autobiographies, 248–249
  subject selection, 248–249
  The Times obituaries 1900, 86
  writers' obituaries, 188–189
World War I, 95, 96–97
  arts, 96–97
World War II, as touchstone, 169
Wortley, The Honorable Mrs. James
  Stuart, 89–90
Writers' obituaries, 181–196
  British contrasted with other nations,
    182, 193–196
  British metropolitan elite, 183–190
  British popular writers, 190–193
  class, 182
  commercial success with literary
    recognition, 190–193
  consecration, 183–187
  education, 182, 186
  expanded canon, 192–193
  gender, 186–187, 191–192
  less securely-consecrated writers,
    187–190
  literary periphery, 193–196
  Nazism, 189–190
  popular culture, 190–193
  position-taking, 181
  producers with declining trajectory,
    184–185
  transmission of hereditary privilege,
    182
  women, 186–187, 191–192
  working class, 188–189

Z
Zatopek, Emil, 227, 228–229
Zola, Emile, 71

Printed in Great Britain
by Amazon